Anonymus

Return of judicial statistics of Ireland 1886

Anonymus

Return of judicial statistics of Ireland 1886

ISBN/EAN: 9783742811226

Manufactured in Europe, USA, Canada, Australia, Japa

Cover: Foto ©Suzi / pixelio.de

Manufactured and distributed by brebook publishing software
(www.brebook.com)

Anonymus

Return of judicial statistics of Ireland 1886

CRIMINAL AND JUDICIAL STATISTICS.

1886.

IRELAND.

PART I.

POLICE—CRIMINAL PROCEEDINGS—PRISONS.

PART II.

CIVIL PROCEEDINGS IN CENTRAL AND LARGER AND SMALLER DISTRICT COURTS.

Presented to both Houses of Parliament by Command of Her Majesty.

DUBLIN:
PRINTED FOR HER MAJESTY'S STATIONERY OFFICE
BY
ALEXANDER THOM & CO. (LIMITED).
And to be purchased, either directly or through any Bookseller, from
Eyre and Spottiswoode, East Harding-street, Fetter-lane, E.C., or 32, Abingdon-street,
Westminster, S.W.; or Adam and Charles Black, 6, North Bridge, Edinburgh; or
Hodges, Figgis, and Co., 104, Grafton-street, Dublin.

1887.

General Register Office,
Charlemont House, Dublin,
5th August, 1887.

Sir,

Adverting to Sir Robert Hamilton's letter of 29th November, 1886, I have the honour to inform you that I have compiled the Report on the Criminal and Judicial Statistics of Ireland for the year 1886, and I now beg to submit the same, together with the Tables appended thereto, for the consideration of His Excellency the Lord Lieutenant.

I remain, Sir,
Your obedient servant,

THOMAS W. GRIMSHAW,
Registrar-General.

Major-General Sir Redvers Buller, V.C., K.C.B., K.C.M.G.
Under Secretary.
&c., &c., &c.

CONTENTS OF REPORT.

PART I.—CRIMINAL STATISTICS.

CHAPTER III.—CRIMINALS AND OTHERS IN CONFINEMENT, AND KNOWN CRIMINALS AT LARGE.

CHAPTER IV.—COST OF THE REPRESSION OF CRIME.

PART II.—JUDICIAL STATISTICS.

CONTENTS OF APPENDIX OF TABLES.

PART I.—CRIMINAL STATISTICS.

I. POLICE TABLES.

II. STATE PRISONS.

III. CRIMINAL PROCEEDINGS AT ASSIZES, THE DUBLIN COMMISSION COURT, AND QUARTER SESSIONS, WITH COSTS.

PART II.—JUDICIAL STATISTICS.—CIVIL PROCEEDINGS.

I. CENTRAL ADMINISTRATION OF JUSTICE.

High Court of Justice.

II. LOCAL ADMINISTRATION OF JUSTICE.

Larger Divisions.

INDEX TO SUBJECTS

IN

REPORT AND TABLES.

B 2

CRIMINAL AND JUDICIAL STATISTICS (IRELAND), 1886.

REPORT.

GENERAL REMARKS.

GENERAL REMARKS.

The information dealt with in the following Report was collected in the usual manner, and has been classified so that it may be in accord with that contained in previous reports upon the same subject. Care has been taken when arranging the various tables and statements that they may, as far as possible, be easily comparable with similar papers published for the other divisions of the United Kingdom.

The Report is, as on former occasions, divided into two principal sections—that relating to the Criminal, and that dealing with the Judicial, Statistics. Each of these portions has been again sub-divided so as to allow of the more important items being referred to in detail.

A general review of the tables contained in the Appendix points to the following conclusions:—

1. That there has been a decrease in the total number of Criminal offences in Ireland in 1886 as compared with 1885.
2. That the improvement as regards the more serious offences (those not determined summarily), noted in the Reports for the four years preceding, has not been maintained, there having been last year an increase of about 5 per cent., as compared with the year 1885, but the number of offences coming under this category is little more than 60 per cent. of the corresponding number for the year 1881; and, allowing for the estimated decrease in the population, the rate last year, per 10,000 persons, was only 15·0 against a rate of 23·1 in 1881.
3. That the number of the less serious offences (those determined summarily) compares favourably with the average for such offences, and is considerably under the number in the year 1885.
4. That the judicial returns present no change of importance.

PART I.—CRIMINAL STATISTICS.

Part I. Criminal Statistics.

Chapter I. *Statistics of Crime.*

Comparison of crime in 1886 with crime in previous years.

Tables 6 and 7.

CHAPTER I.—STATISTICS OF CRIME.

Increase and Decrease of Criminal Offences.—The Criminal offences and charges of all kinds in Ireland are given in the following statement for the year 1886, as compared with each year during the past decade.

As regards charges determined summarily the figures indicate the number of persons proceeded against, including those cases in which the charges were dismissed. In the case of Indictable Offences the figures represent the number of crimes committed.

Year.	Estimated Population in each year.*	Offences and Charges.														
		Indictable, not Disposed of Summarily.					Disposed of Summarily.					Total.				
		Number	Rate per 10,000 Population	Increase or decrease compared with preceding year: In number, Increase	In number, Decrease	In Rate per 10,000 Population	Number	Rate per 10,000 Population	Increase or decrease compared with preceding year: In number, Increase	In number, Decrease	In Rate per 10,000 Population	Number	Rate per 10,000 Population	Increase or decrease compared with preceding year: In number, Increase	In number, Decrease	In Rate per 10,000 Population
1877,	[illegible]	[illegible]	[illegible]	[illegible]	-	[illegible]	[illegible]	[illegible]	[illegible]	-	[illegible]	[illegible]	[illegible]	[illegible]	-	[illegible]
1878,	[illegible]	[illegible]	[illegible]	[illegible]	-	[illegible]	[illegible]	[illegible]	[illegible]	-	[illegible]	[illegible]	[illegible]	[illegible]	-	[illegible]
1879,	[illegible]	[illegible]	[illegible]	[illegible]	-	[illegible]	[illegible]	[illegible]	-	[illegible]	[illegible]	[illegible]	[illegible]	-	[illegible]	[illegible]
1880,	[illegible]	[illegible]	[illegible]	[illegible]	-	[illegible]	[illegible]	[illegible]	-	[illegible]	[illegible]	[illegible]	[illegible]	-	[illegible]	[illegible]
1881,	[illegible]	[illegible]	[illegible]	[illegible]	-	[illegible]	[illegible]	[illegible]	-	[illegible]	[illegible]	[illegible]	[illegible]	-	[illegible]	[illegible]
1882,	[illegible]	[illegible]	[illegible]	-	[illegible]	[illegible]	[illegible]	[illegible]	[illegible]	-	[illegible]	[illegible]	[illegible]	[illegible]	-	[illegible]
1883,	[illegible]	[illegible]	[illegible]	-	[illegible]	[illegible]	[illegible]	[illegible]	[illegible]	-	[illegible]	[illegible]	[illegible]	[illegible]	-	[illegible]
1884,	[illegible]	[illegible]	[illegible]	-	[illegible]	[illegible]	[illegible]	[illegible]	[illegible]	-	[illegible]	[illegible]	[illegible]	[illegible]	-	[illegible]
1885,	[illegible]	[illegible]	[illegible]	-	[illegible]	[illegible]	[illegible]	[illegible]	-	[illegible]	[illegible]	231,313	[illegible]	-	[illegible]	[illegible]
1886,	[illegible]	7,815	15·0	[illegible]	-	[illegible]	[illegible]	[illegible]	-	[illegible]	[illegible]	223,202	456·5	-	8,111	13·2

* Estimated population for the middle of each year from the Registrar-General's Returns.

From this statement it appears that the total number of criminal offences during the year 1886, was 223,202 or 456·5 per 10,000 of the estimated population, as compared with 231,313 or 469·7 per 10,000 of the population in 1885, showing a decrease of 8,111 in number, and a decrease of 13·2 in the rate per 10,000 persons. Offences not disposed of summarily, constituting the more serious group of crimes, are somewhat more numerous than in any of the three years immediately preceding, but show a decrease of 3,291 as compared with the year 1882; and the absolute number (7,815) of these offences, and their ratio to the estimated population (15·0 per 10,000), are below the corresponding averages for the five years ending with 1881. The charges summarily disposed of, which, after having for three years shown a rather marked tendency to increase, declined considerably in 1885, again exhibit a considerable decrease, and are below the average annual number for the last ten years.

General Distribution of Criminal Offences.—The following statement shows the distribution of criminal offences in Ireland by Provinces, Counties, and large Town Districts, such as the Dublin Metropolitan Police District, the Borough of Belfast, &c.

STATEMENT showing the DISTRIBUTION throughout IRELAND of INDICTABLE OFFENCES not DETERMINED SUMMARILY, of OFFENCES DETERMINED SUMMARILY, and of the TOTAL CRIMINAL OFFENCES, for the YEARS 1855 and 1856.

COUNTIES. (Inclusive of Cities, with Dublin and Belfast Police Districts.)	Population in 1851 in thousands	Indictable Offences not Determined Summarily: 1855	1856	1856: Increased	1856: Decreased	1856: Rate per 10,000 Population	Offences Determined Summarily: 1855	1856	1856: Increased	1856: Decreased	1856: Rate per 10,000 Population	Total Criminal Offences: 1855	1856	1856: Increased	1856: Decreased	1856: Rate per 10,000 Population
TOTAL OF IRELAND.	[illegible]	[illegible]	[illegible]	[illegible]	[illegible]	[illegible]	[illegible]	[illegible]	[illegible]	[illegible]	[illegible]	[illegible]	[illegible]	[illegible]	[illegible]	[illegible]
LEINSTER.																
Carlow,	[illegible]	[illegible]	[illegible]	[illegible]	[illegible]	[illegible]	[illegible]	[illegible]	[illegible]	[illegible]	[illegible]	[illegible]	[illegible]	[illegible]	[illegible]	[illegible]
Drogheda Town,	[illegible]	[illegible]	[illegible]	[illegible]	[illegible]	[illegible]	[illegible]	[illegible]	[illegible]	[illegible]	[illegible]	[illegible]	[illegible]	[illegible]	[illegible]	[illegible]
Dublin,	[illegible]	[illegible]	[illegible]	[illegible]	[illegible]	[illegible]	[illegible]	[illegible]	[illegible]	[illegible]	[illegible]	[illegible]	[illegible]	[illegible]	[illegible]	[illegible]
Dublin Metropolitan Police District,	[illegible]	[illegible]	[illegible]	[illegible]	[illegible]	[illegible]	[illegible]	[illegible]	[illegible]	[illegible]	[illegible]	[illegible]	[illegible]	[illegible]	[illegible]	[illegible]
Kildare,	[illegible]	[illegible]	[illegible]	[illegible]	[illegible]	[illegible]	[illegible]	[illegible]	[illegible]	[illegible]	[illegible]	[illegible]	[illegible]	[illegible]	[illegible]	[illegible]
Kilkenny,	[illegible]	[illegible]	[illegible]	[illegible]	[illegible]	[illegible]	[illegible]	[illegible]	[illegible]	[illegible]	[illegible]	[illegible]	[illegible]	[illegible]	[illegible]	[illegible]
King's County,	[illegible]	[illegible]	[illegible]	[illegible]	[illegible]	[illegible]	[illegible]	[illegible]	[illegible]	[illegible]	[illegible]	[illegible]	[illegible]	[illegible]	[illegible]	[illegible]
Longford,	[illegible]	[illegible]	[illegible]	[illegible]	[illegible]	[illegible]	[illegible]	[illegible]	[illegible]	[illegible]	[illegible]	[illegible]	[illegible]	[illegible]	[illegible]	[illegible]
Louth,	[illegible]	[illegible]	[illegible]	[illegible]	[illegible]	[illegible]	[illegible]	[illegible]	[illegible]	[illegible]	[illegible]	[illegible]	[illegible]	[illegible]	[illegible]	[illegible]
Meath,	[illegible]	[illegible]	[illegible]	[illegible]	[illegible]	[illegible]	[illegible]	[illegible]	[illegible]	[illegible]	[illegible]	[illegible]	[illegible]	[illegible]	[illegible]	[illegible]
Queen's County,	[illegible]	[illegible]	[illegible]	[illegible]	[illegible]	[illegible]	[illegible]	[illegible]	[illegible]	[illegible]	[illegible]	[illegible]	[illegible]	[illegible]	[illegible]	[illegible]
Westmeath,	[illegible]	[illegible]	[illegible]	[illegible]	[illegible]	[illegible]	[illegible]	[illegible]	[illegible]	[illegible]	[illegible]	[illegible]	[illegible]	[illegible]	[illegible]	[illegible]
Wexford,	[illegible]	[illegible]	[illegible]	[illegible]	[illegible]	[illegible]	[illegible]	[illegible]	[illegible]	[illegible]	[illegible]	[illegible]	[illegible]	[illegible]	[illegible]	[illegible]
Wicklow,	[illegible]	[illegible]	[illegible]	[illegible]	[illegible]	[illegible]	[illegible]	[illegible]	[illegible]	[illegible]	[illegible]	[illegible]	[illegible]	[illegible]	[illegible]	[illegible]
Total of Leinster,	[illegible]	[illegible]	[illegible]	[illegible]	[illegible]	[illegible]	[illegible]	[illegible]	[illegible]	[illegible]	[illegible]	[illegible]	[illegible]	[illegible]	[illegible]	[illegible]
MUNSTER.																
Clare,	[illegible]	[illegible]	[illegible]	[illegible]	[illegible]	[illegible]	[illegible]	[illegible]	[illegible]	[illegible]	[illegible]	[illegible]	[illegible]	[illegible]	[illegible]	[illegible]
Cork, E.R.,	[illegible]	[illegible]	[illegible]	[illegible]	[illegible]	[illegible]	[illegible]	[illegible]	[illegible]	[illegible]	[illegible]	[illegible]	[illegible]	[illegible]	[illegible]	[illegible]
Cork, W.R.,	[illegible]	[illegible]	[illegible]	[illegible]	[illegible]	[illegible]	[illegible]	[illegible]	[illegible]	[illegible]	[illegible]	[illegible]	[illegible]	[illegible]	[illegible]	[illegible]
Cork City,	[illegible]	[illegible]	[illegible]	[illegible]	[illegible]	[illegible]	[illegible]	[illegible]	[illegible]	[illegible]	[illegible]	[illegible]	[illegible]	[illegible]	[illegible]	[illegible]
Kerry,	[illegible]	[illegible]	[illegible]	[illegible]	[illegible]	[illegible]	[illegible]	[illegible]	[illegible]	[illegible]	[illegible]	[illegible]	[illegible]	[illegible]	[illegible]	[illegible]
Limerick,	[illegible]	[illegible]	[illegible]	[illegible]	[illegible]	[illegible]	[illegible]	[illegible]	[illegible]	[illegible]	[illegible]	[illegible]	[illegible]	[illegible]	[illegible]	[illegible]
Limerick City,	[illegible]	[illegible]	[illegible]	[illegible]	[illegible]	[illegible]	[illegible]	[illegible]	[illegible]	[illegible]	[illegible]	[illegible]	[illegible]	[illegible]	[illegible]	[illegible]
Tipperary, N.R.,	[illegible]	[illegible]	[illegible]	[illegible]	[illegible]	[illegible]	[illegible]	[illegible]	[illegible]	[illegible]	[illegible]	[illegible]	[illegible]	[illegible]	[illegible]	[illegible]
Tipperary, S.R.,	[illegible]	[illegible]	[illegible]	[illegible]	[illegible]	[illegible]	[illegible]	[illegible]	[illegible]	[illegible]	[illegible]	[illegible]	[illegible]	[illegible]	[illegible]	[illegible]
Waterford,	[illegible]	[illegible]	[illegible]	[illegible]	[illegible]	[illegible]	[illegible]	[illegible]	[illegible]	[illegible]	[illegible]	[illegible]	[illegible]	[illegible]	[illegible]	[illegible]
Waterford City,	[illegible]	[illegible]	[illegible]	[illegible]	[illegible]	[illegible]	[illegible]	[illegible]	[illegible]	[illegible]	[illegible]	[illegible]	[illegible]	[illegible]	[illegible]	[illegible]
Total of Munster,	[illegible]	[illegible]	[illegible]	[illegible]	[illegible]	[illegible]	[illegible]	[illegible]	[illegible]	[illegible]	[illegible]	[illegible]	[illegible]	[illegible]	[illegible]	[illegible]
ULSTER.																
Antrim,	[illegible]	[illegible]	[illegible]	[illegible]	[illegible]	[illegible]	[illegible]	[illegible]	[illegible]	[illegible]	[illegible]	[illegible]	[illegible]	[illegible]	[illegible]	[illegible]
Armagh,	[illegible]	[illegible]	[illegible]	[illegible]	[illegible]	[illegible]	[illegible]	[illegible]	[illegible]	[illegible]	[illegible]	[illegible]	[illegible]	[illegible]	[illegible]	[illegible]
Belfast Town,	[illegible]	[illegible]	[illegible]	[illegible]	[illegible]	[illegible]	[illegible]	[illegible]	[illegible]	[illegible]	[illegible]	[illegible]	[illegible]	[illegible]	[illegible]	[illegible]
Carrickfergus Town,	[illegible]	[illegible]	[illegible]	[illegible]	[illegible]	[illegible]	[illegible]	[illegible]	[illegible]	[illegible]	[illegible]	[illegible]	[illegible]	[illegible]	[illegible]	[illegible]
Cavan,	[illegible]	[illegible]	[illegible]	[illegible]	[illegible]	[illegible]	[illegible]	[illegible]	[illegible]	[illegible]	[illegible]	[illegible]	[illegible]	[illegible]	[illegible]	[illegible]
Donegal,	[illegible]	[illegible]	[illegible]	[illegible]	[illegible]	[illegible]	[illegible]	[illegible]	[illegible]	[illegible]	[illegible]	[illegible]	[illegible]	[illegible]	[illegible]	[illegible]
Down,	[illegible]	[illegible]	[illegible]	[illegible]	[illegible]	[illegible]	[illegible]	[illegible]	[illegible]	[illegible]	[illegible]	[illegible]	[illegible]	[illegible]	[illegible]	[illegible]
Fermanagh,	[illegible]	[illegible]	[illegible]	[illegible]	[illegible]	[illegible]	[illegible]	[illegible]	[illegible]	[illegible]	[illegible]	[illegible]	[illegible]	[illegible]	[illegible]	[illegible]
Londonderry,	[illegible]	[illegible]	[illegible]	[illegible]	[illegible]	[illegible]	[illegible]	[illegible]	[illegible]	[illegible]	[illegible]	[illegible]	[illegible]	[illegible]	[illegible]	[illegible]
Monaghan,	[illegible]	[illegible]	[illegible]	[illegible]	[illegible]	[illegible]	[illegible]	[illegible]	[illegible]	[illegible]	[illegible]	[illegible]	[illegible]	[illegible]	[illegible]	[illegible]
Tyrone,	[illegible]	[illegible]	[illegible]	[illegible]	[illegible]	[illegible]	[illegible]	[illegible]	[illegible]	[illegible]	[illegible]	[illegible]	[illegible]	[illegible]	[illegible]	[illegible]
Total of Ulster,	[illegible]	[illegible]	[illegible]	[illegible]	[illegible]	[illegible]	[illegible]	[illegible]	[illegible]	[illegible]	[illegible]	[illegible]	[illegible]	[illegible]	[illegible]	[illegible]
CONNAUGHT.																
Galway, E.R.,	[illegible]	[illegible]	[illegible]	[illegible]	[illegible]	[illegible]	[illegible]	[illegible]	[illegible]	[illegible]	[illegible]	[illegible]	[illegible]	[illegible]	[illegible]	[illegible]
Galway, W.R.,	[illegible]	[illegible]	[illegible]	[illegible]	[illegible]	[illegible]	[illegible]	[illegible]	[illegible]	[illegible]	[illegible]	[illegible]	[illegible]	[illegible]	[illegible]	[illegible]
Galway Town,	[illegible]	[illegible]	[illegible]	[illegible]	[illegible]	[illegible]	[illegible]	[illegible]	[illegible]	[illegible]	[illegible]	[illegible]	[illegible]	[illegible]	[illegible]	[illegible]
Leitrim,	[illegible]	[illegible]	[illegible]	[illegible]	[illegible]	[illegible]	[illegible]	[illegible]	[illegible]	[illegible]	[illegible]	[illegible]	[illegible]	[illegible]	[illegible]	[illegible]
Mayo,	[illegible]	[illegible]	[illegible]	[illegible]	[illegible]	[illegible]	[illegible]	[illegible]	[illegible]	[illegible]	[illegible]	[illegible]	[illegible]	[illegible]	[illegible]	[illegible]
Roscommon,	[illegible]	[illegible]	[illegible]	[illegible]	[illegible]	[illegible]	[illegible]	[illegible]	[illegible]	[illegible]	[illegible]	[illegible]	[illegible]	[illegible]	[illegible]	[illegible]
Sligo,	[illegible]	[illegible]	[illegible]	[illegible]	[illegible]	[illegible]	[illegible]	[illegible]	[illegible]	[illegible]	[illegible]	[illegible]	[illegible]	[illegible]	[illegible]	[illegible]
Total of Connaught,	[illegible]	[illegible]	[illegible]	[illegible]	[illegible]	[illegible]	[illegible]	[illegible]	[illegible]	[illegible]	[illegible]	[illegible]	[illegible]	[illegible]	[illegible]	[illegible]

From this statement it appears that the 233,208 criminal offences in Ireland in 1856 were distributed as follows throughout the four Provinces :—

Part I. Criminal Statistics. — Chapter I. Statistics of Crime. — Distribution of crime.

Leinster, 90,914, or at the rate of 710·8 per 10,000 of the population in 1881; Munster, 54,387, or at the rate of 408·6 per 10,000; Ulster, 54,257, or 311·8 per 10,000; and Connaught, 23,644, or 287·6 per 10,000. Compared with the year 1885, there has been a decrease of criminal cases in Leinster to the extent of 1,636, or 12·8 per 10,000 persons; a decrease of 4,346, or 32·7 per 10,000, in Munster; a decrease of 727, or 4·2 per 10,000, in Ulster; and a decrease of 1,402, or 17·1 per 10,000, in Connaught. The more serious cases (those not determined summarily) have decreased in Leinster, and increased in the other Provinces. The less serious offences (those determined summarily) have decreased in all the provinces, notably in Munster.

Criminal offences show a decrease in the total number in 38 counties and districts, and an increase in 10.

In the following list the counties and districts are arranged in order from that in which there was least crime (in 1886) to that in which there was most:—

1. Donegal.	12. Cavan.	23. Kilkenny.	34. Clare.
2. Antrim.	13. Longford.	24. Galway, E.R.	35. Kerry.
3. Carrickfergus Town.	14. Roscommon.	25. Carlow.	36. Kildare.
4. Mayo.	15. Limerick (County).	26. Louth.	37. Drogheda Town.
5. Down.	16. Cork, E.R.	27. Armagh.	38. Belfast Town.
6. Leitrim.	17. Wicklow.	28. Queen's County.	39. Galway Town.
7. Fermanagh.	18. Galway, W.R.	29. Dublin (County).	40. Limerick City.
8. Wexford.	19. Meath.	30. Tipperary, N.R.	41. Waterford City.
9. Monaghan.	20. King's County.	31. Londonderry.	42. Cork City.
10. Waterford (County).	21. Sligo.	32. Tipperary, S.R.	43. Dublin Metropolitan Police District.
11. Tyrone.	22. Cork, W.R.	33. Westmeath.	

It will be observed that in the above list the seven principal Town Districts occupy the most unfavourable position. This is owing to the greater criminality of town populations, which is more fully demonstrated in the following statement, where the rate of crime to the population in the principal Town Districts is compared with the rate in the adjacent Country Districts.

Excess of crime in urban districts.

Statement showing for the year 1886, the Proportion of Criminal Offences in each 10,000 of Population in the under-mentioned Districts, and the excess of crime in Urban Districts.

Districts.	Offences per 10,000 of Population.			Number of Offences in Urban Districts for every 100 Offences in an equal number of Inhabitants of adjoining Counties.
	In Urban District.	Adjoining County.	Excess in Urban District.	
Dublin Metropolis,	1701·6	352·4	1363·2	483
Cork City,	907·0	304·8	602·2	298
Waterford City,	901·7	271·3	630·4	333
Limerick City,	864·4	323·1	540·3	293
Galway Town,	813·7	311·6	501·2	260
Belfast,	698·6	178·2	518·4	391
Drogheda,	376·7	230·0	226·7	165

It will be observed that the criminal offences in Dublin Metropolis exceeded those among an equal number of the inhabitants of the adjacent County in the proportion of 483 to 100, and that even in Drogheda, where the excess of crime in the Urban over the adjacent Rural District was least, the proportion was as 165 to 100.

Character of persons proceeded against. Table 10.

The character of the persons proceeded against is set forth in the following statement, from which it appears that the character of 16·9 per cent. of those persons was unknown to the Police, and that the character of 88·1 per cent. of the remainder was ascertained to have been previously good.

STATEMENT showing the CHARACTER of PERSONS PROCEEDED AGAINST for CRIMINAL OFFENCES in IRELAND in 1886.

CHARACTER OF PERSONS PROCEEDED AGAINST IN 1886.	IRELAND IN 1886.	
	Total.	Proportion of each Class to the Total Number.
		Per cent.
Total number proceeded against,	190,181	100·
Deduct persons whose character is unknown,	27,188	14·3
Total number whose character is known,	162,993	100·
Previous Good Character,	161,182	68·1
Suspicious Characters,	8,128	4·6
Prostitutes,	4,853	2·4
Vagrants, Tramps, and others without any visible means of subsistence,	1,329	0·4
Habitual Drunkards (not under other heads),	3,440	1·9
Known Thieves,	1,773	1·0

Part I. Criminal Statistics. — Chapter I. — Statement showing the character of persons proceeded against.

NATURE OF CRIMES.

Nature of Crimes.

Distribution of the more serious offences throughout Ireland. Table 6.

In Police Tables 6 and 7 of the Appendix, the nature of the Crimes committed is set forth in detail. The following abstract (see page 20) has been constructed from Table 6, which includes the more serious offences, namely those not dealt with summarily, and gives their distribution throughout Ireland in detail.

The total number of these cases amounted to 7,315, or at the rate of 14·1 per 10,000 of the population, according to the Census of 1881. Of these, 1,456, or 2·8 per 10,000 of the population, were offences against the person; 535, or 1·0 per 10,000, against property with violence; 3,185, or 6·1 per 10,000, against property without violence; 893, or 1·7 per 10,000, were malicious offences against property. Cases of forgery and offences against the currency were only 67, or 0·1 per 10,000, and all other cases amounted to 1,227. It will be observed that the rate per 10,000 of all offences not disposed of summarily was in Leinster 31·1; Munster, 12·3; Ulster, 8·1; and Connaught, 6·9.

Offences against the person.

In the case of *Offences against the Person* the rates per 10,000 of the population were:—for Leinster 5·5 (including 15·6 in the Dublin Metropolitan District), Munster, 2·2; Ulster, 1·8; Connaught, 1·9. The largest number of these offences, both absolutely and relatively, were committed in the Dublin Metropolitan District, amounting to 547, or 15·6 per 10,000; the next largest, in proportion to population, in Cork City and Belfast Town, respectively, amounting to 4·5 per 10,000; the rate in Limerick County was 4·9, in Drogheda Town 4·2, and in the West Riding of Galway 3·7. In all the other counties and districts it was below 3 per 10,000, being below 1·0 in three.

Malicious offences against property.

In the case of *Malicious Offences against Property* it appears that the rates per 10,000 of the population were for Leinster 1·4, Munster 2·9, Ulster 1·1, Connaught 1·6. The highest rate (4·7) was in Limerick County, the next (4·4) in Longford County. The lowest was 0·1 in Antrim County, and the next lowest 0·2 in Down County. In the City of Limerick and the Town of Carrickfergus this class of crime was absent.

Louth, ...
Meath, ...
Queen's County, ...
Westmeath, ...
Wexford, ...
Wicklow, ...

TOTAL OF LEINSTER.

MUNSTER.

Clare, ...
Cork, East Riding, . . .
Cork, West Riding, . . .
Cork City, ...
Kerry, ...
Limerick, ...
Limerick City, ...
Tipperary, North Riding, . .
Tipperary, South Riding, . .
Waterford, ...
Waterford City, ...

TOTAL OF MUNSTER.

ULSTER.

Antrim, ...
Armagh, ...
Belfast Town, ...
Carrickfergus Town, . . .
Cavan, ...
Donegal, ...
Down, ...
Fermanagh, ...
Londonderry, ...
Monaghan, ...
Tyrone, ...

TOTAL OF ULSTER.

CONNAUGHT.

Galway, East Riding, . . .
Galway, West Riding, . . .
Galway Town, . . .
Leitrim, ...
Mayo, ...
Roscommon, ...
Sligo, . . .

Forgery and Offences against the currency.

The cases of *Forgery* and *Offences against the Currency* amounted to the small number of 67, or 0·1 per 10,000 of the population: of these, 28 were in Dublin Metropolitan Police District, 12 in Belfast, 4 in Mayo County, and 3 in Down County.

Miscellaneous offences.

Of offences of the *Miscellaneous class* there were 1,227, or at the rate of 2·4 per 10,000 of the population. The principal portion of this group of crimes is made up of the *offence of Intimidation by Threatening Letters, Notices, or otherwise*: the number of cases (740) of this nature is in excess of the number (710) for the year 1885, which was considerably over the comparatively low numbers for the two preceding years, when there were but 523 and 535 cases respectively, as compared with 2,651 in 1882, and 3,093 in 1881. Of the total number of miscellaneous offences, 241, or 1·9 per 10,000 of the population, were in Leinster, including 99 cases of intimidation by threatening letters, &c. (of which 15 were in King's County, and 28 in Westmeath); 586, or 4·4 per 10,000 inhabitants, were in Munster, including 425 cases of intimidation, of which 160 were in Kerry, 128 in Clare, 49 in the East, and 18 in the West Riding of Cork, 17 in the North, and 12 in the South Riding of Tipperary, and 41 in Limerick County. In Ulster there were 224 miscellaneous offences, or 1·3 per 10,000 of the population; of them, 78 (including 14 in Cavan, and 16 in Londonderry County) were cases of intimidation, and 69 (including 49 in Belfast) were cases of *riot, breach of the peace, &c.* In Connaught the number of miscellaneous offences was 176, or 2·1 per 10,000 of the population, including 138 cases of intimidation, of which 44 were in East Galway, 30 in West Galway, 18 in Mayo, 22 in Roscommon, and 15 in Sligo.

Apprehensions, Table 4.

For the indictable offences not disposed of summarily, there were 4,294 persons apprehended, being equal to 59 per cent. of the number of offences as compared with 52 per cent. in the previous year.

Offences not determined summarily in 1886 compared with previous years. Table 6.

The following summary—also constructed from Table 6—showing the number of offences not determined summarily, classified according to their nature and compared with previous years—will give a fair idea of the variations which have taken place during the past eight years in the number of more serious offences in Ireland:—

OFFENCES	1886	1885	1884	1883	1882	1881	1880	1879
1. Against the Person, . . .	2,458	1,294	1,591	1,187	1,503	1,175	1,369	1,457
2. Against Property with Violence, .	525	359	329	110	540	751	584	592
3. Against Property without Violence,	3,135	3,470	3,801	3,977	4,101	4,018	3,063	4,121
4. Malicious against Property, . .	403	735	713	753	1,280	1,671	1,133	704
5. Forgery and against Currency, .	67	43	48	41	58	60	91	104
6. Not included in foregoing, . .	1,227	1,040	629	597	3,104	3,301	2,367	1,191
Total, ...	7,815	6,961	7,168	7,214	10,606	11,913	8,607	8,059

This statement shows that in 1886 the total number of serious crimes was much below the average for the preceding seven years, and that there was a decrease in some and an increase in other classes of such crimes.

Compared with the year 1885, there was an increase in all classes except *offences against property without violence*, in which there was a decrease of about 10 per cent.

Murders.

A more minute consideration of Table 6 in the Appendix will show that there were 19 cases of *murders of infants*, of which 2 were in Leinster, 7 in Munster, 8 in Ulster, and 2 in Connaught. In the case of *other murders* there were 35 in Ireland, in 1886, as compared with 18 in 1885, 21 in 1884, 17 in 1883, 40 in 1882, 40 in 1881, 22 in 1880, and

Part I. General Statistics. — Chapter I. Statistics of Crime. — Attempts to murder, shooting at, wounding, &c.

22 in 1879. Of these 35 murders, 3 were in Leinster, 12 in Munster, 13 in Ulster, and 7 in Connaught. There was 1 murder each in Dublin County, Kildare, Longford, Cork West Riding, Cork City, Tipperary North Riding, Fermanagh, Galway East Riding, Galway Town, Roscommon, and Sligo; 2 in Tipperary South Riding, and Armagh respectively; 3 each in Clare, Down, and Mayo; 4 in Kerry, and 7 in Belfast Town. There were not any such murders in Carlow County, Drogheda Town, Dublin Metropolitan Police District, Kilkenny, King's County, Louth, Meath, Queen's County, Westmeath, Wexford, or Wicklow, in the Province of Leinster; nor in Cork East Riding, Limerick County, Limerick City, Waterford County, or the City of Waterford, in the Province of Munster; nor in Antrim County, Carrickfergus Town, Cavan County, Donegal, Londonderry, Monaghan, or Tyrone, in the Province of Ulster; nor in Galway West Riding, or Leitrim, in the Province of Connaught. There were 13 *attempts to murder* in 1886, as compared with 5 in 1885, 1 in 1884, 11 in 1883, 35 in 1882, 19 in 1881, 10 in 1880, and 6 in 1879. There were 146 cases of *shooting at, wounding, stabbing, &c., with intent to do bodily harm*, in 1886, compared with 143 in 1885, 152 in 1884, 158 in 1883, 253 in 1882; 246 in 1881; 226 in 1880, and 160 in 1879. The cases of *assault and inflicting bodily harm*, were 720 in 1886, compared with 642 in 1885, 687 in 1884, 488 in 1883, 574 in 1882, 426 in 1881, 418 in 1880, and 530 in 1879. The number of *offences against property with violence* was 685, being 176 in excess of the number for the preceding year, and slightly in excess of the average for the seven years 1879–85.

Offences against property without violence.

In cases of *offences against property without violence*, there was a decline from 3,470 in 1885 to 3,135 last year. As usual, *simple larceny* contributes more than half the crime in this class. It is also again to be noted that a very large proportion of this class of crime is committed in the Dublin Metropolitan Police District. Of the 3,135 offences against property without violence in Ireland, included in Table 6, no less than 2,505, or 80 per cent. were in that District, and of the 1,968 simple larceny cases, 1,733 occurred there.

The classes of *malicious offences against property, offences against the currency* and *miscellaneous offences*, included in Table 6, have already been sufficiently dealt with in the general comments on crime not determined summarily.

Offences disposed of summarily. Table 7.

In Table 7 of the Appendix details are given of the cases determined summarily, which include those usually dealt with in police courts.

These, as previously shown, amount to a total of 215,887, and constitute 97 per cent. of the total crime of the country. It is also in this class that the preponderance of town over rural crime is specially noticeable. Among the offences disposed of summarily the more important are set out in the following statement, and a comparison instituted with the previous year.

	1886.	1885.
Common Assaults, . . .	23,011	22,444
Drunkenness, . . .	79,828	87,133

Thus there has been an increase of 567 in common assaults, and a decrease of 7,305 cases of drunkenness and disorderly conduct in connexion therewith. As these cases constitute more than one half of all the cases dealt with in the police and Petty Sessions courts, are clearly connected with one another, and are the starting points of many other criminal actions, their import is very great when measuring the general condition of the criminal classes.

Habitual drunkards' convictions. Table 11.

In connexion with the statistics of drunkenness, a special return of habitual drunkards (Table 11, page 82) has been compiled, in continuation of a similar Return for the year 1885; it gives the number of persons convicted three times or upwards for being

Part I. Criminal Statistics. — Chapter I. Statistics of Crime. — Habitual Drunkards. Table 11.

The chief value of the habitual drunkenness return is in the light it throws upon the causes of town crime, which has been noticed as excessive. Taking the seven town jurisdictions outside Dublin, of Belfast, Cork, Limerick, Waterford, Galway, Drogheda, and Carrickfergus, with an aggregate population of 391,000, the habitual drunkards were 613, or 15·7 per 10,000 of the population. In the rest of Ireland, outside the Metropolitan district, with a population of 4,434,000, the number was only 1,768, or 4·0 in the 10,000. In the Dublin Metropolitan Police District, with a population of 350,000, the number was 211, or 6·0 per 10,000 population. Compared with 1885 there was an increase in the number in Cork, Limerick, Drogheda, and Carrickfergus, and a decrease in each of the other town jurisdictions, including Dublin. In the rest of Ireland there was a decrease, from 2,127 to 1,768. In all Ireland there was a decrease of 460—viz., from 3,052 to 2,592. Of this total, 2,046 were convictions three times and less than five times, 445 five times and less than ten times, and 101 ten times and upwards. It will be observed from Table 7 that the number of cases of "illegally selling intoxicating drinks" fell from 3,614 in 1885, to 2,139 in 1886.

Illegally Selling Intoxicating Drinks. Table 7.

Cases of *cruelty to animals* were 1,505 in 1885, and 1,322 in 1886. *Offences against Local Acts and Borough By-laws* show an increase, from 15,704 in 1885 to 17,917 in 1886: the latter number includes 13,112 cases in the Dublin Metropolitan Police district. The number of *offences against the Public Health and Nuisances Removal Acts*, was 5,117, or 359 more than in 1885: of the 5,117 charges under these Acts 4,275 were in the Dublin Metropolitan district. In a considerable number of districts no offences against these Acts are recorded. Cases of *unlawful possession of stolen goods* show no appreciable change, the number for 1885 being 1,115, and that for last year 1,107. The *offences against the Highway Act*, including Nuisances on Public Roads, fell from 20,293 in 1885 to 14,654 in 1886. The other statistics contained in Table 7 do not call for any special remark, but, nevertheless, contain many items of considerable interest.

Cruelty to animals. Local Acts and Borough By-laws. Public Health and Nuisances Removal Acts. Unlawful possession of stolen goods. Highway Act.

CHAPTER II.—MODES OF PROCEDURE FOR PUNISHING CRIME.

Chapter II. Procedure.

The Police act as public prosecutors in the great majority of cases in Ireland. In minor cases they undertake the sole duty of prosecuting, and in most of the more serious offences the preliminary proceedings are instituted by them. In all the counties of Ireland, except the County and City of Dublin and the Counties of Kildare and Mayo, there are two Crown Solicitors, one of whom deals with cases at Quarter Sessions, the other with the more serious cases which come before the Judges at Assizes.

Coroners' Courts still deal with cases where criminal offences are involved, and Coroners' Juries frequently find verdicts implicating or exonerating certain persons in cases of homicide, &c. It is not, however, the custom now to bring prisoners charged with homicide, &c., before Coroners' Courts, and in a large number of cases the finding of the Jury relates merely to the cause of death.

A special feature in the administration of Criminal Law in Ireland is the proclamation of certain Districts under special Acts of Parliament. The following is a general statement relating to these Special Acts and the extent of their application in Ireland during the past year.

Under the Act 6 Wm. IV., chap. 13, the following counties were proclaimed as requiring additional Police at the end of 1886:—Clare, Cork, Galway, Kerry, Leitrim, Limerick, Mayo, Roscommon, Tipperary, and Westmeath, as also were portions of the counties of Longford, Sligo, and Waterford.

Districts proclaimed under special Acts. Tables 12, 13, 14.

Part I. Criminal Statistics. — Chapter II. Procedure. — Districts Proclaimed under Special Acts.

Under the Peace Preservation (Ireland) Act, 1881, and the Peace Preservation (Ireland) Continuance Act, 1886, prohibiting the carrying or having arms without a licence, two provinces, viz., Munster and Connaught; all of the province of Leinster except the Counties of Louth and Wicklow, and the City of Kilkenny; and the Town of Belfast, the City of Londonderry, and parts of the Counties of Armagh, Donegal, and Monaghan were proclaimed at the end of 1886. In Ulster the prohibition against carrying arms included the Counties of Cavan, Fermanagh, and Monaghan, one Barony in Down, and five Baronies in Tyrone.

Results of preliminary inquiry as to offences. Table I.

Of 4,294 persons apprehended in 1886 for offences punishable after indictment and trial by jury, 1,696, or 39·5 per cent., were discharged; 235, or 5·5 per cent. were bailed or committed in default of finding bail pending further examination; 2,363, or 55·0 per cent., were committed for trial or admitted to bail pending trial.

Disposal of bills of indictment by grand jury. Table 20.

The result of proceedings in 607 cases brought before Grand Juries was that in 236 cases no bill was found, in 174 cases no prosecution took place, and in 197 bail was accepted, and the cases not tried. In addition to those bailed and not tried, or where there was no prosecution, there were 106 cases in which trials were postponed after disagreement of the juries, &c.

Disposal of persons tried by jury. Table 20.

Of 2,314 persons tried by jury in 1886, 679, or 29·3 per cent. were acquitted; besides 16, or 0·7 per cent. who were found insane or acquitted on the ground of insanity, 1,619, or 70·0 per cent. were convicted.

The following statement shows for the past decade the number of persons tried by jury at Assizes, at the Dublin Commission Court and at Quarter Sessions, and how their cases were disposed of:—

Year.	Tried.	Convicted or Detained as Insane.	Acquitted.	Proportion per cent. of those Tried who were	
				Convicted or Detained as Insane.	Acquitted.
1877, . . .	3,191	2,311	880	72·4	27·6
1878, . . .	3,168	2,306	828	72·1	27·9
1879, . . .	3,364	2,317	1,047	68·9	31·1
1880, . . .	3,153	2,287	1,036	69·6	30·5
1881, . . .	3,850	2,716	1,134	70·5	29·6
1882, . . .	3,163	2,280	882	72·1	27·9
1883, . . .	2,221	1,760	461	79·2	20·8
1884, . . .	2,133	1,564	563	73·4	26·6
1885, . . .	2,155	1,584	571	73·5	26·5
1886, . . .	2,314	1,635	679	70·7	29·3

In the next statement the sentences inflicted on persons convicted, after trial by jury, in 1886, are set out in comparison with similar cases in 1885.

Disposal of Persons Committed for Trial by Jury.

Part I. Criminal Statistics.

Chapter II. Procedure.

Disposal of men and boys for trial by jury compared with disposal of women and girls.

Table 20.

How Disposed of.	1886. Total, 1886.	1886. Men and Boys.	1886. Women and Girls.	1886. Proportion disposed of: Men and Boys.	1886. Proportion disposed of: Women and Girls.	1885. Total, 1885.	1885. Men and Boys.	1885. Women and Girls.	1885. Proportion disposed of: Men and Boys.	1885. Proportion disposed of: Women and Girls.
				Per cent.	Per cent.				Per cent.	Per cent.
Total number of persons sent for trial,	[illegible]	[illegible]	[illegible]	[illegible]	[illegible]	[illegible]	[illegible]	[illegible]	[illegible]	[illegible]
[illegible],	[illegible]	[illegible]	[illegible]	[illegible]	[illegible]	[illegible]	[illegible]	[illegible]	[illegible]	[illegible]
Viz.—[illegible],	[illegible]	[illegible]	[illegible]	[illegible]	[illegible]	[illegible]	[illegible]	[illegible]	[illegible]	[illegible]
No bills found against,	[illegible]	[illegible]	[illegible]	[illegible]	[illegible]	[illegible]	[illegible]	[illegible]	[illegible]	[illegible]
Not prosecuted,	[illegible]	[illegible]	[illegible]	[illegible]	[illegible]	[illegible]	[illegible]	[illegible]	[illegible]	[illegible]
[illegible] postponed after disagreement of jury, etc.	[illegible]	[illegible]	[illegible]	[illegible]	[illegible]	[illegible]	[illegible]	[illegible]	[illegible]	[illegible]
[illegible] tried and disposed of, I and II.,	[illegible]	[illegible]	[illegible]	[illegible] / [illegible]	[illegible] / [illegible]	[illegible]	[illegible]	[illegible]	[illegible] / [illegible]	[illegible] / [illegible]
I. Convicted or detained as insane,	[illegible]	[illegible]	[illegible]	[illegible]	[illegible]	[illegible]	[illegible]	[illegible]	[illegible]	[illegible]
Viz.—Sentenced to death,	[illegible]	[illegible]	[illegible]	[illegible]	[illegible]	[illegible]	[illegible]	[illegible]	[illegible]	[illegible]
Penal servitude.—										
For life,	[illegible]	[illegible]	.	[illegible]	.	[illegible]	[illegible]	.	[illegible]	.
Above 10 years,	[illegible]	[illegible]	[illegible]	[illegible]	[illegible]	[illegible]	[illegible]	.	[illegible]	.
For 10 and above 5 years,	[illegible]	[illegible]	[illegible]	[illegible]	[illegible]	[illegible]	[illegible]	[illegible]	[illegible]	[illegible]
For 5 years,	[illegible]	[illegible]	[illegible]	[illegible]	[illegible]	[illegible]	[illegible]	[illegible]	[illegible]	[illegible]
Found insane, or acquitted on ground of insanity,	[illegible]	[illegible]	[illegible]	[illegible]	[illegible]	[illegible]	[illegible]	[illegible]	[illegible]	[illegible]
Imprisonment.—										
Above 2 years,	[illegible]	[illegible]	[illegible]	[illegible]	[illegible]	[illegible]	[illegible]	[illegible]	[illegible]	[illegible]
For 2 years and above 6 months,	[illegible]	[illegible]	[illegible]	[illegible]	[illegible]	[illegible]	[illegible]	[illegible]	[illegible]	[illegible]
For 6 months and under,	[illegible]	[illegible]	[illegible]	[illegible]	[illegible]	[illegible]	[illegible]	[illegible]	[illegible]	[illegible]
Whipping, fined, discharged on sureties, sentence not passed, or sentence respited,	[illegible]	[illegible]	[illegible]	[illegible]	[illegible]	[illegible]	[illegible]	[illegible]	[illegible]	[illegible]
II. Acquitted on trial,	[illegible]	[illegible]	[illegible]	[illegible]	[illegible]	[illegible]	[illegible]	[illegible]	[illegible]	[illegible]
Sent to Reformatory Schools, included in I.	[illegible]	[illegible]	.	.	.	[illegible]	[illegible]	[illegible]	.	.

* Including one of unsound mind convicted; to be detained in lunatic asylum.

From this it appears that, exclusive of those detained as insane, 1,619 were punished for serious offences in 1886, as compared with 1,573 in 1885, showing an increase of 46. Of these, 1,368 were males, and 251 females, the proportion of females being somewhat less than in 1885. Of the persons convicted, 8 were sentenced to death; 84 (75 males and 9 females) to penal servitude—3 of these were for over 10 years, 34 for above 6 and up to 10 years, and 47 for 5 years; 1,169 (999 males and 170 females) were sentenced to various terms of imprisonment. Thirteen cases (12 males and 1 female) were sent to Reformatory Schools.

The following statement shows the results of proceedings for the punishment of crime dealt with summarily in 1886, as compared with 1885, distinguishing the sexes:—

Proceedings for offences determined summarily: cases of men and boys compared with those of women and girls. Table 9.

DISPOSAL OF PERSONS PROCEEDED AGAINST SUMMARILY.

How disposed of.	Total, 1885.	1885. Men and Boys.	1885. Women and Girls.	1885. Proportion per Cent to Total. Men and Boys.	1885. Proportion per Cent to Total. Women and Girls.	Total, 1886.	1886. Men and Boys.	1886. Women and Girls.	1886. Proportion per Cent to Total. Men and Boys.	1886. Proportion per Cent to Total. Women and Girls.
Total Persons proceeded against,	[illegible]	[illegible]	[illegible]	[illegible]	[illegible]	215,887	[illegible]	[illegible]	[illegible]	[illegible]
Discharged,	30,278	[illegible]	[illegible]	[illegible]	[illegible]	35,913	[illegible]	[illegible]	[illegible]	[illegible]
Total Convicted,	168,071	[illegible]	[illegible]	[illegible]	[illegible]	179,974	148,865	31,109	[illegible]	[illegible]
Unclassed Punishments,	[illegible]	[illegible]	[illegible]	.	.	21,711	17,000	4,711	.	.
Classed Punishments,	[illegible]	[illegible]	[illegible]	[illegible]	[illegible]	158,263	131,865	26,398	[illegible]	[illegible]
Punished and not Committed, viz.:— Total.	[illegible]	[illegible]	[illegible]	[illegible]	[illegible]	139,743	[illegible]	[illegible]	[illegible]	[illegible]
Fined,	[illegible]	[illegible]	[illegible]	[illegible]	[illegible]	135,836	116,187	19,651	[illegible]	[illegible]
To find Sureties or Recognizances,	[illegible]	[illegible]	[illegible]	[illegible]	[illegible]	3,355	2,282	1,073	[illegible]	[illegible]
Delivered to Army or Navy,	[illegible]	[illegible]	.	[illegible]	.	535	535	.	[illegible]	.
Whipped,	[illegible]	[illegible]	.	.	.	15	15	.	.	.
Persons Committed, viz.:— Total.	[illegible]	[illegible]	[illegible]	[illegible]	[illegible]	[illegible]	[illegible]	[illegible]	[illegible]	[illegible]
To Prison, 14 days or under,	[illegible]	[illegible]	[illegible]	[illegible]	[illegible]	7,431	5,279	2,172	[illegible]	[illegible]
" 1 month and above 14 days,	[illegible]	[illegible]	[illegible]	[illegible]	[illegible]	6,621	4,491	2,130	[illegible]	[illegible]
" 2 months and above 1 month,	[illegible]	[illegible]	[illegible]	[illegible]	[illegible]	1,592	1,336	256	[illegible]	[illegible]
" 3 months and above 2 months,	[illegible]	[illegible]	[illegible]	[illegible]	[illegible]	892	608	284	[illegible]	[illegible]
" 6 months and above 3 months,	[illegible]	[illegible]	[illegible]	[illegible]	[illegible]	437	374	63	[illegible]	[illegible]
" Above 6 months,	[illegible]	[illegible]	[illegible]	.	.	39	31	8	.	
To Reformatory Schools,	[illegible]	[illegible]	[illegible]	[illegible]	[illegible]	183	143	40	[illegible]	[illegible]
To Industrial Schools,	[illegible]	[illegible]	[illegible]	[illegible]	[illegible]	1,185	524	661	[illegible]	[illegible]

Of the 215,887 persons proceeded against summarily in 1886, there were 35,913 discharged, and 179,974 convicted, as compared with 30,278 and 168,071 respectively in 1885. Of those convicted in 1886, 148,865 were males and 31,109 females. Of unclassed punishments there were 21,711 (17,000 males and 4,711 females). Of classed punishments there were 158,263 (131,865 males and 26,398 females). Of 139,743 persons not committed, 135,836 (116,187 males and 19,651 females) were fined, 3,355 (2,282 males and 1,073 females) were required to find sureties or recognizances; 535 were given up to the military or naval authorities, and 15 were whipped. Of the persons committed, 7,431 (5,279 males and 2,172 females) were committed to prison for 14 days or under; 6,621 (4,491 males and 2,130 females) for one month and above 14 days; 1,592 (1,336 males and 256 females) for 2 months and over 1 month; 892 (608 males and 284 females) for 3 months and above 2 months; 437 (374 males and 63 females) for 6 months and above 3 months; and 39 (31 males and 8 females) for above 6 months. There were 183 young persons (143 males and 40 females), sent to Reformatory Schools, and 1,185, including 524 males and 661 females, sent to Industrial Schools.

Court for consideration of Crown cases reserved. Table 60.

In the Court for the consideration of Crown cases reserved, constituted under 11 & 12 Vic., cap. 78, there was one case before the Court in 1886; the conviction was affirmed as to two counts and reversed as to one. There were no cases before the Court in 1885.

CHAPTER III.—CRIMINALS AND OTHERS IN CONFINEMENT, AND KNOWN CRIMINALS AT LARGE.

Part I. Criminal Statistics. Chapter III. Criminals, &c., in Confinement and at large.

The statistics of persons in confinement, with a view to punishment for or prevention of crime, include actual criminals, persons accused of criminal offences, debtors, children detained in industrial and reformatory schools, and criminal and dangerous lunatics.

Admissions to different places of detention compared.

In the following statement the number of prisoners, &c., admitted to various places of confinement during the year 1886 is set out:—

Admissions to Places of Detention.	Men and Boys.	Women and Girls.	Total.	Per cent.
Total in all Ireland,	29,813	16,873	45,626	100·
*Into Larger Local Prisons,	23,490	13,808	37,298	81·7
*Into Bridewells,	1,931	378	2,309	5·1
Into Minor Local Prisons,	1,851	439	2,290	5·0
Into Lunatic Asylums (as criminals or dangerous),	1,165	769	1,934	4·2
Into Industrial Schools,	628	904	1,532†	3·4
Into Reformatory Schools,	175	88	263	0·6

* Including ordinary prisoners only. † Of this number 7 were re-committals.

It would thus appear that there were 45,626 persons admitted to places of confinement during the year, but this number is somewhat in excess of the fact, as children sent to Reformatories and some lunatics were confined in Local Prisons prior to their final disposal in schools and lunatic asylums. It must also be noticed that some of the prisoners confined in prison during the year were committed more than once during that period.

Persons in detention at one time compared.

The distribution of persons under detention, at the end of the year 1886, among the different kinds of places of confinement is shown in the following statement:—

Criminals, &c., under Detention at end of 1886.	Men and Boys.	Women and Girls.	Total.	Per cent.
Total in all Ireland,	9,918	7,178	17,096	100·
Ordinary Criminals in Larger Local Prisons,	1,712	671	2,383	13·9
In Bridewells,	11	3	14	0·1
In Minor Local Prisons,	19	8	27	0·1
Debtors, and on Civil Process,	9	1	10	0·1
Convicts,	631	26	657	3·8
Military or Naval Prisoners,	37	-	37	0·2
In Lunatic Asylums (as criminals or dangerous),	3,658	2,372	6,030	35·3
In Reformatories,	781	145	926	5·4
In Industrial Schools,	2,823	4,273	7,096*	41·5

* Not including 61 retained in School, sentence expired.

It appears from this statement that at the close of the year 1886 there were 17,096 persons detained in places of confinement, either for the punishment or the prevention of crime. Among the 17,096 there were 7,096 children in Industrial schools and 6,030 lunatics, making a total of 13,126, or three-fourths of the entire number who were not actual criminals, but were detained as a preventive measure.

PART I. GENERAL SUMMARY. CHAPTER III. Criminals, &c., in Confinement and at large.

Classification of Prisons.

PRISONS.

The Prisons of Ireland, which have since the year 1877 been completely under the control of the General Prisons Board, consist of four classes, namely:—1st. Five Convict Prisons; 2nd. Larger Local Prisons, of which there were 23 at the close of the year 1886; 3rd. Minor Local Prisons, 6 in number, at the same date; 4th. Bridewells which numbered 18.

The State Prisons Tables, Tables 15 to 18, pp. 84-5, give various particulars as to the inmates of those institutions.

The number of commitments of ordinary criminals to larger local prisons in the year 1886, compared with 1885, was as follows:—

—	1885.	1886.	Increase in 1886.
Men and Boys, . .	21,929	23,490	1,561
Women and Girls, . .	13,618	13,808	190
Total, . .	35,537	37,298	1,771

Degree of education of prisoners. Table 15(d).

The state of education of those committed in 1886 is given in the following summary by sexes:—

Degrees of Instruction.	Total of both Sexes.	Men and Boys.	Women and Girls.	Proportion per cent.	
				Males.	Females.
Total, ...	37,298	23,490	13,808	100·	100·
Read and write well, ...	16,033	11,254	4,779	47·9	34·6
Neither read nor write, ...	14,457	7,912	6,545	33·7	47·4
Read, or read and write imperfectly, . .	6,571	4,089	2,482	17·4	18·0
Superior instruction, ...	212	211	1	0·9	0·0
Instruction not ascertained, ...	15	14	1	0·1	0·0

The ignorance of the criminal class is illustrated by these figures: the proportion of ignorance is much greater among the females than among the males.

Re-commitments of Ordinary Criminals. Table 15(e).

From the following statement it appears that of 37,298 commitments to larger local prisons of ordinary criminals, 22,103, or 59·3 per cent., were recommitments. The proportion of recommitments in the case of females is 74 per cent. of the total of that sex, while in the case of males it is only 51 per cent., showing, as in former years, a greater proportion of habitual criminals among female than among male prisoners:—

PART I. CRIMINAL STATISTICS.

CHAPTER II. Criminals, &c., in Confinement and at large.

A more detailed statement is here given as to the number of recommitments of those criminals committed more than once.

Recommitments of ordinary criminals. Table 15 (a).

Number of Times which Persons were previously Committed.	Total of both Sexes.	Men.	Women.	Proportion per cent.		
				Total of both Sexes.	Men.	Women.
Total number of recommitments,	22,103	11,946	10,157	100·	100·	100·
Once previously,	4,656	3,340	1,316	21·1	28·0	13·0
Twice do.,	2,837	1,925	912	12·8	16·1	9·0
Thrice do.,	1,843	1,163	680	8·4	9·7	6·6
Four times previously,	1,549	1,029	520	7·0	8·6	5·1
Five times do.,	977	626	351	4·4	5·2	3·5
Six or seven times previously,	1,613	979	634	7·3	8·2	6·2
Eight, nine, or ten times do.,	1,616	846	770	7·3	7·1	7·6
Above ten times,	7,010	2,016	4,994	31·7	16·9	49·2

From this it appears that of the 22,103 prisoners who were committed more than once, 4,656, or 21·1 per cent., had been previously committed *once*; 2,837, or 12·8 per cent., *twice*; 1,843, or 8·4 per cent., *three times*; 1,549, or 7·0 per cent., *four times*; 977, or 4·4 per cent., *five times*; 1,613, or 7·3 per cent., *six or seven times*; 1,616, or 7·3 per cent., *eight, nine, or ten times*; and 7,010, or 31·7 per cent., *above ten times*. The greater proportion of recommitments among females than males is more fully shown in this than in the previous statement; the percentage of males previously committed above ten times being 16·9 as compared with 49·2 among females.

Age and sex of ordinary prisoners. Table 15 (b).

The following summary shows the age and sex of the ordinary prisoners (other than debtors and persons charged with military and naval offences) committed to the larger Local Prisons in Ireland in 1886, together with the proportions per cent. of each sex at the several age-periods :—

Ages.	Total of both Sexes.	Men and Boys.	Women and Girls.	Proportion per cent.	
				Men and Boys.	Women and Girls.
Total,	36,928	23,120	13,808	100·	100·
Under twelve years,	76	67	9	0·3	0·1
Twelve years and under sixteen,	725	570	155	2·4	1·1
Sixteen years and under twenty-one,	6,303	4,888	1,311	21·3	8·6
Twenty-one years and under thirty,	12,481	8,140	4,341	35·3	31·4
Thirty years and under forty,	8,600	4,608	3,992	19·6	25·9
Forty years and under fifty,	4,929	2,391	2,538	10·3	18·4
Fifty years and under sixty,	2,498	1,451	1,047	6·3	7·6
Sixty years and upwards,	1,385	974	411	4·2	3·0
Age not ascertained,	2	1	1	0·0	0·0

Occupations of ordinary prisoners. Table 15 (c).

The statistics of the occupations of ordinary criminals committed during the year 1886, are given in Table 15 (c), page 84. They show the usual large proportion of

Part I. General Statistics.

prostitutes and unoccupied, women of bad character, the numbers under these heads being 6,094 and 3,447 respectively, out of a total of 18,808 female prisoners.

Chapter III. Criminals, &c., in Confinement and at large.

Criminal and Dangerous Lunatics.

Criminal and Dangerous Lunatics in confinement. Table 27.

The following summary shows the number of persons detained in lunatic asylums, the authority under which they were committed, and the mode of their disposal during the year:—

[illegible]	Lunatics, [illegible]		
	Men.	Women.	Total.
Total number of such Lunatics under detention during year,	4,[illegible]	3,003	7,[illegible]
Under detention at commencement of year,* . .	[illegible]	2,334	4,761
Committed by Justices, under 30 & 31 Vic., c. 118, .	1,083	748	1,831
Received from Prisons under warrant of Lord Lieutenant,	73	17	90
Received from other Asylums, ...	–	–	–
Received under warrant of the Secretary of State for War,	7	–	7
Total number disposed of during year, . . .	1,037	631	1,668
Discharged on becoming sane, on certificate of Resident Medical Superintendent.	167	331	518
Died, ...	315	201	516
Given to their friends, ...	137	83	220
Became ordinary patients on expiration of sentence, .	29	9	38
Removed to workhouses, as sane, . . .	22	11	33
Discharged as sane by warrant of Lord Lieutenant, .	5	2	7
Removed to Prison for trial or punishment, . .	15	3	18
Escaped, ...	1	–	1
Transferred to other Asylums, ...	13	1	14
Remaining under detention at close of year, . .	3,458	2,576	6,0[illegible]

The above statement shows an increase of 286 in the number under detention at the end of 1886, as compared with the number at the commencement of the year.

Grounds of committal. Table 28.

The following summary shows the number of dangerous lunatics committed to asylums in 1886, and the offences which criminal lunatics committed to asylums during the year, were charged with having committed:—

Offences of Lunatics on Grounds of Committal.	Males.	Females.	Total of both Sexes.	Proportion per cent.
Total committed during the year, ...	1,163	769	1,934	100·
Dangerous persons, having intent to commit crime, .	1,083	748	1,831	94·7
Assaults and riot, ...	22	4	26	1·3
Offences against property, ...	26	6	32	1·6
Offences against human life, ...	7	4	11	0·6
Other offences than those here specified, . .	21	5	26	1·5
Vagrants and insane persons without control, . .	6	3	9	0·5

It appears from this table that the lunatics committed as dangerous persons at large having an intent to commit crime, formed 94·7 per cent. of the total number of criminal and dangerous lunatics committed during the year.

The following summary shows the judgments or orders under which criminal and dangerous lunatics were committed to asylums in Ireland in 1886:— Part I. Criminal Statistics. Chapter III. Criminals, &c., in Confinement and at large.

Judgment or Orders of Committal.	Males.	Females.	Total of both Sexes.	Proportion per cent.
Total committed during year,	1,165	769	1,934	100·
Committed to asylums by Justices as dangerous, under stat. 30 & 31 Vic., c. 118, s. 10,	1,085	746	1,831	94·7
Transmitted from prisons by Lord Lieutenant's warrant:—				
Became insane while undergoing sentence of imprisonment,	49	14	63	3·3
Found or declared insane,	9	1	10	0·5
Became insane after committal and before trial,	14	5	19	1·0
Acquitted as insane,	3	1	4	0·2
Committed by Secretary of State for War,	7	—	7	0·4

Criminal and Dangerous Lunatics. Judgment or orders of committal under which detained. Table [illegible].

It appears that 94·7 per cent. of the lunatics were committed direct to asylums by Justices as dangerous with intent to commit crime, and that only 4·9 per cent. were sent by Lord Lieutenant's warrant; 0·4 per cent. were committed by the Secretary of State for War.

Reformatory Schools.

With respect to institutions for the prevention of crime, namely, Reformatory and Industrial Schools, the following statement deals with juvenile criminals under Reformatory control in the year 1886, compared with 1885. Reformatory Schools. Number in confinement. Table [illegible].

Number of Children on the Rolls of Reformatory Schools in Ireland.	End of 1886.			End of 1885.	Increase in 1886.	Decrease in 1886.
	Boys.	Girls.	Total Boys and Girls.	Total.		
In School,	791	145	936	969	—	33
On Licence,	75	1	76	85	—	9
Detained in School, sentence expired,	—	—	—	4	—	4
Absconded, sentence unexpired,	14	—	14	6	8	—
In Prison,	3	—	3	1	2	—
Total,	883	146	1,029	1,065	—	36

From this table it appears that there was a decrease of 36 in the number of children on the rolls of Reformatory schools in Ireland at the end of 1886, as compared with the close of the preceding year. There were 33 less in the schools under sentence; 9 less on licence; and 2 more in prison. At the close of the year 1885 there were 4 persons who were being retained in school after sentence had expired (with their own consent), until provided with employment: at the end of last year there were none so retained. Fourteen of those on the rolls at the close of 1886 had absconded, with sentence unexpired, being an increase of 8 as compared with the number under this heading in 1885.

The total number on the rolls at the close of the year 1886 was 1,029 (883 boys and only 146 girls): the number committed during the year was 203—175 boys and 28 girls—showing an increase of 29 as compared with the committals for the preceding year.

The position of the children committed in 1886 to Reformatories in Ireland, as regards parental control, is shown in the following table:— Degree of parental control. Table [illegible].

—	Boys.	Girls.	Proportion per cent.	
			Boys.	Girls.
Total committed,	175	28	100·	100·
Illegitimate, deserted, or one or both parents destitute or criminal,	63	10	36	36
Under control of parents, other than above,	73	11	42	39
One parent dead,	20	6	11	21
Total orphans,	19	1	11	4

Forty-two per cent. of the boys and 39 per cent. of the girls were under parental control.

PART I.
GENERAL
PROPORTION.

The illegitimate, the deserted, and those having one or both parents destitute or criminal
accounted to 34 per cent. of the boys and an equal proportion of the girls. The orphans
(including those having one parent dead) were only 22 per cent. of boys and 25 per
cent. of girls.

CHAPTER III.
Criminals,
&c., to Com-
mittments and
at large.

Degree of
Education.
Table 12.

The degree of education of children committed to Reformatory Schools is shown in
the following summary :—

—	Boys.	Girls.	Proportion per cent.	
			Boys.	Girls.
Total committed,	115	28	100·	100·
Neither read nor write,	53	12	46·6	42·9
Read, or read and write imperfectly,	40	10	35·4	35·7
Read and write well,	21	6	18·0	21·4
Superior Instruction,	—	—	—	—

Want of
education.

The want of education is seen from this summary, which shows that 46·6 per cent.
of the boys were wholly uneducated; only 18·0 per cent. could read and write well,
while the remainder, 35·4 per cent., had received a small amount of education; and
that of the small number of girls admitted, although 21·4 per cent. could read and
write well; 42·9 per cent. were wholly uneducated, and the remaining 35·7 per cent.
could only read, or read and write imperfectly.

INDUSTRIAL SCHOOLS.

Industrial
schools.
Table 20.

The institutions in which the largest number of persons were in custody at the end of
the year were Industrial Schools.

The total number of Industrial Schools in 1886 is the same as in 1885, namely 66,
of which 26 were in Munster, 19 in Leinster, 12 in Connaught, and 9 in Ulster.

Number in
confinement.

The following summary shows the number of children under warrant of detention in
Industrial Schools in Ireland at the end of 1886, as compared with similar statistics for
the end of 1885 :—

CHILDREN ON THE ROLLS OF INDUSTRIAL SCHOOLS IN IRELAND.	End of 1886.			End of 1885.	Increase.	Decrease.
	Boys.	Girls.	Total.			
In School,	2,823	4,273	7,096	6,553	543	—
On Licence,	487	351	841	857	84	—
Absconded,	11	1	12	11	1	—
Retained in school, sentence expired,	8	43	61	66	—	5
Total,	3,129	4,681	7,810	7,289	521	—

It appears from this table that the number of children on the rolls of Industrial
Schools in Ireland at the end of 1886 (7,810) is higher by 521 than the number
(7,289) at the end of 1885. Of the total number, 7,096 were in the schools undergoing
their sentence of detention, 61 were retained in school by their own consent although
their sentences had expired, 641 were on licence, and 12 had absconded.

Age.

The following figures show the ages of the children placed in these schools in 1886 :—

It appears from these figures that 63 per cent. of the girls and 48 per cent. of the boys are brought under careful training in these schools at the early age of under ten years. *Part I. Criminal Statistics.*

In 1885, 697 boys were sent to Industrial Schools, as compared with 750 girls; and in 1886, 621 boys were sent, as compared with 901 girls.

Table 8 exhibits statistics of the number of known thieves, depredators, receivers of stolen goods, and suspected persons at large and of the houses they frequent. *Thieves, &c., at large. Table 8.*

CHAPTER IV.—COST OF THE REPRESSION OF CRIME.

Chapter IV. Cost of Repressing Crime. Tables 1, 2, 19, 21, 23, 24, 27.

The cost of repression of crime is shown in the following statement:—

Cost of Repression of Crime.	1885.	1886.	Increase.	Decrease.
	£	£	£	£
Total cost,	2,066,812	2,039,055	–	27,757
Police,*	1,554,227	1,533,166	–	21,061
Prosecutions,*	66,231	55,475	–	10,756
Prisons,*	143,640	134,664	–	8,976
Lunatics,†	135,454	137,801	2,347	–
Industrial Schools,†	152,874‡	161,047	8,173	–
Reformatory Schools,†	25,388	24,877	–	511

The following summary shows the Police Force in Ireland in 1886, compared with the number in 1885, at the periods of the year stated in the tables:— *Police Establishments.*

Constabulary and Police.	1885.	1886.	Increase, 1886.	Decrease, 1886.
Royal Irish Constabulary. (Table 1.)				
Effective strength—Officers,	259	263	4	–
Head-Constables, Constables, &c.,	12,396	12,550	154	–
Total,	12,655	12,813	158	–
Dublin Metropolitan Police. (Table 2.)				
Superior Officers,	41	41	–	–
Sergeants and Constables,	1,188	1,176	–	12
Total,	1,229	1,217	–	12
Grand Total,	13,884	14,030	146	–

The number of the Royal Irish Constabulary has been increased by 154 men, and the number of the Dublin Metropolitan Police decreased by 12 men, making a net increase of 146 men in the total Police force§ for Ireland. *Increase in Royal Irish Constabulary and decrease in Dublin Metropolitan Police.*

A column in the first table in the Appendix shows the proportion which the number of effective force of Constabulary bears to the population in the various counties, and in *Tables 1 and 2.*

* For year ended 31st March. † For year ended 31st December.

PART I. GENERAL STATISTICS. — CHAPTER IV. Cost of Repressing Crime. — Police Establishments. Proportion of Police to population. Tables 1 and 2.

towns with a separate Police force, in Ireland. In the following counties the proportion of Police to population is the smallest, as will be seen from the table:—

Antrim, ...	11 in every 10,000 of the population.
Down, ...	11 " "
Londonderry, ...	11 " "
Armagh, ...	12 " "
Tyrone, ...	13 " "

In the following counties in Ireland the proportion of Police is the largest:—

Westmeath, ...	44 in every 10,000 of the population.
Limerick, ...	40 " "
Kerry, ...	38 " "
Meath, ...	37 " "
Tipperary, S.R., ...	35 " "
Galway, ...	34 " "
King's Co., ...	31 " "

The proportion of Police in the principal Cities and Towns is as follows:—

Galway, ...	35 in every 10,000 of the population.
Drogheda, ...	30 " "
Dublin Metropolitan Police District, . .	30 " "
Kilkenny, ...	30 " "
Waterford, ...	29 " "
Belfast Town Force, ...	27 " "
Londonderry, ...	26 " "
Limerick, ...	23 " "
Cork, ...	21 " "

The proportion of Police—excluding County Inspectors and District Inspectors but including Depot and Reserve Force—to the estimated population of Ireland in 1886 was 28 in every 10,000 of the people.

Detectives.

In the Royal Irish Constabulary the members of the different branches of the Force are selected for special duty when necessary; in the Police of the Dublin Metropolitan Police District an entire division consisting of 39 effective men (10 detective officers, 13 Constables, and 16 Sergeants,) 4 Inspectors, and 1 Superintendent, are employed as detectives.

Cost of Establishments. Tables 1 and 2.

The following table shows the total cost of the Police Establishments in Ireland for the year ended 31st March, 1886, as compared with that for the preceding year:—

Cost of Police Establishments.	1885.	1886.	Increase, 1886.	Decrease, 1886.
	£	£	£	£
Total of all Ireland, . .	1,454,[illegible]	1,433,164	-	21,061
Royal Irish Constabulary, .	1,407,[illegible]	1,387,170	-	20,0[illegible]
Dublin Metropolitan Police, .	147,004	145,996	-	1,0[illegible]

This table indicates a decrease of £21,061 in the total cost of the Police Force, following a decrease of £91,650 in the year ended 31st March, 1885.

Extra Constabulary. Table 1, Part IV.

There was a considerable decrease in the demand for extra Constabulary during the year ended 30th September, 1886: the greatest number chargeable in any month was 1,638 in May, 1886, as against 2,280 in October, 1884, 3,077 in October, 1883, 3,300 in November, 1882, 3,248 in September, 1882, and 1,877 in September, 1881; the least number chargeable, 1,438 in November, 1885, was slightly below the minimum for the

The cost of criminal lunatics and dangerous lunatics charged with an intention to commit a crime, is £127,801. Part I. Criminal Statistics. Chapter IV. Cost of Repressing Crime. Cost of Criminal Lunatics in Asylums. Table 27.

In the case of Industrial Schools, the total expenditure returned is £161,047—Imperial Taxes,* £85,579; Local Rates,* £33,166; other sources, £42,654. Cost of Industrial Schools, Table 28.

The following table shows the cost of criminal classes, other than lunatics, in confinement in 1886, as compared with 1885:— Cost of Criminals in Confinement. Tables 19 and 22.

Cost of Criminal Classes in Confinement.	1885.	1886.	Increase, 1886.	Decrease, 1886.
	£	£	£	£
Total of places of confinement,	163,026	161,538	–	6,186
Prisons,†	143,640	138,666	–	5,974
Reformatories,‡	25,386	24,872	–	611

The cost of State Prisons in Ireland (including Convict Prisons, Larger and Minor Local Prisons, and Bridewells), for the year ended 31st March, 1886, was £136,666. State Prisons. Table 12.

As to Reformatories, the total costs in Ireland for the year 1886, are returned as £24,872—£14,968 charged to Imperial Taxes,§ £6,995 to Local Rates,§ and £2,942 to other sources. Reformatories. Table 23.

The form of return as to costs of criminal prosecutions, settled in 1872, has been continued. It brings the information up to 31st March, 1886. Costs of Criminal Prosecutions, Table 31.

Criminal Courts.	Costs of Criminal Prosecutions 1884-85.	Costs of Criminal Prosecutions 1885-86.	Increase, 1885-86.	Decrease, 1885-86.
	£	£	£	£
Total of all Ireland,	66,231	55,473	—	10,758
Assizes and Commission Courts,	48,878	43,191	—	5,687
Quarter Sessions,	12,438	10,763	—	1,670
Petty Sessions, Inquests, and Police Courts,	4,895	2,314	—	2,381

This table shows a decrease in the cost of criminal prosecutions in Ireland in 1885-86 of £10,758, following a decrease of £15,130 in 1884-85.

* The sum (£118,745) entered under "Imperial Taxes" and "Local Rates" includes £363 unexpended at close of year.

† For year ended 31st March. ‡ For year ended 31st December.

§ The sum (£21,963), entered under "Imperial Taxes" and "Local Rates" includes £33 unexpended.

PART II.—JUDICIAL STATISTICS.

Part II. Judicial Statistics.

Arrangement of Tables.

The Tables in this part include Statistics relating to the Civil Jurisdiction of all Courts in Ireland.

The Courts and Offices are divided into those which relate to the Central Administration of Justice, and those which relate to the Local Administration of Justice. The latter are classified into larger and smaller District Administration of Justice, according to the size of the districts into which Ireland is divided for the Special Jurisdiction.

I.—CENTRAL ADMINISTRATION OF JUSTICE.

Central Administration of Justice.

The Central Administration of Justice includes the High Court of Justice, of which there were in 1886 five divisions—Chancery, Queen's Bench, Common Pleas, Exchequer, and the Probate and Matrimonial Division.

Arrangement of Tables.

There are three outlying Courts:—The Court of the Land Commission, the High Court of Admiralty, and the Court of Bankruptcy.

The Central Appellate Jurisdictions, viz., Her Majesty's Court of Appeal, Ireland; Court for Crown Cases Reserved; Court for Cases Reserved for Judges of the Queen's Bench, Common Pleas, and Exchequer Divisions; the Privy Council in Ireland; Her Majesty in Council; and the House of Lords; have been grouped along with the other Central Jurisdictions, as they are closely connected with them.

In the arrangement of the Tables of the different Divisions of the High Court of Justice, the order followed in the English report has been, as far as possible, adopted.

The chief business of the Queen's Bench, Common Pleas, and Exchequer Divisions (the proceedings at the Plea side) is given in consecutive tables.

The proceedings at Jury Trials in Dublin of these three divisions, and the Dublin County Court Appeals, are grouped together, as the business is really transacted on a consolidated plan. With these, the proceedings at chambers before a single Judge, and the applications to have cases of minor importance remitted to County Courts are grouped together.

The Statistics regarding the exclusive jurisdiction of each of the three divisions:—at the Crown side of the Queen's Bench, as to election petitions and acknowledgments of married women in the Common Pleas, and at the Revenue side of the Exchequer, are given last, as the business is so small, compared with that transacted on the Plea side of those divisions.

The offices of Registration of Judgments and Record of Title are grouped together, and along with them is given the Registry of Deeds, as the functions performed by all three are somewhat similar.

The statistics as to the Chancery, Common Law, and Land Judge's Taxing Offices are given in one Table, the offices having been consolidated.

As the business of the Receiver's Office of the Land Judge corresponds with a large part of the business of the Registrar in Lunacy (that relating to the Accounting of Committees of Estates of Lunatics), the statistics of the two offices have been placed together.

The information from the Inland Revenue Department, as to all the law taxes, is

High Court of Justice—Chancery Division.

The following summary shows the Court business in the Chancery Division during the years 1885 and 1886, with the increase or decrease under each head in the latter year.

Court Business in Chancery Division.	1885.	1886.	Increase, 1886.	Decrease, 1886.
Before Lord Chancellor.				
Orders on motions special or from Chambers,	20	19	–	1
Orders on motions of course,	10	16	6	–
Orders on petitions of course,	–	–	–	–
Orders on petitions heard,	7	5	–	2
Causes, actions, &c., heard,	–	–	–	–
Motions for decree or judgment heard,	–	–	–	–
Causes, actions, &c., for further consideration heard,	–	–	–	–
	16	19	3	–
Before Master of the Rolls.				
Orders on motions special or from Chambers,	335	331	–	4
Orders on motions of course,	199	205	6	–
Orders on petitions heard,	93	70	–	23
Causes, actions, &c., heard,	45	51	6	–
Motions for decree or judgment heard,	57	64	7	–
Causes, actions, &c., for further consideration heard,	39	50	11	–
	760	756	–	4
Before Vice-Chancellor.				
Orders on motions special or from Chambers,	330	333	3	–
Orders on motions of course,	159	119	–	40
Orders on petitions heard,	78	75	–	3
Orders on County Court Appeals,	–	10	10	–
Causes, actions, &c., heard,	46	46	–	–
Motions for decree or judgment heard,	50	47	–	3
Causes, actions, &c., for further consideration heard,	55	38	–	17
County Court equity appeals heard, *	8	11	3	–
	751	706	–	45
Total,	1,563	1,517	–	46

This table shows a decrease of Court business of 46 proceedings, following a decrease of 24 in 1885. The arrears at the close of the year were 20 against 26 at the end of 1885.

In the office of the Registrars of the Chancery Division, the total number of Side Bar Orders was 469, or 57 under the number for 1885.

From the County Court equitable jurisdiction, up to £500 property and £30 a year in land, there were 11 Appeals filed, which, with 7 pending at the close of 1885, made 18 for hearing during last year; of these, 14 were heard, with the result that 5 appeals were dismissed, with costs, and 9 decrees of the County Court were reversed or varied; 2 cases were struck out or withdrawn, and 2 were pending at the end of the year.

Part II. Judicial Statistics.

Central Administration of Justice.

Chancery Division.

Business in Court before Lord Chancellor, Master of the Rolls, and Vice-Chancellor. See Tables 28, 39

Registrars' Office. Table 29.

Appeals from Equity Actions in County Courts. Table 30.

Part II. Judicial Statistics. — Central Administration of Justice. — Chancery Division. — Chief Clerks' Returns of proceedings in Chambers Table 31.

The following is a summary of the principal proceedings in the chambers of the Lord Chancellor, the Master of the Rolls, and the Vice-Chancellor :—

Proceedings in Chambers of Chancery Judges.	1885.	1886.	Increase, 1886.	Decrease, 1886.
Summonses :—				
To make Infants Wards,	30	36	6	–
For the Administration of Estates,	101	86	–	15
Under the Charitable Trusts Acts,	–	–	–	–
For appointment of Guardians and maintenance of Infants	35	30	–	5
For other purposes,	532	610	78	–
Other Summonses than to originate Proceedings,	1,918	2,076	158	–
Appointments (by Summonses, &c.), disposed of,	8,101	8,627	526	–
Orders made :—				
Of the Class drawn up by the Registrars,	–	–	–	–
Of the Class drawn up in Chambers,	1,592	1,753	161	–
Orders brought into Chambers for prosecution :—				
Other than Orders for winding up Companies,	391	480	89	–
For winding up Companies,	5	16	11	–
Number of Advertisements issued,	164	199	35	–
Receivers' Accounts passed,	68	41	–	27
Receipts therein,	£138,794	£135,186	–	£3,608
Disbursements and Allowances therein,	£96,307	£135,331	£39,024	–
Accounts passed other than Receivers' Accounts :—				
Number of Accounts,	231	245	14	–
Receipts therein,	£537,046	£2,159,786	£1,622,740	–
Disbursements and allowances therein,	£439,807	£1,891,320	£1,451,513	–

There was a decrease of 20 in Summonses for Administration of Estates, and Appointment of Guardians, from 136 in 1885, to 116 in 1886; and an increase in Summonses other than those to originate proceedings of 158, from 1,918 in 1885, to 2,076 in 1886.

The amount of property passed in accounts rose from £675,340 in 1885, to £2,294,983, being an increase of £1,619,643.

Minor matters in Chambers.

In the Lord Chancellor's, the Master of the Rolls', and the Vice-Chancellor's Chambers there were at the end of the year 1,344 Wards of Court. The new Minor Matters in the year were 31, relating to 59 Minors as compared with 27 new Matters and 52 new Wards in 1885.

Clerk of Records and Writs. Table 32.

The number of actions by writ of summons was 559, showing a decline of 77 from the number (636) in 1885. The proportion of lower scale to higher scale was as 19 to 81 per cent. The originating summonses (189) are 49 more than the summonses filed (140) in 1885. In the Notice Department there were 15,611 original documents, against 15,150 in 1885, and 52,470 copies, against 51,508 in 1885.

Lord Chancellor's Summary. Table 33.

The Lord Chancellor made 88 orders on Petitions as to Commissioners for administering oaths for the High Court of Justice. There were 2 orders on Petitions as to Notaries. The orders as to other Petitions, including Minor Matters, were 86. The warrants for Magistrates were 340, as compared with 313 in 1885; the warrants as to Coroners were 8.

Part II. Judicial Statistics.

Central Administration of Justice.

Chancery Division.

Secretary at the Rolls, Table 33.

The return of the Secretary at the Rolls gives the particulars of 80 petitions set down for hearing before the Master of the Rolls. It appears that 31 of these were under the Trustee Acts, and 22 under the Public Works and Railway Acts.

Crown and Hanaper Office. Table 34

In the Crown and Hanaper Office there were 8,094 official acts during the year 1886, as compared with 8,178 in 1885.

Land Judge.

Registrar's Returns. Table 35.

Under the Land Judge the net rental, or annual value (where given) of Estates sold was £20,967 as compared with £16,730 in 1885, £15,546 in 1884, £19,409 in 1883, £11,695 in 1882, £19,970 in 1881, and £19,698 in 1880, and the purchase money was £296,116, as compared with £241,558 in 1885, £307,274 in 1884, £283,750 in 1883, £203,687 in 1882, £311,256 in 1881, and £329,549 in 1880. The purchase money in 1886 was equal to 14·1 years' purchase on an average of all interests and all tenures. This is below 14·4, the rate in 1885, 19·8 in 1884, 14·9 in 1883, 17·1 in 1882, 15·5 in 1881, 16·5 in 1880, 17·7 in 1879, and 16·9 in 1878, and below the average for 6 years ended 1877, which was 19·4.

The number of cases pending at the end of the year in the Judge's Chamber was 2,409 as compared with 2,209 in 1885.

Record and Affidavit Office. Table 36.

There were 304 petitions filed in 1886, against 236 in 1885, only 62 being by owners. The number of affidavits filed was 4,199, against 4,210 in 1885.

Keeper of Deeds. Table 37.

The number of abstracts of title lodged was 117, and the number of deeds and other documents lodged 4,649.

Sales of Land to Tenants. Table 38.

The sales to tenants under the Irish Land Act of 1870, in which charging orders in favour of the Board of Works for advances to enable them to purchase were made, were 23 in 1885, and 5 in 1886, for £7,353 and £10,758, respectively. Of the 5 sales in 1886, 3 were of holdings under 100 acres, including one holding under 10 acres; the 5 holdings consist of one in Leinster; 2 in Munster; one in Ulster; and one in Connaught.

Queen's Bench, Common Pleas, and Exchequer Divisions.

Distribution of business in Queen's Bench, Common Pleas, and Exchequer Divisions, Tables 39, 40, 41, 42, and 43.

The proceedings at the Plea side of the Queen's Bench, Common Pleas, and Exchequer Divisions are arranged in a single table for each division, although the figures have been supplied by three officers—the Clerk of Writs, the Master, and the Registrar. This has been done to produce tables comparable with those in the English returns.

The writs of summons for the Exchequer Division were, 7,501 in 1885, and 8,452 in 1886; those for the Queen's Bench were 7,502 in 1885, and 8,401 in 1886; and those for the Common Pleas were in 1885, 7,501, and in 1886, 8,427.

The total number of writs of summons for these three divisions showed an increase of 2,776 from 22,504 in 1885, to 25,280 in 1886. The number of cases which actually came to trial by jury in Dublin in 1886 was 277, being 34 under the number in 1885; the amount of money recovered at those trials shows a decrease from £31,806 in 1885, to £19,641 in 1886.

Of the other business of the Queen's Bench, Common Pleas, and Exchequer Divisions, on the Plea side, there were in the Queen's Bench 10,287 affidavits, in the Common Pleas, 7,990, and in the Exchequer 8,630, the total number being 26,907, showing an increase of 4,360 as compared with the number for 1885.

At Chambers there were 134 summonses in the Common Pleas, 183 in the Queen's Bench, and 200 in the Exchequer Division. The motions on notice before a single Judge were, in the Queen's Bench 264, in the Common Pleas 165, and in the Exchequer Division 696. The ex-parte motions, including consent orders, granted before a single Judge, were, in the Queen's Bench 496, in the Exchequer 612, and in the Common Pleas Division 602.

The Judges for Jury trials in Dublin also hear Appeals from the Courts of the Recorder, the County Court Judge for the City and County of Dublin.

The statistics of these appeals or rehearings in 1885 and 1886 are as follows:—

Appeals (Rehearings).		Entered.	Affirmed.	Reversed.	Dismissed, Struck out, &c.	Remaining.
From Decree or Dismiss of Recorder of Dublin City and County Courts (including case stated),	1885,	63	22	7	31	3
	1886,	48	25	6	10	7

The proceedings as to applications to have cases remitted to County Courts are as follows:—

Proceedings under [illegible]	1885.	1886.	Increase, 1886.	Decrease, 1886.
Number of applications to remit to Inferior Courts,	272	299	27	-
Number of applications refused, . . .	45	79	34	–
Number of applications granted, . . .	227	220	-	7
In Cases of Contract under £50.				
Number of applications granted, . . .	114	136	22	-
In Cases of Tort.				
Number of applications granted under sec. 6, .	113	84	-	29

It appears from this table that the number of applications to remit cases to the County Courts, was 299, showing an increase of 27 as compared with the year 1885. Of the 220 applications granted, 136 were in cases of contract and 84 in cases of tort.

Queen's Bench Division.

The Queen's Coroner, Attorney and Master on the Crown side has made his usual return of the business at the Crown side of the Queen's Bench.

Common Pleas Division.

In 1886 there were 3 election petitions; in one case the decision was given in favour of the Petitioner; in another in favour of the Respondent; and in the third case the Petition was abated, by reason of security for costs being declared insufficient on appeal.

In 1886, there were 8 acknowledgments by married women filed, as compared with one in the preceding year. Under the provisions of the Conveyancing Act, 1882 (45 & 46 Vic., cap. 39, sec. 7), no Certificates and Affidavits of Acknowledgments are filed save such as relate to Deeds executed before the commencement of the Act.

No Perpetual Commissioners were appointed in any of the last four years; in 1882 there were five appointments. There were 24 Special Commissions granted in 1886, being a decline of 7 as compared with the number in 1885.

PART II. JUDICIAL STATISTICS. — Central Administration of Justice. — Exchequer Division.

EXCHEQUER DIVISION.

The writs issued on the Revenue side were 510, as compared with 779 in 1885. The Side Bar Rules were 80, as compared with 97 in 1885. The affidavits filed were 194, as compared with 261 in 1885.

Revenue side. Tables 11 and 50.

OFFICES OF REGISTRATION.

The number of judgments, &c., registered in the Registry of Judgments Office in 1886, as compared with the preceding year, was as follows:—

Registry of Judgments Office. Table 51.

Registry of Judgments Office.	1885.	1886.	Increase, 1886.	Decrease, 1886.
Judgments of High Court of Justice registered,	4,832	5,086	251	–
" " re-registered,	631	178	–	453
Revivals,	–	–	–	–
Decrees, Rules, and Orders,	–	–	–	–
Lis pendens,	480	409	–	81
Judgments from Courts in England and Scotland,	18	27	9	–
Total,	5,971	5,851	280	–
Recognizances registered,	600	780	152	–
" re-registered,	67	41	–	26
Crown Bonds registered,	101	63	–	38
" re-registered,	13	24	11	–
Total,	781	856	75	–
Satisfactions of Judgments,	137	92	–	45
Vacates of Recognizances, and Cancellations of Crown Bonds.	177	280	103	–
Negative Searches on £1 Stamps,	–	–	–	–
" " 10s. Stamps,	1,463	1,447	–	16
" " 2s. 6d. Stamps,	73	63	–	10
Total,	1,850	1,882	32	–
Requisitions for library to search made by public,	6,063	6,677	614	–
Stamped Certificates issued,	6,139	6,198	59	–

The figures in the above table show, on the whole, an increase of business in the office. The number of Judgments registered has risen from 4,839 in 1885, to 5,086 in 1886.

Central Administration of Justice.

On comparing the number of judgments registered with the number of executions issued on Judgments in the Queen's Bench, Common Pleas, and Exchequer Divisions, it appears that, whilst 8,818 judgment executions are returned in the proceedings in Masters' Offices as entered up, 5,086 judgments were registered in the Registry of Judgments Office.

Record of Title Office. Table 52.

The total number of estates or properties, the titles to which have been recorded in the Record of Title Office since its establishment in 1865, under Stat. 28 & 29 Vict. c. 88, sec. 67, is 766. The total value is stated to be £2,412,756.

There was no application in the year ended 1st November, 1886, to record land under the 51st section of the Act. There was only one new estate recorded in the Record of Title Office during the year: the value was below £1,000. There were not any proceedings under the Land Debentures Act, 1865.

Bills of Sale. Table 52.

Bills of Sale are registered by the Master of the Queen's Bench Division, and included in his return of business at the Pleas side. They are grouped here with other offices of registration. The number of bills of sale was 806, as compared with 771 in 1885.

Registry of Deeds. Table 53.

The number of deeds registered in the Registry of Deeds Office in the year was 15,904, as compared with 15,476 in 1885. Judgment Mortgage Affidavits are included in this number: they amounted to 653, as compared with 683 in 1885. The searches made by the public were 5,291; those lodged for official search were 2,111, of which 1,186 were negative searches, and 925 common searches. The abstract book, entered up to 24th December in 1885, was, on the 31st of December, 1886, entered up to 22nd December. The lands index, which was complete to 18th of December in 1885, was completed to 16th of December in 1886. The Transcription of Memorials, complete to 9th of November in 1885, was completed to 1st of December in 1886. The negative searches lodged but not made were 38 in 1885, and 34 in 1886, and the common searches lodged but not made numbered 19 in the former and 25 in the latter year.

The negative searches made and ready for delivery but not taken out amounted to 482, and the common searches to 26.

Taxation of Costs.

Chancery, Land Judges, Probate, Common Law. Table 54.

The Costs taxed in the Consolidated Taxing Offices, and certified, amounted to £244,178. The corresponding amount for 1885 was £230,547, which shows an increase of £13,631 for last year.

Administration of Property.

Receivers under Land Judges. Table 55.

There were 158 new receivers appointed by the Land Judges, as compared with 143 in 1885, 164 in 1884, 151 in 1883, 165 in 1882, 118 in 1881, 109 in 1880, 69 in 1879, and 18 in 1878. The total number under the Land Judges at the end of the year was 1,255, as compared with 1,200 at the end of 1885.

The year's rental under the Court of the receivers and guardians who passed accounts, which are filed in the Consolidated Record and Writ Office, is £273,928, of which £152,965 was in minor matters, and £120,963 in other suits.

It appears that there were 690 lettings by proposal without biddings: there was not a single letting by biddings. Of the 690 lettings, 236 were for 7 years, pending the cause, and 454 were for shorter periods.

The chief business in the Lunacy Department in 1886 compared with 1885 was as follows:— PART II. JUDICIAL STATISTICS. — Central Administration of Justice. — Lunacy Department. Table 56.

Lunacy Office.	1886.	1885.	Increase, 1886.	Decrease, 1886.
Orders of the Lord Chancellor, including Fiats confirming Registrars' Reports,	516	420	96	-
Affidavits filed,	574	481	93	-
Reports of Registrar,	169	102	67	-
Accounts, &c., taken and passed by Local Judge,	11	32	-	21
Accounts passed by Registrar,	394	310	84	-
	£	£	£	£
Gross income of Lunatics,	121,500	98,000	-	23,500

This summary indicates an increase of 96 in orders, following an increase of 6 in 1885; and an increase of 93 in affidavits, following a decrease of 27.

The number of lunatics under the control of the Lord Chancellor at the close of 1886 was 230, being 7 more than at the close of 1885.

Probate and Matrimonial Division.

The following is a summary of the business of the Court of Probate in Ireland and the Principal Registry:— Principal Registry. Table 57.

Court of Probate—Principal Registry.	1886.	1885.	Increase, 1886.	Decrease, 1886.
Probates and administrations with Wills annexed,	1,353	1,262	93	-
Administrations without Wills,	581	547	33	-
Total probates and administrations,	2,083	1,909	126	-
Caveats,	549	409	-	23
Causes instituted,	107	115	8	-
Trials by special jury,	15	9	-	6
Trials by common jury,	83	90	-	8
Causes heard without a jury,	71	80	-	1
Court Motions,	645	480	-	165
Petitions disposed of by Judge or Registrar,	75	60	-	10
	£	£	£	£
Total amount of fees received,	3,673	3,489	-	221

From the above it appears that there was an increase of 128 in probates and letters of administration in 1886 as compared with 1885.

The taxation of costs is now included in the returns of the Consolidated Taxing Offices.

A return received from the Comptroller of Stamp Duties shows the amount of duty paid for Grants of Probate and Administration in 1886 to be £183,496, namely, £110,699 in Dublin, and £72,797 in the country districts, as compared with £213,095, namely, £141,210 in Dublin and £71,885 in the country districts, in 1885, being a decrease of £29,599, following an increase of £39,224 in 1885 as compared with 1884. Comptroller of Stamps' Return as to Property under Probate, &c. Table 58.

Part II. Judicial Statistics. — Central Administration of Justice.

Jurisdiction in Matrimonial causes. Table 58. As to matrimonial causes and matters and proceedings under the Legitimacy Declaration Act (Ireland), 1868, it appears that there were 28 petitions filed in matrimonial causes and matters during the year; 20 citations were issued. There were 5 decrees for divorce *a mensâ et thoro*, no decree for restitution of conjugal rights, and no decree of nullity of marriage. There were 61 motions and 9 causes heard in the year. There was no petition under the Legitimacy Act.

High Court of Admiralty.

Admiralty. Tables 60 and 61. The causes instituted in the High Court of Admiralty in Ireland in the year were 31, as compared with 43 in 1885, and 51 in 1884. There were 14 causes pending at end of 1885, making 45 in all to be disposed of.

The motions and summonses heard were 91, final judgments and decrees 9, and instruments, &c., prepared in the Registry 114; showing a total of 214, being under the total in 1885, which amounted to 249, consisting of 123 motions and summonses, 8 judgments and decrees, and 119 instruments, &c., prepared in the Registry.

Court of Bankruptcy.

Bankruptcy. Table 62. In the following summary the principal proceedings in Bankruptcy are compared with those of the preceding year:—

Proceedings in Bankruptcy.	1885.	1886.	Increase, 1886.	Decrease, 1886.
Petitions of Bankruptcy:				
By Creditors, . .	177	196	19	-
By Debtors, . .	12	46	4	–
Petitions for Arrangement, .	253*	266†	13	-
Sittings before the Court, . .	6,091‡	6,384‡	293	–
Sittings before the Chief Registrar, and the Chief Clerk, . .	3,381	4,251	872	–

It appears that the number of petitions of Bankruptcy in 1886 was 242, showing an increase of 23 as compared with the number, 219, in 1885. The petitions for arrangement showed an increase of 13.

Insolvency. Table 61. Although Insolvency jurisdiction was abolished from 1st of January, 1873, by the Debtors (Ireland) Act of 1872, there were still, at the end of thirteen years, a few proceedings in winding up the cases previously in the Court.

Proceedings in Insolvency.	1885.	1886.	Increase, 1886.	Decrease, 1886.
Petitions in which dividends were declared, ...	1	4	3	-
Sittings before the Court in Dublin for all purposes in Insolvency, .	6	13	7	-
„ before the First Clerk or other Officer, . . .	3	9	6	-

Details regarding the state of the Bankruptcies and Insolvencies under the charge of each Official Assignee in 1886 are given in Table 62.

Finance.

Accountant-General's Office. In Chancery and Probate business § the Accountant-General carried over (in cash and securities) on 1st of October £3,697,695,‖ being £65,974 in excess of the amount carried over on the corresponding day in 1885.

Table 66.

* This number includes 23 Private Arrangements turned into Bankruptcy.

† „ „ 38 „ „

‡ This does not include "Motions of Course" made before the Judges.

§ See note on page 121.

‖ £1,[illegible] being adopted as the value of $[illegible],000 in foreign currency.

Part II. Judicial Statistics.

Central Administration of Justice.

Table 66 contains particulars regarding the Receipts and Payments of the Accountant-General of the Supreme Court of Judicature in Ireland, in respect of the funds of suitors in said Court, and a statement of Liabilities and Assets in respect of such funds, also particulars of securities in Court.

Law Taxes. Table 67.

A Return has been obtained from the Inland Revenue Department of the Law Taxes levied in connexion with the High Court of Justice: see Table 67.

Appellate Jurisdiction.

The Proceedings in the Supreme Courts of Appeal, in 1886, are shown in Tables 68–73.

Her Majesty's Court of Appeal, Ireland. Table 68.

During the year 89 appeals from final judgments from Divisions of the High Court of Justice were heard and judgment delivered by Her Majesty's Court of Appeal in Ireland, 18 of which Appeals were from the Chancery Division, 7 from the Queen's Bench, 5 from the Common Pleas, 9 from the Exchequer Division, and 1 from the Probate and Matrimonial Causes Division. There were 41 appeals from interlocutory orders from Divisions of the High Court of Justice heard, viz.:—16 from the Chancery Division, 8 from the Queen's Bench, 7 from the Common Pleas, and 8 from the Exchequer Division. Sixty-one appeals from other Judges or Courts were heard, 8 of which were from the Judges in Bankruptcy, 1 from the High Court of Admiralty; 41 were Registry of Voters Appeals, and 11 were appeals from the Irish Land Commission. There were also 21 original motions heard. The Judgments delivered were 143. In 70 of these the Judgment below was affirmed; in 30 it was reversed; in 6 reversed with declaration, direction, or finding; and in 17 cases varied.

Privy Council, Ireland. Table 71.

There were 12 applications before the Privy Council in Ireland under the Labourers (Ireland) Act, 1883, for confirmation of Provisional Orders made by the Local Government Board for Ireland: in 1 case the Order was confirmed, in 7 cases the Orders were varied, 1 case was withdrawn, and 3 cases were pending at the close of the year. There were also before the Council 3 applications (including 2 remaining from 1885) under the "Tramways and Public Companies (Ireland) Act, 1853;" 9 applications under the "Tramways (Ireland) Acts, 1860 and 1861, and 1 under the "Fairs (Ireland) Act, 1868."

Her Majesty in Council. Table 72.

There were no appeals from Ireland to Her Majesty in Council.

House of Lords. Table 73.

The number of Appeals from Ireland presented to the House of Lords in 1886 was 5; 3 were in matters of Real Property, and 2 in matters of Personal Property. Three Causes were dismissed for want of prosecution. Three Judgments were delivered during the year, at the close of which 1 Cause stood over for judgment, and 1 for hearing.

Tables 69 and 70.

There were 2 appeals before the Judges of the Common Law Divisions, as to Presentment and other Cases not within the 11 & 12 Vic., cap. 78: particulars regarding these cases are given in Table 70. There was 1 appeal before the Court for Crown Cases Reserved. See Table 69.

Local Administration of Justice—Larger Districts.

II.—LOCAL ADMINISTRATION OF JUSTICE—LARGER DISTRICTS.

The tables in this part are arranged chiefly according to the degree of localization carried out in the different jurisdictions.

Local Courts of Admiralty. Table 74.

Admiralty jurisdiction:—In Belfast in 1886 there were 6 actions or proceedings, and in Cork 18.

Part II. Judicial Statistics.

Local Administration of Justice—Larger Districts.

District Probate Registries. Table 73.

In the District Registries of the Court of Probate the chief business in 1885 and 1886 was as follows:—

Court of Probate—District Registries.	1885.	1886.	Increase, 1886.	Decrease, 1886.
Granted in Common Form:				
Probates, ...	1,693	1,605	-	88
Letters of administration—(Intestate Widows' Acts)	18	16	-	2
" —others, ...	1,313	1,301	-	12
Letters of administration with the Will annexed,	316	309	-	7
Granted under direction of Judge:				
Probates, ...	17	20	3	-
Letters of administration, ...	12	17	5	-
Letters of administration with the Will annexed,	8	15	7	-
Granted on Decrees of County Court Judges:				
Probates, ...	20	17	-	3
Letters of administration, ...	4	3	-	1
Letters of administration with Will annexed, .	4	3	-	1
Recalled or varied:				
Probates, ...	1	-	-	1
Letters of administration, ...	5	-	-	5
Total granted, &c., ...	3,408	3,308	-	100
	£	£	£	£
Total amount of fees received, . .	9,101	8,198	-	903
Amount of duty on Schedules lodged for grants, ...	74,039	70,880	-	3,159

Number of probates of wills and letters of administration in Ireland.

There has been a decrease of 94 in the number of wills proved and letters of administration granted, in 1886, at the District Registries, of which there are eleven. The aggregate number at both Central and District Registries (5,314) is 82 over the number (5,462) in 1885.

Proving of Wills where assets small, through Officers of Inland Revenue.

The 33rd section of the Customs and Inland Revenue Act of 1881, affords local facilities for obtaining grants of probate or letters of administration, where the gross value of the personal estate of the deceased does not exceed £300. In 1886 there were in Ireland 111 towns where officers of Inland Revenue were authorized to deal with applications under this Act. These, with Dublin and the 11 District Probate Registry Towns, give 123 towns for proving wills of not more than £300 assets.

Proceedings on Circuit.

Jury Trials. Tables 76, 77, and 78.

There are now only five circuits in Ireland, but Assizes are still held in thirty-three towns. Six of these towns are counties of cities and towns with distinct Grand and Petit Juries and Officers. The Grand and Petit Jurors of the county of the town of Carrickfergus are brought to Belfast for assize purposes, but those of Drogheda are not brought to Dundalk, the county town of Louth. The causes entered for trial on circuit in 1886 were 200 as compared with 241 in 1885. The amount recovered fell from £12,061 in 1885 to £7,086 in 1886.

Appeals from County Court

PART II. JUDICIAL STATISTICS. — *Local Administration of Justice—Larger Districts.*

There were in 1886, 16 objections to Presentments heard by Judges, and 26 special directions given.

Railway, Tramway, and other traverses on circuit. Table 79.

The railway traverses under the Railway Acts, which have been returned, were 20 in number. The amount claimed in those cases where verdicts were given was £7,494, the amount found by verdict was £3,174. There were 11 tramway traverses under Tramway Acts; the amount claimed in cases where verdicts were given was £1,040, and the amount found by verdict £402. The traverses other than railway and tramway traverses in 1886, were 97 in number—£16,427 was claimed in the cases where verdicts were given, and £4,730 found by verdict.

Fines on Jurors on circuit. Table 79.

The memorials from persons fined for non-attendance as Jurors, after falling from 150 in 1879, to 137 in 1880, rose in 1881 to 163, and fell to 84 in 1882, to 83 in 1883 and 1884, and to 72 in 1885: in 1886 they numbered 75. The fines appealed from in cases heard rose from £398 in 1880 to £776 in 1881, fell to £166 in 1882, rose to £364 in 1883, and to £425 in 1884, fell to £372 in 1885, and rose to £473 in 1886: with the exception of £1 all of the last named sum was remitted. In 1885 and 1884, all the fines in cases heard were remitted, and in 1883 they were reduced to £3, as compared with £19 in 1882, £88 in 1881, and £92 in 1880.

COUNTY COURTS.

Process served. Table 81.

Returns have been obtained from the Process Servers, who are appointed under statute by the County Court Judges and Recorders, and whose salary is annually voted by Parliament. Out of the entire number of 850 Process Servers, all but 33, or less than 4 per cent., have made returns.

The Civil Bill ejectments served by these officers are 21,064 as compared with 18,592 in 1885, 22,528 in 1884, 22,708 in 1883, 19,035 in 1882, 13,621 in 1881, 10,633 in 1880, and 9,703 in 1879; the number of replevins 294 as compared with 430 in 1885, 312 in 1884, 269 in 1883, 407 in 1882, 412 in 1881, 378 in 1880, and 459 in 1879; and the number of other civil bills 214,823, as compared with 226,153 in 1885, 236,394 in 1884, 231,762 in 1883, 220,948 in 1882, 240,366 in 1881, 289,358 in 1880, and 347,909 in 1879.

County Court Proceedings. Table 82.

The statistics of proceedings (other than at Equity or Land Sessions, or under Local Admiralty Jurisdiction Act) in the Courts of County Court Judges and Courts of Recorders whether ejectments, causes remitted from the Superior Courts, or other suits, have been collected into one Table.

Ejectments.

In ejectments entered there was an increase of 4,041 in 1886, following a decrease of 3,009 in 1885, and an increase of 1,129 in 1884.

	Ejectments Entered.
For 1886, . .	18,352
For 1885, . .	14,311
Increase in 1886, .	4,041

Causes Remitted.

In cases remitted from the Superior Courts which were entered below there was a decrease from 313 in 1885 to 259 in 1886: in 1884 the number was 265. In other suits there was an increase of 2,567, from 89,338 in 1885, to 91,905 in 1886, following a decrease of 3,067 between 1884 and 1885. There were only 105 cases disposed of by a jury.

Ordinary Civil Bills.

The amount decreed in the Civil Bill Courts in 1886 was £312,950 in ejectment cases, and £345,715 in other suits, making £658,665.* Compared with 1885, the amount decreed in ejectment cases shows an increase of £119,574 and the amount decreed in other suits an increase of £26,718. The costs adjudged to plaintiffs amounted to £70,407, being £10,965 over the amount in 1885. Of these costs, £32,062 was in ejectment cases, and £38,345 in other suits.

* Including £706 at Land Sessions, under the Landlord and Tenant (Ireland) Act, 1870, the total was £659,371.

PART II. JUDICIAL STATISTICS. — Local Administration of Justice. — County Courts, &c.

Local equitable matters or proceedings. Table 82.

The Equitable Jurisdiction cases for 1886 (exclusive of Lunacy Proceedings), were 610 as compared with 797 cases for 1885. The aggregate amount of the subject matter in dispute, so far as returned, was £61,905 as compared with £75,415 in 1885.

County Court Lunacy Jurisdiction. Table 83.

In County Court Lunacy Cases, under the jurisdiction conferred by the Lunacy Act of 1880, there were 43 orders made. The subject matter (so far as returned) in these orders goes to make up the £61,905 referred to above.

Ejectments executed by Sheriffs. Table 84.

A classification of the ejectments executed by Sheriffs and Special Bailiffs according as they came from the High Court of Justice or the County Court, gives the following results:—

	High Court.				County Courts.			
	1885.	1886.	Increase.	Decrease.	1885.	1886.	Increase.	Decrease.
Ejectments executed, .	685	931	246	–	3,873	4,175	302	–
Leinster, . . .	310	336	26	–	586	781	195	–
Munster, . . .	202	346	144	..	1,021	1,254	230	–
Ulster, . . .	95	174	79	–	1,296	1,113	–	183
Connaught, . .	78	75	–	3	964	1,027	63	–

The ejectments executed show an increase of 548—from 4,558 in 1885 to 5,106 last year following a decrease of 1,340 in 1885 as compared with 1884.

In the ejectments from the High Court which were executed there was an increase of 246, following a decrease of 200 in 1885, a decrease of 101 in 1884, a decrease of 491 in 1883, and increases in each of the three preceding years, viz.—56 in 1882, 446 in 1881, 49 in 1880.

County Court Ejectment Suits and Executions compared

The County Court Ejectment Suits entered and lodged increased from 9,856 in 1880, to 11,772 in 1881, and to 16,835 in 1882; fell to 14,744 in 1883, rose to 15,873 in 1884, fell to 12,870 in 1885, and rose last year to 16,911, being an increase of 4,041 as compared with 1885.

The executions of County Court ejectments by the Sheriff show an increase of 302—from 3,873 in 1885 to 4,175 in 1886. The number for 1885 was 1,140 under that for 1884.

Fourteen thousand five hundred and thirty-five Civil Bill decrees and dismisses are returned as executed by Sheriffs, and 6,569 by Special Bailiffs, or 21,104 in all.

Warrants against Cottier Tenants and Weekly Tenants. Table 89. Summary recovery of possession of tenements overheld in towns.

The warrants to Special Bailiffs under Act 23 & 24 Vic., c. 154 (summary recovery of possession of tenements), were 767 in 1885, and 886 in 1886. The warrants to Special Bailiffs under 14 & 15 Vic., cap. 92, s. 15 (summary recovery of possession of tenements overheld in towns), 14,701, show an increase of 1,939 from 12,762 in 1885.

Ejectments executed for non-payment of rent and others in 1886 and 1885, compared. Table 84.

The following is a Summary of the Returns of Sheriffs as to execution of ejectments, classed so as to show the proportion that were and were not for non-payment of rent:—

	Ejectments for Non-payment of Rent.				Ejectments for Other Causes.			
	1885.	1886.	Increase, 1886.	Decrease, 1886.	1885.	1886.	Increase, 1886.	Decrease, 1886.
Ireland, . .	3,796	4,592	796	—	762	514	—	248
Leinster, . .	716	997	281	—	133	100	—	33
Munster . .	985	1,531	546	..	141	49	—	102
Ulster, . .	1,131	993	--	138	270	294	24	—
Connaught, .	914	1,021	107	—	96	61	—	47

From this Table it appears that there was an increase of 796 in ejectments for non-payment of rent (following a decrease of 1,287 in 1885), and a decrease of 248 in

The statistics as to the proceedings under the Landlord and Tenant Act of 1870, are shown in the following table:—

Cases disposed of at Land Sessions.	1885.	1886.	Increase in 1886.	Decrease in 1886.
Total number of cases, . . .	20	22	2	–
Confirmation of leases, . .	–	–	–	–
Registration of improvements, . .	1	–	–	1
Other cases:—	19	22	3	–
Decrees, . . .	8	8	–	–
Dismisses, ...	4	4	–	–
Otherwise disposed of, . .	3	6	3	–
Pending at end of year, . .	4	4	–	–

Part II. Judicial Statistics. — Land Administration of Justice — Land Districts. — County Courts. — Land Sessions. Table 84.

It appears from this table that there was an increase of 2 in the number of cases from 20 in 1885 to 22 in 1886. This followed a decrease of 6 in 1885, 17 in 1884, 104 in 1883, 143 in 1882, 58 in 1881, 61 in 1880, 146 in 1879, and 41 in 1878. The number of cases now is less than 4 per cent. of the number in 1878.

There were no applications for confirmation of leases in either 1885 or 1886.

The decrees in 1886, were 8, and the dismisses 4.

In the 8 land claim cases in which there were decrees, the total amount adjudged on the decrees was £709, being £1,435 less than in 1885. The following table shows the distribution of the amount in the different provinces in 1885 and 1886 for comparison:— Decrees.

Decrees at Land Sessions.	Gross Amount of Decrees.		Number of Decrees.		Average Gross Sum adjudged in each case.	
	1885.	1886.	1885.	1886.	1885.	1886.
	£	£			£	£
Total of Ireland, . . .	2,144	709	8	8	268	89
Leinster, . . .	1,416	–	3	–	472	–
Munster, . . .	596	341	3	2	199	172
Ulster, . . .	132	298	2	5	66	59
Connaught, . . .	–	70	–	1	–	70

It appears from this table that the average gross amount awarded, without deducting allowances for set-off to landlord, for dilapidation, rent, &c., was in all Ireland £89, as compared with £268 in 1885. In Ulster it was £59, as compared with £66 in 1885; in Munster £172, as compared with £199 in 1885. There were no decrees in Leinster in 1886, and but one (for £70) in Connaught; in 1885 there were three decrees in Leinster, for amounts averaging £472, and none in Connaught.

The following Table showing the distribution of the £3,912 claimed in cases where decrees were made, into provinces and counties, with the amount decreed in each province and county, and the ratio of the amount decreed to the sum claimed is given

Part II. Judicial Statistics. — Land Administration of Justice.— Larger Districts. — County Courts. — Land Sessions.

PROCEEDINGS IN 1886 UNDER LANDLORD AND TENANT (IRELAND) ACT, 1870.

Province and County.	Amount: Claimed where Decrees made.	Amount: Decreed.	Percentage in Amount decreed of Amount claimed.	Province and County.	Amount: Claimed where Decrees made.	Amount: Decreed.	Percentage in Amount decreed of Amount claimed.
	£	£	Per cent.	MUNSTER—con.	£	£	Per cent.
IRELAND, . .	3,912	709	18	Limerick, . .	–	–	–
				Tipperary, .	–	–	–
LEINSTER, . .	–	–	–	Waterford, .	364	194	53
Carlow, . .	–	–	–	ULSTER, . .	1,943	283	15
Dublin, . .	–	–	–				
Kildare, . .	–	–	–	Antrim, . .	1,503	183	9
Kilkenny, . .	–	–	–	Armagh, . .	131	20	16
King's County, .	–	–	–	Cavan, . .	–	–	–
Longford, . .	–	–	–	Donegal, . .	–	–	–
Louth, . .	–	–	–	Down, . .	–	–	–
Meath, . .	–	–	–	Fermanagh, .	–	–	–
Queen's County,	–	–	–	Londonderry, .	309	143	46
Westmeath, .	–	–	–	Monaghan, .	–	–	–
Wexford, . .	–	–	–	Tyrone, . .	–	–	–
Wicklow, . .	–	–	–				
				CONNAUGHT, .	302	70	23
MUNSTER, .	1,697	344	20				
				Galway, . .	–	–	–
Clare, . .	1,333	150	11	Leitrim, . .	–	–	–
Cork, E. R., .	–	–	–	Mayo, . .	295	70	24
Cork, W. R., .	–	–	–	Roscommon, .	–	–	–
Kerry, . .	–	–	–	Sligo, . .	–	–	–

It appears from this Table that in all Ireland the amount decreed, £709, was 18 per cent. of the amount claimed in cases where decrees were made—£3,912. In 1885, the sum decreed was £2,144 or 44 per cent. of the amount claimed in those cases where decrees were made.

Land Commission Court. — Table 63.

COURT OF THE IRISH LAND COMMISSION.

The Commissioners appointed under the "Land Law (Ireland) Act, 1881," have many functions of a judicial character, therefore it is necessary in this Report to refer to the judicial portion of their proceedings, and it is convenient here to refer to the subject as they are somewhat allied to those under the Act of 1870—dealt with above—and are mainly determined in the Courts of the Sub-Commissions which are most properly dealt with as part of the local administration of justice.

It is unnecessary to give here a detailed account of the business of the Court of the Land Commission as the Reports of the Commissioners contain full information on the

The following statement shows generally the extent and nature of the proceedings in connexion with the Court of the Land Commission during the year 1886 :—

Nature of Proceedings.	No. of Cases.	Nature of Proceedings.	No. of Cases.
Applications to have fair rents fixed :—		Miscellaneous originating notices :—	
1. In court—		Pending at beginning of year,	250
Pending at beginning of year,	6,455	Number lodged during 1886,	100
Entered and lodged during 1886,	7,340*	Disposed of,	74
Rents fixed,	3,690	Pending at end of year,	256
Dismissed or struck out,	455	Appeals re Fair Rent, &c. :—	
Withdrawn,	68	Pending at beginning of year,	6,250
Pending at end of year,	7,565*	Number lodged during 1886,	1,673
2. Out of court—		Heard,	1,264
Agreements fixing fair rents,	5,558	Withdrawn,	2,347
		Pending at end of year,	4,781‡
Applications to have leases declared void :—		Result of Appeals heard :	
Pending at beginning of year,†	77	Decisions below, reversed,	60
Declared void,	—	Do. do., confirmed,	750
Dismissed and struck out,	2	Rents fixed below, increased,	94
Withdrawn or compromised,	—	Do. do., reduced,	538
Pending at end of year,	75		

The following statement shows the sums of money dealt with by the Court in fixing fair rents in the year 1886 :—

Fair Rents Fixed	Former Rent.			Judicial Rent.			Amount of Reduction.			Rate per Cent.
	£	s.	d.	£	s.	d.	£	s.	d.	
In court,	35,391	9	10½	28,996	6	0	16,323	1	10½	29·6
Out of court,	84,786	14	9¾	66,163	7	0¾	9,621	7	9¾	11·3
Total,	120,178	1	8½	94,160	13	0¾	26,017	15	7¾	21·6

Part II. Judicial Statistics. — *Land Administration of Justice—Larger Districts.*

From these statements it appears that during the year 1886 "fair rents" were fixed in 6,024 cases (2,698 in court and 3,326 out of court), the "former rent" of the holdings dealt with in these cases being in round numbers £120,178, and the "judicial rents" registered by the Court for these holdings being £94,161 showing a reduction of £26,017 or 21·6 per cent. of the "former rent." Some of the "judicial rents" included in the above are liable to variation on appeal.

Land Commission Court.

The number of cases of appeal from the Land Court to the Court of Appeal, and how these were disposed of, will be found in Table 69 of Appendix, and are dealt with at page 45 under the head of Appellate Jurisdiction.

Proceedings of Sheriffs.

Proceedings of Sheriffs.

The proceedings of Sheriffs in the year of their office 1886-7, including those having relation to Jurors summoned, and those already referred to, are set forth in detail in Tables 86 and 88.

Jurors.

Revision of Jurors Lists and correction of Jurors Books, Table 87.

The revision of the General Jurors Lists resulted in the striking off of 41,017 out of 107,094 persons, or 38 per cent.; there were only 19 persons added by Revision Court.

Besides those struck off on revision there were 274 exempted by Clerks of the Peace, and 71 were struck off by Judges. This gives the total number of Jurors on the corrected General Jurors Books (when handed to the Sheriffs) in all Ireland as 65,751. 59,522 Jurors were on rated qualification, 3,009 were £10 freeholders, 2,933 were £20 leaseholders, 276 Directors or Managers of Public Companies, and 11 Harbour Commissioners.

In the case of 16,057 persons on the Special Jurors Lists, 5,779 persons were struck off by Revision Court, 142 exempted by the Clerks of the Peace, and 12 struck off by Judges; 197 were added by Revision Court, so that there was a net reduction of 5,736, or 36 per cent. When handed to the Sheriffs the books showed 10,321 Special Jurors.

Jurors summoned, Table 88.

Along with the jurors summoned by Sheriffs are included the jurors summoned to the Recorder's Court in the case of the boroughs of Belfast and Londonderry, which have separate Courts of Sessions of the Peace, although these are summoned by the Clerk of the Peace of the borough.

The total number of jurors returned as summoned in the year is 47,273, as compared with 52,789 in 1885. Of the number for 1886, 6,149 were Grand Jurors* for Assizes, Commissions, and Superior Courts; 6,669 were Grand Jurors for Quarter Sessions; 3,460* were Special Jurors for Assizes, Commissions and Superior Courts; 13,416 were Petit and Common Jurors for Assizes, Commissions and Superior Courts; 16,839 were Petit Jurors for Quarter Sessions; 1,417 were Jurors in Civil Bill cases before County Court Judges or Recorders; and 110 were Jurors for other purposes.

Part II. Judicial Statistics.

Local Administration of Justice.

In the following summary the statistics of appeals at Quarter Sessions are compared with the figures for 1885:—

Appeals from Magistrates at Quarter Sessions. Table 90.

Appeals at Quarter Sessions.	1885.	1886.	Increase, 1886.	Decrease, 1886.
Appeals from Magistrates:—				
Affirmed, ...	335	304	–	31
Reversed, ...	177	183	6	–
Varied, ...	70	64	–	6
Otherwise disposed of (including cases where there was no appearance), . . .	120	86	–	34
Total, ...	704	637	–	67

The number of appeals from Magistrates heard at Quarter Sessions, as appears from the above figures, was 67 less in 1886 than in 1885. There had been an increase of 19 in 1885, an increase of 63 in 1884, a decrease of 63 in 1883, and an increase of 57 in 1882. Of the appeals heard and decided in Court during 1886, in 304 cases the previous decisions were affirmed, in 183 reversed, and in 64 varied.

Spirit Licences.

Spirit Licences.

The number of licences granted at other Quarter Sessions than the annual licensing Sessions was 676, which, with the number granted or confirmed at the Annual Sessions (1,675), makes 2,351 in all, and of these 474 were on original application, compared with 519 in 1885.

SMALLER DISTRICT ADMINISTRATION OF JUSTICE.

Local Charter Courts.

Local Charter Courts. Table 91.

The following summary shows the business in 1886 in the eight Local Charter Courts, viz.:—Clonmel Court of Conscience, Drogheda Court of Conscience, Dublin Lord Mayor's Court, Dublin Court of Conscience, Kilkenny Court of Conscience, Limerick Court of Conscience, Londonderry Court of Conscience, and Wexford Court of Conscience. There were summonses issued, 4,774, against 4,947 in 1885; causes heard, 3,235; decisions for plaintiff, 2,446; for defendant, 388; otherwise disposed of, 401

Petty Sessions Courts.

Petty Sessions Courts. Table 89. Civil proceedings.

Table 89 in the Appendix shows the civil business at the Courts of Petty Sessions. The summonses issued were 131,016, which shows a decrease of 4,720 as compared with the number in 1885, following a decrease of 5,396 in 1885 as compared with 1884.

Civil cases at Petty Sessions other than proceedings against cottier and weekly tenants were disposed of as follows:—

	1885.	1886.	Increase in 1886.	Decrease in 1886.
Summonses issued, . .	110,805	104,291	—	6,514
Complaints heard, . .	63,193	58,239	—	4,954
Decrees made, . .	46,973	43,797	—	3,176
Warrants issued, . .	11,819	11,356	—	463

Proceedings against cottier tenants.

The table also shows the proceedings relating to cottier tenants under the Landlord and Tenant Act, 1860, (Stat. 23 & 24 Vic., c. 154,) under which cottier tenements of less than half an acre, under £5 rent, and repaired by landlord, may be summarily

Part II. Judicial Statistics. — Local Administration of Justice—Smaller Districts. — Petty Sessions Courts. — Proceedings against Cottier and Weekly Tenants. Table 58.

The proceedings against cottier and weekly tenants and against servants, herdsmen, and caretakers in 1886 appear from the returns to have been as follows:—

[illegible]	[illegible]	[illegible]	[illegible]	[illegible]
Cottier Tenants. Under Stat. 23 & 24 Vic., c. 154.				
For Waste (sec. 84),	58	45	886	82
For Non-payment of Rent (sec. 85),	113	63		
Caretakers, Servants, and Cottier Tenants.				
For Overholding (sec. 86),	1,858	1,307		
Weekly Tenants. Under Stat. 14 & 15 Vic., c. 92.				
For Overholding in Towns (sec. 15),	34,861	17,920	14,701	101
Total,	36,719	19,330	15,587	183

Non-attendance of Magistrates. Table 59.

The returns further indicate the number of occasions on which, in consequence of the non-attendance of Magistrates, Petty Sessions were not held. This number (695), as compared with 13,549 days on which Petty Sessions Courts other than Dublin Police Courts were held, gives a proportion of 5·1 per cent.; but this proportion is differently distributed, and reaches 11·5 per cent. in the province of Connaught, as appears from the following table:—

Provinces.	[illegible]	[illegible]	[illegible]
			Per cent.
Leinster, (162* Courts),	139	3,473*	4·0
Munster, (165 „),	233	4,659	5·0
Ulster, (169 „),	70	3,216	2·2
Connaught, (111 „),	253	2,203	11·5
Total (607 Courts),*	695	13,549*	5·1

* Not including 2 Metropolitan Police District Courts (where local Magistrates cannot sit) which sat on 12 days.

In Leinster the postponements fell from 169 in 1885 to 139 in 1886, being a decrease of 30; in Munster they rose 23 or from 210 to 233; in Ulster there was a decrease of 8 postponements, namely from 78 to 70, and in Connaught the number rose from 205 in 1885 to 253, being an increase of 48. The net increase for all Ireland was 33.

THOMAS W. GRIMSHAW,

Registrar-General.

Part I.—[illegible]							Cost of [illegible]										
[illegible]	Other Superior Officers.	[illegible]	Clerks.	[illegible]	[illegible]	Total.	Salaries and Pay.	Allowances and Contingent Expenses.	Clothing and Accoutrements.	[illegible]	Horses, Forage, &c.	[illegible] Charges, &c.	Other Miscellaneous Charges.	Total Cost.	Proportion paid by Counties for additional Number of Men.	Proportion paid by [illegible]	Proportion paid by Her Majesty's Treasury.
[illegible]	[illegible]	[illegible]	[illegible]	[illegible]	[illegible]	[illegible]	£ s. d.	£ s. d.	£ s. d.	£ s. d.	£ s. d.	£ s. d.	£ s. d.	£ s. d.	£ s. d.	£ s. d.	£ s. d.

PART III.—EFFECTIVE STRENGTH of the FORCE in COUNTIES, and in COUNTIES of CITIES and of TOWNS, on the [illegible] day of September, [illegible].

Counties, and Counties of Cities and of Towns, with Depot of Ireland.	County and Town Inspectors.	District Inspectors.	Head Constables.	Sergeants, Acting Sergeants, and Constables.	Total of Effective Strength—Head Constables, Sergeants, Acting Sergeants, and Constables.	Population according to Census of 1861.	Number of Effective Constabulary per [illegible] of Population.
Antrim,	[illegible]	[illegible]	[illegible]	[illegible]	[illegible]	[illegible]	[illegible]
Armagh,	[illegible]	[illegible]	[illegible]	[illegible]	[illegible]	[illegible]	[illegible]
Carlow,	[illegible]	[illegible]	[illegible]	[illegible]	[illegible]	[illegible]	[illegible]
Cavan,	[illegible]	[illegible]	[illegible]	[illegible]	[illegible]	[illegible]	[illegible]
Clare,	[illegible]	[illegible]	[illegible]	[illegible]	[illegible]	[illegible]	[illegible]
Cork, East Riding,	[illegible]	[illegible]	[illegible]	[illegible]	[illegible]	[illegible]	[illegible]
Cork, West Riding,	[illegible]	[illegible]	[illegible]	[illegible]	[illegible]	[illegible]	[illegible]
Donegal,	[illegible]	[illegible]	[illegible]	[illegible]	[illegible]	[illegible]	[illegible]
Down,	[illegible]	[illegible]	[illegible]	[illegible]	[illegible]	[illegible]	[illegible]
Dublin,	[illegible]	[illegible]	[illegible]	[illegible]	[illegible]	[illegible]	[illegible]
Fermanagh,	[illegible]	[illegible]	[illegible]	[illegible]	[illegible]	[illegible]	[illegible]
Galway, East Riding,	[illegible]	[illegible]	[illegible]	[illegible]	[illegible]	[illegible]	[illegible]
Galway, West Riding,	[illegible]	[illegible]	[illegible]	[illegible]	[illegible]	[illegible]	[illegible]
Kerry,	[illegible]	[illegible]	[illegible]	[illegible]	[illegible]	[illegible]	[illegible]
Kildare,	[illegible]	[illegible]	[illegible]	[illegible]	[illegible]	[illegible]	[illegible]
Kilkenny,	[illegible]	[illegible]	[illegible]	[illegible]	[illegible]	[illegible]	[illegible]
King's,	[illegible]	[illegible]	[illegible]	[illegible]	[illegible]	[illegible]	[illegible]
Leitrim,	[illegible]	[illegible]	[illegible]	[illegible]	[illegible]	[illegible]	[illegible]
Limerick,	[illegible]	[illegible]	[illegible]	[illegible]	[illegible]	[illegible]	[illegible]
Londonderry,	[illegible]	[illegible]	[illegible]	[illegible]	[illegible]	[illegible]	[illegible]
Longford,	[illegible]	[illegible]	[illegible]	[illegible]	[illegible]	[illegible]	[illegible]
Louth,	[illegible]	[illegible]	[illegible]	[illegible]	[illegible]	[illegible]	[illegible]
Mayo,	[illegible]	[illegible]	[illegible]	[illegible]	[illegible]	[illegible]	[illegible]
Meath,	[illegible]	[illegible]	[illegible]	[illegible]	[illegible]	[illegible]	[illegible]
Monaghan,	[illegible]	[illegible]	[illegible]	[illegible]	[illegible]	[illegible]	[illegible]
Queen's,	[illegible]	[illegible]	[illegible]	[illegible]	[illegible]	[illegible]	[illegible]
Roscommon,	[illegible]	[illegible]	[illegible]	[illegible]	[illegible]	[illegible]	[illegible]
Sligo,	[illegible]	[illegible]	[illegible]	[illegible]	[illegible]	[illegible]	[illegible]
Tipperary, North Riding,	[illegible]	[illegible]	[illegible]	[illegible]	[illegible]	[illegible]	[illegible]
Tipperary, South Riding,	[illegible]	[illegible]	[illegible]	[illegible]	[illegible]	[illegible]	[illegible]
Tyrone,	[illegible]	[illegible]	[illegible]	[illegible]	[illegible]	[illegible]	[illegible]
Waterford,	[illegible]	[illegible]	[illegible]	[illegible]	[illegible]	[illegible]	[illegible]
Westmeath,	[illegible]	[illegible]	[illegible]	[illegible]	[illegible]	[illegible]	[illegible]
Wexford,	[illegible]	[illegible]	[illegible]	[illegible]	[illegible]	[illegible]	[illegible]
Wicklow,	[illegible]	[illegible]	[illegible]	[illegible]	[illegible]	[illegible]	[illegible]
CITIES AND TOWNS.							
Carrickfergus,	[illegible]	[illegible]	[illegible]	[illegible]	[illegible]	[illegible]	[illegible]
Cork,	[illegible]	[illegible]	[illegible]	[illegible]	[illegible]	[illegible]	[illegible]
Drogheda,	[illegible]	[illegible]	[illegible]	[illegible]	[illegible]	[illegible]	[illegible]
Galway,	[illegible]	[illegible]	[illegible]	[illegible]	[illegible]	[illegible]	[illegible]
Kilkenny,	[illegible]	[illegible]	[illegible]	[illegible]	[illegible]	[illegible]	[illegible]
Limerick,	[illegible]	[illegible]	[illegible]	[illegible]	[illegible]	[illegible]	[illegible]
Londonderry,	[illegible]	[illegible]	[illegible]	[illegible]	[illegible]	[illegible]	[illegible]
Waterford,	[illegible]	[illegible]	[illegible]	[illegible]	[illegible]	[illegible]	[illegible]
Total,	[illegible]	[illegible]	[illegible]	[illegible]	[illegible]	[illegible]	[illegible]
Belfast Town Force,	[illegible]	[illegible]	[illegible]	[illegible]	[illegible]	[illegible]	[illegible]
Reserve Force,	[illegible]	[illegible]	[illegible]	[illegible]	[illegible]	[illegible]	[illegible]
Depot,	[illegible]	[illegible]	[illegible]	[illegible]	[illegible]	[illegible]	[illegible]
Total,	[illegible]	[illegible]	[illegible]	[illegible]	[illegible]	[illegible]	[illegible]

[illegible]

[illegible]

PART IV.—AMOUNT CHARGED to COUNTIES and COUNTIES of CITIES and of TOWNS for EXTRA FORCE, in the Year ended [illegible] September, [illegible].

Greatest Number of Extra Men chargeable in the Year [illegible], in the month of [illegible], [illegible]	Least Number of Extra Men chargeable in the Year [illegible], in the Month of [illegible], [illegible]	Monthly average of Extra Men during the Year, [illegible]

Part I.

	[illegible]	[illegible]	[illegible]	[illegible]	[illegible]	[illegible]	Total.	Salaries and Pay.	[illegible] and Contingent Expenses.	Clothing and [illegible]	[illegible]	[illegible]	[illegible] Charges
								£. s. d.	£. s. d.	£. s. d.	£. s. d.	£. s. d.	£. s.
[illegible]	[illegible]	[illegible]	[illegible]	[illegible]	[illegible]	[illegible]	[illegible]						
								[illegible]	[illegible]	[illegible]	[illegible]	[illegible]	[illegible]

Part II.—[illegible]

[illegible]							

PART III.—DUBLIN POLICE COURTS.

PART III.	Number of Courts	Establishment: Magistrates	Clerks	Police Officers and Constables	Messengers	Total	Cost of Establishment: 1 Salaries and Pay	2 Fuel and Light	3 Rents, Repairs, and Miscellaneous Charges	4 [illegible]	5 Other Miscellaneous Charges	6 Gross Cost	7 [illegible] paid by Her Majesty's Treasury
							£ s. d.	£ s. d.	£ s. d.	£ s. d.	£ s. d.	£ s. d.	£ s. d.
Police Courts, . . .	[illegible]	[illegible]	[illegible]	[illegible]	[illegible]	[illegible]	[illegible]	[illegible]	[illegible]	[illegible]	[illegible]	[illegible]	[illegible]

PART IV.—EFFECTIVE STRENGTH OF THE FORCE, IN DIVISIONS, ON [illegible] MARCH, [illegible].

Divisions.	Superintendents	Inspectors	Sergeants	Constables	Detective Officers	Total Effective Strength	Population according to Census of [illegible]	Number of Effective Strength per 10,000 of Population
1. A, [illegible]	[illegible]	[illegible]	[illegible]	[illegible]	—	[illegible]	[illegible]	[illegible]
2. B, [illegible]	[illegible]	[illegible]	[illegible]	[illegible]	—	[illegible]	[illegible]	[illegible]
3. C, [illegible]	[illegible]	[illegible]	[illegible]	[illegible]	—	[illegible]	[illegible]	[illegible]
4. D, [illegible]	[illegible]	[illegible]	[illegible]	[illegible]	—	[illegible]	[illegible]	[illegible]
5. E, [illegible]	[illegible]	[illegible]	[illegible]	[illegible]	—	[illegible]	[illegible]	[illegible]
6. F, [illegible]	[illegible]	[illegible]	[illegible]	[illegible]	—	[illegible]	[illegible]	[illegible]
7. G, [illegible]	[illegible]	[illegible]	[illegible]	[illegible]	[illegible]	[illegible]	—	—
Total, . . .	[illegible]	[illegible]	[illegible]	[illegible]	[illegible]	[illegible]	[illegible]	[illegible]

* [illegible]

† [illegible]

‡ [illegible]

IRELAND.

PROVINCE, COUNTY, COUNTY OF CITY OR OF TOWN.	Known Thieves and Depredators				Receivers of Stolen Goods				Suspected Persons				[illegible]				[illegible]	[illegible]			[illegible]	[illegible]
	Under 16 years		16 years and above		Under 16 years		16 years and above		Under 16 years		16 years and above		Under 16 years		16 years and above			[illegible]	[illegible]	[illegible]		
LEINSTER:	M.	W.	M.	W.	M.	W.	M.	W.	M.	W.	M.	W.	M.	W.	M.	W.						
Carlow,	[illegible]	[illegible]	[illegible]	[illegible]	[illegible]	[illegible]	[illegible]	[illegible]	[illegible]	[illegible]	[illegible]	[illegible]	[illegible]	[illegible]	[illegible]	[illegible]	[illegible]	[illegible]	[illegible]	[illegible]	[illegible]	[illegible]
Drogheda, Town of,	[illegible]	[illegible]	[illegible]	[illegible]	[illegible]	[illegible]	[illegible]	[illegible]	[illegible]	[illegible]	[illegible]	[illegible]	[illegible]	[illegible]	[illegible]	[illegible]	[illegible]	[illegible]	[illegible]	[illegible]	[illegible]	[illegible]
Dublin County,	[illegible]	[illegible]	[illegible]	[illegible]	[illegible]	[illegible]	[illegible]	[illegible]	[illegible]	[illegible]	[illegible]	[illegible]	[illegible]	[illegible]	[illegible]	[illegible]	[illegible]	[illegible]	[illegible]	[illegible]	[illegible]	[illegible]
Dublin City (and part of County) Metropolitan Police District—Divisions—																						
A,	[illegible]	[illegible]	[illegible]	[illegible]	[illegible]	[illegible]	[illegible]	[illegible]	[illegible]	[illegible]	[illegible]	[illegible]	[illegible]	[illegible]	[illegible]	[illegible]	[illegible]	[illegible]	[illegible]	[illegible]	[illegible]	[illegible]
B,	[illegible]	[illegible]	[illegible]	[illegible]	[illegible]	[illegible]	[illegible]	[illegible]	[illegible]	[illegible]	[illegible]	[illegible]	[illegible]	[illegible]	[illegible]	[illegible]	[illegible]	[illegible]	[illegible]	[illegible]	[illegible]	[illegible]
C,	[illegible]	[illegible]	[illegible]	[illegible]	[illegible]	[illegible]	[illegible]	[illegible]	[illegible]	[illegible]	[illegible]	[illegible]	[illegible]	[illegible]	[illegible]	[illegible]	[illegible]	[illegible]	[illegible]	[illegible]	[illegible]	[illegible]
D,	[illegible]	[illegible]	[illegible]	[illegible]	[illegible]	[illegible]	[illegible]	[illegible]	[illegible]	[illegible]	[illegible]	[illegible]	[illegible]	[illegible]	[illegible]	[illegible]	[illegible]	[illegible]	[illegible]	[illegible]	[illegible]	[illegible]
E,	[illegible]	[illegible]	[illegible]	[illegible]	[illegible]	[illegible]	[illegible]	[illegible]	[illegible]	[illegible]	[illegible]	[illegible]	[illegible]	[illegible]	[illegible]	[illegible]	[illegible]	[illegible]	[illegible]	[illegible]	[illegible]	[illegible]
F,	[illegible]	[illegible]	[illegible]	[illegible]	[illegible]	[illegible]	[illegible]	[illegible]	[illegible]	[illegible]	[illegible]	[illegible]	[illegible]	[illegible]	[illegible]	[illegible]	[illegible]	[illegible]	[illegible]	[illegible]	[illegible]	[illegible]
Total of Metropolitan Police District,	[illegible]	[illegible]	[illegible]	[illegible]	[illegible]	[illegible]	[illegible]	[illegible]	[illegible]	[illegible]	[illegible]	[illegible]	[illegible]	[illegible]	[illegible]	[illegible]	[illegible]	[illegible]	[illegible]	[illegible]	[illegible]	[illegible]
Kildare,	[illegible]	[illegible]	[illegible]	[illegible]	[illegible]	[illegible]	[illegible]	[illegible]	[illegible]	[illegible]	[illegible]	[illegible]	[illegible]	[illegible]	[illegible]	[illegible]	[illegible]	[illegible]	[illegible]	[illegible]	[illegible]	[illegible]
Kilkenny,	[illegible]	[illegible]	[illegible]	[illegible]	[illegible]	[illegible]	[illegible]	[illegible]	[illegible]	[illegible]	[illegible]	[illegible]	[illegible]	[illegible]	[illegible]	[illegible]	[illegible]	[illegible]	[illegible]	[illegible]	[illegible]	[illegible]
King's County,	[illegible]	[illegible]	[illegible]	[illegible]	[illegible]	[illegible]	[illegible]	[illegible]	[illegible]	[illegible]	[illegible]	[illegible]	[illegible]	[illegible]	[illegible]	[illegible]	[illegible]	[illegible]	[illegible]	[illegible]	[illegible]	[illegible]
Longford,	[illegible]	[illegible]	[illegible]	[illegible]	[illegible]	[illegible]	[illegible]	[illegible]	[illegible]	[illegible]	[illegible]	[illegible]	[illegible]	[illegible]	[illegible]	[illegible]	[illegible]	[illegible]	[illegible]	[illegible]	[illegible]	[illegible]
Louth,	[illegible]	[illegible]	[illegible]	[illegible]	[illegible]	[illegible]	[illegible]	[illegible]	[illegible]	[illegible]	[illegible]	[illegible]	[illegible]	[illegible]	[illegible]	[illegible]	[illegible]	[illegible]	[illegible]	[illegible]	[illegible]	[illegible]
Meath,	[illegible]	[illegible]	[illegible]	[illegible]	[illegible]	[illegible]	[illegible]	[illegible]	[illegible]	[illegible]	[illegible]	[illegible]	[illegible]	[illegible]	[illegible]	[illegible]	[illegible]	[illegible]	[illegible]	[illegible]	[illegible]	[illegible]
Queen's County,	[illegible]	[illegible]	[illegible]	[illegible]	[illegible]	[illegible]	[illegible]	[illegible]	[illegible]	[illegible]	[illegible]	[illegible]	[illegible]	[illegible]	[illegible]	[illegible]	[illegible]	[illegible]	[illegible]	[illegible]	[illegible]	[illegible]
Westmeath,	[illegible]	[illegible]	[illegible]	[illegible]	[illegible]	[illegible]	[illegible]	[illegible]	[illegible]	[illegible]	[illegible]	[illegible]	[illegible]	[illegible]	[illegible]	[illegible]	[illegible]	[illegible]	[illegible]	[illegible]	[illegible]	[illegible]
Wexford,	[illegible]	[illegible]	[illegible]	[illegible]	[illegible]	[illegible]	[illegible]	[illegible]	[illegible]	[illegible]	[illegible]	[illegible]	[illegible]	[illegible]	[illegible]	[illegible]	[illegible]	[illegible]	[illegible]	[illegible]	[illegible]	[illegible]
Wicklow,	[illegible]	[illegible]	[illegible]	[illegible]	[illegible]	[illegible]	[illegible]	[illegible]	[illegible]	[illegible]	[illegible]	[illegible]	[illegible]	[illegible]	[illegible]	[illegible]	[illegible]	[illegible]	[illegible]	[illegible]	[illegible]	[illegible]
Total of Province,	[illegible]	[illegible]	[illegible]	[illegible]	[illegible]	[illegible]	[illegible]	[illegible]	[illegible]	[illegible]	[illegible]	[illegible]	[illegible]	[illegible]	[illegible]	[illegible]	[illegible]	[illegible]	[illegible]	[illegible]	[illegible]	[illegible]

Munster.																						
Clare,	[illegible]	[illegible]	[illegible]	[illegible]	[illegible]	[illegible]	[illegible]	[illegible]	[illegible]	[illegible]	[illegible]	[illegible]	[illegible]	[illegible]	[illegible]	[illegible]	[illegible]	[illegible]	[illegible]	[illegible]	[illegible]	[illegible]
Cork, E. R.,	[illegible]	[illegible]	[illegible]	[illegible]	[illegible]	[illegible]	[illegible]	[illegible]	[illegible]	[illegible]	[illegible]	[illegible]	[illegible]	[illegible]	[illegible]	[illegible]	[illegible]	[illegible]	[illegible]	[illegible]	[illegible]	[illegible]
Cork, W. R.,	[illegible]	[illegible]	[illegible]	[illegible]	[illegible]	[illegible]	[illegible]	[illegible]	[illegible]	[illegible]	[illegible]	[illegible]	[illegible]	[illegible]	[illegible]	[illegible]	[illegible]	[illegible]	[illegible]	[illegible]	[illegible]	[illegible]
Cork City,	[illegible]	[illegible]	[illegible]	[illegible]	[illegible]	[illegible]	[illegible]	[illegible]	[illegible]	[illegible]	[illegible]	[illegible]	[illegible]	[illegible]	[illegible]	[illegible]	[illegible]	[illegible]	[illegible]	[illegible]	[illegible]	[illegible]
Kerry,	[illegible]	[illegible]	[illegible]	[illegible]	[illegible]	[illegible]	[illegible]	[illegible]	[illegible]	[illegible]	[illegible]	[illegible]	[illegible]	[illegible]	[illegible]	[illegible]	[illegible]	[illegible]	[illegible]	[illegible]	[illegible]	[illegible]
Limerick,	[illegible]	[illegible]	[illegible]	[illegible]	[illegible]	[illegible]	[illegible]	[illegible]	[illegible]	[illegible]	[illegible]	[illegible]	[illegible]	[illegible]	[illegible]	[illegible]	[illegible]	[illegible]	[illegible]	[illegible]	[illegible]	[illegible]
Limerick City,	[illegible]	[illegible]	[illegible]	[illegible]	[illegible]	[illegible]	[illegible]	[illegible]	[illegible]	[illegible]	[illegible]	[illegible]	[illegible]	[illegible]	[illegible]	[illegible]	[illegible]	[illegible]	[illegible]	[illegible]	[illegible]	[illegible]
Tipperary, N. R.,	[illegible]	[illegible]	[illegible]	[illegible]	[illegible]	[illegible]	[illegible]	[illegible]	[illegible]	[illegible]	[illegible]	[illegible]	[illegible]	[illegible]	[illegible]	[illegible]	[illegible]	[illegible]	[illegible]	[illegible]	[illegible]	[illegible]
Tipperary, S. R.,	[illegible]	[illegible]	[illegible]	[illegible]	[illegible]	[illegible]	[illegible]	[illegible]	[illegible]	[illegible]	[illegible]	[illegible]	[illegible]	[illegible]	[illegible]	[illegible]	[illegible]	[illegible]	[illegible]	[illegible]	[illegible]	[illegible]
Waterford,	[illegible]	[illegible]	[illegible]	[illegible]	[illegible]	[illegible]	[illegible]	[illegible]	[illegible]	[illegible]	[illegible]	[illegible]	[illegible]	[illegible]	[illegible]	[illegible]	[illegible]	[illegible]	[illegible]	[illegible]	[illegible]	[illegible]
Waterford City,	[illegible]	[illegible]	[illegible]	[illegible]	[illegible]	[illegible]	[illegible]	[illegible]	[illegible]	[illegible]	[illegible]	[illegible]	[illegible]	[illegible]	[illegible]	[illegible]	[illegible]	[illegible]	[illegible]	[illegible]	[illegible]	[illegible]
Total of Province,	[illegible]	[illegible]	[illegible]	[illegible]	[illegible]	[illegible]	[illegible]	[illegible]	[illegible]	[illegible]	[illegible]	[illegible]	[illegible]	[illegible]	[illegible]	[illegible]	[illegible]	[illegible]	[illegible]	[illegible]	[illegible]	[illegible]
Ulster.																						
Antrim,	[illegible]	[illegible]	[illegible]	[illegible]	[illegible]	[illegible]	[illegible]	[illegible]	[illegible]	[illegible]	[illegible]	[illegible]	[illegible]	[illegible]	[illegible]	[illegible]	[illegible]	[illegible]	[illegible]	[illegible]	[illegible]	[illegible]
Armagh,	[illegible]	[illegible]	[illegible]	[illegible]	[illegible]	[illegible]	[illegible]	[illegible]	[illegible]	[illegible]	[illegible]	[illegible]	[illegible]	[illegible]	[illegible]	[illegible]	[illegible]	[illegible]	[illegible]	[illegible]	[illegible]	[illegible]
Belfast, Town of,	[illegible]	[illegible]	[illegible]	[illegible]	[illegible]	[illegible]	[illegible]	[illegible]	[illegible]	[illegible]	[illegible]	[illegible]	[illegible]	[illegible]	[illegible]	[illegible]	[illegible]	[illegible]	[illegible]	[illegible]	[illegible]	[illegible]
Carrickfergus, Town of,	[illegible]	[illegible]	[illegible]	[illegible]	[illegible]	[illegible]	[illegible]	[illegible]	[illegible]	[illegible]	[illegible]	[illegible]	[illegible]	[illegible]	[illegible]	[illegible]	[illegible]	[illegible]	[illegible]	[illegible]	[illegible]	[illegible]
Cavan,	[illegible]	[illegible]	[illegible]	[illegible]	[illegible]	[illegible]	[illegible]	[illegible]	[illegible]	[illegible]	[illegible]	[illegible]	[illegible]	[illegible]	[illegible]	[illegible]	[illegible]	[illegible]	[illegible]	[illegible]	[illegible]	[illegible]
Donegal,	[illegible]	[illegible]	[illegible]	[illegible]	[illegible]	[illegible]	[illegible]	[illegible]	[illegible]	[illegible]	[illegible]	[illegible]	[illegible]	[illegible]	[illegible]	[illegible]	[illegible]	[illegible]	[illegible]	[illegible]	[illegible]	[illegible]
Down,	[illegible]	[illegible]	[illegible]	[illegible]	[illegible]	[illegible]	[illegible]	[illegible]	[illegible]	[illegible]	[illegible]	[illegible]	[illegible]	[illegible]	[illegible]	[illegible]	[illegible]	[illegible]	[illegible]	[illegible]	[illegible]	[illegible]
Fermanagh,	[illegible]	[illegible]	[illegible]	[illegible]	[illegible]	[illegible]	[illegible]	[illegible]	[illegible]	[illegible]	[illegible]	[illegible]	[illegible]	[illegible]	[illegible]	[illegible]	[illegible]	[illegible]	[illegible]	[illegible]	[illegible]	[illegible]
Londonderry,	[illegible]	[illegible]	[illegible]	[illegible]	[illegible]	[illegible]	[illegible]	[illegible]	[illegible]	[illegible]	[illegible]	[illegible]	[illegible]	[illegible]	[illegible]	[illegible]	[illegible]	[illegible]	[illegible]	[illegible]	[illegible]	[illegible]
Monaghan,	[illegible]	[illegible]	[illegible]	[illegible]	[illegible]	[illegible]	[illegible]	[illegible]	[illegible]	[illegible]	[illegible]	[illegible]	[illegible]	[illegible]	[illegible]	[illegible]	[illegible]	[illegible]	[illegible]	[illegible]	[illegible]	[illegible]
Tyrone,	[illegible]	[illegible]	[illegible]	[illegible]	[illegible]	[illegible]	[illegible]	[illegible]	[illegible]	[illegible]	[illegible]	[illegible]	[illegible]	[illegible]	[illegible]	[illegible]	[illegible]	[illegible]	[illegible]	[illegible]	[illegible]	[illegible]
Total of Province,	[illegible]	[illegible]	[illegible]	[illegible]	[illegible]	[illegible]	[illegible]	[illegible]	[illegible]	[illegible]	[illegible]	[illegible]	[illegible]	[illegible]	[illegible]	[illegible]	[illegible]	[illegible]	[illegible]	[illegible]	[illegible]	[illegible]
Connaught.																						
Galway, E. R.,	[illegible]	[illegible]	[illegible]	[illegible]	[illegible]	[illegible]	[illegible]	[illegible]	[illegible]	[illegible]	[illegible]	[illegible]	[illegible]	[illegible]	[illegible]	[illegible]	[illegible]	[illegible]	[illegible]	[illegible]	[illegible]	[illegible]
Galway, W. R.,	[illegible]	[illegible]	[illegible]	[illegible]	[illegible]	[illegible]	[illegible]	[illegible]	[illegible]	[illegible]	[illegible]	[illegible]	[illegible]	[illegible]	[illegible]	[illegible]	[illegible]	[illegible]	[illegible]	[illegible]	[illegible]	[illegible]
Galway, Town of,	[illegible]	[illegible]	[illegible]	[illegible]	[illegible]	[illegible]	[illegible]	[illegible]	[illegible]	[illegible]	[illegible]	[illegible]	[illegible]	[illegible]	[illegible]	[illegible]	[illegible]	[illegible]	[illegible]	[illegible]	[illegible]	[illegible]
Leitrim,	[illegible]	[illegible]	[illegible]	[illegible]	[illegible]	[illegible]	[illegible]	[illegible]	[illegible]	[illegible]	[illegible]	[illegible]	[illegible]	[illegible]	[illegible]	[illegible]	[illegible]	[illegible]	[illegible]	[illegible]	[illegible]	[illegible]
Mayo,	[illegible]	[illegible]	[illegible]	[illegible]	[illegible]	[illegible]	[illegible]	[illegible]	[illegible]	[illegible]	[illegible]	[illegible]	[illegible]	[illegible]	[illegible]	[illegible]	[illegible]	[illegible]	[illegible]	[illegible]	[illegible]	[illegible]
Roscommon,	[illegible]	[illegible]	[illegible]	[illegible]	[illegible]	[illegible]	[illegible]	[illegible]	[illegible]	[illegible]	[illegible]	[illegible]	[illegible]	[illegible]	[illegible]	[illegible]	[illegible]	[illegible]	[illegible]	[illegible]	[illegible]	[illegible]
Sligo,	[illegible]	[illegible]	[illegible]	[illegible]	[illegible]	[illegible]	[illegible]	[illegible]	[illegible]	[illegible]	[illegible]	[illegible]	[illegible]	[illegible]	[illegible]	[illegible]	[illegible]	[illegible]	[illegible]	[illegible]	[illegible]	[illegible]
Total of Province,	[illegible]	[illegible]	[illegible]	[illegible]	[illegible]	[illegible]	[illegible]	[illegible]	[illegible]	[illegible]	[illegible]	[illegible]	[illegible]	[illegible]	[illegible]	[illegible]	[illegible]	[illegible]	[illegible]	[illegible]	[illegible]	[illegible]
Total of Ireland,	[illegible]	[illegible]	[illegible]	[illegible]	[illegible]	[illegible]	[illegible]	[illegible]	[illegible]	[illegible]	[illegible]	[illegible]	[illegible]	[illegible]	[illegible]	[illegible]	[illegible]	[illegible]	[illegible]	[illegible]	[illegible]	[illegible]

TABLE 4.—RETURN OF INDICTABLE OFFENCES (not Disposed of Summarily). Number of Crimes Committed in each Police District (so far as known to the Police), the Number of Persons Apprehended, and the Disposal of the Charges against them, in the Year ended 31st December, [illegible].

Province, County, County of City or of Town.	Number of Crimes Committed					Number of Persons Apprehended					Disposal of the Persons Apprehended													
	Jan. Feb. March.	April, May, June.	July, August, Sept.	Oct. Nov. Dec.	Total Crimes.	Jan. Feb. March.	April, May, June.	July, August, Sept.	Oct. Nov. Dec.	Total Persons.	Bailed		Discharged: For want of Evidence		Discharged: For want of Prosecution		[illegible]		[illegible]		[illegible]		Committed for Trial.	
											M.	W.	M.	W.	M.	W.	M.	W.	M.	W.	M.	W.	M.	W.
LEINSTER:																								
Carlow,	[illegible]	[illegible]	[illegible]	[illegible]	[illegible]	[illegible]	[illegible]	[illegible]	[illegible]	[illegible]	[illegible]	[illegible]	[illegible]	[illegible]	[illegible]	[illegible]	[illegible]	[illegible]	[illegible]	[illegible]	[illegible]	[illegible]	[illegible]	[illegible]
Drogheda, Town of,	[illegible]	[illegible]	[illegible]	[illegible]	[illegible]	[illegible]	[illegible]	[illegible]	[illegible]	[illegible]	[illegible]	[illegible]	[illegible]	[illegible]	[illegible]	[illegible]	[illegible]	[illegible]	[illegible]	[illegible]	[illegible]	[illegible]	[illegible]	[illegible]
Dublin County (part of),	[illegible]	[illegible]	[illegible]	[illegible]	[illegible]	[illegible]	[illegible]	[illegible]	[illegible]	[illegible]	[illegible]	[illegible]	[illegible]	[illegible]	[illegible]	[illegible]	[illegible]	[illegible]	[illegible]	[illegible]	[illegible]	[illegible]	[illegible]	[illegible]
Dublin City (and part of County) Metropolitan Police District—Divisions																								
A,	[illegible]	[illegible]	[illegible]	[illegible]	[illegible]	[illegible]	[illegible]	[illegible]	[illegible]	[illegible]	[illegible]	[illegible]	[illegible]	[illegible]	[illegible]	[illegible]	[illegible]	[illegible]	[illegible]	[illegible]	[illegible]	[illegible]	[illegible]	[illegible]
B,	[illegible]	[illegible]	[illegible]	[illegible]	[illegible]	[illegible]	[illegible]	[illegible]	[illegible]	[illegible]	[illegible]	[illegible]	[illegible]	[illegible]	[illegible]	[illegible]	[illegible]	[illegible]	[illegible]	[illegible]	[illegible]	[illegible]	[illegible]	[illegible]
C,	[illegible]	[illegible]	[illegible]	[illegible]	[illegible]	[illegible]	[illegible]	[illegible]	[illegible]	[illegible]	[illegible]	[illegible]	[illegible]	[illegible]	[illegible]	[illegible]	[illegible]	[illegible]	[illegible]	[illegible]	[illegible]	[illegible]	[illegible]	[illegible]
D,	[illegible]	[illegible]	[illegible]	[illegible]	[illegible]	[illegible]	[illegible]	[illegible]	[illegible]	[illegible]	[illegible]	[illegible]	[illegible]	[illegible]	[illegible]	[illegible]	[illegible]	[illegible]	[illegible]	[illegible]	[illegible]	[illegible]	[illegible]	[illegible]
E,	[illegible]	[illegible]	[illegible]	[illegible]	[illegible]	[illegible]	[illegible]	[illegible]	[illegible]	[illegible]	[illegible]	[illegible]	[illegible]	[illegible]	[illegible]	[illegible]	[illegible]	[illegible]	[illegible]	[illegible]	[illegible]	[illegible]	[illegible]	[illegible]
F,	[illegible]	[illegible]	[illegible]	[illegible]	[illegible]	[illegible]	[illegible]	[illegible]	[illegible]	[illegible]	[illegible]	[illegible]	[illegible]	[illegible]	[illegible]	[illegible]	[illegible]	[illegible]	[illegible]	[illegible]	[illegible]	[illegible]	[illegible]	[illegible]
Total of Met. Police District,	[illegible]	[illegible]	[illegible]	[illegible]	[illegible]	[illegible]	[illegible]	[illegible]	[illegible]	[illegible]	[illegible]	[illegible]	[illegible]	[illegible]	[illegible]	[illegible]	[illegible]	[illegible]	[illegible]	[illegible]	[illegible]	[illegible]	[illegible]	[illegible]
Kildare,	[illegible]	[illegible]	[illegible]	[illegible]	[illegible]	[illegible]	[illegible]	[illegible]	[illegible]	[illegible]	[illegible]	[illegible]	[illegible]	[illegible]	[illegible]	[illegible]	[illegible]	[illegible]	[illegible]	[illegible]	[illegible]	[illegible]	[illegible]	[illegible]
Kilkenny,	[illegible]	[illegible]	[illegible]	[illegible]	[illegible]	[illegible]	[illegible]	[illegible]	[illegible]	[illegible]	[illegible]	[illegible]	[illegible]	[illegible]	[illegible]	[illegible]	[illegible]	[illegible]	[illegible]	[illegible]	[illegible]	[illegible]	[illegible]	[illegible]
King's County,	[illegible]	[illegible]	[illegible]	[illegible]	[illegible]	[illegible]	[illegible]	[illegible]	[illegible]	[illegible]	[illegible]	[illegible]	[illegible]	[illegible]	[illegible]	[illegible]	[illegible]	[illegible]	[illegible]	[illegible]	[illegible]	[illegible]	[illegible]	[illegible]
Longford,	[illegible]	[illegible]	[illegible]	[illegible]	[illegible]	[illegible]	[illegible]	[illegible]	[illegible]	[illegible]	[illegible]	[illegible]	[illegible]	[illegible]	[illegible]	[illegible]	[illegible]	[illegible]	[illegible]	[illegible]	[illegible]	[illegible]	[illegible]	[illegible]
Louth,	[illegible]	[illegible]	[illegible]	[illegible]	[illegible]	[illegible]	[illegible]	[illegible]	[illegible]	[illegible]	[illegible]	[illegible]	[illegible]	[illegible]	[illegible]	[illegible]	[illegible]	[illegible]	[illegible]	[illegible]	[illegible]	[illegible]	[illegible]	[illegible]
Meath,	[illegible]	[illegible]	[illegible]	[illegible]	[illegible]	[illegible]	[illegible]	[illegible]	[illegible]	[illegible]	[illegible]	[illegible]	[illegible]	[illegible]	[illegible]	[illegible]	[illegible]	[illegible]	[illegible]	[illegible]	[illegible]	[illegible]	[illegible]	[illegible]
Queen's County,	[illegible]	[illegible]	[illegible]	[illegible]	[illegible]	[illegible]	[illegible]	[illegible]	[illegible]	[illegible]	[illegible]	[illegible]	[illegible]	[illegible]	[illegible]	[illegible]	[illegible]	[illegible]	[illegible]	[illegible]	[illegible]	[illegible]	[illegible]	[illegible]
Westmeath,	[illegible]	[illegible]	[illegible]	[illegible]	[illegible]	[illegible]	[illegible]	[illegible]	[illegible]	[illegible]	[illegible]	[illegible]	[illegible]	[illegible]	[illegible]	[illegible]	[illegible]	[illegible]	[illegible]	[illegible]	[illegible]	[illegible]	[illegible]	[illegible]
Wexford,	[illegible]	[illegible]	[illegible]	[illegible]	[illegible]	[illegible]	[illegible]	[illegible]	[illegible]	[illegible]	[illegible]	[illegible]	[illegible]	[illegible]	[illegible]	[illegible]	[illegible]	[illegible]	[illegible]	[illegible]	[illegible]	[illegible]	[illegible]	[illegible]
Wicklow,	[illegible]	[illegible]	[illegible]	[illegible]	[illegible]	[illegible]	[illegible]	[illegible]	[illegible]	[illegible]	[illegible]	[illegible]	[illegible]	[illegible]	[illegible]	[illegible]	[illegible]	[illegible]	[illegible]	[illegible]	[illegible]	[illegible]	[illegible]	[illegible]
Total of Leinster,	[illegible]	[illegible]	[illegible]	[illegible]	[illegible]	[illegible]	[illegible]	[illegible]	[illegible]	[illegible]	[illegible]	[illegible]	[illegible]	[illegible]	[illegible]	[illegible]	[illegible]	[illegible]	[illegible]	[illegible]	[illegible]	[illegible]	[illegible]	[illegible]
MUNSTER:																								
Clare,	[illegible]	[illegible]	[illegible]	[illegible]	[illegible]	[illegible]	[illegible]	[illegible]	[illegible]	[illegible]	[illegible]	[illegible]	[illegible]	[illegible]	[illegible]	[illegible]	[illegible]	[illegible]	[illegible]	[illegible]	[illegible]	[illegible]	[illegible]	[illegible]
Cork, East Riding,	[illegible]	[illegible]	[illegible]	[illegible]	[illegible]	[illegible]	[illegible]	[illegible]	[illegible]	[illegible]	[illegible]	[illegible]	[illegible]	[illegible]	[illegible]	[illegible]	[illegible]	[illegible]	[illegible]	[illegible]	[illegible]	[illegible]	[illegible]	[illegible]

Cork, West Riding,	[illegible]	[illegible]	[illegible]	[illegible]	[illegible]	[illegible]	[illegible]	[illegible]	[illegible]	[illegible]	[illegible]	[illegible]	[illegible]	[illegible]	[illegible]	[illegible]	[illegible]	[illegible]	[illegible]	[illegible]	[illegible]	[illegible]	[illegible]	[illegible]
Cork City,	[illegible]	[illegible]	[illegible]	[illegible]	[illegible]	[illegible]	[illegible]	[illegible]	[illegible]	[illegible]	[illegible]	[illegible]	[illegible]	[illegible]	[illegible]	[illegible]	[illegible]	[illegible]	[illegible]	[illegible]	[illegible]	[illegible]	[illegible]	[illegible]
Kerry,	[illegible]	[illegible]	[illegible]	[illegible]	[illegible]	[illegible]	[illegible]	[illegible]	[illegible]	[illegible]	[illegible]	[illegible]	[illegible]	[illegible]	[illegible]	[illegible]	[illegible]	[illegible]	[illegible]	[illegible]	[illegible]	[illegible]	[illegible]	[illegible]
Limerick,	[illegible]	[illegible]	[illegible]	[illegible]	[illegible]	[illegible]	[illegible]	[illegible]	[illegible]	[illegible]	[illegible]	[illegible]	[illegible]	[illegible]	[illegible]	[illegible]	[illegible]	[illegible]	[illegible]	[illegible]	[illegible]	[illegible]	[illegible]	[illegible]
Limerick City,	[illegible]	[illegible]	[illegible]	[illegible]	[illegible]	[illegible]	[illegible]	[illegible]	[illegible]	[illegible]	[illegible]	[illegible]	[illegible]	[illegible]	[illegible]	[illegible]	[illegible]	[illegible]	[illegible]	[illegible]	[illegible]	[illegible]	[illegible]	[illegible]
Tipperary, North Riding,	[illegible]	[illegible]	[illegible]	[illegible]	[illegible]	[illegible]	[illegible]	[illegible]	[illegible]	[illegible]	[illegible]	[illegible]	[illegible]	[illegible]	[illegible]	[illegible]	[illegible]	[illegible]	[illegible]	[illegible]	[illegible]	[illegible]	[illegible]	[illegible]
Tipperary, South Riding,	[illegible]	[illegible]	[illegible]	[illegible]	[illegible]	[illegible]	[illegible]	[illegible]	[illegible]	[illegible]	[illegible]	[illegible]	[illegible]	[illegible]	[illegible]	[illegible]	[illegible]	[illegible]	[illegible]	[illegible]	[illegible]	[illegible]	[illegible]	[illegible]
Waterford,	[illegible]	[illegible]	[illegible]	[illegible]	[illegible]	[illegible]	[illegible]	[illegible]	[illegible]	[illegible]	[illegible]	[illegible]	[illegible]	[illegible]	[illegible]	[illegible]	[illegible]	[illegible]	[illegible]	[illegible]	[illegible]	[illegible]	[illegible]	[illegible]
Waterford City,	[illegible]	[illegible]	[illegible]	[illegible]	[illegible]	[illegible]	[illegible]	[illegible]	[illegible]	[illegible]	[illegible]	[illegible]	[illegible]	[illegible]	[illegible]	[illegible]	[illegible]	[illegible]	[illegible]	[illegible]	[illegible]	[illegible]	[illegible]	[illegible]
Total of Province,	[illegible]	[illegible]	[illegible]	[illegible]	[illegible]	[illegible]	[illegible]	[illegible]	[illegible]	[illegible]	[illegible]	[illegible]	[illegible]	[illegible]	[illegible]	[illegible]	[illegible]	[illegible]	[illegible]	[illegible]	[illegible]	[illegible]	[illegible]	[illegible]
Ulster:																								
Antrim,	[illegible]	[illegible]	[illegible]	[illegible]	[illegible]	[illegible]	[illegible]	[illegible]	[illegible]	[illegible]	[illegible]	[illegible]	[illegible]	[illegible]	[illegible]	[illegible]	[illegible]	[illegible]	[illegible]	[illegible]	[illegible]	[illegible]	[illegible]	[illegible]
Armagh,	[illegible]	[illegible]	[illegible]	[illegible]	[illegible]	[illegible]	[illegible]	[illegible]	[illegible]	[illegible]	[illegible]	[illegible]	[illegible]	[illegible]	[illegible]	[illegible]	[illegible]	[illegible]	[illegible]	[illegible]	[illegible]	[illegible]	[illegible]	[illegible]
Belfast, Town of,	[illegible]	[illegible]	[illegible]	[illegible]	[illegible]	[illegible]	[illegible]	[illegible]	[illegible]	[illegible]	[illegible]	[illegible]	[illegible]	[illegible]	[illegible]	[illegible]	[illegible]	[illegible]	[illegible]	[illegible]	[illegible]	[illegible]	[illegible]	[illegible]
Carrickfergus, Town of,	[illegible]	[illegible]	[illegible]	[illegible]	[illegible]	[illegible]	[illegible]	[illegible]	[illegible]	[illegible]	[illegible]	[illegible]	[illegible]	[illegible]	[illegible]	[illegible]	[illegible]	[illegible]	[illegible]	[illegible]	[illegible]	[illegible]	[illegible]	[illegible]
Cavan,	[illegible]	[illegible]	[illegible]	[illegible]	[illegible]	[illegible]	[illegible]	[illegible]	[illegible]	[illegible]	[illegible]	[illegible]	[illegible]	[illegible]	[illegible]	[illegible]	[illegible]	[illegible]	[illegible]	[illegible]	[illegible]	[illegible]	[illegible]	[illegible]
Donegal,	[illegible]	[illegible]	[illegible]	[illegible]	[illegible]	[illegible]	[illegible]	[illegible]	[illegible]	[illegible]	[illegible]	[illegible]	[illegible]	[illegible]	[illegible]	[illegible]	[illegible]	[illegible]	[illegible]	[illegible]	[illegible]	[illegible]	[illegible]	[illegible]
Down,	[illegible]	[illegible]	[illegible]	[illegible]	[illegible]	[illegible]	[illegible]	[illegible]	[illegible]	[illegible]	[illegible]	[illegible]	[illegible]	[illegible]	[illegible]	[illegible]	[illegible]	[illegible]	[illegible]	[illegible]	[illegible]	[illegible]	[illegible]	[illegible]
Fermanagh,	[illegible]	[illegible]	[illegible]	[illegible]	[illegible]	[illegible]	[illegible]	[illegible]	[illegible]	[illegible]	[illegible]	[illegible]	[illegible]	[illegible]	[illegible]	[illegible]	[illegible]	[illegible]	[illegible]	[illegible]	[illegible]	[illegible]	[illegible]	[illegible]
Londonderry,	[illegible]	[illegible]	[illegible]	[illegible]	[illegible]	[illegible]	[illegible]	[illegible]	[illegible]	[illegible]	[illegible]	[illegible]	[illegible]	[illegible]	[illegible]	[illegible]	[illegible]	[illegible]	[illegible]	[illegible]	[illegible]	[illegible]	[illegible]	[illegible]
Monaghan,	[illegible]	[illegible]	[illegible]	[illegible]	[illegible]	[illegible]	[illegible]	[illegible]	[illegible]	[illegible]	[illegible]	[illegible]	[illegible]	[illegible]	[illegible]	[illegible]	[illegible]	[illegible]	[illegible]	[illegible]	[illegible]	[illegible]	[illegible]	[illegible]
Tyrone,	[illegible]	[illegible]	[illegible]	[illegible]	[illegible]	[illegible]	[illegible]	[illegible]	[illegible]	[illegible]	[illegible]	[illegible]	[illegible]	[illegible]	[illegible]	[illegible]	[illegible]	[illegible]	[illegible]	[illegible]	[illegible]	[illegible]	[illegible]	[illegible]
Total of Province,	[illegible]	[illegible]	[illegible]	[illegible]	[illegible]	[illegible]	[illegible]	[illegible]	[illegible]	[illegible]	[illegible]	[illegible]	[illegible]	[illegible]	[illegible]	[illegible]	[illegible]	[illegible]	[illegible]	[illegible]	[illegible]	[illegible]	[illegible]	[illegible]
Connaught:																								
Galway, East Riding,	[illegible]	[illegible]	[illegible]	[illegible]	[illegible]	[illegible]	[illegible]	[illegible]	[illegible]	[illegible]	[illegible]	[illegible]	[illegible]	[illegible]	[illegible]	[illegible]	[illegible]	[illegible]	[illegible]	[illegible]	[illegible]	[illegible]	[illegible]	[illegible]
Galway, West Riding,	[illegible]	[illegible]	[illegible]	[illegible]	[illegible]	[illegible]	[illegible]	[illegible]	[illegible]	[illegible]	[illegible]	[illegible]	[illegible]	[illegible]	[illegible]	[illegible]	[illegible]	[illegible]	[illegible]	[illegible]	[illegible]	[illegible]	[illegible]	[illegible]
Galway, Town of,	[illegible]	[illegible]	[illegible]	[illegible]	[illegible]	[illegible]	[illegible]	[illegible]	[illegible]	[illegible]	[illegible]	[illegible]	[illegible]	[illegible]	[illegible]	[illegible]	[illegible]	[illegible]	[illegible]	[illegible]	[illegible]	[illegible]	[illegible]	[illegible]
Leitrim,	[illegible]	[illegible]	[illegible]	[illegible]	[illegible]	[illegible]	[illegible]	[illegible]	[illegible]	[illegible]	[illegible]	[illegible]	[illegible]	[illegible]	[illegible]	[illegible]	[illegible]	[illegible]	[illegible]	[illegible]	[illegible]	[illegible]	[illegible]	[illegible]
Mayo,	[illegible]	[illegible]	[illegible]	[illegible]	[illegible]	[illegible]	[illegible]	[illegible]	[illegible]	[illegible]	[illegible]	[illegible]	[illegible]	[illegible]	[illegible]	[illegible]	[illegible]	[illegible]	[illegible]	[illegible]	[illegible]	[illegible]	[illegible]	[illegible]
Roscommon,	[illegible]	[illegible]	[illegible]	[illegible]	[illegible]	[illegible]	[illegible]	[illegible]	[illegible]	[illegible]	[illegible]	[illegible]	[illegible]	[illegible]	[illegible]	[illegible]	[illegible]	[illegible]	[illegible]	[illegible]	[illegible]	[illegible]	[illegible]	[illegible]
Sligo,	[illegible]	[illegible]	[illegible]	[illegible]	[illegible]	[illegible]	[illegible]	[illegible]	[illegible]	[illegible]	[illegible]	[illegible]	[illegible]	[illegible]	[illegible]	[illegible]	[illegible]	[illegible]	[illegible]	[illegible]	[illegible]	[illegible]	[illegible]	[illegible]
Total of Province,	[illegible]	[illegible]	[illegible]	[illegible]	[illegible]	[illegible]	[illegible]	[illegible]	[illegible]	[illegible]	[illegible]	[illegible]	[illegible]	[illegible]	[illegible]	[illegible]	[illegible]	[illegible]	[illegible]	[illegible]	[illegible]	[illegible]	[illegible]	[illegible]
Total of Ireland,	[illegible]	[illegible]	[illegible]	[illegible]	[illegible]	[illegible]	[illegible]	[illegible]	[illegible]	[illegible]	[illegible]	[illegible]	[illegible]	[illegible]	[illegible]	[illegible]	[illegible]	[illegible]	[illegible]	[illegible]	[illegible]	[illegible]	[illegible]	[illegible]

[illegible]	[illegible]	[illegible]	[illegible]	[illegible]	[illegible]	[illegible]	[illegible]	[illegible]	[illegible]	[illegible]	[illegible]	[illegible]	[illegible]	[illegible]	[illegible]	[illegible]	[illegible]	[illegible]	[illegible]	[illegible]	[illegible]	[illegible]	[illegible]	[illegible]
Embezzlement,	[illegible]	[illegible]	[illegible]	[illegible]	[illegible]	[illegible]	[illegible]	[illegible]	[illegible]	[illegible]	[illegible]	[illegible]	[illegible]	[illegible]	[illegible]	[illegible]	[illegible]	[illegible]	[illegible]	[illegible]	[illegible]	[illegible]	[illegible]	[illegible]
Larceny by Servants in the Post Office,	[illegible]	[illegible]	[illegible]	[illegible]	[illegible]	[illegible]	[illegible]	[illegible]	[illegible]	[illegible]	[illegible]	[illegible]	[illegible]	[illegible]	[illegible]	[illegible]	[illegible]	[illegible]	[illegible]	[illegible]	[illegible]	[illegible]	[illegible]	[illegible]
Receiving Stolen Goods,	[illegible]	[illegible]	[illegible]	[illegible]	[illegible]	[illegible]	[illegible]	[illegible]	[illegible]	[illegible]	[illegible]	[illegible]	[illegible]	[illegible]	[illegible]	[illegible]	[illegible]	[illegible]	[illegible]	[illegible]	[illegible]	[illegible]	[illegible]	[illegible]
Fraudulently obtaining Goods by false pretences, and attempts to defraud,	[illegible]	[illegible]	[illegible]	[illegible]	[illegible]	[illegible]	[illegible]	[illegible]	[illegible]	[illegible]	[illegible]	[illegible]	[illegible]	[illegible]	[illegible]	[illegible]	[illegible]	[illegible]	[illegible]	[illegible]	[illegible]	[illegible]	[illegible]	[illegible]
Total of No. 3.	[illegible]	[illegible]	[illegible]	[illegible]	[illegible]	[illegible]	[illegible]	[illegible]	[illegible]	[illegible]	[illegible]	[illegible]	[illegible]	[illegible]	[illegible]	[illegible]	[illegible]	[illegible]	[illegible]	[illegible]	[illegible]	[illegible]	[illegible]	[illegible]
No. 4.—Malicious Offences against Property																								
Arson and other Wilful Burning,	[illegible]	[illegible]	[illegible]	[illegible]	[illegible]	[illegible]	[illegible]	[illegible]	[illegible]	[illegible]	[illegible]	[illegible]	[illegible]	[illegible]	[illegible]	[illegible]	[illegible]	[illegible]	[illegible]	[illegible]	[illegible]	[illegible]	[illegible]	[illegible]
Felonious Riot, and demolishing Buildings, &c.,	[illegible]	[illegible]	[illegible]	[illegible]	[illegible]	[illegible]	[illegible]	[illegible]	[illegible]	[illegible]	[illegible]	[illegible]	[illegible]	[illegible]	[illegible]	[illegible]	[illegible]	[illegible]	[illegible]	[illegible]	[illegible]	[illegible]	[illegible]	[illegible]
Destroying Goods in process of Manufacture,	[illegible]	[illegible]	[illegible]	[illegible]	[illegible]	[illegible]	[illegible]	[illegible]	[illegible]	[illegible]	[illegible]	[illegible]	[illegible]	[illegible]	[illegible]	[illegible]	[illegible]	[illegible]	[illegible]	[illegible]	[illegible]	[illegible]	[illegible]	[illegible]
Destroying Trees, Shrubs, &c., [illegible],	[illegible]	[illegible]	[illegible]	[illegible]	[illegible]	[illegible]	[illegible]	[illegible]	[illegible]	[illegible]	[illegible]	[illegible]	[illegible]	[illegible]	[illegible]	[illegible]	[illegible]	[illegible]	[illegible]	[illegible]	[illegible]	[illegible]	[illegible]	[illegible]
Killing and Maiming Cattle,	[illegible]	[illegible]	[illegible]	[illegible]	[illegible]	[illegible]	[illegible]	[illegible]	[illegible]	[illegible]	[illegible]	[illegible]	[illegible]	[illegible]	[illegible]	[illegible]	[illegible]	[illegible]	[illegible]	[illegible]	[illegible]	[illegible]	[illegible]	[illegible]
Malicious Injuries to Property according to value,	[illegible]	[illegible]	[illegible]	[illegible]	[illegible]	[illegible]	[illegible]	[illegible]	[illegible]	[illegible]	[illegible]	[illegible]	[illegible]	[illegible]	[illegible]	[illegible]	[illegible]	[illegible]	[illegible]	[illegible]	[illegible]	[illegible]	[illegible]	[illegible]
Other Wilful and Malicious Injuries to Property,	[illegible]	[illegible]	[illegible]	[illegible]	[illegible]	[illegible]	[illegible]	[illegible]	[illegible]	[illegible]	[illegible]	[illegible]	[illegible]	[illegible]	[illegible]	[illegible]	[illegible]	[illegible]	[illegible]	[illegible]	[illegible]	[illegible]	[illegible]	[illegible]
Total of No. 4.	[illegible]	[illegible]	[illegible]	[illegible]	[illegible]	[illegible]	[illegible]	[illegible]	[illegible]	[illegible]	[illegible]	[illegible]	[illegible]	[illegible]	[illegible]	[illegible]	[illegible]	[illegible]	[illegible]	[illegible]	[illegible]	[illegible]	[illegible]	[illegible]
No. 5.—Forgery and Offences against the Currency																								
Forging and uttering Forged Instruments,	[illegible]	[illegible]	[illegible]	[illegible]	[illegible]	[illegible]	[illegible]	[illegible]	[illegible]	[illegible]	[illegible]	[illegible]	[illegible]	[illegible]	[illegible]	[illegible]	[illegible]	[illegible]	[illegible]	[illegible]	[illegible]	[illegible]	[illegible]	[illegible]
Having in possession Forged Bank Notes,	[illegible]	[illegible]	[illegible]	[illegible]	[illegible]	[illegible]	[illegible]	[illegible]	[illegible]	[illegible]	[illegible]	[illegible]	[illegible]	[illegible]	[illegible]	[illegible]	[illegible]	[illegible]	[illegible]	[illegible]	[illegible]	[illegible]	[illegible]	[illegible]
Coining, and having implements of Coining in possession,	[illegible]	[illegible]	[illegible]	[illegible]	[illegible]	[illegible]	[illegible]	[illegible]	[illegible]	[illegible]	[illegible]	[illegible]	[illegible]	[illegible]	[illegible]	[illegible]	[illegible]	[illegible]	[illegible]	[illegible]	[illegible]	[illegible]	[illegible]	[illegible]
Uttering, putting off, and having in possession Counterfeit Coin,	[illegible]	[illegible]	[illegible]	[illegible]	[illegible]	[illegible]	[illegible]	[illegible]	[illegible]	[illegible]	[illegible]	[illegible]	[illegible]	[illegible]	[illegible]	[illegible]	[illegible]	[illegible]	[illegible]	[illegible]	[illegible]	[illegible]	[illegible]	[illegible]
Total of No. 5.	[illegible]	[illegible]	[illegible]	[illegible]	[illegible]	[illegible]	[illegible]	[illegible]	[illegible]	[illegible]	[illegible]	[illegible]	[illegible]	[illegible]	[illegible]	[illegible]	[illegible]	[illegible]	[illegible]	[illegible]	[illegible]	[illegible]	[illegible]	[illegible]
No. 6.—Offences not included in the above Classes																								
Offences against the Queen's authority and person,	[illegible]	[illegible]	[illegible]	[illegible]	[illegible]	[illegible]	[illegible]	[illegible]	[illegible]	[illegible]	[illegible]	[illegible]	[illegible]	[illegible]	[illegible]	[illegible]	[illegible]	[illegible]	[illegible]	[illegible]	[illegible]	[illegible]	[illegible]	[illegible]
Intimidation by Threatening Letters, Notices, or otherwise,	[illegible]	[illegible]	[illegible]	[illegible]	[illegible]	[illegible]	[illegible]	[illegible]	[illegible]	[illegible]	[illegible]	[illegible]	[illegible]	[illegible]	[illegible]	[illegible]	[illegible]	[illegible]	[illegible]	[illegible]	[illegible]	[illegible]	[illegible]	[illegible]
Having Arms or Ammunition without license in a Proclaimed District,	[illegible]	[illegible]	[illegible]	[illegible]	[illegible]	[illegible]	[illegible]	[illegible]	[illegible]	[illegible]	[illegible]	[illegible]	[illegible]	[illegible]	[illegible]	[illegible]	[illegible]	[illegible]	[illegible]	[illegible]	[illegible]	[illegible]	[illegible]	[illegible]
Offences against the Game Laws,	[illegible]	[illegible]	[illegible]	[illegible]	[illegible]	[illegible]	[illegible]	[illegible]	[illegible]	[illegible]	[illegible]	[illegible]	[illegible]	[illegible]	[illegible]	[illegible]	[illegible]	[illegible]	[illegible]	[illegible]	[illegible]	[illegible]	[illegible]	[illegible]
Being at large under sentence of Transportation or Penal Servitude,	[illegible]	[illegible]	[illegible]	[illegible]	[illegible]	[illegible]	[illegible]	[illegible]	[illegible]	[illegible]	[illegible]	[illegible]	[illegible]	[illegible]	[illegible]	[illegible]	[illegible]	[illegible]	[illegible]	[illegible]	[illegible]	[illegible]	[illegible]	[illegible]
Perjury, and Subornation of Perjury,	[illegible]	[illegible]	[illegible]	[illegible]	[illegible]	[illegible]	[illegible]	[illegible]	[illegible]	[illegible]	[illegible]	[illegible]	[illegible]	[illegible]	[illegible]	[illegible]	[illegible]	[illegible]	[illegible]	[illegible]	[illegible]	[illegible]	[illegible]	[illegible]
Riot, Breach of the Peace, &c.,	[illegible]	[illegible]	[illegible]	[illegible]	[illegible]	[illegible]	[illegible]	[illegible]	[illegible]	[illegible]	[illegible]	[illegible]	[illegible]	[illegible]	[illegible]	[illegible]	[illegible]	[illegible]	[illegible]	[illegible]	[illegible]	[illegible]	[illegible]	[illegible]
Keeping Disorderly Houses,	[illegible]	[illegible]	[illegible]	[illegible]	[illegible]	[illegible]	[illegible]	[illegible]	[illegible]	[illegible]	[illegible]	[illegible]	[illegible]	[illegible]	[illegible]	[illegible]	[illegible]	[illegible]	[illegible]	[illegible]	[illegible]	[illegible]	[illegible]	[illegible]
Indecently Exposing the Person,	[illegible]	[illegible]	[illegible]	[illegible]	[illegible]	[illegible]	[illegible]	[illegible]	[illegible]	[illegible]	[illegible]	[illegible]	[illegible]	[illegible]	[illegible]	[illegible]	[illegible]	[illegible]	[illegible]	[illegible]	[illegible]	[illegible]	[illegible]	[illegible]
Suicide, attempting to commit,	[illegible]	[illegible]	[illegible]	[illegible]	[illegible]	[illegible]	[illegible]	[illegible]	[illegible]	[illegible]	[illegible]	[illegible]	[illegible]	[illegible]	[illegible]	[illegible]	[illegible]	[illegible]	[illegible]	[illegible]	[illegible]	[illegible]	[illegible]	[illegible]
Other Felonies not included in the above,	[illegible]	[illegible]	[illegible]	[illegible]	[illegible]	[illegible]	[illegible]	[illegible]	[illegible]	[illegible]	[illegible]	[illegible]	[illegible]	[illegible]	[illegible]	[illegible]	[illegible]	[illegible]	[illegible]	[illegible]	[illegible]	[illegible]	[illegible]	[illegible]
Other Misdemeanours not included in the above,	[illegible]	[illegible]	[illegible]	[illegible]	[illegible]	[illegible]	[illegible]	[illegible]	[illegible]	[illegible]	[illegible]	[illegible]	[illegible]	[illegible]	[illegible]	[illegible]	[illegible]	[illegible]	[illegible]	[illegible]	[illegible]	[illegible]	[illegible]	[illegible]
Total of No. 6.	[illegible]	[illegible]	[illegible]	[illegible]	[illegible]	[illegible]	[illegible]	[illegible]	[illegible]	[illegible]	[illegible]	[illegible]	[illegible]	[illegible]	[illegible]	[illegible]	[illegible]	[illegible]	[illegible]	[illegible]	[illegible]	[illegible]	[illegible]	[illegible]
General Total.	[illegible]	[illegible]	[illegible]	[illegible]	[illegible]	[illegible]	[illegible]	[illegible]	[illegible]	[illegible]	[illegible]	[illegible]	[illegible]	[illegible]	[illegible]	[illegible]	[illegible]	[illegible]	[illegible]	[illegible]	[illegible]	[illegible]	[illegible]	[illegible]

TABLE 4.—RETURN OF INDICTABLE OFFENCES (not Disposed of Summarily). Nature of the Crimes Committed, made by the

NATURE OF CRIMES.	Figures (Total and by Counties)
Class 1.—Offences against the Person.	
Murder of Infants aged one year and under.	[illegible]
Other Murders.	[illegible]
Attempts to Murder.	[illegible]
Shooting at, Wounding, Stabbing, &c., to do bodily harm.	[illegible]
Manslaughter.	[illegible]
Concealing the Birth of Infants.	[illegible]
Sodomy and Bestiality.	[illegible]
—— Attempts to commit, and other unnatural Misdemeanours.	[illegible]
Rape.	[illegible]
—— Assaults, with intent to ravish and abuse.	[illegible]
Bigamy.	[illegible]
Child Stealing.	[illegible]
Unlawfully Abandoning Children under two years of age.	[illegible]
Endangering the safety of Passengers on Railways.	[illegible]
Assaults inflicting bodily harm.	[illegible]
Assaults, common.	[illegible]
Assaults on Peace Officers.	[illegible]
Total of No. 1.	[illegible]
No. 2.—Offences against Property with Violence.	
Burglary.	[illegible]
Burglary and Housebreaking.	[illegible]
Breaking into Shops, Warehouses, &c.	[illegible]
Attempts to Break into Houses, Shops, Warehouses, &c.	[illegible]
Robbery.	[illegible]
Attempts to rob, and demanding Money by Menaces.	[illegible]
Total of No. 2.	[illegible]
No. 3.—Offences against Property without Violence.	
Cattle Stealing.	[illegible]
Horse Stealing.	[illegible]
Sheep Stealing.	[illegible]
Larceny to the value of £5 in Dwelling-houses.	[illegible]
Larceny from the Person.	[illegible]
Larceny by Servants.	[illegible]
Larceny, Simple.	[illegible]
Larceny on Rivers, Canals, Wharfs, &c.	[illegible]
Stealing Fixtures, Shrubs growing, &c.	[illegible]
Attempts to Steal.	[illegible]
Embezzlement.	[illegible]
Larceny by Servants in the Post Office.	[illegible]
Receiving Stolen Goods.	[illegible]
Fraudulently obtaining Goods by false pretences, and attempts to defraud.	[illegible]
Total of No. 3.	[illegible]
No. 4.—Malicious Offences against Property.	
Arson and other Wilful Burning.	[illegible]
Damaging Roads and Agricultural Buildings, &c.	[illegible]
Destroying Goods in Process of Manufacture.	[illegible]
Destroying Trees, Shrubs, &c., growing.	[illegible]
Killing and Maiming Cattle.	[illegible]
Malicious Injuries to Property exceeding £5 in value.	[illegible]
Other Wilful and Malicious Injuries to Property.	[illegible]
Total of No. 4.	[illegible]
No. 5.—Forgery and Offences against the Currency.	
Forging and uttering Forged Instruments.	[illegible]
Having in possession Forged Bank Notes.	[illegible]
Coining, and having Implements of Coining in possession.	[illegible]
Uttering, putting off, and having in possession Counterfeit Coin.	[illegible]
Total of No. 5.	[illegible]
No. 6.—Offences not included in the above Classes.	
Offences against the Queen's authority and person.	[illegible]
Intimidation by Threatening Letters, Notices, or otherwise.	[illegible]
Having Arms or Ammunition without Licence in a Proclaimed District.	[illegible]
Being at large under Sentence of Transportation or Penal Servitude.	[illegible]
Perjury, and Subornation of Perjury.	[illegible]
Libel, Breach of the Peace, &c.	[illegible]
Indecently Exposing the Person.	[illegible]
Nuisance, Vagrancy, &c.	[illegible]
Other Felonies not included in the above.	[illegible]
Other Misdemeanours not included in the above.	[illegible]
Total of No. 6.	[illegible]
GENERAL TOTAL.	[illegible]

[illegible] in each County, and County of City or of Town, so far as known to the Police, in the Year ended 31st December, [illegible], [illegible]

Nature of Crimes	[illegible]	[illegible]	[illegible]	[illegible]	[illegible]	[illegible]	[illegible]	[illegible]	[illegible]	[illegible]	[illegible]	[illegible]	[illegible]	[illegible]
No. 1.—Offences against the Person.														
Murder of Infants under one year old.	[illegible]	[illegible]	[illegible]	[illegible]	[illegible]	[illegible]	[illegible]	[illegible]	[illegible]	[illegible]	[illegible]	[illegible]	[illegible]	[illegible]
Other Murders.	[illegible]	[illegible]	[illegible]	[illegible]	[illegible]	[illegible]	[illegible]	[illegible]	[illegible]	[illegible]	[illegible]	[illegible]	[illegible]	[illegible]
Attempts to Murder.	[illegible]	[illegible]	[illegible]	[illegible]	[illegible]	[illegible]	[illegible]	[illegible]	[illegible]	[illegible]	[illegible]	[illegible]	[illegible]	[illegible]
Shooting at, Wounding, Stabbing, &c., to do bodily harm.	[illegible]	[illegible]	[illegible]	[illegible]	[illegible]	[illegible]	[illegible]	[illegible]	[illegible]	[illegible]	[illegible]	[illegible]	[illegible]	[illegible]
Manslaughter.	[illegible]	[illegible]	[illegible]	[illegible]	[illegible]	[illegible]	[illegible]	[illegible]	[illegible]	[illegible]	[illegible]	[illegible]	[illegible]	[illegible]
Concealing the Birth of Infants.	[illegible]	[illegible]	[illegible]	[illegible]	[illegible]	[illegible]	[illegible]	[illegible]	[illegible]	[illegible]	[illegible]	[illegible]	[illegible]	[illegible]
Sodomy and Bestiality.	[illegible]	[illegible]	[illegible]	[illegible]	[illegible]	[illegible]	[illegible]	[illegible]	[illegible]	[illegible]	[illegible]	[illegible]	[illegible]	[illegible]
——— Attempts to commit, and other unnatural Misdemeanours.	[illegible]	[illegible]	[illegible]	[illegible]	[illegible]	[illegible]	[illegible]	[illegible]	[illegible]	[illegible]	[illegible]	[illegible]	[illegible]	[illegible]
Rape.	[illegible]	[illegible]	[illegible]	[illegible]	[illegible]	[illegible]	[illegible]	[illegible]	[illegible]	[illegible]	[illegible]	[illegible]	[illegible]	[illegible]
——— Assaults, with intent to ravish and abuse.	[illegible]	[illegible]	[illegible]	[illegible]	[illegible]	[illegible]	[illegible]	[illegible]	[illegible]	[illegible]	[illegible]	[illegible]	[illegible]	[illegible]
Bigamy.	[illegible]	[illegible]	[illegible]	[illegible]	[illegible]	[illegible]	[illegible]	[illegible]	[illegible]	[illegible]	[illegible]	[illegible]	[illegible]	[illegible]
Child Stealing.	[illegible]	[illegible]	[illegible]	[illegible]	[illegible]	[illegible]	[illegible]	[illegible]	[illegible]	[illegible]	[illegible]	[illegible]	[illegible]	[illegible]
Unlawfully abandoning Children under two years of age.	[illegible]	[illegible]	[illegible]	[illegible]	[illegible]	[illegible]	[illegible]	[illegible]	[illegible]	[illegible]	[illegible]	[illegible]	[illegible]	[illegible]
Endangering the safety of Passengers on Railways.	[illegible]	[illegible]	[illegible]	[illegible]	[illegible]	[illegible]	[illegible]	[illegible]	[illegible]	[illegible]	[illegible]	[illegible]	[illegible]	[illegible]
Assaults, inflicting bodily harm.	[illegible]	[illegible]	[illegible]	[illegible]	[illegible]	[illegible]	[illegible]	[illegible]	[illegible]	[illegible]	[illegible]	[illegible]	[illegible]	[illegible]
Assaults, common.	[illegible]	[illegible]	[illegible]	[illegible]	[illegible]	[illegible]	[illegible]	[illegible]	[illegible]	[illegible]	[illegible]	[illegible]	[illegible]	[illegible]
Assaults on Peace Officers.	[illegible]	[illegible]	[illegible]	[illegible]	[illegible]	[illegible]	[illegible]	[illegible]	[illegible]	[illegible]	[illegible]	[illegible]	[illegible]	[illegible]
Total of No. 1.	[illegible]	[illegible]	[illegible]	[illegible]	[illegible]	[illegible]	[illegible]	[illegible]	[illegible]	[illegible]	[illegible]	[illegible]	[illegible]	[illegible]
No. 2.—Offences against Property with Violence.														
Sacrilege.	[illegible]	[illegible]	[illegible]	[illegible]	[illegible]	[illegible]	[illegible]	[illegible]	[illegible]	[illegible]	[illegible]	[illegible]	[illegible]	[illegible]
Burglary and Housebreaking.	[illegible]	[illegible]	[illegible]	[illegible]	[illegible]	[illegible]	[illegible]	[illegible]	[illegible]	[illegible]	[illegible]	[illegible]	[illegible]	[illegible]
Breaking into Shops, Warehouses, &c.	[illegible]	[illegible]	[illegible]	[illegible]	[illegible]	[illegible]	[illegible]	[illegible]	[illegible]	[illegible]	[illegible]	[illegible]	[illegible]	[illegible]
Attempts to break into Houses, Shops, Warehouses, &c.	[illegible]	[illegible]	[illegible]	[illegible]	[illegible]	[illegible]	[illegible]	[illegible]	[illegible]	[illegible]	[illegible]	[illegible]	[illegible]	[illegible]
Robbery.	[illegible]	[illegible]	[illegible]	[illegible]	[illegible]	[illegible]	[illegible]	[illegible]	[illegible]	[illegible]	[illegible]	[illegible]	[illegible]	[illegible]
Attempts to rob and demanding Money by menaces.	[illegible]	[illegible]	[illegible]	[illegible]	[illegible]	[illegible]	[illegible]	[illegible]	[illegible]	[illegible]	[illegible]	[illegible]	[illegible]	[illegible]
Total of No. 2.	[illegible]	[illegible]	[illegible]	[illegible]	[illegible]	[illegible]	[illegible]	[illegible]	[illegible]	[illegible]	[illegible]	[illegible]	[illegible]	[illegible]
No. 3.—Offences against Property without Violence.														
Cattle Stealing.	[illegible]	[illegible]	[illegible]	[illegible]	[illegible]	[illegible]	[illegible]	[illegible]	[illegible]	[illegible]	[illegible]	[illegible]	[illegible]	[illegible]
Horse Stealing.	[illegible]	[illegible]	[illegible]	[illegible]	[illegible]	[illegible]	[illegible]	[illegible]	[illegible]	[illegible]	[illegible]	[illegible]	[illegible]	[illegible]
Sheep Stealing.	[illegible]	[illegible]	[illegible]	[illegible]	[illegible]	[illegible]	[illegible]	[illegible]	[illegible]	[illegible]	[illegible]	[illegible]	[illegible]	[illegible]
Larceny to the value of £5 in Dwelling-houses.	[illegible]	[illegible]	[illegible]	[illegible]	[illegible]	[illegible]	[illegible]	[illegible]	[illegible]	[illegible]	[illegible]	[illegible]	[illegible]	[illegible]
Larceny from the Person.	[illegible]	[illegible]	[illegible]	[illegible]	[illegible]	[illegible]	[illegible]	[illegible]	[illegible]	[illegible]	[illegible]	[illegible]	[illegible]	[illegible]
Larceny by Servants.	[illegible]	[illegible]	[illegible]	[illegible]	[illegible]	[illegible]	[illegible]	[illegible]	[illegible]	[illegible]	[illegible]	[illegible]	[illegible]	[illegible]
Larceny, simple.	[illegible]	[illegible]	[illegible]	[illegible]	[illegible]	[illegible]	[illegible]	[illegible]	[illegible]	[illegible]	[illegible]	[illegible]	[illegible]	[illegible]
Larceny [illegible]	[illegible]	[illegible]	[illegible]	[illegible]	[illegible]	[illegible]	[illegible]	[illegible]	[illegible]	[illegible]	[illegible]	[illegible]	[illegible]	[illegible]
Stealing Fixtures, [illegible]	[illegible]	[illegible]	[illegible]	[illegible]	[illegible]	[illegible]	[illegible]	[illegible]	[illegible]	[illegible]	[illegible]	[illegible]	[illegible]	[illegible]
Attempts to Steal.	[illegible]	[illegible]	[illegible]	[illegible]	[illegible]	[illegible]	[illegible]	[illegible]	[illegible]	[illegible]	[illegible]	[illegible]	[illegible]	[illegible]
Embezzlement.	[illegible]	[illegible]	[illegible]	[illegible]	[illegible]	[illegible]	[illegible]	[illegible]	[illegible]	[illegible]	[illegible]	[illegible]	[illegible]	[illegible]
Larceny by Servants in the Post Office.	[illegible]	[illegible]	[illegible]	[illegible]	[illegible]	[illegible]	[illegible]	[illegible]	[illegible]	[illegible]	[illegible]	[illegible]	[illegible]	[illegible]
Receiving Stolen Goods.	[illegible]	[illegible]	[illegible]	[illegible]	[illegible]	[illegible]	[illegible]	[illegible]	[illegible]	[illegible]	[illegible]	[illegible]	[illegible]	[illegible]
Fraudulently obtaining Goods by false pretences, and attempts to defraud.	[illegible]	[illegible]	[illegible]	[illegible]	[illegible]	[illegible]	[illegible]	[illegible]	[illegible]	[illegible]	[illegible]	[illegible]	[illegible]	[illegible]
Total of No. 3.	[illegible]	[illegible]	[illegible]	[illegible]	[illegible]	[illegible]	[illegible]	[illegible]	[illegible]	[illegible]	[illegible]	[illegible]	[illegible]	[illegible]
No. 4.—Malicious Offences against Property.														
Arson and other Wilful Burning.	[illegible]	[illegible]	[illegible]	[illegible]	[illegible]	[illegible]	[illegible]	[illegible]	[illegible]	[illegible]	[illegible]	[illegible]	[illegible]	[illegible]
[illegible]	[illegible]	[illegible]	[illegible]	[illegible]	[illegible]	[illegible]	[illegible]	[illegible]	[illegible]	[illegible]	[illegible]	[illegible]	[illegible]	[illegible]
[illegible]	[illegible]	[illegible]	[illegible]	[illegible]	[illegible]	[illegible]	[illegible]	[illegible]	[illegible]	[illegible]	[illegible]	[illegible]	[illegible]	[illegible]
Destroying Trees, Shrubs, &c., growing.	[illegible]	[illegible]	[illegible]	[illegible]	[illegible]	[illegible]	[illegible]	[illegible]	[illegible]	[illegible]	[illegible]	[illegible]	[illegible]	[illegible]
Killing and Maiming Cattle.	[illegible]	[illegible]	[illegible]	[illegible]	[illegible]	[illegible]	[illegible]	[illegible]	[illegible]	[illegible]	[illegible]	[illegible]	[illegible]	[illegible]
Malicious Injuries to Property exceeding £5 in value.	[illegible]	[illegible]	[illegible]	[illegible]	[illegible]	[illegible]	[illegible]	[illegible]	[illegible]	[illegible]	[illegible]	[illegible]	[illegible]	[illegible]
Other Wilful and Malicious Injuries to Property.	[illegible]	[illegible]	[illegible]	[illegible]	[illegible]	[illegible]	[illegible]	[illegible]	[illegible]	[illegible]	[illegible]	[illegible]	[illegible]	[illegible]
Total of No. 4.	[illegible]	[illegible]	[illegible]	[illegible]	[illegible]	[illegible]	[illegible]	[illegible]	[illegible]	[illegible]	[illegible]	[illegible]	[illegible]	[illegible]
No. 5.—Forgery and Offences against the Currency.														
Forging and uttering Forged Instruments.	[illegible]	[illegible]	[illegible]	[illegible]	[illegible]	[illegible]	[illegible]	[illegible]	[illegible]	[illegible]	[illegible]	[illegible]	[illegible]	[illegible]
[illegible]	[illegible]	[illegible]	[illegible]	[illegible]	[illegible]	[illegible]	[illegible]	[illegible]	[illegible]	[illegible]	[illegible]	[illegible]	[illegible]	[illegible]
Coining, and having Instruments for Coining in Possession.	[illegible]	[illegible]	[illegible]	[illegible]	[illegible]	[illegible]	[illegible]	[illegible]	[illegible]	[illegible]	[illegible]	[illegible]	[illegible]	[illegible]
Uttering, passing off, and having in possession Counterfeit Coin.	[illegible]	[illegible]	[illegible]	[illegible]	[illegible]	[illegible]	[illegible]	[illegible]	[illegible]	[illegible]	[illegible]	[illegible]	[illegible]	[illegible]
Total of No. 5.	[illegible]	[illegible]	[illegible]	[illegible]	[illegible]	[illegible]	[illegible]	[illegible]	[illegible]	[illegible]	[illegible]	[illegible]	[illegible]	[illegible]
No. 6.—Offences not included in the above Classes.														
Offences against the Queen's authority and person.	[illegible]	[illegible]	[illegible]	[illegible]	[illegible]	[illegible]	[illegible]	[illegible]	[illegible]	[illegible]	[illegible]	[illegible]	[illegible]	[illegible]
Intimidation by Threatening Letters, Notices, or otherwise.	[illegible]	[illegible]	[illegible]	[illegible]	[illegible]	[illegible]	[illegible]	[illegible]	[illegible]	[illegible]	[illegible]	[illegible]	[illegible]	[illegible]
Having Arms in [illegible] without Licence in Proclaimed Districts.	[illegible]	[illegible]	[illegible]	[illegible]	[illegible]	[illegible]	[illegible]	[illegible]	[illegible]	[illegible]	[illegible]	[illegible]	[illegible]	[illegible]
Being at large, under Sentence of Transportation or Penal Servitude.	[illegible]	[illegible]	[illegible]	[illegible]	[illegible]	[illegible]	[illegible]	[illegible]	[illegible]	[illegible]	[illegible]	[illegible]	[illegible]	[illegible]
Perjury, and Subornation of Perjury.	[illegible]	[illegible]	[illegible]	[illegible]	[illegible]	[illegible]	[illegible]	[illegible]	[illegible]	[illegible]	[illegible]	[illegible]	[illegible]	[illegible]
Riot, Breach of the Peace, &c.	[illegible]	[illegible]	[illegible]	[illegible]	[illegible]	[illegible]	[illegible]	[illegible]	[illegible]	[illegible]	[illegible]	[illegible]	[illegible]	[illegible]
Unlawfully Exposing the Person.	[illegible]	[illegible]	[illegible]	[illegible]	[illegible]	[illegible]	[illegible]	[illegible]	[illegible]	[illegible]	[illegible]	[illegible]	[illegible]	[illegible]
[illegible]	[illegible]	[illegible]	[illegible]	[illegible]	[illegible]	[illegible]	[illegible]	[illegible]	[illegible]	[illegible]	[illegible]	[illegible]	[illegible]	[illegible]
Other Felonies not included in the above.	[illegible]	[illegible]	[illegible]	[illegible]	[illegible]	[illegible]	[illegible]	[illegible]	[illegible]	[illegible]	[illegible]	[illegible]	[illegible]	[illegible]
Other Misdemeanours not included in the above.	[illegible]	[illegible]	[illegible]	[illegible]	[illegible]	[illegible]	[illegible]	[illegible]	[illegible]	[illegible]	[illegible]	[illegible]	[illegible]	[illegible]
Total of No. 6.	[illegible]	[illegible]	[illegible]	[illegible]	[illegible]	[illegible]	[illegible]	[illegible]	[illegible]	[illegible]	[illegible]	[illegible]	[illegible]	[illegible]
General Total.	[illegible]	[illegible]	[illegible]	[illegible]	[illegible]	[illegible]	[illegible]	[illegible]	[illegible]	[illegible]	[illegible]	[illegible]	[illegible]	[illegible]

TABLE [illegible]—continued.—RETURN OF INDICTABLE OFFENCES [illegible]. Nature of the Crime [illegible] December, 18[illegible], [illegible]

NATURE OF CRIMES.	[illegible]	[illegible]	[illegible]	[illegible]	[illegible]	[illegible]	[illegible]	[illegible]	[illegible]	[illegible]
No. 1.—Offences against the Person.										
Murder of Infants under one year old,	[illegible]	[illegible]	[illegible]	[illegible]	[illegible]	[illegible]	[illegible]	[illegible]	[illegible]	[illegible]
Other Murders,	[illegible]	[illegible]	[illegible]	[illegible]	[illegible]	[illegible]	[illegible]	[illegible]	[illegible]	[illegible]
Attempts to Murder,	[illegible]	[illegible]	[illegible]	[illegible]	[illegible]	[illegible]	[illegible]	[illegible]	[illegible]	[illegible]
Shooting at, Wounding, Stabbing, &c., to do bodily harm,	[illegible]	[illegible]	[illegible]	[illegible]	[illegible]	[illegible]	[illegible]	[illegible]	[illegible]	[illegible]
Manslaughter,	[illegible]	[illegible]	[illegible]	[illegible]	[illegible]	[illegible]	[illegible]	[illegible]	[illegible]	[illegible]
Concealing the Birth of Infants,	[illegible]	[illegible]	[illegible]	[illegible]	[illegible]	[illegible]	[illegible]	[illegible]	[illegible]	[illegible]
Sodomy and Bestiality,	[illegible]	[illegible]	[illegible]	[illegible]	[illegible]	[illegible]	[illegible]	[illegible]	[illegible]	[illegible]
—— Attempts to commit, and other unnatural Misdemeanors,	[illegible]	[illegible]	[illegible]	[illegible]	[illegible]	[illegible]	[illegible]	[illegible]	[illegible]	[illegible]
Rape,	[illegible]	[illegible]	[illegible]	[illegible]	[illegible]	[illegible]	[illegible]	[illegible]	[illegible]	[illegible]
—— Assaults, with intent to ravish and abuse,	[illegible]	[illegible]	[illegible]	[illegible]	[illegible]	[illegible]	[illegible]	[illegible]	[illegible]	[illegible]
Bigamy,	[illegible]	[illegible]	[illegible]	[illegible]	[illegible]	[illegible]	[illegible]	[illegible]	[illegible]	[illegible]
Child Stealing,	[illegible]	[illegible]	[illegible]	[illegible]	[illegible]	[illegible]	[illegible]	[illegible]	[illegible]	[illegible]
Unlawfully abandoning Children under two years of age,	[illegible]	[illegible]	[illegible]	[illegible]	[illegible]	[illegible]	[illegible]	[illegible]	[illegible]	[illegible]
Endangering the safety of Passengers on Railways,	[illegible]	[illegible]	[illegible]	[illegible]	[illegible]	[illegible]	[illegible]	[illegible]	[illegible]	[illegible]
Assault and inflicting bodily harm,	[illegible]	[illegible]	[illegible]	[illegible]	[illegible]	[illegible]	[illegible]	[illegible]	[illegible]	[illegible]
Assaults, common,	[illegible]	[illegible]	[illegible]	[illegible]	[illegible]	[illegible]	[illegible]	[illegible]	[illegible]	[illegible]
Assaults on Peace Officers,	[illegible]	[illegible]	[illegible]	[illegible]	[illegible]	[illegible]	[illegible]	[illegible]	[illegible]	[illegible]
Total of No. 1,	[illegible]	[illegible]	[illegible]	[illegible]	[illegible]	[illegible]	[illegible]	[illegible]	[illegible]	[illegible]
No. 2.—Offences against Property with Violence.										
Burglary,	[illegible]	[illegible]	[illegible]	[illegible]	[illegible]	[illegible]	[illegible]	[illegible]	[illegible]	[illegible]
Burglary and Housebreaking,	[illegible]	[illegible]	[illegible]	[illegible]	[illegible]	[illegible]	[illegible]	[illegible]	[illegible]	[illegible]
Breaking into Shops, Warehouses, &c.,	[illegible]	[illegible]	[illegible]	[illegible]	[illegible]	[illegible]	[illegible]	[illegible]	[illegible]	[illegible]
Attempts to break into Houses, Shops, Warehouses, &c.,	[illegible]	[illegible]	[illegible]	[illegible]	[illegible]	[illegible]	[illegible]	[illegible]	[illegible]	[illegible]
Robbery,	[illegible]	[illegible]	[illegible]	[illegible]	[illegible]	[illegible]	[illegible]	[illegible]	[illegible]	[illegible]
Attempts to rob, and demanding Money by [illegible],	[illegible]	[illegible]	[illegible]	[illegible]	[illegible]	[illegible]	[illegible]	[illegible]	[illegible]	[illegible]
Total of No. 2,	[illegible]	7	[illegible]	[illegible]	[illegible]	[illegible]	[illegible]	[illegible]	[illegible]	[illegible]
No. 3.—Offences against Property without Violence.										
Cattle Stealing,	[illegible]	[illegible]	[illegible]	[illegible]	[illegible]	[illegible]	[illegible]	[illegible]	[illegible]	[illegible]
Horse Stealing,	[illegible]	[illegible]	[illegible]	[illegible]	[illegible]	[illegible]	[illegible]	[illegible]	[illegible]	[illegible]
Sheep Stealing,	[illegible]	[illegible]	[illegible]	[illegible]	[illegible]	[illegible]	[illegible]	[illegible]	[illegible]	[illegible]
Larceny to the value of £5 in Dwelling-houses,	[illegible]	[illegible]	[illegible]	[illegible]	[illegible]	[illegible]	[illegible]	[illegible]	[illegible]	[illegible]
Larceny from the Person,	[illegible]	[illegible]	[illegible]	[illegible]	[illegible]	[illegible]	[illegible]	[illegible]	[illegible]	[illegible]
Larceny by Servants,	[illegible]	[illegible]	[illegible]	[illegible]	[illegible]	[illegible]	[illegible]	[illegible]	[illegible]	[illegible]
Larceny, simple,	[illegible]	[illegible]	[illegible]	[illegible]	[illegible]	[illegible]	[illegible]	[illegible]	[illegible]	[illegible]
Larceny on Rivers, Canals, Wharfs, &c.,	[illegible]	[illegible]	[illegible]	[illegible]	[illegible]	[illegible]	[illegible]	[illegible]	[illegible]	[illegible]
Stealing Fixtures, Shrubs growing, &c.,	[illegible]	[illegible]	[illegible]	[illegible]	[illegible]	[illegible]	[illegible]	[illegible]	[illegible]	[illegible]
Attempts to Steal,	[illegible]	[illegible]	[illegible]	[illegible]	[illegible]	[illegible]	[illegible]	[illegible]	[illegible]	[illegible]
Embezzlements,	[illegible]	[illegible]	[illegible]	[illegible]	[illegible]	[illegible]	[illegible]	[illegible]	[illegible]	[illegible]
Larceny by Servants of the Post Office,	[illegible]	[illegible]	[illegible]	[illegible]	[illegible]	[illegible]	[illegible]	[illegible]	[illegible]	[illegible]
Receiving Stolen Goods,	[illegible]	[illegible]	[illegible]	[illegible]	[illegible]	[illegible]	[illegible]	[illegible]	[illegible]	[illegible]
Fraudulently obtaining Goods by false pretences and attempts to defraud,	[illegible]	[illegible]	[illegible]	[illegible]	[illegible]	[illegible]	[illegible]	[illegible]	[illegible]	[illegible]
Total of No. 3,	[illegible]	[illegible]	[illegible]	[illegible]	[illegible]	[illegible]	[illegible]	[illegible]	[illegible]	[illegible]
No. 4.—Malicious Offences against Property.										
Arson and other Wilful Burning,	[illegible]	[illegible]	[illegible]	[illegible]	[illegible]	[illegible]	[illegible]	[illegible]	[illegible]	[illegible]
[illegible] Buildings, &c.,	[illegible]	[illegible]	[illegible]	[illegible]	[illegible]	[illegible]	[illegible]	[illegible]	[illegible]	[illegible]
[illegible] of Vegetation,	[illegible]	[illegible]	[illegible]	[illegible]	[illegible]	[illegible]	[illegible]	[illegible]	[illegible]	[illegible]
Destroying Trees, Shrubs, &c. growing,	[illegible]	[illegible]	[illegible]	[illegible]	[illegible]	[illegible]	[illegible]	[illegible]	[illegible]	[illegible]
Killing and Maiming Cattle,	[illegible]	[illegible]	[illegible]	[illegible]	[illegible]	[illegible]	[illegible]	[illegible]	[illegible]	[illegible]
Malicious Injuries to Property exceeding £5 in value,	[illegible]	[illegible]	[illegible]	[illegible]	[illegible]	[illegible]	[illegible]	[illegible]	[illegible]	[illegible]
Other Wilful and Malicious Injuries to Property,	[illegible]	[illegible]	[illegible]	[illegible]	[illegible]	[illegible]	[illegible]	[illegible]	[illegible]	[illegible]
Total of No. 4,	[illegible]	[illegible]	[illegible]	[illegible]	[illegible]	[illegible]	[illegible]	[illegible]	[illegible]	[illegible]
No. 5.—Forgery and Offences against the Currency.										
Forgery and uttering Forged Instruments,	[illegible]	[illegible]	[illegible]	[illegible]	[illegible]	[illegible]	[illegible]	[illegible]	[illegible]	[illegible]
[illegible] Forged Bank Notes,	[illegible]	[illegible]	[illegible]	[illegible]	[illegible]	[illegible]	[illegible]	[illegible]	[illegible]	[illegible]
Coining, and having Implements for Coining in possession,	[illegible]	[illegible]	[illegible]	[illegible]	[illegible]	[illegible]	[illegible]	[illegible]	[illegible]	[illegible]
Uttering, putting off, and having in possession Counterfeit Coin,	[illegible]	[illegible]	[illegible]	[illegible]	[illegible]	[illegible]	[illegible]	[illegible]	[illegible]	[illegible]
Total of No. 5,	[illegible]	[illegible]	[illegible]	[illegible]	[illegible]	[illegible]	[illegible]	[illegible]	[illegible]	[illegible]
No. 6.—Offences not included in the above Classes.										
Offences against the Queen's authority and Person,	[illegible]	[illegible]	[illegible]	[illegible]	[illegible]	[illegible]	[illegible]	[illegible]	[illegible]	[illegible]
Intimidation by Threatening Letters, Notices, or otherwise,	[illegible]	[illegible]	[illegible]	[illegible]	[illegible]	[illegible]	[illegible]	[illegible]	[illegible]	[illegible]
Having Arms or Ammunition without Licence in a Proclaimed District,	[illegible]	[illegible]	[illegible]	[illegible]	[illegible]	[illegible]	[illegible]	[illegible]	[illegible]	[illegible]
Being at large under Sentence of Transportation or Penal Servitude,	[illegible]	[illegible]	[illegible]	[illegible]	[illegible]	[illegible]	[illegible]	[illegible]	[illegible]	[illegible]
Perjury, and Subornation of Perjury,	[illegible]	[illegible]	[illegible]	[illegible]	[illegible]	[illegible]	[illegible]	[illegible]	[illegible]	[illegible]
Riot, Breach of the Peace, &c.,	[illegible]	[illegible]	[illegible]	[illegible]	[illegible]	[illegible]	[illegible]	[illegible]	[illegible]	[illegible]
Indecently Exposing the Person,	[illegible]	[illegible]	[illegible]	[illegible]	[illegible]	[illegible]	[illegible]	[illegible]	[illegible]	[illegible]
Suicide, attempting to commit,	[illegible]	[illegible]	[illegible]	[illegible]	[illegible]	[illegible]	[illegible]	[illegible]	[illegible]	[illegible]
Other Felonies not included in the above,	[illegible]	[illegible]	[illegible]	[illegible]	[illegible]	[illegible]	[illegible]	[illegible]	[illegible]	[illegible]
Other Misdemeanors not included in the above,	[illegible]	[illegible]	[illegible]	[illegible]	[illegible]	[illegible]	[illegible]	[illegible]	[illegible]	[illegible]
Total of No. 6,	[illegible]	[illegible]	[illegible]	[illegible]	[illegible]	[illegible]	[illegible]	[illegible]	[illegible]	[illegible]
GENERAL TOTAL,	[illegible]	[illegible]	[illegible]	[illegible]	[illegible]	[illegible]	[illegible]	[illegible]	[illegible]	[illegible]

[illegible] Committed in each County, and County of City or of Town, so far as Known to the Police, in the Year ended [illegible] by the Inspector-General.

[illegible]	[illegible]	[illegible]	Galway, E.R.	Galway, W.R.	Galway Town	Leitrim	Mayo	Roscommon	Sligo	NATURE OF CRIMES
										No. 1.—Offences against the Person.
[illegible]	[illegible]	[illegible]	[illegible]	[illegible]	[illegible]	[illegible]	[illegible]	[illegible]	[illegible]	Murder of Infants under one year old
[illegible]	[illegible]	[illegible]	[illegible]	[illegible]	[illegible]	[illegible]	[illegible]	[illegible]	[illegible]	Other Murders
[illegible]	[illegible]	[illegible]	[illegible]	[illegible]	[illegible]	[illegible]	[illegible]	[illegible]	[illegible]	Attempts to Murder
[illegible]	[illegible]	[illegible]	[illegible]	[illegible]	[illegible]	[illegible]	[illegible]	[illegible]	[illegible]	Shooting at, Wounding, Stabbing, &c., to do bodily harm
[illegible]	[illegible]	[illegible]	[illegible]	[illegible]	[illegible]	[illegible]	[illegible]	[illegible]	[illegible]	Manslaughter
[illegible]	[illegible]	[illegible]	[illegible]	[illegible]	[illegible]	[illegible]	[illegible]	[illegible]	[illegible]	Concealing the Birth of Infants
[illegible]	[illegible]	[illegible]	[illegible]	[illegible]	[illegible]	[illegible]	[illegible]	[illegible]	[illegible]	Sodomy and Bestiality
[illegible]	[illegible]	[illegible]	[illegible]	[illegible]	[illegible]	[illegible]	[illegible]	[illegible]	[illegible]	—— Attempts to commit, and other unnatural Misdemeanors
[illegible]	[illegible]	[illegible]	[illegible]	[illegible]	[illegible]	[illegible]	[illegible]	[illegible]	[illegible]	Rape
[illegible]	[illegible]	[illegible]	[illegible]	[illegible]	[illegible]	[illegible]	[illegible]	[illegible]	[illegible]	—— Assaults with intent to ravish and abuse
[illegible]	[illegible]	[illegible]	[illegible]	[illegible]	[illegible]	[illegible]	[illegible]	[illegible]	[illegible]	Bigamy
[illegible]	[illegible]	[illegible]	[illegible]	[illegible]	[illegible]	[illegible]	[illegible]	[illegible]	[illegible]	Child Stealing
[illegible]	[illegible]	[illegible]	[illegible]	[illegible]	[illegible]	[illegible]	[illegible]	[illegible]	[illegible]	Unlawfully abandoning Children under two years of age
[illegible]	[illegible]	[illegible]	[illegible]	[illegible]	[illegible]	[illegible]	[illegible]	[illegible]	[illegible]	Endangering the safety of Passengers on Railways
[illegible]	[illegible]	[illegible]	[illegible]	[illegible]	[illegible]	[illegible]	[illegible]	[illegible]	[illegible]	Assaults and inflicting bodily harm
[illegible]	[illegible]	[illegible]	[illegible]	[illegible]	[illegible]	[illegible]	[illegible]	[illegible]	[illegible]	Assaults, common
[illegible]	[illegible]	[illegible]	[illegible]	[illegible]	[illegible]	[illegible]	[illegible]	[illegible]	[illegible]	Assaults on Peace Officers
[illegible]	[illegible]	[illegible]	[illegible]	[illegible]	[illegible]	[illegible]	[illegible]	[illegible]	[illegible]	Total of No. 1.
										No. 2.—Offences against Property with Violence.
[illegible]	[illegible]	[illegible]	[illegible]	[illegible]	[illegible]	[illegible]	[illegible]	[illegible]	[illegible]	Burglary
[illegible]	[illegible]	[illegible]	[illegible]	[illegible]	[illegible]	[illegible]	[illegible]	[illegible]	[illegible]	Burglary and Housebreaking
[illegible]	[illegible]	[illegible]	[illegible]	[illegible]	[illegible]	[illegible]	[illegible]	[illegible]	[illegible]	Breaking into Shops, Warehouses, &c.
[illegible]	[illegible]	[illegible]	[illegible]	[illegible]	[illegible]	[illegible]	[illegible]	[illegible]	[illegible]	Attempts to break into Houses, Shops, Warehouses, &c.
[illegible]	[illegible]	[illegible]	[illegible]	[illegible]	[illegible]	[illegible]	[illegible]	[illegible]	[illegible]	Robbery
[illegible]	[illegible]	[illegible]	[illegible]	[illegible]	[illegible]	[illegible]	[illegible]	[illegible]	[illegible]	Attempts to rob, and demanding Money by Menaces
[illegible]	[illegible]	[illegible]	[illegible]	[illegible]	[illegible]	[illegible]	[illegible]	[illegible]	[illegible]	Total of No. 2.
										No. 3.—Offences against Property without Violence.
[illegible]	[illegible]	[illegible]	[illegible]	[illegible]	[illegible]	[illegible]	[illegible]	[illegible]	[illegible]	Cattle Stealing
[illegible]	[illegible]	[illegible]	[illegible]	[illegible]	[illegible]	[illegible]	[illegible]	[illegible]	[illegible]	Horse Stealing
[illegible]	[illegible]	[illegible]	[illegible]	[illegible]	[illegible]	[illegible]	[illegible]	[illegible]	[illegible]	Sheep Stealing
[illegible]	[illegible]	[illegible]	[illegible]	[illegible]	[illegible]	[illegible]	[illegible]	[illegible]	[illegible]	Larceny to the value of £5 in Dwelling-houses
[illegible]	[illegible]	[illegible]	[illegible]	[illegible]	[illegible]	[illegible]	[illegible]	[illegible]	[illegible]	Larceny from the Person
[illegible]	[illegible]	[illegible]	[illegible]	[illegible]	[illegible]	[illegible]	[illegible]	[illegible]	[illegible]	Larceny by Servants
[illegible]	[illegible]	[illegible]	[illegible]	[illegible]	[illegible]	[illegible]	[illegible]	[illegible]	[illegible]	Larceny, Simple
[illegible]	[illegible]	[illegible]	[illegible]	[illegible]	[illegible]	[illegible]	[illegible]	[illegible]	[illegible]	Larceny on Board, Canals, Wharfs, &c.
[illegible]	[illegible]	[illegible]	[illegible]	[illegible]	[illegible]	[illegible]	[illegible]	[illegible]	[illegible]	Stealing Fixtures, Goods, growing, &c.
[illegible]	[illegible]	[illegible]	[illegible]	[illegible]	[illegible]	[illegible]	[illegible]	[illegible]	[illegible]	Attempts to Steal
[illegible]	[illegible]	[illegible]	[illegible]	[illegible]	[illegible]	[illegible]	[illegible]	[illegible]	[illegible]	Embezzlement
[illegible]	[illegible]	[illegible]	[illegible]	[illegible]	[illegible]	[illegible]	[illegible]	[illegible]	[illegible]	Larceny by Servants in the Post Office
[illegible]	[illegible]	[illegible]	[illegible]	[illegible]	[illegible]	[illegible]	[illegible]	[illegible]	[illegible]	Receiving Stolen Goods
[illegible]	[illegible]	[illegible]	[illegible]	[illegible]	[illegible]	[illegible]	[illegible]	[illegible]	[illegible]	Fraudulently obtaining Goods by false pretences, and attempts to defraud
[illegible]	[illegible]	[illegible]	[illegible]	[illegible]	[illegible]	[illegible]	[illegible]	[illegible]	[illegible]	Total of No. 3.
										No. 4.—Malicious Offences against Property.
[illegible]	[illegible]	[illegible]	[illegible]	[illegible]	[illegible]	[illegible]	[illegible]	[illegible]	[illegible]	Arson and other Wilful Burning
[illegible]	[illegible]	[illegible]	[illegible]	[illegible]	[illegible]	[illegible]	[illegible]	[illegible]	[illegible]	[illegible]
[illegible]	[illegible]	[illegible]	[illegible]	[illegible]	[illegible]	[illegible]	[illegible]	[illegible]	[illegible]	[illegible]
[illegible]	[illegible]	[illegible]	[illegible]	[illegible]	[illegible]	[illegible]	[illegible]	[illegible]	[illegible]	[illegible]
[illegible]	[illegible]	[illegible]	[illegible]	[illegible]	[illegible]	[illegible]	[illegible]	[illegible]	[illegible]	Killing and Maiming Cattle
[illegible]	[illegible]	[illegible]	[illegible]	[illegible]	[illegible]	[illegible]	[illegible]	[illegible]	[illegible]	Malicious Injuries to Property exceeding £5 in value
[illegible]	[illegible]	[illegible]	[illegible]	[illegible]	[illegible]	[illegible]	[illegible]	[illegible]	[illegible]	Other Wilful and Malicious Injuries to Property
[illegible]	[illegible]	[illegible]	[illegible]	[illegible]	[illegible]	[illegible]	[illegible]	[illegible]	[illegible]	Total of No. 4.
										No. 5.—Forgery and Offences against the Currency.
[illegible]	[illegible]	[illegible]	[illegible]	[illegible]	[illegible]	[illegible]	[illegible]	[illegible]	[illegible]	Forging and uttering Forged Instruments
[illegible]	[illegible]	[illegible]	[illegible]	[illegible]	[illegible]	[illegible]	[illegible]	[illegible]	[illegible]	[illegible]
[illegible]	[illegible]	[illegible]	[illegible]	[illegible]	[illegible]	[illegible]	[illegible]	[illegible]	[illegible]	Coining, and having Implements for Coining in possession
[illegible]	[illegible]	[illegible]	[illegible]	[illegible]	[illegible]	[illegible]	[illegible]	[illegible]	[illegible]	Uttering, putting off, and having in possession Counterfeit Coin
[illegible]	[illegible]	[illegible]	[illegible]	[illegible]	[illegible]	[illegible]	[illegible]	[illegible]	[illegible]	Total of No. 5.
										No. 6.—Offences not included in the above Classes.
[illegible]	[illegible]	[illegible]	[illegible]	[illegible]	[illegible]	[illegible]	[illegible]	[illegible]	[illegible]	Offences against the Queen's authority and person
[illegible]	[illegible]	[illegible]	[illegible]	[illegible]	[illegible]	[illegible]	[illegible]	[illegible]	[illegible]	Intimidation by Threatening Letters, Notices or otherwise
[illegible]	[illegible]	[illegible]	[illegible]	[illegible]	[illegible]	[illegible]	[illegible]	[illegible]	[illegible]	Having Arms or Ammunition without Licence in a Proclaimed District
[illegible]	[illegible]	[illegible]	[illegible]	[illegible]	[illegible]	[illegible]	[illegible]	[illegible]	[illegible]	Being at large under sentence of Transportation or Penal Servitude
[illegible]	[illegible]	[illegible]	[illegible]	[illegible]	[illegible]	[illegible]	[illegible]	[illegible]	[illegible]	Perjury and Subornation of Perjury
[illegible]	[illegible]	[illegible]	[illegible]	[illegible]	[illegible]	[illegible]	[illegible]	[illegible]	[illegible]	Riot, Breach of the Peace, &c.
[illegible]	[illegible]	[illegible]	[illegible]	[illegible]	[illegible]	[illegible]	[illegible]	[illegible]	[illegible]	Indecently Exposing the Person
[illegible]	[illegible]	[illegible]	[illegible]	[illegible]	[illegible]	[illegible]	[illegible]	[illegible]	[illegible]	Suicide, attempting to commit
[illegible]	[illegible]	[illegible]	[illegible]	[illegible]	[illegible]	[illegible]	[illegible]	[illegible]	[illegible]	Other Felonies not included in the above
[illegible]	[illegible]	[illegible]	[illegible]	[illegible]	[illegible]	[illegible]	[illegible]	[illegible]	[illegible]	Other Misdemeanors not included in the above
[illegible]	[illegible]	[illegible]	[illegible]	[illegible]	[illegible]	[illegible]	[illegible]	[illegible]	[illegible]	Total of No. 6.
[illegible]	[illegible]	[illegible]	[illegible]	[illegible]	[illegible]	[illegible]	[illegible]	[illegible]	[illegible]	GENERAL TOTAL.

OFFENCES PUNISHABLE BY [illegible]	[illegible]	[illegible]											
		[illegible]	[illegible]	[illegible]	[illegible]	[illegible]	[illegible]	[illegible]	[illegible]	[illegible]	[illegible]	[illegible]	[illegible]
Adulteration of Food, &c., Act,	[illegible]	[illegible]	[illegible]	[illegible]	[illegible]	[illegible]	[illegible]	[illegible]	[illegible]	[illegible]	[illegible]	[illegible]	[illegible]
Assaults, Aggravated, on Women and Children,	[illegible]	[illegible]	[illegible]	[illegible]	[illegible]	[illegible]	[illegible]	[illegible]	[illegible]	[illegible]	[illegible]	[illegible]	[illegible]
—— on Peace Officers, Gamekeepers, [illegible], &c.	[illegible]	[illegible]	[illegible]	[illegible]	[illegible]	[illegible]	[illegible]	[illegible]	[illegible]	[illegible]	[illegible]	[illegible]	[illegible]
—— Common,	[illegible]	[illegible]	[illegible]	[illegible]	[illegible]	[illegible]	[illegible]	[illegible]	[illegible]	[illegible]	[illegible]	[illegible]	[illegible]
Bastardy Orders, disobeying,	[illegible]	[illegible]	[illegible]	[illegible]	[illegible]	[illegible]	[illegible]	[illegible]	[illegible]	[illegible]	[illegible]	[illegible]	[illegible]
Breaches of the Peace, [illegible], &c.	[illegible]	[illegible]	[illegible]	[illegible]	[illegible]	[illegible]	[illegible]	[illegible]	[illegible]	[illegible]	[illegible]	[illegible]	[illegible]
Cattle Plague Orders, Offences against,	[illegible]	[illegible]	[illegible]	[illegible]	[illegible]	[illegible]	[illegible]	[illegible]	[illegible]	[illegible]	[illegible]	[illegible]	[illegible]
Chimney Sweepers Act, Offences against,	[illegible]	[illegible]	[illegible]	[illegible]	[illegible]	[illegible]	[illegible]	[illegible]	[illegible]	[illegible]	[illegible]	[illegible]	[illegible]
Cruelty to Animals,	[illegible]	[illegible]	[illegible]	[illegible]	[illegible]	[illegible]	[illegible]	[illegible]	[illegible]	[illegible]	[illegible]	[illegible]	[illegible]
[illegible]	[illegible]	[illegible]	[illegible]	[illegible]	[illegible]	[illegible]	[illegible]	[illegible]	[illegible]	[illegible]	[illegible]	[illegible]	[illegible]
Employers' and Workmen's Act, 1875,	[illegible]	[illegible]	[illegible]	[illegible]	[illegible]	[illegible]	[illegible]	[illegible]	[illegible]	[illegible]	[illegible]	[illegible]	[illegible]
Factory Acts, Offences against,	[illegible]	[illegible]	[illegible]	[illegible]	[illegible]	[illegible]	[illegible]	[illegible]	[illegible]	[illegible]	[illegible]	[illegible]	[illegible]
Fisheries Acts, Offences against,	[illegible]	[illegible]	[illegible]	[illegible]	[illegible]	[illegible]	[illegible]	[illegible]	[illegible]	[illegible]	[illegible]	[illegible]	[illegible]
Game Laws, Offences against, viz.—													
Trespassing in the day-time in pursuit of Game,	[illegible]	[illegible]	[illegible]	[illegible]	[illegible]	[illegible]	[illegible]	[illegible]	[illegible]	[illegible]	[illegible]	[illegible]	[illegible]
Night Poaching and destroying Game,	[illegible]	[illegible]	[illegible]	[illegible]	[illegible]	[illegible]	[illegible]	[illegible]	[illegible]	[illegible]	[illegible]	[illegible]	[illegible]
Illegally selling or buying Game,	[illegible]	[illegible]	[illegible]	[illegible]	[illegible]	[illegible]	[illegible]	[illegible]	[illegible]	[illegible]	[illegible]	[illegible]	[illegible]
Poaching Acts, [illegible],	[illegible]	[illegible]	[illegible]	[illegible]	[illegible]	[illegible]	[illegible]	[illegible]	[illegible]	[illegible]	[illegible]	[illegible]	[illegible]
Other Offences against the Game Acts,	[illegible]	[illegible]	[illegible]	[illegible]	[illegible]	[illegible]	[illegible]	[illegible]	[illegible]	[illegible]	[illegible]	[illegible]	[illegible]
Licensing Acts, [illegible], Offences against, viz.—													
Drunkenness, and Drunk and Disorderly,	[illegible]	[illegible]	[illegible]	[illegible]	[illegible]	[illegible]	[illegible]	[illegible]	[illegible]	[illegible]	[illegible]	[illegible]	[illegible]
Permitting Drunkenness and Disorderly Conduct in Licensed House,	[illegible]	[illegible]	[illegible]	[illegible]	[illegible]	[illegible]	[illegible]	[illegible]	[illegible]	[illegible]	[illegible]	[illegible]	[illegible]
Illegally selling Intoxicating Liquors,	[illegible]	[illegible]	[illegible]	[illegible]	[illegible]	[illegible]	[illegible]	[illegible]	[illegible]	[illegible]	[illegible]	[illegible]	[illegible]
Adulteration of Intoxicating Liquors,	[illegible]	[illegible]	[illegible]	[illegible]	[illegible]	[illegible]	[illegible]	[illegible]	[illegible]	[illegible]	[illegible]	[illegible]	[illegible]
Beerhouse Acts, Offences against,	[illegible]	[illegible]	[illegible]	[illegible]	[illegible]	[illegible]	[illegible]	[illegible]	[illegible]	[illegible]	[illegible]	[illegible]	[illegible]
Other Offences under the Licensing Acts,	[illegible]	[illegible]	[illegible]	[illegible]	[illegible]	[illegible]	[illegible]	[illegible]	[illegible]	[illegible]	[illegible]	[illegible]	[illegible]
Lord's Day Act, Offences against,	[illegible]	[illegible]	[illegible]	[illegible]	[illegible]	[illegible]	[illegible]	[illegible]	[illegible]	[illegible]	[illegible]	[illegible]	[illegible]
Local Acts and Borough By-Laws, Offences against,	[illegible]	[illegible]	[illegible]	[illegible]	[illegible]	[illegible]	[illegible]	[illegible]	[illegible]	[illegible]	[illegible]	[illegible]	[illegible]
Malicious Damage to Fences, Walls, Crops, &c.	[illegible]	[illegible]	[illegible]	[illegible]	[illegible]	[illegible]	[illegible]	[illegible]	[illegible]	[illegible]	[illegible]	[illegible]	[illegible]
—— Fruit and Vegetable Productions,	[illegible]	[illegible]	[illegible]	[illegible]	[illegible]	[illegible]	[illegible]	[illegible]	[illegible]	[illegible]	[illegible]	[illegible]	[illegible]
—— Trees, Shrubs, &c.	[illegible]	[illegible]	[illegible]	[illegible]	[illegible]	[illegible]	[illegible]	[illegible]	[illegible]	[illegible]	[illegible]	[illegible]	[illegible]
Other Malicious and Wilful Damage, and Trespass,	[illegible]	[illegible]	[illegible]	[illegible]	[illegible]	[illegible]	[illegible]	[illegible]	[illegible]	[illegible]	[illegible]	[illegible]	[illegible]
Military Acts, Offences against, viz.—													
Army Act,	[illegible]	[illegible]	[illegible]	[illegible]	[illegible]	[illegible]	[illegible]	[illegible]	[illegible]	[illegible]	[illegible]	[illegible]	[illegible]
Navy Act,	[illegible]	[illegible]	[illegible]	[illegible]	[illegible]	[illegible]	[illegible]	[illegible]	[illegible]	[illegible]	[illegible]	[illegible]	[illegible]
Militia Act,	[illegible]	[illegible]	[illegible]	[illegible]	[illegible]	[illegible]	[illegible]	[illegible]	[illegible]	[illegible]	[illegible]	[illegible]	[illegible]
[illegible] Acts, Offences against,	[illegible]	[illegible]	[illegible]	[illegible]	[illegible]	[illegible]	[illegible]	[illegible]	[illegible]	[illegible]	[illegible]	[illegible]	[illegible]
Nuisances, and Offences against Health, viz.—													
Public Health Acts,	[illegible]	[illegible]	[illegible]	[illegible]	[illegible]	[illegible]	[illegible]	[illegible]	[illegible]	[illegible]	[illegible]	[illegible]	[illegible]
[illegible] Acts,	[illegible]	[illegible]	[illegible]	[illegible]	[illegible]	[illegible]	[illegible]	[illegible]	[illegible]	[illegible]	[illegible]	[illegible]	[illegible]
[illegible] Acts,	[illegible]	[illegible]	[illegible]	[illegible]	[illegible]	[illegible]	[illegible]	[illegible]	[illegible]	[illegible]	[illegible]	[illegible]	[illegible]
Nuisances Removal Act,	[illegible]	[illegible]	[illegible]	[illegible]	[illegible]	[illegible]	[illegible]	[illegible]	[illegible]	[illegible]	[illegible]	[illegible]	[illegible]
Common Lodging Houses Acts,	[illegible]	[illegible]	[illegible]	[illegible]	[illegible]	[illegible]	[illegible]	[illegible]	[illegible]	[illegible]	[illegible]	[illegible]	[illegible]
Selling and exposing for sale unsound Food,	[illegible]	[illegible]	[illegible]	[illegible]	[illegible]	[illegible]	[illegible]	[illegible]	[illegible]	[illegible]	[illegible]	[illegible]	[illegible]
Other Sanitary offences,	[illegible]	[illegible]	[illegible]	[illegible]	[illegible]	[illegible]	[illegible]	[illegible]	[illegible]	[illegible]	[illegible]	[illegible]	[illegible]
Pawnbrokers Act, Offences against, viz.—													
By Pawnbrokers,	[illegible]	[illegible]	[illegible]	[illegible]	[illegible]	[illegible]	[illegible]	[illegible]	[illegible]	[illegible]	[illegible]	[illegible]	[illegible]
By persons unlawfully pledging or disposing,	[illegible]	[illegible]	[illegible]	[illegible]	[illegible]	[illegible]	[illegible]	[illegible]	[illegible]	[illegible]	[illegible]	[illegible]	[illegible]
Other Offences,	[illegible]	[illegible]	[illegible]	[illegible]	[illegible]	[illegible]	[illegible]	[illegible]	[illegible]	[illegible]	[illegible]	[illegible]	[illegible]
Police Acts, Offences against, viz.—													
Unlawfully possessing Goods,	[illegible]	[illegible]	[illegible]	[illegible]	[illegible]	[illegible]	[illegible]	[illegible]	[illegible]	[illegible]	[illegible]	[illegible]	[illegible]
Offences [illegible],	[illegible]	[illegible]	[illegible]	[illegible]	[illegible]	[illegible]	[illegible]	[illegible]	[illegible]	[illegible]	[illegible]	[illegible]	[illegible]
Constables neglecting their Duty,	[illegible]	[illegible]	[illegible]	[illegible]	[illegible]	[illegible]	[illegible]	[illegible]	[illegible]	[illegible]	[illegible]	[illegible]	[illegible]
Other Offences (not falling under other special heads),	[illegible]	[illegible]	[illegible]	[illegible]	[illegible]	[illegible]	[illegible]	[illegible]	[illegible]	[illegible]	[illegible]	[illegible]	[illegible]
Prevention of Crime Act, 1871, Sec. 7 (Special Offences by Persons under supervision),	[illegible]	[illegible]	[illegible]	[illegible]	[illegible]	[illegible]	[illegible]	[illegible]	[illegible]	[illegible]	[illegible]	[illegible]	[illegible]
Poor Law Acts, Offences against, viz.—													
Desertion or Neglecting to support Family,	[illegible]	[illegible]	[illegible]	[illegible]	[illegible]	[illegible]	[illegible]	[illegible]	[illegible]	[illegible]	[illegible]	[illegible]	[illegible]
Disorderly Conduct in Workhouses,	[illegible]	[illegible]	[illegible]	[illegible]	[illegible]	[illegible]	[illegible]	[illegible]	[illegible]	[illegible]	[illegible]	[illegible]	[illegible]
Destroying Workhouse Clothing, Bedding, &c.,	[illegible]	[illegible]	[illegible]	[illegible]	[illegible]	[illegible]	[illegible]	[illegible]	[illegible]	[illegible]	[illegible]	[illegible]	[illegible]
Refreshment Houses and Wine Licences Act,	[illegible]	[illegible]	[illegible]	[illegible]	[illegible]	[illegible]	[illegible]	[illegible]	[illegible]	[illegible]	[illegible]	[illegible]	[illegible]
Revenue Laws, Offences against, viz.—													
Customs Acts,	[illegible]	[illegible]	[illegible]	[illegible]	[illegible]	[illegible]	[illegible]	[illegible]	[illegible]	[illegible]	[illegible]	[illegible]	[illegible]
Excise Acts (including Hawkers and Pedlars Act),	[illegible]	[illegible]	[illegible]	[illegible]	[illegible]	[illegible]	[illegible]	[illegible]	[illegible]	[illegible]	[illegible]	[illegible]	[illegible]
Salmon Fisheries Act, Offences against,	[illegible]	[illegible]	[illegible]	[illegible]	[illegible]	[illegible]	[illegible]	[illegible]	[illegible]	[illegible]	[illegible]	[illegible]	[illegible]
Stealing, or Attempts to Steal, viz.—													
Larceny, by children under 16 years (Juvenile Offenders Act),	[illegible]	[illegible]	[illegible]	[illegible]	[illegible]	[illegible]	[illegible]	[illegible]	[illegible]	[illegible]	[illegible]	[illegible]	[illegible]
Larceny, under value of 5s., and on pleading Guilty (Criminal Justice Act),	[illegible]	[illegible]	[illegible]	[illegible]	[illegible]	[illegible]	[illegible]	[illegible]	[illegible]	[illegible]	[illegible]	[illegible]	[illegible]
Larceny above value of 5s., on pleading Guilty (Criminal Justice Act),	[illegible]	[illegible]	[illegible]	[illegible]	[illegible]	[illegible]	[illegible]	[illegible]	[illegible]	[illegible]	[illegible]	[illegible]	[illegible]
Larceny, or Larceny from Person, attempting to commit (Criminal Justice Act),	[illegible]	[illegible]	[illegible]	[illegible]	[illegible]	[illegible]	[illegible]	[illegible]	[illegible]	[illegible]	[illegible]	[illegible]	[illegible]
Dogs, Birds, or Beasts, &c.,	[illegible]	[illegible]	[illegible]	[illegible]	[illegible]	[illegible]	[illegible]	[illegible]	[illegible]	[illegible]	[illegible]	[illegible]	[illegible]
Fruit or Vegetable Productions,	[illegible]	[illegible]	[illegible]	[illegible]	[illegible]	[illegible]	[illegible]	[illegible]	[illegible]	[illegible]	[illegible]	[illegible]	[illegible]
Plants, Wood, &c.,	[illegible]	[illegible]	[illegible]	[illegible]	[illegible]	[illegible]	[illegible]	[illegible]	[illegible]	[illegible]	[illegible]	[illegible]	[illegible]
Trees, Shrubs, &c.,	[illegible]	[illegible]	[illegible]	[illegible]	[illegible]	[illegible]	[illegible]	[illegible]	[illegible]	[illegible]	[illegible]	[illegible]	[illegible]
Vagrant Act, Offences against, viz.—													
Prostitutes,	[illegible]	[illegible]	[illegible]	[illegible]	[illegible]	[illegible]	[illegible]	[illegible]	[illegible]	[illegible]	[illegible]	[illegible]	[illegible]
Beggars,	[illegible]	[illegible]	[illegible]	[illegible]	[illegible]	[illegible]	[illegible]	[illegible]	[illegible]	[illegible]	[illegible]	[illegible]	[illegible]
[illegible] no visible Means of Subsistence, &c.	[illegible]	[illegible]	[illegible]	[illegible]	[illegible]	[illegible]	[illegible]	[illegible]	[illegible]	[illegible]	[illegible]	[illegible]	[illegible]
Having Implements for Housebreaking, &c.	[illegible]	[illegible]	[illegible]	[illegible]	[illegible]	[illegible]	[illegible]	[illegible]	[illegible]	[illegible]	[illegible]	[illegible]	[illegible]
Found in enclosed Premises for unlawful purposes,	[illegible]	[illegible]	[illegible]	[illegible]	[illegible]	[illegible]	[illegible]	[illegible]	[illegible]	[illegible]	[illegible]	[illegible]	[illegible]
Frequenting Places of Public Resort, &c., to commit Felony,	[illegible]	[illegible]	[illegible]	[illegible]	[illegible]	[illegible]	[illegible]	[illegible]	[illegible]	[illegible]	[illegible]	[illegible]	[illegible]
Incorrigible Rogues,	[illegible]	[illegible]	[illegible]	[illegible]	[illegible]	[illegible]	[illegible]	[illegible]	[illegible]	[illegible]	[illegible]	[illegible]	[illegible]
Other Offences under Vagrant Act,	[illegible]	[illegible]	[illegible]	[illegible]	[illegible]	[illegible]	[illegible]	[illegible]	[illegible]	[illegible]	[illegible]	[illegible]	[illegible]
Vaccination Acts, Offences against,	[illegible]	[illegible]	[illegible]	[illegible]	[illegible]	[illegible]	[illegible]	[illegible]	[illegible]	[illegible]	[illegible]	[illegible]	[illegible]
[illegible] Acts, Offences against, viz.—													
Stage and Hackney Carriage Acts,	[illegible]	[illegible]	[illegible]	[illegible]	[illegible]	[illegible]	[illegible]	[illegible]	[illegible]	[illegible]	[illegible]	[illegible]	[illegible]
Highway Act (including Road Encroachments),	[illegible]	[illegible]	[illegible]	[illegible]	[illegible]	[illegible]	[illegible]	[illegible]	[illegible]	[illegible]	[illegible]	[illegible]	[illegible]
[illegible] Act,	[illegible]	[illegible]	[illegible]	[illegible]	[illegible]	[illegible]	[illegible]	[illegible]	[illegible]	[illegible]	[illegible]	[illegible]	[illegible]
Railway Acts,	[illegible]	[illegible]	[illegible]	[illegible]	[illegible]	[illegible]	[illegible]	[illegible]	[illegible]	[illegible]	[illegible]	[illegible]	[illegible]
Weights and Measures Act, Offences against,	[illegible]	[illegible]	[illegible]	[illegible]	[illegible]	[illegible]	[illegible]	[illegible]	[illegible]	[illegible]	[illegible]	[illegible]	[illegible]
Other Offences (not included within the above heads),	[illegible]	[illegible]	[illegible]	[illegible]	[illegible]	[illegible]	[illegible]	[illegible]	[illegible]	[illegible]	[illegible]	[illegible]	[illegible]
Total,	[illegible]	[illegible]	[illegible]	[illegible]	[illegible]	[illegible]	[illegible]	[illegible]	[illegible]	[illegible]	[illegible]	[illegible]	[illegible]

Total Number of [illegible] Prosecutions against before Justices, in each County, and County of City or of Town, [illegible] December, 186[illegible], made by the Inspector-General.

Counties [illegible] (16 columns, all figures illegible)	OFFENCES PUNISHABLE BY JUSTICES.
[illegible]	Adulteration of Food, &c., Act.
[illegible]	Assaults, Aggravated, on Women and Children.
[illegible]	—— on Peace Officers, [illegible] &c.
[illegible]	—— Common.
[illegible]	[illegible]
[illegible]	[illegible] of the Peace, [illegible] &c.
[illegible]	[illegible] Offences against.
[illegible]	[illegible] Act, Offences against.
[illegible]	Cruelty to Animals.
[illegible]	[illegible]
[illegible]	Employers' and Workmen's Act, 18[illegible].
[illegible]	Fishery Acts, Offences against.
[illegible]	[illegible] Acts, Offences against.
[illegible]	Game Acts, Offences against, viz.:—
[illegible]	Trespassing in the day time in pursuit of Game.
[illegible]	[illegible]
[illegible]	[illegible] selling or buying Game.
[illegible]	[illegible] Acts, [illegible]
[illegible]	Other Offences against the Game Acts.
[illegible]	[illegible] Acts, [illegible] Offences against, viz.:—
[illegible]	Drunkenness, and Drunk and Disorderly.
[illegible]	[illegible] Drunkenness and Disorderly Conduct at Licensed Houses.
[illegible]	[illegible]
[illegible]	[illegible]
[illegible]	[illegible] Acts, Offences against.
[illegible]	Other Offences under the [illegible] Acts.
[illegible]	Lord's Day Act, Offences against.
[illegible]	Local Acts and [illegible] Bye-Laws, Offences against.
[illegible]	[illegible] Fences, Walls, Gates, &c.
[illegible]	—— Fruit and Vegetable Productions.
[illegible]	—— Trees, Shrubs, &c.
[illegible]	Other [illegible] Damage, and Trespass.
[illegible]	[illegible] Acts, Offences against, viz.:—
[illegible]	Army Act.
[illegible]	Navy Act.
[illegible]	Militia Act.
[illegible]	[illegible] Acts, Offences against.
[illegible]	[illegible], and Offences against Health, viz.:—
[illegible]	Public Health Acts.
[illegible]	[illegible] Acts.
[illegible]	Sewer Acts.
[illegible]	[illegible] Act.
[illegible]	Common Lodging Houses Acts.
[illegible]	[illegible] for sale [illegible]
[illegible]	Other Sanitary Offences.
[illegible]	[illegible] Act, Offences against, viz.:—
[illegible]	By [illegible]
[illegible]	By persons unlawfully pledging or disposing.
[illegible]	Other Offences.
[illegible]	Police Acts, Offences against, viz.:—
[illegible]	Unlawfully possessing Goods.
[illegible]	[illegible]
[illegible]	[illegible]
[illegible]	Other Offences [illegible] under other special heads.
[illegible]	Prevention of Crime Act, [illegible] Offences by Persons [illegible]
[illegible]	Poor Law Acts, Offences against, viz.:—
[illegible]	Deserting or [illegible] to support Family.
[illegible]	[illegible] in Workhouses.
[illegible]	[illegible] Workhouse Clothing, [illegible], &c.
[illegible]	[illegible] and Wine Licences Act.
[illegible] Laws, Offences against, viz.:—	
[illegible]	[illegible] Acts.
[illegible]	[illegible] Acts [illegible] and [illegible] Act.
[illegible]	[illegible] Act, Offences against.
[illegible]	[illegible], viz.:—
[illegible]	Larceny, [illegible] Act.
[illegible]	Larceny, [illegible] value of [illegible], and on pleading Guilty ([illegible] Justices Act).
[illegible]	Larceny above value of [illegible], on pleading Guilty ([illegible] Justices Act).
[illegible]	Larceny or Larceny [illegible], attempting to [illegible] ([illegible] Justices Act).
[illegible]	[illegible]
[illegible]	Fruit or Vegetable Productions.
[illegible]	[illegible]
[illegible]	[illegible]
[illegible]	[illegible] Act, Offences against, viz.:—
[illegible]	[illegible]
[illegible]	[illegible]
[illegible]	[illegible]
[illegible]	[illegible]
[illegible]	Found on enclosed Premises for unlawful purposes.
[illegible]	[illegible]
[illegible]	[illegible]
[illegible]	Other Offences under Vagrant Act.
[illegible]	Vaccination Acts, Offences against.
[illegible]	[illegible] Acts, Offences against, viz.:—
[illegible]	[illegible] Carriage Acts.
[illegible]	[illegible] Act ([illegible])
[illegible]	[illegible] Act.
[illegible]	[illegible] Acts.
[illegible]	Weights and Measures Act, Offences against.
[illegible]	Other Offences not included under the above heads.
[illegible]	Total.

[illegible] BY PETTY [illegible]

	[illegible]	[illegible]
[illegible] Act,	[illegible]	[illegible]
[illegible] on Women and Children,	[illegible]	[illegible]
[illegible]	[illegible]	[illegible]
[illegible]	[illegible]	[illegible]
[illegible]	[illegible]	[illegible]
[illegible]	[illegible]	[illegible]
[illegible] Offences against,	[illegible]	[illegible]
[illegible]	[illegible]	[illegible]
[illegible] Act, 1872,	[illegible]	[illegible]
[illegible]	[illegible]	[illegible]
[illegible]	[illegible]	[illegible]
[illegible]	[illegible]	[illegible]
[illegible]	[illegible]	[illegible]
[illegible] Game Acts,	[illegible]	[illegible]
[illegible] Drunk and Disorderly,	[illegible]	[illegible]
[illegible] and Disorderly Conduct in [illegible]	[illegible]	[illegible]
[illegible]	[illegible]	[illegible]
[illegible] under the Licensing Acts,	[illegible]	[illegible]
[illegible] By-Laws, Offences against,	[illegible]	[illegible]
[illegible]	[illegible]	[illegible]
[illegible]	[illegible]	[illegible]
[illegible] Offences against,	[illegible]	[illegible]
[illegible] Public Health, [illegible]	[illegible]	[illegible]
[illegible] Act,	[illegible]	[illegible]
[illegible]	[illegible]	[illegible]
[illegible]	[illegible]	[illegible]
[illegible]	[illegible]	[illegible]
[illegible]	[illegible]	[illegible]
[illegible] Act, [illegible]	[illegible]	[illegible]
[illegible]	[illegible]	[illegible]
[illegible] Wine Licences Act,	[illegible]	[illegible]
[illegible]	[illegible]	[illegible]

TABLE I.—OFFENCES DETERMINED SUMMARILY. [illegible]

[illegible]	[illegible]						
	[illegible]			[illegible]		[illegible]	
	M.	W.	M. & W.	M.	W.	M.	W.
[illegible]	[illegible]	[illegible]	[illegible]	[illegible]	[illegible]	[illegible]	[illegible]
Total	[illegible]	[illegible]	[illegible]	[illegible]	[illegible]	[illegible]	[illegible]

... were proceeded against Summarily before Justices, in the Year ended 31st December, [illegible], and the Results ... by the Inspectors-General.

Fined. M.	Fined. W.	Whipped. M.	Whipped. W.	To find Sureties or Recognizances. M.	To find Sureties or Recognizances. W.	Delivered to Army or Navy. M.	Other Punishments. M.	Other Punishments. W.	OFFENCES PUNISHABLE BY JUSTICES.
[illegible]	[illegible]	[illegible]	[illegible]	[illegible]	[illegible]	[illegible]	[illegible]	[illegible]	Adulteration of Food, &c., Act.
[illegible]	[illegible]	[illegible]	[illegible]	[illegible]	[illegible]	[illegible]	[illegible]	[illegible]	Assaults, Aggravated, on Women and Children.
[illegible]	[illegible]	[illegible]	[illegible]	[illegible]	[illegible]	[illegible]	[illegible]	[illegible]	——— on Peace Officers, Resisting, Obstructing, &c.
[illegible]	[illegible]	[illegible]	[illegible]	[illegible]	[illegible]	[illegible]	[illegible]	[illegible]	——— Common
[illegible]	[illegible]	[illegible]	[illegible]	[illegible]	[illegible]	[illegible]	[illegible]	[illegible]	Bastardy Orders, Disobeying
[illegible]	[illegible]	[illegible]	[illegible]	[illegible]	[illegible]	[illegible]	[illegible]	[illegible]	Breaches of the Peace, want of Sureties, &c.
[illegible]	[illegible]	[illegible]	[illegible]	[illegible]	[illegible]	[illegible]	[illegible]	[illegible]	Cattle Plague Orders, Offences against
[illegible]	[illegible]	[illegible]	[illegible]	[illegible]	[illegible]	[illegible]	[illegible]	[illegible]	Chimney Sweepers Act, Offences against
[illegible]	[illegible]	[illegible]	[illegible]	[illegible]	[illegible]	[illegible]	[illegible]	[illegible]	Cruelty to Animals.
[illegible]	[illegible]	[illegible]	[illegible]	[illegible]	[illegible]	[illegible]	[illegible]	[illegible]	Embezzlement
[illegible]	[illegible]	[illegible]	[illegible]	[illegible]	[illegible]	[illegible]	[illegible]	[illegible]	Employers' and Workmen's Act, 1875.
[illegible]	[illegible]	[illegible]	[illegible]	[illegible]	[illegible]	[illegible]	[illegible]	[illegible]	Factory Acts, Offences against
[illegible]	[illegible]	[illegible]	[illegible]	[illegible]	[illegible]	[illegible]	[illegible]	[illegible]	Fisheries Acts, Offences against
									Game Laws, Offences against, viz.:—
[illegible]	[illegible]	[illegible]	[illegible]	[illegible]	[illegible]	[illegible]	[illegible]	[illegible]	Trespassing in the daytime in pursuit of Game
[illegible]	[illegible]	[illegible]	[illegible]	[illegible]	[illegible]	[illegible]	[illegible]	[illegible]	Night Poaching and destroying Game.
[illegible]	[illegible]	[illegible]	[illegible]	[illegible]	[illegible]	[illegible]	[illegible]	[illegible]	Illegally selling or buying Game.
[illegible]	[illegible]	[illegible]	[illegible]	[illegible]	[illegible]	[illegible]	[illegible]	[illegible]	Poaching Acts [illegible]
[illegible]	[illegible]	[illegible]	[illegible]	[illegible]	[illegible]	[illegible]	[illegible]	[illegible]	Other Offences against the Game Laws
									Licensing Acts, [illegible], Offences against, viz.:—
[illegible]	[illegible]	[illegible]	[illegible]	[illegible]	[illegible]	[illegible]	[illegible]	[illegible]	Drunkenness and Drunk and Disorderly
[illegible]	[illegible]	[illegible]	[illegible]	[illegible]	[illegible]	[illegible]	[illegible]	[illegible]	Permitting Drunkenness and Disorderly Conduct in Licensed Houses
[illegible]	[illegible]	[illegible]	[illegible]	[illegible]	[illegible]	[illegible]	[illegible]	[illegible]	Illegally selling Intoxicating Drinks
[illegible]	[illegible]	[illegible]	[illegible]	[illegible]	[illegible]	[illegible]	[illegible]	[illegible]	Adulteration of Intoxicating Liquors
[illegible]	[illegible]	[illegible]	[illegible]	[illegible]	[illegible]	[illegible]	[illegible]	[illegible]	Sunday [illegible] Acts, Offences against
[illegible]	[illegible]	[illegible]	[illegible]	[illegible]	[illegible]	[illegible]	[illegible]	[illegible]	Other Offences under the Licensing Acts.
[illegible]	[illegible]	[illegible]	[illegible]	[illegible]	[illegible]	[illegible]	[illegible]	[illegible]	Lord's Day Act, Offences against
[illegible]	[illegible]	[illegible]	[illegible]	[illegible]	[illegible]	[illegible]	[illegible]	[illegible]	Local Acts and Borough By Laws, Offences against
[illegible]	[illegible]	[illegible]	[illegible]	[illegible]	[illegible]	[illegible]	[illegible]	[illegible]	Maliciously destroying Fences, Walls, Gates, &c.
[illegible]	[illegible]	[illegible]	[illegible]	[illegible]	[illegible]	[illegible]	[illegible]	[illegible]	——— Trees and Vegetable Productions
[illegible]	[illegible]	[illegible]	[illegible]	[illegible]	[illegible]	[illegible]	[illegible]	[illegible]	——— Trees, Shrubs, &c.
[illegible]	[illegible]	[illegible]	[illegible]	[illegible]	[illegible]	[illegible]	[illegible]	[illegible]	Other Malicious and Wilful Damage and Trespass.
									Military Laws, Offences against, viz.:—
[illegible]	[illegible]	[illegible]	[illegible]	[illegible]	[illegible]	[illegible]	[illegible]	[illegible]	Army Act
[illegible]	[illegible]	[illegible]	[illegible]	[illegible]	[illegible]	[illegible]	[illegible]	[illegible]	Navy Act
[illegible]	[illegible]	[illegible]	[illegible]	[illegible]	[illegible]	[illegible]	[illegible]	[illegible]	Militia Act.
[illegible]	[illegible]	[illegible]	[illegible]	[illegible]	[illegible]	[illegible]	[illegible]	[illegible]	Merchant Shipping Acts, Offences against
									Nuisances, and Offences against Public Health, viz.:—
[illegible]	[illegible]	[illegible]	[illegible]	[illegible]	[illegible]	[illegible]	[illegible]	[illegible]	Public Health Acts
[illegible]	[illegible]	[illegible]	[illegible]	[illegible]	[illegible]	[illegible]	[illegible]	[illegible]	Smoke Acts
[illegible]	[illegible]	[illegible]	[illegible]	[illegible]	[illegible]	[illegible]	[illegible]	[illegible]	Sewers Acts
[illegible]	[illegible]	[illegible]	[illegible]	[illegible]	[illegible]	[illegible]	[illegible]	[illegible]	[illegible] Act
[illegible]	[illegible]	[illegible]	[illegible]	[illegible]	[illegible]	[illegible]	[illegible]	[illegible]	Common Lodging Houses Acts
[illegible]	[illegible]	[illegible]	[illegible]	[illegible]	[illegible]	[illegible]	[illegible]	[illegible]	Selling and exposing for sale unsound Food.
[illegible]	[illegible]	[illegible]	[illegible]	[illegible]	[illegible]	[illegible]	[illegible]	[illegible]	Other Sanitary Offences
									Pawnbrokers Act, Offences against, viz.:—
[illegible]	[illegible]	[illegible]	[illegible]	[illegible]	[illegible]	[illegible]	[illegible]	[illegible]	By Pawnbrokers
[illegible]	[illegible]	[illegible]	[illegible]	[illegible]	[illegible]	[illegible]	[illegible]	[illegible]	By persons unlawfully pledging or disposing
[illegible]	[illegible]	[illegible]	[illegible]	[illegible]	[illegible]	[illegible]	[illegible]	[illegible]	Other Offences.
									Police Acts, Offences against, viz.:—
[illegible]	[illegible]	[illegible]	[illegible]	[illegible]	[illegible]	[illegible]	[illegible]	[illegible]	Disorderly prostitutes [illegible]
[illegible]	[illegible]	[illegible]	[illegible]	[illegible]	[illegible]	[illegible]	[illegible]	[illegible]	Offences punishable as Misdemeanours
[illegible]	[illegible]	[illegible]	[illegible]	[illegible]	[illegible]	[illegible]	[illegible]	[illegible]	Constables neglecting their Duty
[illegible]	[illegible]	[illegible]	[illegible]	[illegible]	[illegible]	[illegible]	[illegible]	[illegible]	Other Offences not falling under other general heads.
[illegible]	[illegible]	[illegible]	[illegible]	[illegible]	[illegible]	[illegible]	[illegible]	[illegible]	Prevention of Crimes Act, 1871, sec. 7 (Special Offences by Persons under supervision)
									Poor Law Acts, Offences against, viz.:—
[illegible]	[illegible]	[illegible]	[illegible]	[illegible]	[illegible]	[illegible]	[illegible]	[illegible]	Deserting or Neglecting to support Family
[illegible]	[illegible]	[illegible]	[illegible]	[illegible]	[illegible]	[illegible]	[illegible]	[illegible]	Refractory Conduct in Workhouses.
[illegible]	[illegible]	[illegible]	[illegible]	[illegible]	[illegible]	[illegible]	[illegible]	[illegible]	Destroying Workhouse Clothes, [illegible]
[illegible]	[illegible]	[illegible]	[illegible]	[illegible]	[illegible]	[illegible]	[illegible]	[illegible]	[illegible] Acts.
									Revenue Laws, Offences against, viz.:—
[illegible]	[illegible]	[illegible]	[illegible]	[illegible]	[illegible]	[illegible]	[illegible]	[illegible]	Customs Acts
[illegible]	[illegible]	[illegible]	[illegible]	[illegible]	[illegible]	[illegible]	[illegible]	[illegible]	Excise Acts [illegible]
[illegible]	[illegible]	[illegible]	[illegible]	[illegible]	[illegible]	[illegible]	[illegible]	[illegible]	Salmon Fisheries Act, Offences against
									Stealing, or Attempts to Steal, viz.:—
[illegible]	[illegible]	[illegible]	[illegible]	[illegible]	[illegible]	[illegible]	[illegible]	[illegible]	Larceny, by Offenders under 16 years (Juvenile Offenders Act)
[illegible]	[illegible]	[illegible]	[illegible]	[illegible]	[illegible]	[illegible]	[illegible]	[illegible]	Larceny, under value of 5s., and on pleading Guilty (Criminal Justice Act)
[illegible]	[illegible]	[illegible]	[illegible]	[illegible]	[illegible]	[illegible]	[illegible]	[illegible]	Larceny, above value of 5s., on pleading Guilty (Criminal Justice Act)
[illegible]	[illegible]	[illegible]	[illegible]	[illegible]	[illegible]	[illegible]	[illegible]	[illegible]	Larceny, or Larceny from Person, [illegible] (Criminal Justice Act)
[illegible]	[illegible]	[illegible]	[illegible]	[illegible]	[illegible]	[illegible]	[illegible]	[illegible]	Dogs, Birds, or Beasts, &c.
[illegible]	[illegible]	[illegible]	[illegible]	[illegible]	[illegible]	[illegible]	[illegible]	[illegible]	Fruit or Vegetable Productions.
[illegible]	[illegible]	[illegible]	[illegible]	[illegible]	[illegible]	[illegible]	[illegible]	[illegible]	Timber, Wood, &c.
[illegible]	[illegible]	[illegible]	[illegible]	[illegible]	[illegible]	[illegible]	[illegible]	[illegible]	Trees, Shrubs, &c.
									Vagrant Act, Offences against, viz.:—
[illegible]	[illegible]	[illegible]	[illegible]	[illegible]	[illegible]	[illegible]	[illegible]	[illegible]	Prostitutes.
[illegible]	[illegible]	[illegible]	[illegible]	[illegible]	[illegible]	[illegible]	[illegible]	[illegible]	Beggars
[illegible]	[illegible]	[illegible]	[illegible]	[illegible]	[illegible]	[illegible]	[illegible]	[illegible]	Sleeping out [illegible]
[illegible]	[illegible]	[illegible]	[illegible]	[illegible]	[illegible]	[illegible]	[illegible]	[illegible]	Having implements for Housebreaking, &c.
[illegible]	[illegible]	[illegible]	[illegible]	[illegible]	[illegible]	[illegible]	[illegible]	[illegible]	Found in enclosed Premises for unlawful purposes
[illegible]	[illegible]	[illegible]	[illegible]	[illegible]	[illegible]	[illegible]	[illegible]	[illegible]	Frequenting Places of Public Resort, &c., to commit Felony
[illegible]	[illegible]	[illegible]	[illegible]	[illegible]	[illegible]	[illegible]	[illegible]	[illegible]	Incorrigible Rogues.
[illegible]	[illegible]	[illegible]	[illegible]	[illegible]	[illegible]	[illegible]	[illegible]	[illegible]	Other Offences under Vagrant Act
[illegible]	[illegible]	[illegible]	[illegible]	[illegible]	[illegible]	[illegible]	[illegible]	[illegible]	Vaccination Acts, Offences against
									Ways Acts, Offences against, viz.:—
[illegible]	[illegible]	[illegible]	[illegible]	[illegible]	[illegible]	[illegible]	[illegible]	[illegible]	Highway and Turnpike Acts.
[illegible]	[illegible]	[illegible]	[illegible]	[illegible]	[illegible]	[illegible]	[illegible]	[illegible]	Highway Act [illegible]
[illegible]	[illegible]	[illegible]	[illegible]	[illegible]	[illegible]	[illegible]	[illegible]	[illegible]	[illegible] Act.
[illegible]	[illegible]	[illegible]	[illegible]	[illegible]	[illegible]	[illegible]	[illegible]	[illegible]	Railway Acts.
[illegible]	[illegible]	[illegible]	[illegible]	[illegible]	[illegible]	[illegible]	[illegible]	[illegible]	Weights and Measures Act, Offences against
[illegible]	[illegible]	[illegible]	[illegible]	[illegible]	[illegible]	[illegible]	[illegible]	[illegible]	Other Offences (not included under the above heads)
[illegible]	[illegible]	[illegible]	[illegible]	[illegible]	[illegible]	[illegible]	[illegible]	[illegible]	TOTAL.

IRELAND.

PROVINCE, COUNTY, COUNTY OF CITY OR OF TOWN.	M	W	M & W	M	W	M	W	M	W	M	W	M	W	M	W	M	W	M	W	M	W	M	W	M	W	M	W	M	W	M	M	W
LEINSTER:																																
Carlow,	[illegible]	[illegible]	[illegible]	[illegible]	[illegible]	[illegible]	[illegible]	[illegible]	[illegible]	[illegible]	[illegible]	[illegible]	[illegible]	[illegible]	[illegible]	[illegible]	[illegible]	[illegible]	[illegible]	[illegible]	[illegible]	[illegible]	[illegible]	[illegible]	[illegible]	[illegible]	[illegible]	[illegible]	[illegible]	[illegible]	[illegible]	[illegible]	[illegible]
Drogheda, Town of,	[illegible]	[illegible]	[illegible]	[illegible]	[illegible]	[illegible]	[illegible]	[illegible]	[illegible]	[illegible]	[illegible]	[illegible]	[illegible]	[illegible]	[illegible]	[illegible]	[illegible]	[illegible]	[illegible]	[illegible]	[illegible]	[illegible]	[illegible]	[illegible]	[illegible]	[illegible]	[illegible]	[illegible]	[illegible]	[illegible]	[illegible]	[illegible]	[illegible]
Dublin County,	[illegible]	[illegible]	[illegible]	[illegible]	[illegible]	[illegible]	[illegible]	[illegible]	[illegible]	[illegible]	[illegible]	[illegible]	[illegible]	[illegible]	[illegible]	[illegible]	[illegible]	[illegible]	[illegible]	[illegible]	[illegible]	[illegible]	[illegible]	[illegible]	[illegible]	[illegible]	[illegible]	[illegible]	[illegible]	[illegible]	[illegible]	[illegible]	[illegible]
Dublin City (and part of County) Metropolitan Police District. Divisions:—																																
A,	[illegible]	[illegible]	[illegible]	[illegible]	[illegible]	[illegible]	[illegible]	[illegible]	[illegible]	[illegible]	[illegible]	[illegible]	[illegible]	[illegible]	[illegible]	[illegible]	[illegible]	[illegible]	[illegible]	[illegible]	[illegible]	[illegible]	[illegible]	[illegible]	[illegible]	[illegible]	[illegible]	[illegible]	[illegible]	[illegible]	[illegible]	[illegible]	[illegible]
B,	[illegible]	[illegible]	[illegible]	[illegible]	[illegible]	[illegible]	[illegible]	[illegible]	[illegible]	[illegible]	[illegible]	[illegible]	[illegible]	[illegible]	[illegible]	[illegible]	[illegible]	[illegible]	[illegible]	[illegible]	[illegible]	[illegible]	[illegible]	[illegible]	[illegible]	[illegible]	[illegible]	[illegible]	[illegible]	[illegible]	[illegible]	[illegible]	[illegible]
C,	[illegible]	[illegible]	[illegible]	[illegible]	[illegible]	[illegible]	[illegible]	[illegible]	[illegible]	[illegible]	[illegible]	[illegible]	[illegible]	[illegible]	[illegible]	[illegible]	[illegible]	[illegible]	[illegible]	[illegible]	[illegible]	[illegible]	[illegible]	[illegible]	[illegible]	[illegible]	[illegible]	[illegible]	[illegible]	[illegible]	[illegible]	[illegible]	[illegible]
D,	[illegible]	[illegible]	[illegible]	[illegible]	[illegible]	[illegible]	[illegible]	[illegible]	[illegible]	[illegible]	[illegible]	[illegible]	[illegible]	[illegible]	[illegible]	[illegible]	[illegible]	[illegible]	[illegible]	[illegible]	[illegible]	[illegible]	[illegible]	[illegible]	[illegible]	[illegible]	[illegible]	[illegible]	[illegible]	[illegible]	[illegible]	[illegible]	[illegible]
E,	[illegible]	[illegible]	[illegible]	[illegible]	[illegible]	[illegible]	[illegible]	[illegible]	[illegible]	[illegible]	[illegible]	[illegible]	[illegible]	[illegible]	[illegible]	[illegible]	[illegible]	[illegible]	[illegible]	[illegible]	[illegible]	[illegible]	[illegible]	[illegible]	[illegible]	[illegible]	[illegible]	[illegible]	[illegible]	[illegible]	[illegible]	[illegible]	[illegible]
F,	[illegible]	[illegible]	[illegible]	[illegible]	[illegible]	[illegible]	[illegible]	[illegible]	[illegible]	[illegible]	[illegible]	[illegible]	[illegible]	[illegible]	[illegible]	[illegible]	[illegible]	[illegible]	[illegible]	[illegible]	[illegible]	[illegible]	[illegible]	[illegible]	[illegible]	[illegible]	[illegible]	[illegible]	[illegible]	[illegible]	[illegible]	[illegible]	[illegible]
Total of Metropolitan Police District,	[illegible]	[illegible]	[illegible]	[illegible]	[illegible]	[illegible]	[illegible]	[illegible]	[illegible]	[illegible]	[illegible]	[illegible]	[illegible]	[illegible]	[illegible]	[illegible]	[illegible]	[illegible]	[illegible]	[illegible]	[illegible]	[illegible]	[illegible]	[illegible]	[illegible]	[illegible]	[illegible]	[illegible]	[illegible]	[illegible]	[illegible]	[illegible]	[illegible]
Kildare,	[illegible]	[illegible]	[illegible]	[illegible]	[illegible]	[illegible]	[illegible]	[illegible]	[illegible]	[illegible]	[illegible]	[illegible]	[illegible]	[illegible]	[illegible]	[illegible]	[illegible]	[illegible]	[illegible]	[illegible]	[illegible]	[illegible]	[illegible]	[illegible]	[illegible]	[illegible]	[illegible]	[illegible]	[illegible]	[illegible]	[illegible]	[illegible]	[illegible]
Kilkenny,	[illegible]	[illegible]	[illegible]	[illegible]	[illegible]	[illegible]	[illegible]	[illegible]	[illegible]	[illegible]	[illegible]	[illegible]	[illegible]	[illegible]	[illegible]	[illegible]	[illegible]	[illegible]	[illegible]	[illegible]	[illegible]	[illegible]	[illegible]	[illegible]	[illegible]	[illegible]	[illegible]	[illegible]	[illegible]	[illegible]	[illegible]	[illegible]	[illegible]
King's County,	[illegible]	[illegible]	[illegible]	[illegible]	[illegible]	[illegible]	[illegible]	[illegible]	[illegible]	[illegible]	[illegible]	[illegible]	[illegible]	[illegible]	[illegible]	[illegible]	[illegible]	[illegible]	[illegible]	[illegible]	[illegible]	[illegible]	[illegible]	[illegible]	[illegible]	[illegible]	[illegible]	[illegible]	[illegible]	[illegible]	[illegible]	[illegible]	[illegible]
Longford,	[illegible]	[illegible]	[illegible]	[illegible]	[illegible]	[illegible]	[illegible]	[illegible]	[illegible]	[illegible]	[illegible]	[illegible]	[illegible]	[illegible]	[illegible]	[illegible]	[illegible]	[illegible]	[illegible]	[illegible]	[illegible]	[illegible]	[illegible]	[illegible]	[illegible]	[illegible]	[illegible]	[illegible]	[illegible]	[illegible]	[illegible]	[illegible]	[illegible]
Louth,	[illegible]	[illegible]	[illegible]	[illegible]	[illegible]	[illegible]	[illegible]	[illegible]	[illegible]	[illegible]	[illegible]	[illegible]	[illegible]	[illegible]	[illegible]	[illegible]	[illegible]	[illegible]	[illegible]	[illegible]	[illegible]	[illegible]	[illegible]	[illegible]	[illegible]	[illegible]	[illegible]	[illegible]	[illegible]	[illegible]	[illegible]	[illegible]	[illegible]
Meath,	[illegible]	[illegible]	[illegible]	[illegible]	[illegible]	[illegible]	[illegible]	[illegible]	[illegible]	[illegible]	[illegible]	[illegible]	[illegible]	[illegible]	[illegible]	[illegible]	[illegible]	[illegible]	[illegible]	[illegible]	[illegible]	[illegible]	[illegible]	[illegible]	[illegible]	[illegible]	[illegible]	[illegible]	[illegible]	[illegible]	[illegible]	[illegible]	[illegible]
Queen's County,	[illegible]	[illegible]	[illegible]	[illegible]	[illegible]	[illegible]	[illegible]	[illegible]	[illegible]	[illegible]	[illegible]	[illegible]	[illegible]	[illegible]	[illegible]	[illegible]	[illegible]	[illegible]	[illegible]	[illegible]	[illegible]	[illegible]	[illegible]	[illegible]	[illegible]	[illegible]	[illegible]	[illegible]	[illegible]	[illegible]	[illegible]	[illegible]	[illegible]
Westmeath,	[illegible]	[illegible]	[illegible]	[illegible]	[illegible]	[illegible]	[illegible]	[illegible]	[illegible]	[illegible]	[illegible]	[illegible]	[illegible]	[illegible]	[illegible]	[illegible]	[illegible]	[illegible]	[illegible]	[illegible]	[illegible]	[illegible]	[illegible]	[illegible]	[illegible]	[illegible]	[illegible]	[illegible]	[illegible]	[illegible]	[illegible]	[illegible]	[illegible]
Wexford,	[illegible]	[illegible]	[illegible]	[illegible]	[illegible]	[illegible]	[illegible]	[illegible]	[illegible]	[illegible]	[illegible]	[illegible]	[illegible]	[illegible]	[illegible]	[illegible]	[illegible]	[illegible]	[illegible]	[illegible]	[illegible]	[illegible]	[illegible]	[illegible]	[illegible]	[illegible]	[illegible]	[illegible]	[illegible]	[illegible]	[illegible]	[illegible]	[illegible]
Wicklow,	[illegible]	[illegible]	[illegible]	[illegible]	[illegible]	[illegible]	[illegible]	[illegible]	[illegible]	[illegible]	[illegible]	[illegible]	[illegible]	[illegible]	[illegible]	[illegible]	[illegible]	[illegible]	[illegible]	[illegible]	[illegible]	[illegible]	[illegible]	[illegible]	[illegible]	[illegible]	[illegible]	[illegible]	[illegible]	[illegible]	[illegible]	[illegible]	[illegible]

Munster:																																
Clare	[illegible]	[illegible]	[illegible]	[illegible]	[illegible]	[illegible]	[illegible]	[illegible]	[illegible]	[illegible]	[illegible]	[illegible]	[illegible]	[illegible]	[illegible]	[illegible]	[illegible]	[illegible]	[illegible]	[illegible]	[illegible]	[illegible]	[illegible]	[illegible]	[illegible]	[illegible]	[illegible]	[illegible]	[illegible]	[illegible]	[illegible]	[illegible]
Cork, E. R.	[illegible]	[illegible]	[illegible]	[illegible]	[illegible]	[illegible]	[illegible]	[illegible]	[illegible]	[illegible]	[illegible]	[illegible]	[illegible]	[illegible]	[illegible]	[illegible]	[illegible]	[illegible]	[illegible]	[illegible]	[illegible]	[illegible]	[illegible]	[illegible]	[illegible]	[illegible]	[illegible]	[illegible]	[illegible]	[illegible]	[illegible]	[illegible]
Cork, W. R.	[illegible]	[illegible]	[illegible]	[illegible]	[illegible]	[illegible]	[illegible]	[illegible]	[illegible]	[illegible]	[illegible]	[illegible]	[illegible]	[illegible]	[illegible]	[illegible]	[illegible]	[illegible]	[illegible]	[illegible]	[illegible]	[illegible]	[illegible]	[illegible]	[illegible]	[illegible]	[illegible]	[illegible]	[illegible]	[illegible]	[illegible]	[illegible]
Cork City	[illegible]	[illegible]	[illegible]	[illegible]	[illegible]	[illegible]	[illegible]	[illegible]	[illegible]	[illegible]	[illegible]	[illegible]	[illegible]	[illegible]	[illegible]	[illegible]	[illegible]	[illegible]	[illegible]	[illegible]	[illegible]	[illegible]	[illegible]	[illegible]	[illegible]	[illegible]	[illegible]	[illegible]	[illegible]	[illegible]	[illegible]	[illegible]
Kerry	[illegible]	[illegible]	[illegible]	[illegible]	[illegible]	[illegible]	[illegible]	[illegible]	[illegible]	[illegible]	[illegible]	[illegible]	[illegible]	[illegible]	[illegible]	[illegible]	[illegible]	[illegible]	[illegible]	[illegible]	[illegible]	[illegible]	[illegible]	[illegible]	[illegible]	[illegible]	[illegible]	[illegible]	[illegible]	[illegible]	[illegible]	[illegible]
Limerick	[illegible]	[illegible]	[illegible]	[illegible]	[illegible]	[illegible]	[illegible]	[illegible]	[illegible]	[illegible]	[illegible]	[illegible]	[illegible]	[illegible]	[illegible]	[illegible]	[illegible]	[illegible]	[illegible]	[illegible]	[illegible]	[illegible]	[illegible]	[illegible]	[illegible]	[illegible]	[illegible]	[illegible]	[illegible]	[illegible]	[illegible]	[illegible]
Limerick City	[illegible]	[illegible]	[illegible]	[illegible]	[illegible]	[illegible]	[illegible]	[illegible]	[illegible]	[illegible]	[illegible]	[illegible]	[illegible]	[illegible]	[illegible]	[illegible]	[illegible]	[illegible]	[illegible]	[illegible]	[illegible]	[illegible]	[illegible]	[illegible]	[illegible]	[illegible]	[illegible]	[illegible]	[illegible]	[illegible]	[illegible]	[illegible]
Tipperary, N. R.	[illegible]	[illegible]	[illegible]	[illegible]	[illegible]	[illegible]	[illegible]	[illegible]	[illegible]	[illegible]	[illegible]	[illegible]	[illegible]	[illegible]	[illegible]	[illegible]	[illegible]	[illegible]	[illegible]	[illegible]	[illegible]	[illegible]	[illegible]	[illegible]	[illegible]	[illegible]	[illegible]	[illegible]	[illegible]	[illegible]	[illegible]	[illegible]
Tipperary, S. R.	[illegible]	[illegible]	[illegible]	[illegible]	[illegible]	[illegible]	[illegible]	[illegible]	[illegible]	[illegible]	[illegible]	[illegible]	[illegible]	[illegible]	[illegible]	[illegible]	[illegible]	[illegible]	[illegible]	[illegible]	[illegible]	[illegible]	[illegible]	[illegible]	[illegible]	[illegible]	[illegible]	[illegible]	[illegible]	[illegible]	[illegible]	[illegible]
Waterford	[illegible]	[illegible]	[illegible]	[illegible]	[illegible]	[illegible]	[illegible]	[illegible]	[illegible]	[illegible]	[illegible]	[illegible]	[illegible]	[illegible]	[illegible]	[illegible]	[illegible]	[illegible]	[illegible]	[illegible]	[illegible]	[illegible]	[illegible]	[illegible]	[illegible]	[illegible]	[illegible]	[illegible]	[illegible]	[illegible]	[illegible]	[illegible]
Waterford City	[illegible]	[illegible]	[illegible]	[illegible]	[illegible]	[illegible]	[illegible]	[illegible]	[illegible]	[illegible]	[illegible]	[illegible]	[illegible]	[illegible]	[illegible]	[illegible]	[illegible]	[illegible]	[illegible]	[illegible]	[illegible]	[illegible]	[illegible]	[illegible]	[illegible]	[illegible]	[illegible]	[illegible]	[illegible]	[illegible]	[illegible]	[illegible]
Total of Province	[illegible]	[illegible]	[illegible]	[illegible]	[illegible]	[illegible]	[illegible]	[illegible]	[illegible]	[illegible]	[illegible]	[illegible]	[illegible]	[illegible]	[illegible]	[illegible]	[illegible]	[illegible]	[illegible]	[illegible]	[illegible]	[illegible]	[illegible]	[illegible]	[illegible]	[illegible]	[illegible]	[illegible]	[illegible]	[illegible]	[illegible]	[illegible]
Ulster:																																
Antrim	[illegible]	[illegible]	[illegible]	[illegible]	[illegible]	[illegible]	[illegible]	[illegible]	[illegible]	[illegible]	[illegible]	[illegible]	[illegible]	[illegible]	[illegible]	[illegible]	[illegible]	[illegible]	[illegible]	[illegible]	[illegible]	[illegible]	[illegible]	[illegible]	[illegible]	[illegible]	[illegible]	[illegible]	[illegible]	[illegible]	[illegible]	[illegible]
Armagh	[illegible]	[illegible]	[illegible]	[illegible]	[illegible]	[illegible]	[illegible]	[illegible]	[illegible]	[illegible]	[illegible]	[illegible]	[illegible]	[illegible]	[illegible]	[illegible]	[illegible]	[illegible]	[illegible]	[illegible]	[illegible]	[illegible]	[illegible]	[illegible]	[illegible]	[illegible]	[illegible]	[illegible]	[illegible]	[illegible]	[illegible]	[illegible]
Belfast, Town of	[illegible]	[illegible]	[illegible]	[illegible]	[illegible]	[illegible]	[illegible]	[illegible]	[illegible]	[illegible]	[illegible]	[illegible]	[illegible]	[illegible]	[illegible]	[illegible]	[illegible]	[illegible]	[illegible]	[illegible]	[illegible]	[illegible]	[illegible]	[illegible]	[illegible]	[illegible]	[illegible]	[illegible]	[illegible]	[illegible]	[illegible]	[illegible]
Carrickfergus, Town of	[illegible]	[illegible]	[illegible]	[illegible]	[illegible]	[illegible]	[illegible]	[illegible]	[illegible]	[illegible]	[illegible]	[illegible]	[illegible]	[illegible]	[illegible]	[illegible]	[illegible]	[illegible]	[illegible]	[illegible]	[illegible]	[illegible]	[illegible]	[illegible]	[illegible]	[illegible]	[illegible]	[illegible]	[illegible]	[illegible]	[illegible]	[illegible]
Cavan	[illegible]	[illegible]	[illegible]	[illegible]	[illegible]	[illegible]	[illegible]	[illegible]	[illegible]	[illegible]	[illegible]	[illegible]	[illegible]	[illegible]	[illegible]	[illegible]	[illegible]	[illegible]	[illegible]	[illegible]	[illegible]	[illegible]	[illegible]	[illegible]	[illegible]	[illegible]	[illegible]	[illegible]	[illegible]	[illegible]	[illegible]	[illegible]
Donegal	[illegible]	[illegible]	[illegible]	[illegible]	[illegible]	[illegible]	[illegible]	[illegible]	[illegible]	[illegible]	[illegible]	[illegible]	[illegible]	[illegible]	[illegible]	[illegible]	[illegible]	[illegible]	[illegible]	[illegible]	[illegible]	[illegible]	[illegible]	[illegible]	[illegible]	[illegible]	[illegible]	[illegible]	[illegible]	[illegible]	[illegible]	[illegible]
Down	[illegible]	[illegible]	[illegible]	[illegible]	[illegible]	[illegible]	[illegible]	[illegible]	[illegible]	[illegible]	[illegible]	[illegible]	[illegible]	[illegible]	[illegible]	[illegible]	[illegible]	[illegible]	[illegible]	[illegible]	[illegible]	[illegible]	[illegible]	[illegible]	[illegible]	[illegible]	[illegible]	[illegible]	[illegible]	[illegible]	[illegible]	[illegible]
Fermanagh	[illegible]	[illegible]	[illegible]	[illegible]	[illegible]	[illegible]	[illegible]	[illegible]	[illegible]	[illegible]	[illegible]	[illegible]	[illegible]	[illegible]	[illegible]	[illegible]	[illegible]	[illegible]	[illegible]	[illegible]	[illegible]	[illegible]	[illegible]	[illegible]	[illegible]	[illegible]	[illegible]	[illegible]	[illegible]	[illegible]	[illegible]	[illegible]
Londonderry	[illegible]	[illegible]	[illegible]	[illegible]	[illegible]	[illegible]	[illegible]	[illegible]	[illegible]	[illegible]	[illegible]	[illegible]	[illegible]	[illegible]	[illegible]	[illegible]	[illegible]	[illegible]	[illegible]	[illegible]	[illegible]	[illegible]	[illegible]	[illegible]	[illegible]	[illegible]	[illegible]	[illegible]	[illegible]	[illegible]	[illegible]	[illegible]
Monaghan	[illegible]	[illegible]	[illegible]	[illegible]	[illegible]	[illegible]	[illegible]	[illegible]	[illegible]	[illegible]	[illegible]	[illegible]	[illegible]	[illegible]	[illegible]	[illegible]	[illegible]	[illegible]	[illegible]	[illegible]	[illegible]	[illegible]	[illegible]	[illegible]	[illegible]	[illegible]	[illegible]	[illegible]	[illegible]	[illegible]	[illegible]	[illegible]
Tyrone	[illegible]	[illegible]	[illegible]	[illegible]	[illegible]	[illegible]	[illegible]	[illegible]	[illegible]	[illegible]	[illegible]	[illegible]	[illegible]	[illegible]	[illegible]	[illegible]	[illegible]	[illegible]	[illegible]	[illegible]	[illegible]	[illegible]	[illegible]	[illegible]	[illegible]	[illegible]	[illegible]	[illegible]	[illegible]	[illegible]	[illegible]	[illegible]
Total of Province	[illegible]	[illegible]	[illegible]	[illegible]	[illegible]	[illegible]	[illegible]	[illegible]	[illegible]	[illegible]	[illegible]	[illegible]	[illegible]	[illegible]	[illegible]	[illegible]	[illegible]	[illegible]	[illegible]	[illegible]	[illegible]	[illegible]	[illegible]	[illegible]	[illegible]	[illegible]	[illegible]	[illegible]	[illegible]	[illegible]	[illegible]	[illegible]
Connaught:																																
Galway, E. R.	[illegible]	[illegible]	[illegible]	[illegible]	[illegible]	[illegible]	[illegible]	[illegible]	[illegible]	[illegible]	[illegible]	[illegible]	[illegible]	[illegible]	[illegible]	[illegible]	[illegible]	[illegible]	[illegible]	[illegible]	[illegible]	[illegible]	[illegible]	[illegible]	[illegible]	[illegible]	[illegible]	[illegible]	[illegible]	[illegible]	[illegible]	[illegible]
Galway, W. R.	[illegible]	[illegible]	[illegible]	[illegible]	[illegible]	[illegible]	[illegible]	[illegible]	[illegible]	[illegible]	[illegible]	[illegible]	[illegible]	[illegible]	[illegible]	[illegible]	[illegible]	[illegible]	[illegible]	[illegible]	[illegible]	[illegible]	[illegible]	[illegible]	[illegible]	[illegible]	[illegible]	[illegible]	[illegible]	[illegible]	[illegible]	[illegible]
Galway, Town of	[illegible]	[illegible]	[illegible]	[illegible]	[illegible]	[illegible]	[illegible]	[illegible]	[illegible]	[illegible]	[illegible]	[illegible]	[illegible]	[illegible]	[illegible]	[illegible]	[illegible]	[illegible]	[illegible]	[illegible]	[illegible]	[illegible]	[illegible]	[illegible]	[illegible]	[illegible]	[illegible]	[illegible]	[illegible]	[illegible]	[illegible]	[illegible]
Leitrim	[illegible]	[illegible]	[illegible]	[illegible]	[illegible]	[illegible]	[illegible]	[illegible]	[illegible]	[illegible]	[illegible]	[illegible]	[illegible]	[illegible]	[illegible]	[illegible]	[illegible]	[illegible]	[illegible]	[illegible]	[illegible]	[illegible]	[illegible]	[illegible]	[illegible]	[illegible]	[illegible]	[illegible]	[illegible]	[illegible]	[illegible]	[illegible]
Mayo	[illegible]	[illegible]	[illegible]	[illegible]	[illegible]	[illegible]	[illegible]	[illegible]	[illegible]	[illegible]	[illegible]	[illegible]	[illegible]	[illegible]	[illegible]	[illegible]	[illegible]	[illegible]	[illegible]	[illegible]	[illegible]	[illegible]	[illegible]	[illegible]	[illegible]	[illegible]	[illegible]	[illegible]	[illegible]	[illegible]	[illegible]	[illegible]
Roscommon	[illegible]	[illegible]	[illegible]	[illegible]	[illegible]	[illegible]	[illegible]	[illegible]	[illegible]	[illegible]	[illegible]	[illegible]	[illegible]	[illegible]	[illegible]	[illegible]	[illegible]	[illegible]	[illegible]	[illegible]	[illegible]	[illegible]	[illegible]	[illegible]	[illegible]	[illegible]	[illegible]	[illegible]	[illegible]	[illegible]	[illegible]	[illegible]
Sligo	[illegible]	[illegible]	[illegible]	[illegible]	[illegible]	[illegible]	[illegible]	[illegible]	[illegible]	[illegible]	[illegible]	[illegible]	[illegible]	[illegible]	[illegible]	[illegible]	[illegible]	[illegible]	[illegible]	[illegible]	[illegible]	[illegible]	[illegible]	[illegible]	[illegible]	[illegible]	[illegible]	[illegible]	[illegible]	[illegible]	[illegible]	[illegible]
Total of Province	[illegible]	[illegible]	[illegible]	[illegible]	[illegible]	[illegible]	[illegible]	[illegible]	[illegible]	[illegible]	[illegible]	[illegible]	[illegible]	[illegible]	[illegible]	[illegible]	[illegible]	[illegible]	[illegible]	[illegible]	[illegible]	[illegible]	[illegible]	[illegible]	[illegible]	[illegible]	[illegible]	[illegible]	[illegible]	[illegible]	[illegible]	[illegible]
Total of Ireland	[illegible]	[illegible]	[illegible]	[illegible]	[illegible]	[illegible]	[illegible]	[illegible]	[illegible]	[illegible]	[illegible]	[illegible]	[illegible]	[illegible]	[illegible]	[illegible]	[illegible]	[illegible]	[illegible]	[illegible]	[illegible]	[illegible]	[illegible]	[illegible]	[illegible]	[illegible]	[illegible]	[illegible]	[illegible]	[illegible]	[illegible]	[illegible]

TABLE 16.—RETURN OF CLASS OF PERSONS PROCEEDED AGAINST in each Police District, on Indictment and Summarily in the Year ended 31st December, [illegible].

PROVINCE, COUNTY, RIDING OF COUNTY, CITY OR TOWN.	I.—Class of Persons Proceeded Against on Indictment. Known Thieves		Prostitutes	Vagrants, Tramps, and others without visible means of subsistence		Suspicious Characters		[illegible]		Persons of good Character		Character unknown		Total		
	M.	W.	W.	M.	W.	M.	W.	M.	W.	M.	W.	M.	W.	M.	W.	M. & W.
LEINSTER.																
Carlow,	[illegible]	[illegible]	[illegible]	[illegible]	[illegible]	[illegible]	[illegible]	[illegible]	[illegible]	[illegible]	[illegible]	[illegible]	[illegible]	[illegible]	[illegible]	[illegible]
Drogheda Town,	[illegible]	[illegible]	[illegible]	[illegible]	[illegible]	[illegible]	[illegible]	[illegible]	[illegible]	[illegible]	[illegible]	[illegible]	[illegible]	[illegible]	[illegible]	[illegible]
Dublin County, part of,	[illegible]	[illegible]	[illegible]	[illegible]	[illegible]	[illegible]	[illegible]	[illegible]	[illegible]	[illegible]	[illegible]	[illegible]	[illegible]	[illegible]	[illegible]	[illegible]
Dublin City (and part of County) Metropolitan Police District, Divisions—																
A,	[illegible]	[illegible]	[illegible]	[illegible]	[illegible]	[illegible]	[illegible]	[illegible]	[illegible]	[illegible]	[illegible]	[illegible]	[illegible]	[illegible]	[illegible]	[illegible]
B,	[illegible]	[illegible]	[illegible]	[illegible]	[illegible]	[illegible]	[illegible]	[illegible]	[illegible]	[illegible]	[illegible]	[illegible]	[illegible]	[illegible]	[illegible]	[illegible]
C,	[illegible]	[illegible]	[illegible]	[illegible]	[illegible]	[illegible]	[illegible]	[illegible]	[illegible]	[illegible]	[illegible]	[illegible]	[illegible]	[illegible]	[illegible]	[illegible]
D,	[illegible]	[illegible]	[illegible]	[illegible]	[illegible]	[illegible]	[illegible]	[illegible]	[illegible]	[illegible]	[illegible]	[illegible]	[illegible]	[illegible]	[illegible]	[illegible]
E,	[illegible]	[illegible]	[illegible]	[illegible]	[illegible]	[illegible]	[illegible]	[illegible]	[illegible]	[illegible]	[illegible]	[illegible]	[illegible]	[illegible]	[illegible]	[illegible]
F,	[illegible]	[illegible]	[illegible]	[illegible]	[illegible]	[illegible]	[illegible]	[illegible]	[illegible]	[illegible]	[illegible]	[illegible]	[illegible]	[illegible]	[illegible]	[illegible]
Total of Metropolitan Police District,	[illegible]	[illegible]	[illegible]	[illegible]	[illegible]	[illegible]	[illegible]	[illegible]	[illegible]	[illegible]	[illegible]	[illegible]	[illegible]	[illegible]	[illegible]	[illegible]
Kildare,	[illegible]	[illegible]	[illegible]	[illegible]	[illegible]	[illegible]	[illegible]	[illegible]	[illegible]	[illegible]	[illegible]	[illegible]	[illegible]	[illegible]	[illegible]	[illegible]
Kilkenny,	[illegible]	[illegible]	[illegible]	[illegible]	[illegible]	[illegible]	[illegible]	[illegible]	[illegible]	[illegible]	[illegible]	[illegible]	[illegible]	[illegible]	[illegible]	[illegible]
King's County,	[illegible]	[illegible]	[illegible]	[illegible]	[illegible]	[illegible]	[illegible]	[illegible]	[illegible]	[illegible]	[illegible]	[illegible]	[illegible]	[illegible]	[illegible]	[illegible]
Longford,	[illegible]	[illegible]	[illegible]	[illegible]	[illegible]	[illegible]	[illegible]	[illegible]	[illegible]	[illegible]	[illegible]	[illegible]	[illegible]	[illegible]	[illegible]	[illegible]
Louth,	[illegible]	[illegible]	[illegible]	[illegible]	[illegible]	[illegible]	[illegible]	[illegible]	[illegible]	[illegible]	[illegible]	[illegible]	[illegible]	[illegible]	[illegible]	[illegible]
Meath,	[illegible]	[illegible]	[illegible]	[illegible]	[illegible]	[illegible]	[illegible]	[illegible]	[illegible]	[illegible]	[illegible]	[illegible]	[illegible]	[illegible]	[illegible]	[illegible]
Queen's County,	[illegible]	[illegible]	[illegible]	[illegible]	[illegible]	[illegible]	[illegible]	[illegible]	[illegible]	[illegible]	[illegible]	[illegible]	[illegible]	[illegible]	[illegible]	[illegible]
Westmeath,	[illegible]	[illegible]	[illegible]	[illegible]	[illegible]	[illegible]	[illegible]	[illegible]	[illegible]	[illegible]	[illegible]	[illegible]	[illegible]	[illegible]	[illegible]	[illegible]
Wexford,	[illegible]	[illegible]	[illegible]	[illegible]	[illegible]	[illegible]	[illegible]	[illegible]	[illegible]	[illegible]	[illegible]	[illegible]	[illegible]	[illegible]	[illegible]	[illegible]
Wicklow,	[illegible]	[illegible]	[illegible]	[illegible]	[illegible]	[illegible]	[illegible]	[illegible]	[illegible]	[illegible]	[illegible]	[illegible]	[illegible]	[illegible]	[illegible]	[illegible]
Total of Province,	[illegible]	[illegible]	[illegible]	[illegible]	[illegible]	[illegible]	[illegible]	[illegible]	[illegible]	[illegible]	[illegible]	[illegible]	[illegible]	[illegible]	[illegible]	[illegible]
MUNSTER:																
Clare,	[illegible]	[illegible]	[illegible]	[illegible]	[illegible]	[illegible]	[illegible]	[illegible]	[illegible]	[illegible]	[illegible]	[illegible]	[illegible]	[illegible]	[illegible]	[illegible]
Cork, East Riding,	[illegible]	[illegible]	[illegible]	[illegible]	[illegible]	[illegible]	[illegible]	[illegible]	[illegible]	[illegible]	[illegible]	[illegible]	[illegible]	[illegible]	[illegible]	[illegible]
Cork, West Riding,	[illegible]	[illegible]	[illegible]	[illegible]	[illegible]	[illegible]	[illegible]	[illegible]	[illegible]	[illegible]	[illegible]	[illegible]	[illegible]	[illegible]	[illegible]	[illegible]

PROVINCE, COUNTY, RIDING OF COUNTY, CITY OR TOWN.	II.—Class of Persons Proceeded Against Summarily. Known Thieves		Prostitutes	Vagrants, Tramps, and others without visible means of subsistence		Suspicious Characters		[illegible]		Persons of good Character		Character unknown		Total		
	M.	W.	W.	M.	W.	M.	W.	M.	W.	M.	W.	M.	W.	M.	W.	M. & W.
LEINSTER.																
Carlow,	[illegible]	[illegible]	[illegible]	[illegible]	[illegible]	[illegible]	[illegible]	[illegible]	[illegible]	[illegible]	[illegible]	[illegible]	[illegible]	[illegible]	[illegible]	[illegible]
Drogheda Town,	[illegible]	[illegible]	[illegible]	[illegible]	[illegible]	[illegible]	[illegible]	[illegible]	[illegible]	[illegible]	[illegible]	[illegible]	[illegible]	[illegible]	[illegible]	[illegible]
Dublin County, part of,	[illegible]	[illegible]	[illegible]	[illegible]	[illegible]	[illegible]	[illegible]	[illegible]	[illegible]	[illegible]	[illegible]	[illegible]	[illegible]	[illegible]	[illegible]	[illegible]
Dublin City (and part of County) Metropolitan Police District, Divisions—																
A,	[illegible]	[illegible]	[illegible]	[illegible]	[illegible]	[illegible]	[illegible]	[illegible]	[illegible]	[illegible]	[illegible]	[illegible]	[illegible]	[illegible]	[illegible]	[illegible]
B,	[illegible]	[illegible]	[illegible]	[illegible]	[illegible]	[illegible]	[illegible]	[illegible]	[illegible]	[illegible]	[illegible]	[illegible]	[illegible]	[illegible]	[illegible]	[illegible]
C,	[illegible]	[illegible]	[illegible]	[illegible]	[illegible]	[illegible]	[illegible]	[illegible]	[illegible]	[illegible]	[illegible]	[illegible]	[illegible]	[illegible]	[illegible]	[illegible]
D,	[illegible]	[illegible]	[illegible]	[illegible]	[illegible]	[illegible]	[illegible]	[illegible]	[illegible]	[illegible]	[illegible]	[illegible]	[illegible]	[illegible]	[illegible]	[illegible]
E,	[illegible]	[illegible]	[illegible]	[illegible]	[illegible]	[illegible]	[illegible]	[illegible]	[illegible]	[illegible]	[illegible]	[illegible]	[illegible]	[illegible]	[illegible]	[illegible]
F,	[illegible]	[illegible]	[illegible]	[illegible]	[illegible]	[illegible]	[illegible]	[illegible]	[illegible]	[illegible]	[illegible]	[illegible]	[illegible]	[illegible]	[illegible]	[illegible]
Total of Metropolitan Police District,	[illegible]	[illegible]	[illegible]	[illegible]	[illegible]	[illegible]	[illegible]	[illegible]	[illegible]	[illegible]	[illegible]	[illegible]	[illegible]	[illegible]	[illegible]	[illegible]
Kildare,	[illegible]	[illegible]	[illegible]	[illegible]	[illegible]	[illegible]	[illegible]	[illegible]	[illegible]	[illegible]	[illegible]	[illegible]	[illegible]	[illegible]	[illegible]	[illegible]
Kilkenny,	[illegible]	[illegible]	[illegible]	[illegible]	[illegible]	[illegible]	[illegible]	[illegible]	[illegible]	[illegible]	[illegible]	[illegible]	[illegible]	[illegible]	[illegible]	[illegible]
King's County,	[illegible]	[illegible]	[illegible]	[illegible]	[illegible]	[illegible]	[illegible]	[illegible]	[illegible]	[illegible]	[illegible]	[illegible]	[illegible]	[illegible]	[illegible]	[illegible]
Longford,	[illegible]	[illegible]	[illegible]	[illegible]	[illegible]	[illegible]	[illegible]	[illegible]	[illegible]	[illegible]	[illegible]	[illegible]	[illegible]	[illegible]	[illegible]	[illegible]
Louth,	[illegible]	[illegible]	[illegible]	[illegible]	[illegible]	[illegible]	[illegible]	[illegible]	[illegible]	[illegible]	[illegible]	[illegible]	[illegible]	[illegible]	[illegible]	[illegible]
Meath,	[illegible]	[illegible]	[illegible]	[illegible]	[illegible]	[illegible]	[illegible]	[illegible]	[illegible]	[illegible]	[illegible]	[illegible]	[illegible]	[illegible]	[illegible]	[illegible]
Queen's County,	[illegible]	[illegible]	[illegible]	[illegible]	[illegible]	[illegible]	[illegible]	[illegible]	[illegible]	[illegible]	[illegible]	[illegible]	[illegible]	[illegible]	[illegible]	[illegible]
Westmeath,	[illegible]	[illegible]	[illegible]	[illegible]	[illegible]	[illegible]	[illegible]	[illegible]	[illegible]	[illegible]	[illegible]	[illegible]	[illegible]	[illegible]	[illegible]	[illegible]
Wexford,	[illegible]	[illegible]	[illegible]	[illegible]	[illegible]	[illegible]	[illegible]	[illegible]	[illegible]	[illegible]	[illegible]	[illegible]	[illegible]	[illegible]	[illegible]	[illegible]
Wicklow,	[illegible]	[illegible]	[illegible]	[illegible]	[illegible]	[illegible]	[illegible]	[illegible]	[illegible]	[illegible]	[illegible]	[illegible]	[illegible]	[illegible]	[illegible]	[illegible]
Total of Province,	[illegible]	[illegible]	[illegible]	[illegible]	[illegible]	[illegible]	[illegible]	[illegible]	[illegible]	[illegible]	[illegible]	[illegible]	[illegible]	[illegible]	[illegible]	[illegible]
MUNSTER:																
Clare,	[illegible]	[illegible]	[illegible]	[illegible]	[illegible]	[illegible]	[illegible]	[illegible]	[illegible]	[illegible]	[illegible]	[illegible]	[illegible]	[illegible]	[illegible]	[illegible]
Cork, East Riding,	[illegible]	[illegible]	[illegible]	[illegible]	[illegible]	[illegible]	[illegible]	[illegible]	[illegible]	[illegible]	[illegible]	[illegible]	[illegible]	[illegible]	[illegible]	[illegible]
Cork, West Riding,	[illegible]	[illegible]	[illegible]	[illegible]	[illegible]	[illegible]	[illegible]	[illegible]	[illegible]	[illegible]	[illegible]	[illegible]	[illegible]	[illegible]	[illegible]	[illegible]

Cork City,	[illegible]
Kerry,	[illegible]
Limerick,	[illegible]
Limerick City,	[illegible]
Tipperary, North Riding,	[illegible]
Tipperary, South Riding,	[illegible]
Waterford,	[illegible]
Waterford City,	[illegible]
Total of Munster,	[illegible]
Ulster.	
Antrim,	[illegible]
Armagh,	[illegible]
Belfast, Town of,	[illegible]
Carrickfergus, Town of,	[illegible]
Cavan,	[illegible]
Donegal,	[illegible]
Down,	[illegible]
Fermanagh,	[illegible]
Londonderry,	[illegible]
Monaghan,	[illegible]
Tyrone,	[illegible]
Total of Ulster,	[illegible]
Connaught.	
Galway, East Riding,	[illegible]
Galway, West Riding,	[illegible]
Galway, Town of,	[illegible]
Leitrim,	[illegible]
Mayo,	[illegible]
Roscommon,	[illegible]
Sligo,	[illegible]
Total of Connaught,	[illegible]
Total of Ireland,	[illegible]

* To be entered as an Habitual Drunkard in this column a person must have been convicted of Drunkenness at least three times within the twelve months up to and ending with the date of the Proceeding on Indictment which led to his being [illegible] to the [illegible].

† To be entered as an Habitual Drunkard in this column a person must have been convicted of Drunkenness at least three times within twelve months up to and ending with the date of the Summary Proceeding which led to his being [illegible] [illegible] [illegible] with Summary Proceeding [illegible] [illegible] [illegible] [illegible] to be [illegible] as one of the three [illegible].

TABLE 11.—RETURN of Persons Convicted three times and upwards, of being Drunk or Drunk and Disorderly, during the year ended 31st December, 188[illegible] (as far as known to the Police).

Province, County, County of City or of Town, and Police District.	Number Convicted 3 times and less than 7	Number Convicted 7 times and less than 10	Number Convicted 10 times and upwards	Total
Leinster:				
Carlow,	[illegible]	[illegible]	[illegible]	[illegible]
Drogheda, Town of,	[illegible]	[illegible]	[illegible]	[illegible]
Dublin County (part of),	[illegible]	[illegible]	[illegible]	[illegible]
Dublin City (and part of County) Metropolitan Police District.—Divisions:				
A,	[illegible]	[illegible]	[illegible]	[illegible]
B,	[illegible]	[illegible]	[illegible]	[illegible]
C,	[illegible]	[illegible]	[illegible]	[illegible]
D,	[illegible]	[illegible]	[illegible]	[illegible]
E,	[illegible]	[illegible]	[illegible]	[illegible]
F,	[illegible]	[illegible]	[illegible]	[illegible]
Total of Metropolitan,	[illegible]	[illegible]	[illegible]	[illegible]
Kildare,	[illegible]	[illegible]	[illegible]	[illegible]
Kilkenny,	[illegible]	[illegible]	[illegible]	[illegible]
King's County,	[illegible]	[illegible]	[illegible]	[illegible]
Longford,	[illegible]	[illegible]	[illegible]	[illegible]
Louth,	[illegible]	[illegible]	[illegible]	[illegible]
Meath,	[illegible]	[illegible]	[illegible]	[illegible]
Queen's County,	[illegible]	[illegible]	[illegible]	[illegible]
Westmeath,	[illegible]	[illegible]	[illegible]	[illegible]
Wexford,	[illegible]	[illegible]	[illegible]	[illegible]
Wicklow,	[illegible]	[illegible]	[illegible]	[illegible]
Total of Province,	[illegible]	[illegible]	[illegible]	[illegible]
Munster:				
Clare,	[illegible]	[illegible]	[illegible]	[illegible]
Cork, East Riding,	[illegible]	[illegible]	[illegible]	[illegible]
Cork, West Riding,	[illegible]	[illegible]	[illegible]	[illegible]
Cork City,	[illegible]	[illegible]	[illegible]	[illegible]
Kerry,	[illegible]	[illegible]	[illegible]	[illegible]

Province, County, County of City or of Town, and Police District.	Number Convicted 3 times and less than 7	Number Convicted 7 times and less than 10	Number Convicted 10 times and upwards	Total
Munster—continued.				
Limerick,	[illegible]	[illegible]	[illegible]	[illegible]
Limerick City,	[illegible]	[illegible]	[illegible]	[illegible]
Tipperary, North Riding,	[illegible]	[illegible]	[illegible]	[illegible]
Tipperary, South Riding,	[illegible]	[illegible]	[illegible]	[illegible]
Waterford,	[illegible]	[illegible]	[illegible]	[illegible]
Waterford City,	[illegible]	[illegible]	[illegible]	[illegible]
Total of Province,	[illegible]	[illegible]	[illegible]	[illegible]
Ulster:				
Antrim,	[illegible]	[illegible]	[illegible]	[illegible]
Armagh,	[illegible]	[illegible]	[illegible]	[illegible]
Belfast, Town of,	[illegible]	[illegible]	[illegible]	[illegible]
Carrickfergus, Town of,	[illegible]	[illegible]	[illegible]	[illegible]
Cavan,	[illegible]	[illegible]	[illegible]	[illegible]
Donegal,	[illegible]	[illegible]	[illegible]	[illegible]
Down,	[illegible]	[illegible]	[illegible]	[illegible]
Fermanagh,	[illegible]	[illegible]	[illegible]	[illegible]
Londonderry,	[illegible]	[illegible]	[illegible]	[illegible]
Monaghan,	[illegible]	[illegible]	[illegible]	[illegible]
Tyrone,	[illegible]	[illegible]	[illegible]	[illegible]
Total of Province,	[illegible]	[illegible]	[illegible]	[illegible]
Connaught:				
Galway, East Riding,	[illegible]	[illegible]	[illegible]	[illegible]
Galway, West Riding,	[illegible]	[illegible]	[illegible]	[illegible]
Galway Town,	[illegible]	[illegible]	[illegible]	[illegible]
Leitrim,	[illegible]	[illegible]	[illegible]	[illegible]
Mayo,	[illegible]	[illegible]	[illegible]	[illegible]
Roscommon,	[illegible]	[illegible]	[illegible]	[illegible]
Sligo,	[illegible]	[illegible]	[illegible]	[illegible]
Total of Province,	[illegible]	[illegible]	[illegible]	[illegible]
Total of Ireland,	[illegible]	[illegible]	[illegible]	[illegible]

TABLES SHOWING DISTRICTS PROCLAIMED.

TABLE [illegible].—RETURN showing the several DISTRICTS which were subject to PROCLAMATIONS IN COUNCIL under 4 WM. IV., CAP. [illegible], SEC. [illegible], on the 31st December, 188[illegible].

County.	Proclaimed District.	Date of Proclamation.
Clare,	The County,	[illegible] January, [illegible]
Cork, (a)	[illegible]	1 April, [illegible]
Galway,	[illegible]	1 October, [illegible]
Kerry,	[illegible]	[illegible] October, [illegible]
Leitrim,	[illegible]	[illegible] December, [illegible]
Limerick,	[illegible]	[illegible] December, [illegible]
Longford,	The County of Longford,	[illegible] February, [illegible]
Mayo,	The County,	[illegible] October, [illegible]
Roscommon, (b)	[illegible]	[illegible] February, [illegible]
Sligo,	The Baronies of Carbury, Tyreragh, Corran, and Leyney,	[illegible] January, [illegible]
	The Barony of [illegible],	[illegible] April, [illegible]
Tipperary, (c)	The County,	[illegible] July, [illegible]
Waterford,	The Baronies of [illegible] and [illegible], [illegible], [illegible], [illegible], [illegible], and Upperthird,	[illegible] February, [illegible]
Westmeath,	The County,	[illegible] December, [illegible]

(a) Portions of the County were proclaimed on [illegible] October, [illegible], and [illegible] March, [illegible].
(b) Ditto, ditto, [illegible] January, [illegible].
(c) Ditto, ditto, [illegible] February, [illegible].

THE PEACE PRESERVATION (IRELAND) ACT, 18[illegible], AND THE PEACE PRESERVATION (IRELAND) CONTINUANCE ACT, 18[illegible].

TABLE 1[illegible].—RETURN No. I, showing the several DISTRICTS which were under the operation of PROCLAMATIONS IN COUNCIL under the above Acts, prohibiting the CARRYING OR HAVING OF ARMS, &c., on the 31st December, 18[illegible].

County, &c.	Proclaimed District.	Date of Proclamation.
Armagh,	The Parishes of [illegible], [illegible], [illegible], [illegible], and [illegible],	[illegible] March, 18[illegible].
Belfast,	The Borough,	[illegible] July, 18[illegible].
Carlow,	The County,	27 December, 18[illegible].
Clare,	"	[illegible] April, "
Cork,	"	" "
Cork City,	The County of the City,	" "
Donegal,	The Baronies of [illegible], [illegible], and [illegible] East, and the Parishes of [illegible], [illegible] Lower, [illegible] or [illegible], and [illegible], in the Barony of [illegible] West,	" "
Drogheda,	The County of the Town,	27 December, "
Dublin,	The County,	" "
Dublin City,	The Metropolitan Police District, (a)	" "
Galway,	The County,	[illegible] April, "
Galway Town,	The County of the Town,	" "
Kerry,	The County,	" "
Kildare,	"	27 December, "
Kilkenny,	" (b)	[illegible] May, "
King's,	"	[illegible] June, "
Leitrim,	"	[illegible] April, "
Limerick,	"	" "
Limerick City,	The County of the City,	" "
Londonderry City,	The Borough,	[illegible] July, 18[illegible].
Longford,	The County,	[illegible] April, 18[illegible].
Mayo,	"	" "
Meath,	"	27 December, "
Monaghan,	The Baronies of [illegible] and [illegible], and Parish of [illegible],	[illegible] August, 18[illegible].
Queen's,	The County,	[illegible] April, 18[illegible].
Roscommon,	"	" "
Sligo,	"	" "
Tipperary,	" (c)	[illegible] December, "
Westmeath,	"	" "
Waterford City,	The County of the City,	" "
Waterford,	The County,	[illegible] April, "
Wexford,	"	27 December, "

(a) This District was proclaimed against the carrying of Arms, &c., on the [illegible] May, 18[illegible].
(b) A portion of the County was proclaimed on the [illegible] of April, 18[illegible].
(c) The North Riding was proclaimed against the carrying of Arms, &c., on the [illegible] April, 18[illegible].

TABLE 1[illegible].—RETURN No. II, showing the several DISTRICTS which were under the operation of PROCLAMATIONS IN COUNCIL under the above Acts, prohibiting the CARRYING OF ARMS, &c., on the 31st December, 18[illegible].

County, &c.	Proclaimed District.	Date of Proclamation.
Armagh,	That part of the Parish of Newry in which is situate that portion of the town of Newry which is in the County Armagh, and also that part of the Barony of Lower Orior which is contiguous to the aforesaid part of the Parish of Newry.	[illegible] December, 18[illegible].
Cavan,	The County,	[illegible] April, 18[illegible].
Down,	The Barony or Lordship of Newry,	[illegible] November, 18[illegible].
Fermanagh,	The County,	[illegible] December, "
Monaghan,	The County, (a)	[illegible] April, 18[illegible].
Tyrone,	The Baronies of Dungannon Upper and Middle,	[illegible] May, "
	The Baronies of Omagh East, Omagh West, and Clogher,	[illegible] December, 18[illegible].

(a) The Baronies of Farney and Cremorne and the Parish of [illegible] were proclaimed for having or carrying Arms, &c., on [illegible] August, 18[illegible].

TABLE [illegible].—STATE PRISONS.—CLASSIFICATION of ORDINARY CRIMINALS Convicted during the year [illegible], reported by General Prisons Board

(a.) As to Frequency of Commitment.	Number of First Committed Ordinary Criminals (M.)	(W.)	Number of Commitments of Ordinary Criminals other than First Commitments (M.)	(W.)	Second (M.)	(W.)	Third (M.)	(W.)	Fourth (M.)	(W.)	Fifth (M.)	(W.)	Sixth (M.)	(W.)	Seventh (M.)	(W.)	Eighth (M.)	(W.)	Ninth (M.)	(W.)	Tenth (M.)	(W.)	Eleventh (M.)	(W.)	Twelfth and upwards (M.)	(W.)	Number of Persons [illegible] (M.)	(W.)
Number in all Larger Local Prisons.	[illegible]	[illegible]	[illegible]	[illegible]	[illegible]	[illegible]	[illegible]	[illegible]	[illegible]	[illegible]	[illegible]	[illegible]	[illegible]	[illegible]	[illegible]	[illegible]	[illegible]	[illegible]	[illegible]	[illegible]	[illegible]	[illegible]	[illegible]	[illegible]	[illegible]	[illegible]	[illegible]	[illegible]

(b.) As to Age and Sex.	Under 16 Years (M.)	(W.)	[illegible] (M.)	(W.)	[illegible] (M.)	(W.)	[illegible] (M.)	(W.)	[illegible] (M.)	(W.)	[illegible] (M.)	(W.)	[illegible] (M.)	(W.)	[illegible] (M.)	(W.)	Age not ascertained (M.)	(W.)
Number in all Larger Local Prisons.	[illegible]	[illegible]	[illegible]	[illegible]	[illegible]	[illegible]	[illegible]	[illegible]	[illegible]	[illegible]	[illegible]	[illegible]	[illegible]	[illegible]	[illegible]	[illegible]	[illegible]	[illegible]

(c.) As to Birthplace.	[illegible]	[illegible]	[illegible]	[illegible]	[illegible]	[illegible]	[illegible]
Number in all Larger Local Prisons.	[illegible]	[illegible]	[illegible]	[illegible]	[illegible]	[illegible]	[illegible]

(d.) As to Degree of Instruction.	Neither Read nor Write (M.)	(W.)	Read, or Read and Write imperfectly (M.)	(W.)	Read and Write well (M.)	(W.)	Superior Instruction (M.)	(W.)	Instruction not ascertained (M.)	(W.)
Number in all Larger Local Prisons.	[illegible]	[illegible]	[illegible]	[illegible]	[illegible]	[illegible]	[illegible]	[illegible]	[illegible]	[illegible]

(e.) As to Class of Occupation.	No Occupation (M.)	(W.)	Domestic Servants (M.)	(W.)	Labourers, [illegible] (M.)	(W.)	Factory Workers (M.)	(W.)	Mechanics and Skilled Workers (M.)	(W.)	[illegible] (M.)	(W.)	[illegible] (M.)	(W.)	Shopkeepers and Dealers (M.)	(W.)	Professional Employments (M.)	(W.)	Soldiers, Sailors, [illegible] (M.)	Prostitutes (W.)	Occupation not [illegible] (M.)	(W.)
Number in all Larger Local Prisons	[illegible]	[illegible]	[illegible]	[illegible]	[illegible]	[illegible]	[illegible]	[illegible]	[illegible]	[illegible]	[illegible]	[illegible]	[illegible]	[illegible]	[illegible]	[illegible]	[illegible]	[illegible]	[illegible]	[illegible]	[illegible]	[illegible]

TABLE [illegible].—CRIMINAL PROCEEDINGS AT ASSIZES, COMMISSION, AND QUARTER SESSIONS—[illegible] RESULT of the PROCEEDINGS—[illegible]

EACH OFFENCE and CLASS of OFFENCES the NUMBER of PERSONS for TRIAL in the Year 1866, and [illegible] by Clerks of the Crown and Clerks of the Peace.

Insane, to be detained: Found Insane on Arraignment		Acquitted on ground of Insanity		Convicted: Death		Penal Servitude: Life		Above 15 Years		15 Years and above 10 Years		10 Years and above 6 Years		[illegible] Years		OFFENCES charged on Commitment or Indictment, and of which Persons tried were Convicted or Acquitted.
M.	W.	M.	W.	M.	W.	M.	W.	M.	W.	M.	W.	M.	W.	M.	W.			
																		No. 1.—Offences against the Person.
[illegible]	[illegible]	[illegible]	[illegible]	[illegible]	[illegible]	[illegible]	[illegible]	[illegible]	[illegible]	[illegible]	[illegible]	[illegible]	[illegible]	[illegible]	[illegible]	[illegible]	[illegible]	Murder of Infants aged one year and under
[illegible]	[illegible]	[illegible]	[illegible]	[illegible]	[illegible]	[illegible]	[illegible]	[illegible]	[illegible]	[illegible]	[illegible]	[illegible]	[illegible]	[illegible]	[illegible]	[illegible]	[illegible]	Other Murders
[illegible]	[illegible]	[illegible]	[illegible]	[illegible]	[illegible]	[illegible]	[illegible]	[illegible]	[illegible]	[illegible]	[illegible]	[illegible]	[illegible]	[illegible]	[illegible]	[illegible]	[illegible]	Attempts to murder.
[illegible]	[illegible]	[illegible]	[illegible]	[illegible]	[illegible]	[illegible]	[illegible]	[illegible]	[illegible]	[illegible]	[illegible]	[illegible]	[illegible]	[illegible]	[illegible]	[illegible]	[illegible]	[illegible] to Murder
[illegible]	[illegible]	[illegible]	[illegible]	[illegible]	[illegible]	[illegible]	[illegible]	[illegible]	[illegible]	[illegible]	[illegible]	[illegible]	[illegible]	[illegible]	[illegible]	[illegible]	[illegible]	Shooting at, Wounding, Stabbing, &c., to do bodily harm
[illegible]	[illegible]	[illegible]	[illegible]	[illegible]	[illegible]	[illegible]	[illegible]	[illegible]	[illegible]	[illegible]	[illegible]	[illegible]	[illegible]	[illegible]	[illegible]	[illegible]	[illegible]	Manslaughter.
[illegible]	[illegible]	[illegible]	[illegible]	[illegible]	[illegible]	[illegible]	[illegible]	[illegible]	[illegible]	[illegible]	[illegible]	[illegible]	[illegible]	[illegible]	[illegible]	[illegible]	[illegible]	Attempts to procure Miscarriage.
[illegible]	[illegible]	[illegible]	[illegible]	[illegible]	[illegible]	[illegible]	[illegible]	[illegible]	[illegible]	[illegible]	[illegible]	[illegible]	[illegible]	[illegible]	[illegible]	[illegible]	[illegible]	Concealing the Birth of Infants
[illegible]	[illegible]	[illegible]	[illegible]	[illegible]	[illegible]	[illegible]	[illegible]	[illegible]	[illegible]	[illegible]	[illegible]	[illegible]	[illegible]	[illegible]	[illegible]	[illegible]	[illegible]	Having Carnal Knowledge with Female under 10 years of age
[illegible]	[illegible]	[illegible]	[illegible]	[illegible]	[illegible]	[illegible]	[illegible]	[illegible]	[illegible]	[illegible]	[illegible]	[illegible]	[illegible]	[illegible]	[illegible]	[illegible]	[illegible]	Attempts to have same.
[illegible]	[illegible]	[illegible]	[illegible]	[illegible]	[illegible]	[illegible]	[illegible]	[illegible]	[illegible]	[illegible]	[illegible]	[illegible]	[illegible]	[illegible]	[illegible]	[illegible]	[illegible]	Sodomy, &c., attempts to Commit, and other unnatural Offences
[illegible]	[illegible]	[illegible]	[illegible]	[illegible]	[illegible]	[illegible]	[illegible]	[illegible]	[illegible]	[illegible]	[illegible]	[illegible]	[illegible]	[illegible]	[illegible]	[illegible]	[illegible]	Rape
[illegible]	[illegible]	[illegible]	[illegible]	[illegible]	[illegible]	[illegible]	[illegible]	[illegible]	[illegible]	[illegible]	[illegible]	[illegible]	[illegible]	[illegible]	[illegible]	[illegible]	[illegible]	—— Assaults, with intent to ravish and abuse.
[illegible]	[illegible]	[illegible]	[illegible]	[illegible]	[illegible]	[illegible]	[illegible]	[illegible]	[illegible]	[illegible]	[illegible]	[illegible]	[illegible]	[illegible]	[illegible]	[illegible]	[illegible]	Bigamy.
[illegible]	[illegible]	[illegible]	[illegible]	[illegible]	[illegible]	[illegible]	[illegible]	[illegible]	[illegible]	[illegible]	[illegible]	[illegible]	[illegible]	[illegible]	[illegible]	[illegible]	[illegible]	Child Stealing.
[illegible]	[illegible]	[illegible]	[illegible]	[illegible]	[illegible]	[illegible]	[illegible]	[illegible]	[illegible]	[illegible]	[illegible]	[illegible]	[illegible]	[illegible]	[illegible]	[illegible]	[illegible]	Offences by abandoning Children under two years of age
[illegible]	[illegible]	[illegible]	[illegible]	[illegible]	[illegible]	[illegible]	[illegible]	[illegible]	[illegible]	[illegible]	[illegible]	[illegible]	[illegible]	[illegible]	[illegible]	[illegible]	[illegible]	Endangering the Safety of Passengers on Railways.
[illegible]	[illegible]	[illegible]	[illegible]	[illegible]	[illegible]	[illegible]	[illegible]	[illegible]	[illegible]	[illegible]	[illegible]	[illegible]	[illegible]	[illegible]	[illegible]	[illegible]	[illegible]	Assaults and inflicting bodily harm.
[illegible]	[illegible]	[illegible]	[illegible]	[illegible]	[illegible]	[illegible]	[illegible]	[illegible]	[illegible]	[illegible]	[illegible]	[illegible]	[illegible]	[illegible]	[illegible]	[illegible]	[illegible]	Assaults, Common
[illegible]	[illegible]	[illegible]	[illegible]	[illegible]	[illegible]	[illegible]	[illegible]	[illegible]	[illegible]	[illegible]	[illegible]	[illegible]	[illegible]	[illegible]	[illegible]	[illegible]	[illegible]	Assaults on Peace Officers
[illegible]	[illegible]	[illegible]	[illegible]	[illegible]	[illegible]	[illegible]	[illegible]	[illegible]	[illegible]	[illegible]	[illegible]	[illegible]	[illegible]	[illegible]	[illegible]	[illegible]	[illegible]	Total of No. 1.
																		No. 2.—Offences against Property, with Violence.
[illegible]	[illegible]	[illegible]	[illegible]	[illegible]	[illegible]	[illegible]	[illegible]	[illegible]	[illegible]	[illegible]	[illegible]	[illegible]	[illegible]	[illegible]	[illegible]	[illegible]	[illegible]	Sacrilege
[illegible]	[illegible]	[illegible]	[illegible]	[illegible]	[illegible]	[illegible]	[illegible]	[illegible]	[illegible]	[illegible]	[illegible]	[illegible]	[illegible]	[illegible]	[illegible]	[illegible]	[illegible]	Burglary and Housebreaking
[illegible]	[illegible]	[illegible]	[illegible]	[illegible]	[illegible]	[illegible]	[illegible]	[illegible]	[illegible]	[illegible]	[illegible]	[illegible]	[illegible]	[illegible]	[illegible]	[illegible]	[illegible]	Breaking into Shops, Warehouses, &c.
[illegible]	[illegible]	[illegible]	[illegible]	[illegible]	[illegible]	[illegible]	[illegible]	[illegible]	[illegible]	[illegible]	[illegible]	[illegible]	[illegible]	[illegible]	[illegible]	[illegible]	[illegible]	Attempts to Break into Houses, Shops, Warehouses, &c.
[illegible]	[illegible]	[illegible]	[illegible]	[illegible]	[illegible]	[illegible]	[illegible]	[illegible]	[illegible]	[illegible]	[illegible]	[illegible]	[illegible]	[illegible]	[illegible]	[illegible]	[illegible]	Robbery.
[illegible]	[illegible]	[illegible]	[illegible]	[illegible]	[illegible]	[illegible]	[illegible]	[illegible]	[illegible]	[illegible]	[illegible]	[illegible]	[illegible]	[illegible]	[illegible]	[illegible]	[illegible]	Attempts to rob, and demanding Money by Menaces
[illegible]	[illegible]	[illegible]	[illegible]	[illegible]	[illegible]	[illegible]	[illegible]	[illegible]	[illegible]	[illegible]	[illegible]	[illegible]	[illegible]	[illegible]	[illegible]	[illegible]	[illegible]	Total of No. 2.
																		No. 3.—Offences against Property, without Violence.
[illegible]	[illegible]	[illegible]	[illegible]	[illegible]	[illegible]	[illegible]	[illegible]	[illegible]	[illegible]	[illegible]	[illegible]	[illegible]	[illegible]	[illegible]	[illegible]	[illegible]	[illegible]	Cattle Stealing
[illegible]	[illegible]	[illegible]	[illegible]	[illegible]	[illegible]	[illegible]	[illegible]	[illegible]	[illegible]	[illegible]	[illegible]	[illegible]	[illegible]	[illegible]	[illegible]	[illegible]	[illegible]	Horse Stealing.
[illegible]	[illegible]	[illegible]	[illegible]	[illegible]	[illegible]	[illegible]	[illegible]	[illegible]	[illegible]	[illegible]	[illegible]	[illegible]	[illegible]	[illegible]	[illegible]	[illegible]	[illegible]	Sheep Stealing
[illegible]	[illegible]	[illegible]	[illegible]	[illegible]	[illegible]	[illegible]	[illegible]	[illegible]	[illegible]	[illegible]	[illegible]	[illegible]	[illegible]	[illegible]	[illegible]	[illegible]	[illegible]	Larceny, to the value of £5, in Dwelling-houses.
[illegible]	[illegible]	[illegible]	[illegible]	[illegible]	[illegible]	[illegible]	[illegible]	[illegible]	[illegible]	[illegible]	[illegible]	[illegible]	[illegible]	[illegible]	[illegible]	[illegible]	[illegible]	Larceny from the Person
[illegible]	[illegible]	[illegible]	[illegible]	[illegible]	[illegible]	[illegible]	[illegible]	[illegible]	[illegible]	[illegible]	[illegible]	[illegible]	[illegible]	[illegible]	[illegible]	[illegible]	[illegible]	Larceny, by Servants
[illegible]	[illegible]	[illegible]	[illegible]	[illegible]	[illegible]	[illegible]	[illegible]	[illegible]	[illegible]	[illegible]	[illegible]	[illegible]	[illegible]	[illegible]	[illegible]	[illegible]	[illegible]	Larceny, Simple
[illegible]	[illegible]	[illegible]	[illegible]	[illegible]	[illegible]	[illegible]	[illegible]	[illegible]	[illegible]	[illegible]	[illegible]	[illegible]	[illegible]	[illegible]	[illegible]	[illegible]	[illegible]	Larceny on Rivers, Canals, Wharfs, &c.
[illegible]	[illegible]	[illegible]	[illegible]	[illegible]	[illegible]	[illegible]	[illegible]	[illegible]	[illegible]	[illegible]	[illegible]	[illegible]	[illegible]	[illegible]	[illegible]	[illegible]	[illegible]	Stealing Fixtures, Public property, &c.
[illegible]	[illegible]	[illegible]	[illegible]	[illegible]	[illegible]	[illegible]	[illegible]	[illegible]	[illegible]	[illegible]	[illegible]	[illegible]	[illegible]	[illegible]	[illegible]	[illegible]	[illegible]	Attempts to Steal
[illegible]	[illegible]	[illegible]	[illegible]	[illegible]	[illegible]	[illegible]	[illegible]	[illegible]	[illegible]	[illegible]	[illegible]	[illegible]	[illegible]	[illegible]	[illegible]	[illegible]	[illegible]	Embezzlement
[illegible]	[illegible]	[illegible]	[illegible]	[illegible]	[illegible]	[illegible]	[illegible]	[illegible]	[illegible]	[illegible]	[illegible]	[illegible]	[illegible]	[illegible]	[illegible]	[illegible]	[illegible]	Larceny by Servants in the Post Office
[illegible]	[illegible]	[illegible]	[illegible]	[illegible]	[illegible]	[illegible]	[illegible]	[illegible]	[illegible]	[illegible]	[illegible]	[illegible]	[illegible]	[illegible]	[illegible]	[illegible]	[illegible]	Receiving Stolen Goods
[illegible]	[illegible]	[illegible]	[illegible]	[illegible]	[illegible]	[illegible]	[illegible]	[illegible]	[illegible]	[illegible]	[illegible]	[illegible]	[illegible]	[illegible]	[illegible]	[illegible]	[illegible]	Fraudulently obtaining Goods by false pretences, and attempts to do.
[illegible]	[illegible]	[illegible]	[illegible]	[illegible]	[illegible]	[illegible]	[illegible]	[illegible]	[illegible]	[illegible]	[illegible]	[illegible]	[illegible]	[illegible]	[illegible]	[illegible]	[illegible]	Total of No. 3.
																		No. 4.—Malicious Offences against Property.
[illegible]	[illegible]	[illegible]	[illegible]	[illegible]	[illegible]	[illegible]	[illegible]	[illegible]	[illegible]	[illegible]	[illegible]	[illegible]	[illegible]	[illegible]	[illegible]	[illegible]	[illegible]	Arson and other Wilful Burning
[illegible]	[illegible]	[illegible]	[illegible]	[illegible]	[illegible]	[illegible]	[illegible]	[illegible]	[illegible]	[illegible]	[illegible]	[illegible]	[illegible]	[illegible]	[illegible]	[illegible]	[illegible]	Felonious Riot and demolishing Buildings, &c.
[illegible]	[illegible]	[illegible]	[illegible]	[illegible]	[illegible]	[illegible]	[illegible]	[illegible]	[illegible]	[illegible]	[illegible]	[illegible]	[illegible]	[illegible]	[illegible]	[illegible]	[illegible]	Destroying Goods in process of Manufacture.
[illegible]	[illegible]	[illegible]	[illegible]	[illegible]	[illegible]	[illegible]	[illegible]	[illegible]	[illegible]	[illegible]	[illegible]	[illegible]	[illegible]	[illegible]	[illegible]	[illegible]	[illegible]	Destroying Trees, Shrubs, &c., growing.
[illegible]	[illegible]	[illegible]	[illegible]	[illegible]	[illegible]	[illegible]	[illegible]	[illegible]	[illegible]	[illegible]	[illegible]	[illegible]	[illegible]	[illegible]	[illegible]	[illegible]	[illegible]	Killing and Maiming Cattle
[illegible]	[illegible]	[illegible]	[illegible]	[illegible]	[illegible]	[illegible]	[illegible]	[illegible]	[illegible]	[illegible]	[illegible]	[illegible]	[illegible]	[illegible]	[illegible]	[illegible]	[illegible]	Malicious Injuries to Property exceeding £5 in value.
[illegible]	[illegible]	[illegible]	[illegible]	[illegible]	[illegible]	[illegible]	[illegible]	[illegible]	[illegible]	[illegible]	[illegible]	[illegible]	[illegible]	[illegible]	[illegible]	[illegible]	[illegible]	Other Wilful and Malicious Injuries to Property
[illegible]	[illegible]	[illegible]	[illegible]	[illegible]	[illegible]	[illegible]	[illegible]	[illegible]	[illegible]	[illegible]	[illegible]	[illegible]	[illegible]	[illegible]	[illegible]	[illegible]	[illegible]	Total of No. 4.
																		No. 5.—Forgery and Offences against the Currency.
[illegible]	[illegible]	[illegible]	[illegible]	[illegible]	[illegible]	[illegible]	[illegible]	[illegible]	[illegible]	[illegible]	[illegible]	[illegible]	[illegible]	[illegible]	[illegible]	[illegible]	[illegible]	Forging and uttering Forged Instruments
[illegible]	[illegible]	[illegible]	[illegible]	[illegible]	[illegible]	[illegible]	[illegible]	[illegible]	[illegible]	[illegible]	[illegible]	[illegible]	[illegible]	[illegible]	[illegible]	[illegible]	[illegible]	Having in Possession Forged Bank Notes
[illegible]	[illegible]	[illegible]	[illegible]	[illegible]	[illegible]	[illegible]	[illegible]	[illegible]	[illegible]	[illegible]	[illegible]	[illegible]	[illegible]	[illegible]	[illegible]	[illegible]	[illegible]	Coining, and having in possession Implements for Coining
[illegible]	[illegible]	[illegible]	[illegible]	[illegible]	[illegible]	[illegible]	[illegible]	[illegible]	[illegible]	[illegible]	[illegible]	[illegible]	[illegible]	[illegible]	[illegible]	[illegible]	[illegible]	Uttering, possessing, &c., and having in possession Counterfeit Coin.
[illegible]	[illegible]	[illegible]	[illegible]	[illegible]	[illegible]	[illegible]	[illegible]	[illegible]	[illegible]	[illegible]	[illegible]	[illegible]	[illegible]	[illegible]	[illegible]	[illegible]	[illegible]	Total of No. 5.
																		No. 6.—Offences not included in the above Classes.
[illegible]	[illegible]	[illegible]	[illegible]	[illegible]	[illegible]	[illegible]	[illegible]	[illegible]	[illegible]	[illegible]	[illegible]	[illegible]	[illegible]	[illegible]	[illegible]	[illegible]	[illegible]	Prison Breach
[illegible]	[illegible]	[illegible]	[illegible]	[illegible]	[illegible]	[illegible]	[illegible]	[illegible]	[illegible]	[illegible]	[illegible]	[illegible]	[illegible]	[illegible]	[illegible]	[illegible]	[illegible]	Offences against the Queen's Authority and Person
[illegible]	[illegible]	[illegible]	[illegible]	[illegible]	[illegible]	[illegible]	[illegible]	[illegible]	[illegible]	[illegible]	[illegible]	[illegible]	[illegible]	[illegible]	[illegible]	[illegible]	[illegible]	Extortion by Threatening Letters, &c.
[illegible]	[illegible]	[illegible]	[illegible]	[illegible]	[illegible]	[illegible]	[illegible]	[illegible]	[illegible]	[illegible]	[illegible]	[illegible]	[illegible]	[illegible]	[illegible]	[illegible]	[illegible]	Having Arms or Ammunition without Licence in a Proclaimed District
[illegible]	[illegible]	[illegible]	[illegible]	[illegible]	[illegible]	[illegible]	[illegible]	[illegible]	[illegible]	[illegible]	[illegible]	[illegible]	[illegible]	[illegible]	[illegible]	[illegible]	[illegible]	Offences against the Game Laws.
[illegible]	[illegible]	[illegible]	[illegible]	[illegible]	[illegible]	[illegible]	[illegible]	[illegible]	[illegible]	[illegible]	[illegible]	[illegible]	[illegible]	[illegible]	[illegible]	[illegible]	[illegible]	Being at large under Sentence of Transportation or Penal Servitude
[illegible]	[illegible]	[illegible]	[illegible]	[illegible]	[illegible]	[illegible]	[illegible]	[illegible]	[illegible]	[illegible]	[illegible]	[illegible]	[illegible]	[illegible]	[illegible]	[illegible]	[illegible]	Perjury, and Subornation of Perjury.
[illegible]	[illegible]	[illegible]	[illegible]	[illegible]	[illegible]	[illegible]	[illegible]	[illegible]	[illegible]	[illegible]	[illegible]	[illegible]	[illegible]	[illegible]	[illegible]	[illegible]	[illegible]	Riot, Breach of the Peace, &c.
[illegible]	[illegible]	[illegible]	[illegible]	[illegible]	[illegible]	[illegible]	[illegible]	[illegible]	[illegible]	[illegible]	[illegible]	[illegible]	[illegible]	[illegible]	[illegible]	[illegible]	[illegible]	Keeping Disorderly Houses
[illegible]	[illegible]	[illegible]	[illegible]	[illegible]	[illegible]	[illegible]	[illegible]	[illegible]	[illegible]	[illegible]	[illegible]	[illegible]	[illegible]	[illegible]	[illegible]	[illegible]	[illegible]	Indecently Exposing the Person.
[illegible]	[illegible]	[illegible]	[illegible]	[illegible]	[illegible]	[illegible]	[illegible]	[illegible]	[illegible]	[illegible]	[illegible]	[illegible]	[illegible]	[illegible]	[illegible]	[illegible]	[illegible]	Suicide, attempting to commit.
[illegible]	[illegible]	[illegible]	[illegible]	[illegible]	[illegible]	[illegible]	[illegible]	[illegible]	[illegible]	[illegible]	[illegible]	[illegible]	[illegible]	[illegible]	[illegible]	[illegible]	[illegible]	Other Offences not included in the above.
[illegible]	[illegible]	[illegible]	[illegible]	[illegible]	[illegible]	[illegible]	[illegible]	[illegible]	[illegible]	[illegible]	[illegible]	[illegible]	[illegible]	[illegible]	[illegible]	[illegible]	[illegible]	Other Misdemeanours not included in the above
[illegible]	[illegible]	[illegible]	[illegible]	[illegible]	[illegible]	[illegible]	[illegible]	[illegible]	[illegible]	[illegible]	[illegible]	[illegible]	[illegible]	[illegible]	[illegible]	[illegible]	[illegible]	Assault and Rescue, &c.
[illegible]	[illegible]	[illegible]	[illegible]	[illegible]	[illegible]	[illegible]	[illegible]	[illegible]	[illegible]	[illegible]	[illegible]	[illegible]	[illegible]	[illegible]	[illegible]	[illegible]	[illegible]	Total of No. 6.
[illegible]	[illegible]	[illegible]	[illegible]	[illegible]	[illegible]	[illegible]	[illegible]	[illegible]	[illegible]	[illegible]	[illegible]	[illegible]	[illegible]	[illegible]	[illegible]	[illegible]	[illegible]	GRAND TOTAL.

(continued on next page)

Showing for EACH OFFENCE and CLASS of OFFENCES the NUMBER of PERSONS for TRIAL in the Year 18[illegible] made by Clerks of the Crown and Clerks of the Peace.

[illegible] and Fined. M.	W.	[illegible] Conviction. M.	W.	Removed to Reformatory Schools, (included in the [illegible]) M.	W.	[illegible] of Capital [illegible]. M.	W.	Cases of Commutation of Sentence of Death. M.	W.	[illegible] Pardon. M.	W.	OFFENCES Charged on Commitment or Indictment, and of which those Tried were Convicted or Acquitted.
												No. 1.—Offences against the Person.
.	-	[illegible]	[illegible]	.	.	.	.	[illegible]	[illegible]	.	.	Murder of Infants under One year and under.
.	.	.	.	.	.	.	.	.	.	.	.	Other Murders.
.	.	.	.	.	.	.	.	.	.	.	.	Accessory to murder.
.	.	[illegible]	[illegible]	.	.	.	.	.	.	.	.	Attempts to Murder.
.	.	[illegible]	[illegible]	.	.	.	.	.	.	.	.	Shooting at, Wounding, Stabbing, &c., to do bodily harm.
.	.	.	[illegible]	.	.	.	.	.	.	.	.	Manslaughter.
.	[illegible]	.	[illegible]	.	.	.	.	.	.	.	.	Attempts to procure Miscarriage.
.	.	[illegible]	.	.	.	.	.	.	.	.	.	Concealing the Birth of Infants.
.	.	.	.	.	.	.	.	.	.	.	.	Having Criminal Connection with Female under 12 years of age.
.	.	[illegible]	.	.	.	.	.	.	.	.	.	Attempts to have same.
.	.	[illegible]	.	.	.	.	.	.	.	.	.	Sodomy, &c., Attempts to Commit, and other unnatural Misdemeanours.
.	.	[illegible]	.	.	.	.	.	.	.	.	.	Rape.
.	.	[illegible]	.	.	.	.	.	.	.	.	.	——, Assaults, with intent to ravish and abuse.
.	.	[illegible]	.	.	.	.	.	.	.	.	.	Bigamy.
.	.	.	[illegible]	.	.	.	.	.	.	.	.	Child Stealing.
[illegible]	[illegible]	[illegible]	[illegible]	.	.	.	.	.	.	.	.	Unlawfully Abandoning Children under two years of age.
[illegible]	.	[illegible]	[illegible]	.	.	.	.	.	.	.	.	Endangering the Safety of Passengers on Railways.
.	.	[illegible]	[illegible]	.	.	.	.	.	.	.	.	Assaults and inflicting bodily harm.
.	.	.	.	.	.	.	.	.	.	.	.	Assaults, Common.
.	.	.	.	.	.	.	.	.	.	.	.	Assaults on Peace Officers.
[illegible]	[illegible]	[illegible]	[illegible]	.	.	.	.	[illegible]	[illegible]	.	.	Total of No. 1.
												No. 2.—Offences against Property, with Violence.
.	.	[illegible]	.	.	.	.	.	.	.	.	.	Sacrilege.
.	.	[illegible]	[illegible]	[illegible]	.	.	.	.	.	.	.	Burglary and Housebreaking.
.	.	[illegible]	[illegible]	[illegible]	.	.	.	.	.	.	.	Breaking into Shops, Warehouses, &c.
.	.	.	.	.	.	.	.	.	.	.	.	Attempts to break into Houses, Shops, Warehouses, &c.
.	.	[illegible]	[illegible]	[illegible]	.	.	.	.	.	.	.	Robbery.
.	.	[illegible]	.	.	.	.	.	.	.	.	.	Attempts to rob, and demanding Money by Menaces.
.	.	[illegible]	[illegible]	[illegible]	.	.	.	.	.	.	.	Total of No. 2.
												No. 3.—Offences against Property, without Violence.
.	.	[illegible]	.	.	.	.	.	.	.	.	.	Cattle Stealing.
.	.	[illegible]	.	.	.	.	.	.	.	.	.	Horse Stealing.
.	.	[illegible]	.	.	.	.	.	.	.	.	.	Sheep Stealing.
.	.	[illegible]	[illegible]	.	.	.	.	.	.	.	.	Larceny, to the value of 5l., in Dwelling house.
[illegible]	.	[illegible]	[illegible]	.	.	.	.	.	.	.	.	Larceny, from the Person.
.	.	[illegible]	.	.	.	.	.	.	.	.	.	Larceny, by Servants.
[illegible]	[illegible]	[illegible]	[illegible]	[illegible]	.	.	.	.	.	.	.	Larceny, Simple.
[illegible]	.	[illegible]	.	.	.	.	.	.	.	.	.	Larceny on Rivers, Canals, Wharfs, &c.
.	-	[illegible]	-	.	.	.	.	.	.	.	.	Stealing Fixtures, Shrubs growing, &c.
.	.	[illegible]	.	.	.	.	.	.	.	.	.	Attempts to Steal.
.	.	[illegible]	.	.	.	.	.	.	.	.	.	Embezzlement.
.	.	[illegible]	.	.	.	.	.	.	.	.	.	Larceny by Servants in the Post Office.
.	.	[illegible]	[illegible]	[illegible]	[illegible]	.	.	.	.	.	.	Receiving Stolen Goods.
[illegible]	.	[illegible]	[illegible]	.	.	.	.	.	.	.	.	Fraudulently obtaining Goods by false pretences, and attempts to defraud.
[illegible]	[illegible]	[illegible]	[illegible]	[illegible]	[illegible]	-	.	.	.	.	.	Total of No. 3.
												No. 4.—Malicious Offences against Property.
-	.	[illegible]	[illegible]	.	.	.	.	.	.	.	.	Arson and other Wilful Burnings.
.	.	.	.	.	.	.	.	.	.	.	.	[illegible]
.	.	.	.	.	.	.	.	.	.	.	.	[illegible] Goods in process of Manufacture.
.	.	[illegible]	.	.	.	.	.	.	.	.	.	Destroying Trees, Shrubs, &c., growing.
.	.	[illegible]	.	.	.	.	.	.	.	.	.	Killing and Maiming Cattle.
[illegible]	.	[illegible]	[illegible]	.	.	.	.	.	.	.	.	Malicious Injuries to Property exceeding 5l. in value.
.	.	[illegible]	.	.	.	.	.	.	.	.	.	Other Wilful and Malicious Injuries to Property.
[illegible]	.	[illegible]	[illegible]	.	.	.	.	.	.	.	.	Total of No. 4.
												No. 5.—Forgery and Offences against the Currency.
-	.	[illegible]	[illegible]	.	.	.	.	.	.	.	.	Forging and uttering Forged Instruments.
.	.	.	.	.	.	.	.	.	.	.	.	[illegible] Forged Bank Notes.
.	.	[illegible]	.	.	.	.	.	.	.	.	.	Coining, and having in possession Implements for Coining.
.	.	[illegible]	[illegible]	[illegible]	.	.	.	.	.	.	.	Uttering, putting off, and having in possession Counterfeit Coin.
.	.	[illegible]	.	[illegible]	.	.	.	.	.	.	.	Total of No. 5.
												No. 6.—Offences not included in the above Classes.
.	.	[illegible]	[illegible]	.	.	.	.	.	.	.	.	Prison Breach.
.	.	[illegible]	[illegible]	.	.	.	.	.	.	.	.	Offences against the Queen's Authority and Person.
.	.	[illegible]	.	.	.	.	.	.	.	.	.	Intimidation by Threatening Letters, Notices, or otherwise.
.	.	.	.	.	.	.	.	.	.	.	.	Having Arms or Ammunition without Licence in a Proclaimed District.
.	.	.	.	.	.	.	.	.	.	.	.	Offences against the Game Laws.
.	.	[illegible]	.	.	.	.	.	.	.	.	.	Being at large under Sentence of Transportation, or Penal Servitude.
.	.	[illegible]	.	.	.	.	.	.	.	.	.	Perjury, and Subornation of Perjury.
[illegible]	.	[illegible]	[illegible]	.	.	.	.	.	.	.	.	Riot, Breach of the Peace, &c.
.	.	.	-	.	.	.	.	.	.	.	.	Keeping Disorderly Houses.
.	.	[illegible]	.	.	.	.	.	.	.	.	.	Indecently Exposing the Person.
.	.	[illegible]	[illegible]	.	.	.	.	.	.	.	.	[illegible]
.	.	[illegible]	[illegible]	.	.	.	.	.	.	.	.	Other Felonies not included in the above.
[illegible]	[illegible]	[illegible]	[illegible]	.	.	.	.	.	.	.	.	Other Misdemeanours not included in the above.
.	-	[illegible]	[illegible]	.	.	.	.	.	.	.	.	Assault and Rescue, &c.
[illegible]	[illegible]	[illegible]	[illegible]	.	.	.	.	.	.	.	.	Total of No. 6.
[illegible]	[illegible]	1,[illegible]	[illegible]	[illegible]	[illegible]	.	.	[illegible]	[illegible]	.	.	GRAND TOTAL.

[illegible]	[illegible]	[illegible]	[illegible]	[illegible]		[illegible]	[illegible]	[illegible]
[illegible]	[illegible]	[illegible]	[illegible]	[illegible]	[illegible]	[illegible]	[illegible]	[illegible]
[illegible]	[illegible]	[illegible]	[illegible]	[illegible]	[illegible]	[illegible]	[illegible]	[illegible]
[illegible]	[illegible]	[illegible]	[illegible]	[illegible]	[illegible]	[illegible]	[illegible]	[illegible]
[illegible]	[illegible]	[illegible]	[illegible]	[illegible]	[illegible]	[illegible]	[illegible]	[illegible]
[illegible]	[illegible]	[illegible]	[illegible]	[illegible]	[illegible]	[illegible]	[illegible]	[illegible]
[illegible]	[illegible]	[illegible]	[illegible]	[illegible]	[illegible]	[illegible]	[illegible]	[illegible]
[illegible]	[illegible]	[illegible]	[illegible]	[illegible]	[illegible]	[illegible]	[illegible]	[illegible]
[illegible]	[illegible]	[illegible]	[illegible]	[illegible]	[illegible]	[illegible]	[illegible]	[illegible]
[illegible]	[illegible]	[illegible]	[illegible]	[illegible]		—		
[illegible]	[illegible]	—				—		
[illegible]	[illegible]	[illegible]	[illegible]	[illegible]	[illegible]	[illegible]	[illegible]	[illegible]
[illegible]	[illegible]				[illegible]	[illegible]	[illegible]	[illegible]
[illegible]	[illegible]	[illegible]	[illegible]	[illegible]	[illegible]	[illegible]	[illegible]	[illegible]
[illegible]	[illegible]	[illegible]	[illegible]	[illegible]	[illegible]	[illegible]	[illegible]	[illegible]
[illegible]	[illegible]	[illegible]	[illegible]	[illegible]	[illegible]	[illegible]	[illegible]	[illegible]
[illegible]	[illegible]	[illegible]	[illegible]	[illegible]	[illegible]	[illegible]	[illegible]	[illegible]
[illegible]	[illegible]	[illegible]	[illegible]	[illegible]	[illegible]	[illegible]	[illegible]	[illegible]
[illegible]	[illegible]	[illegible]	[illegible]	[illegible]	[illegible]	[illegible]	[illegible]	[illegible]
[illegible]	[illegible]	[illegible]	[illegible]	[illegible]	[illegible]	[illegible]	[illegible]	[illegible]
[illegible]	[illegible]	[illegible]	[illegible]	[illegible]	[illegible]	[illegible]	[illegible]	[illegible]
[illegible]	[illegible]				[illegible]	[illegible]	[illegible]	[illegible]
[illegible]	[illegible]	[illegible]	[illegible]	[illegible]	[illegible]	[illegible]	[illegible]	[illegible]
[illegible]	[illegible]	[illegible]	[illegible]	[illegible]	[illegible]	[illegible]	[illegible]	[illegible]
[illegible]	[illegible]	[illegible]	[illegible]	[illegible]	[illegible]	[illegible]	[illegible]	[illegible]
[illegible]	[illegible]	[illegible]	[illegible]	[illegible]	[illegible]	[illegible]	[illegible]	[illegible]
[illegible]	[illegible]	[illegible]	[illegible]	[illegible]	[illegible]	[illegible]	[illegible]	[illegible]
[illegible]	[illegible]	[illegible]	[illegible]	[illegible]	[illegible]	[illegible]	[illegible]	[illegible]
[illegible]	[illegible]	[illegible]	[illegible]	[illegible]	[illegible]	[illegible]	[illegible]	[illegible]
[illegible]	[illegible]	[illegible]	[illegible]	[illegible]	[illegible]	[illegible]	[illegible]	[illegible]
[illegible]	[illegible]	[illegible]	[illegible]	[illegible]	[illegible]	[illegible]	[illegible]	[illegible]
[illegible]	[illegible]				[illegible]	[illegible]	[illegible]	[illegible]
[illegible]	[illegible]	[illegible]	[illegible]	[illegible]	[illegible]	[illegible]	[illegible]	[illegible]
[illegible]	[illegible]	[illegible]	[illegible]	[illegible]	[illegible]	[illegible]	[illegible]	[illegible]

by Her Majesty's Treasury for Criminal Prosecutions at Assizes, the Dublin Commission Court, and Quarter Sessions,
Amount of Costs under each Head, from Returns made by Crown Solicitors and County and City Presiding Officers.

Amount paid through County and City Presiding Officers								Total.	Counties, and Counties of Cities and of Towns.
At Assizes.		At Quarter Sessions.		At Petty Sessions and Police Courts.		Under the Criminal Justice Act, 14 & 15 Vic., c. 93, ...			
Number of Prosecutors and Witnesses Paid.	Amount Paid.	Number of Prosecutors and Witnesses Paid.	Amount Paid.	Number of Prosecutors and Witnesses Paid.	Amount Paid.	Number of Prosecutors and Witnesses Paid.	Amount Paid.		
	£ s. d.		£ s. d.		£ s. d.		£ s. d.	£ s. d.	
[illegible]	[illegible]	[illegible]	[illegible]	[illegible]	[illegible]	.	—	[illegible]	Antrim, including Co. of Town of Carrickfergus.
[illegible]	[illegible]	[illegible]	[illegible]	[illegible]	[illegible]	.	—	[illegible]	Armagh.
[illegible]	[illegible]	[illegible]	[illegible]	[illegible]	[illegible]	.	—	[illegible]	Carlow.
[illegible]	[illegible]	[illegible]	[illegible]	.	—	.	—	[illegible]	Cavan.
[illegible]	[illegible]	[illegible]	[illegible]	[illegible]	[illegible]	.	—	[illegible]	Clare.
[illegible]	[illegible]	[illegible]	[illegible]	[illegible]	[illegible]	.	—	[illegible]	Cork County.
[illegible]	[illegible]	[illegible]	[illegible]	[illegible]	[illegible]	.	—		Cork City.
[illegible]	[illegible]	[illegible]	[illegible]	[illegible]	[illegible]	.	—	[illegible]	Donegal.
[illegible]	[illegible]	[illegible]	[illegible]	[illegible]	[illegible]	.	—	[illegible]	Down.
[illegible]	[illegible]	[illegible]	[illegible]	[illegible]	[illegible]	.	—	[illegible]	Drogheda Town.
[illegible]	[illegible]	[illegible]	[illegible]	[illegible]	[illegible]	.	—	[illegible]	Dublin County.
[illegible]	[illegible]	[illegible]	[illegible]	[illegible]	[illegible]	.	—		Dublin City.
[illegible]	[illegible]	[illegible]	[illegible]	[illegible]	[illegible]	.	—	[illegible]	Fermanagh.
[illegible]	[illegible]	[illegible]	[illegible]	.	—	.	—	[illegible]	Galway County.
[illegible]	[illegible]	[illegible]	[illegible]	.	—	.	—		Galway Town.
[illegible]	[illegible]	[illegible]	[illegible]	[illegible]	[illegible]	.	—	[illegible]	Kerry.
[illegible]	[illegible]	[illegible]	[illegible]	[illegible]	[illegible]	.	—	[illegible]	Kildare.
[illegible]	[illegible]	[illegible]	[illegible]	[illegible]	[illegible]	.	—	[illegible]	Kilkenny County.
[illegible]	[illegible]	[illegible]	[illegible]	[illegible]	[illegible]	.	—		Kilkenny City.
[illegible]	[illegible]	[illegible]	[illegible]	[illegible]	[illegible]	.	—	[illegible]	King's County.
[illegible]	[illegible]	[illegible]	[illegible]	.	—	.	—	[illegible]	Leitrim.
[illegible]	[illegible]	[illegible]	[illegible]	.	—	[illegible]	[illegible]	[illegible]	Limerick County.
[illegible]	[illegible]	[illegible]	[illegible]	[illegible]	[illegible]	.	—		Limerick City.
[illegible]	[illegible]	[illegible]	[illegible]	[illegible]	[illegible]	.	—	[illegible]	Londonderry.
[illegible]	[illegible]	[illegible]	[illegible]	.	—	.	—	[illegible]	Longford.
[illegible]	[illegible]	[illegible]	[illegible]	[illegible]	[illegible]	.	—	[illegible]	Louth.
[illegible]	[illegible]	[illegible]	[illegible]	[illegible]	[illegible]	.	—	[illegible]	Mayo.
[illegible]	[illegible]	[illegible]	[illegible]	[illegible]	[illegible]	.	—	[illegible]	Meath.
[illegible]	[illegible]	[illegible]	[illegible]	[illegible]	[illegible]	.	—	[illegible]	Monaghan.
[illegible]	[illegible]	[illegible]	[illegible]	[illegible]	[illegible]	.	—	[illegible]	Queen's County.
[illegible]	[illegible]	[illegible]	[illegible]	.	—	.	—	[illegible]	Roscommon.
[illegible]	[illegible]	[illegible]	[illegible]	[illegible]	[illegible]	.	—	[illegible]	Sligo.
[illegible]	[illegible]	[illegible]	[illegible]	.	—	[illegible]	[illegible]	[illegible]	Tipperary, North Riding.
[illegible]	[illegible]	[illegible]	[illegible]	.	—	[illegible]	[illegible]		Tipperary, South Riding.
[illegible]	[illegible]	[illegible]	[illegible]	.	—	.	—	[illegible]	Tyrone.
[illegible]	[illegible]	[illegible]	[illegible]	[illegible]	[illegible]	.	—	[illegible]	Waterford County.
[illegible]	[illegible]	[illegible]	[illegible]	[illegible]	[illegible]	.	—		Waterford City.
[illegible]	[illegible]	[illegible]	[illegible]	[illegible]	[illegible]	.	—	[illegible]	Westmeath.
[illegible]	[illegible]	[illegible]	[illegible]	[illegible]	[illegible]	.	—	[illegible]	Wexford.
[illegible]	[illegible]	[illegible]	[illegible]	[illegible]	[illegible]	.	—	[illegible]	Wicklow.
[illegible]	[illegible]	[illegible]	[illegible]	[illegible]	[illegible]	[illegible]	[illegible]	[illegible]	Total.

TABLE II.—REFORMATORY SCHOOLS.—RETURN showing the NUMBER of BOYS and GIRLS UNDER DETENTION, COMMITTED, DISCHARGED, and REMOVED in the Year [illegible], made by the Inspector of Reformatories and Industrial Schools.

Certified Schools to which the Commitments were made, with the Date of Certificate, and Religion of Children receivable in School.	Under Detention at Beginning of Year: In School	On Licence	In Prison	[illegible]	[illegible]	Total	Admitted in Year: [illegible]	[illegible]	Discharged or Removed in Year: [illegible]	[illegible]	Died	Total [illegible]	Under Detention at Close of Year: In School	On Licence	In Prison	[illegible]	[illegible]	Total	Average number of [illegible]	[illegible]	[illegible] Imperial Taxes	Local Taxes	Other Sources
Boys.																				£ s. d.	£ s. d.	£ s. d.	£ s. d.
Malone, Belfast, County Antrim, 13th March, 1860 (Protestant).	167	8	.	9	.	184	51	.	.	35	.	36	165	5	.	6	.	186	[illegible]	[illegible]	[illegible]	[illegible]	[illegible]
St. Patrick's, Upton, County Cork, 4th July, 1859 (Roman Catholic).	148	4	.	1	.	153	59	.	.	47	1	48	157	8	.	2	.	163	[illegible]	[illegible]	[illegible]	[illegible]	[illegible]
[illegible], Dublin, [illegible] December, 18[illegible] (Protestant).	[illegible]	8	.	.	1	[illegible]	6	.	.	7	.	7	[illegible]	8	9	1	.	[illegible]	[illegible]	[illegible]	[illegible]	[illegible]	[illegible]
King's County Reformatory School, Philipstown, 22nd December, 18[illegible] (Roman Catholic).	[illegible]	22	1	1	3	[illegible]	17	.	.	[illegible]	.	[illegible]	[illegible]	27	.	5	.	[illegible]	[illegible]	[illegible]	[illegible]	[illegible]	—
St. Kevin's, Glencree, County Wicklow, 17th April, 18[illegible] (Roman Catholic).	[illegible]	11	.	.	.	[illegible]	[illegible]	.	.	31	1	32	[illegible]	16	.	3	.	[illegible]	[illegible]	[illegible]	[illegible]	[illegible]	[illegible]
Total Boys,	[illegible]	[illegible]	1	[illegible]	3	[illegible]	111	.	.	[illegible]	2	[illegible]	[illegible]	[illegible]	9	14	.	[illegible]	[illegible]	[illegible]	[illegible]	[illegible]	[illegible]
Girls.																							
[illegible], Cork-street, Dublin, 13th April, 18[illegible] (Protestant).	11	.				13	1	.	.	6	1	8	16	.	.	.	.	[illegible]	37	[illegible]	[illegible]	[illegible]	[illegible]
High Park, Drumcondra, County Dublin, 21st December, 18[illegible] (Roman Catholic).	13	.	.		.	[illegible]	11	.	1	[illegible]	.	[illegible]	[illegible]	1	.	.	.	[illegible]	[illegible]	[illegible]	[illegible]	[illegible]	[illegible]
St. Joseph's, Limerick, [illegible] January, 18[illegible] (Roman Catholic).	[illegible]	.				[illegible]	4	1		8	.	7	[illegible]	.	.	.	.	[illegible]	[illegible]	[illegible]	[illegible]	[illegible]	[illegible]
[illegible] Lake, Monaghan, [illegible] July, 18[illegible] (Roman Catholic).	[illegible]	.			4	[illegible]	4	1	.	[illegible]	.	[illegible]	[illegible]	.	.	.	.	[illegible]	[illegible]	[illegible]	[illegible]	[illegible]	[illegible]
Total Girls,	[illegible]	.	.		3	[illegible]	[illegible]	3	2	[illegible]	1	[illegible]	[illegible]	1	.	.	.	[illegible]	[illegible]	[illegible]	[illegible]	[illegible]	[illegible]
Total Boys and Girls,	[illegible]	[illegible]	1	[illegible]	[illegible]	[illegible]	[illegible]	3	2	[illegible]	4	[illegible]	[illegible]	[illegible]	9	14	.	[illegible]	[illegible]	[illegible]	[illegible]	[illegible]	[illegible]

* [illegible]

TABLE 14.—REFORMATORY SCHOOLS.—RETURN showing OCCASION of COMMITTALS and SENTENCES passed upon BOYS and GIRLS RECEIVED during the Year 1866. Made by the Inspector of Reformatories and Industrial Schools.

CERTIFIED SCHOOLS (in which the first offences were made, with the date of Certificate, and Religion of the Inmates)	Committed on Indictment (Committals)	Summarily Convicted	Total Committed	Sentences: Previous Imprisonment: 14 Days	Between 14 days and 1 Month	1 Month and above	2 Months and above	Above 3 Months	Years of Committal to Reformatory Schools: [illegible] Years	[illegible] Years and above	[illegible] Years and above	[illegible] Years and above
Boys.												
Malone, Belfast, [illegible] March, 18[illegible] (Protestant)	[illegible]	[illegible]	[illegible]	[illegible]	.	.	-	-	[illegible]	-	.	[illegible]
St. Patrick's, Upton, County Cork, [illegible] July, 18[illegible] (Roman Catholic)	[illegible]	[illegible]	[illegible]	[illegible]	.	.	.	-	[illegible]	[illegible]	.	[illegible]
[illegible], Dublin, [illegible] (Protestant)	-	[illegible]	[illegible]	[illegible]	-	.	.	.	.	-	.	[illegible]
[illegible], King's County, [illegible] (Roman Catholic)	[illegible]	[illegible]	[illegible]	[illegible]	[illegible]	.	.	.	[illegible]	-	[illegible]	[illegible]
St. [illegible], [illegible] April, 18[illegible] (Roman Catholic)	[illegible]	[illegible]	[illegible]	[illegible]	[illegible]	-	.	.	[illegible]	[illegible]	[illegible]	[illegible]
Total Boys,	[illegible]	[illegible]	[illegible]	[illegible]	[illegible]	-	.	.	[illegible]	[illegible]	[illegible]	[illegible]
Girls.												
[illegible], Dublin, [illegible] April, 18[illegible] (Protestant)	.	[illegible]	[illegible]	[illegible]	.	-	-	.	.	-	.	[illegible]
High Park, [illegible], County Dublin, [illegible] (Roman Catholic)	[illegible]	[illegible]	[illegible]	[illegible]	.	-	.	-	[illegible]	[illegible]	-	[illegible]
St. Joseph's, Limerick, [illegible] (Roman Catholic)	.	[illegible]	[illegible]	[illegible]	-	.	.	.	[illegible]	[illegible]	[illegible]	[illegible]
[illegible], [illegible] July, 18[illegible] (Roman Catholic)	.	[illegible]	[illegible]	[illegible]	.	.	.	.	.	-	.	[illegible]
Total Girls,	[illegible]	[illegible]	[illegible]	[illegible]	.	-	.	.	[illegible]	[illegible]	[illegible]	[illegible]
Total Boys and Girls,	[illegible]	[illegible]	[illegible]	[illegible]	[illegible]	-	.	.	[illegible]	[illegible]	[illegible]	[illegible]
Total Roman Catholics,	[illegible]	[illegible]	[illegible]	[illegible]	[illegible]	.	.	.	[illegible]	[illegible]	[illegible]	[illegible]
Total Protestants,	[illegible]	[illegible]	[illegible]	[illegible]	.	.	.	.	[illegible]	.	.	[illegible]

TABLE 15.—REFORMATORY SCHOOLS.—RETURN of OFFENCES of which the BOYS and GIRLS were CONVICTED, who were RECEIVED under Stat. 21 & 22 Vic., c. 103, into REFORMATORY SCHOOLS during the Year 1866. Made by the Inspector of Reformatories and Industrial Schools.

OFFENCES	Boys: [illegible]	[illegible]	[illegible]	[illegible]	[illegible]	Girls: [illegible]	[illegible]	[illegible]	[illegible]	Total Committed in Year: B.	G.	B & G
Larceny and Petty Theft,	[illegible]	[illegible]	[illegible]	[illegible]	[illegible]	-	[illegible]	[illegible]	[illegible]	[illegible]	[illegible]	[illegible]
" of Poultry,	.	-	.	.	.	.	.	.	.	.	.	.
" by Servant,	.	-	.	[illegible]	[illegible]	.	-	.	.	[illegible]	-	[illegible]
" from Person,	.	.	.	[illegible]	[illegible]	.	.	.	.	[illegible]	.	[illegible]
" in Dwelling house,	[illegible]	.	.	[illegible]	.	[illegible]	.	.	-	[illegible]	[illegible]	[illegible]
Attempt to Steal,	.	.	[illegible]	[illegible]	[illegible]	.	[illegible]	.	.	[illegible]	[illegible]	[illegible]
Unlawful Possession of Goods,	.	.	.	[illegible]	[illegible]	.	[illegible]	.	.	[illegible]	[illegible]	[illegible]
Receiving Stolen Goods,	.	.	-	.	.	.	.	.	.	.	.	.
Fraudulent Offences,	[illegible]	[illegible]	.	[illegible]	[illegible]	.	[illegible]	.	.	[illegible]	[illegible]	[illegible]
Embezzlement,	.	.	.	-	[illegible]	.	.	.	.	[illegible]	-	[illegible]
Horse Stealing,	.	.	[illegible]	.	-	.	.	.	-	[illegible]	.	[illegible]
Sheep Stealing,	.	-	.	.	.	.	.	.	.	.	-	.
Cattle Stealing,	.	.	.	.	.	.	.	.	.	.	.	.
Housebreaking, Shopbreaking, &c.,	[illegible]	[illegible]	.	[illegible]	.	.	.	.	.	[illegible]	.	[illegible]
Burglary,	.	.	.	-	.	.	-	.	.	.	-	.
Robbery on the Highway,	.	.	.	.	[illegible]	.	.	.	.	[illegible]	-	[illegible]
Attempt to Break into Houses, &c.,	.	-	.	.	-	.	.	.	.	.	.	.
Arson and Wilful Burning,	.	.	.	.	.	.	.	.	.	.	.	.
Wilful Damage and other Malicious Offences,	.	.	.	[illegible]	[illegible]	.	.	.	.	[illegible]	.	[illegible]
Assaults,	[illegible]	[illegible]	.	[illegible]	[illegible]	-	[illegible]	.	.	[illegible]	[illegible]	[illegible]
Assault with intent to Ravish,	.	.	.	.	.	.	.	.	.	.	.	.
Forgery,	.	.	.	.	.	.	.	.	.	.	.	.
Uttering Counterfeit Coin,	.	.	.	.	.	.	.	.	.	.	.	.
Vagrancy,	.	[illegible]	.	.	.	.	[illegible]	.	.	[illegible]	[illegible]	[illegible]
Other Offences,	.	[illegible]	.	[illegible]	[illegible]	.	.	.	[illegible]	[illegible]	[illegible]	[illegible]
Total,	[illegible]	[illegible]	[illegible]	[illegible]	[illegible]	[illegible]	[illegible]	[illegible]	[illegible]	[illegible]	[illegible]	[illegible]

TABLE [illegible].—INDUSTRIAL SCHOOLS.—RETURN showing the NUMBER under DETENTION, COMMITTED, DISCHARGED, REMOVED, or TRANSFERRED, in the Year 18[illegible], with the COSTS, under Stat. [illegible] Vic., c. [illegible]. Made by the Inspector of Reformatories and Industrial Schools.

INDUSTRIAL SCHOOLS, ARRANGED IN COUNTIES.	[illegible]	[illegible]	[illegible]	[illegible]	[illegible]	[illegible]	[illegible]	[illegible]	[illegible]	[illegible]	[illegible]	[illegible]	[illegible]	[illegible]	[illegible]	[illegible]	[illegible]	[illegible]	[illegible]	[illegible]	[illegible]	[illegible]	[illegible]	[illegible]	[illegible]	[illegible]	[illegible]	[illegible]	[illegible]	[illegible]	[illegible]
GIRLS.																															
Antrim:																															
Hampton House (Protestant)	[illegible]	[illegible]	[illegible]	[illegible]	[illegible]	[illegible]	[illegible]	[illegible]	[illegible]	[illegible]	[illegible]	[illegible]	[illegible]	[illegible]	[illegible]	[illegible]	[illegible]	[illegible]	[illegible]	[illegible]	[illegible]	[illegible]	[illegible]	[illegible]	[illegible]	[illegible]	[illegible]	[illegible]	[illegible]	[illegible]	[illegible]
St. Patrick's (R.C.)	[illegible]	[illegible]	[illegible]	[illegible]	[illegible]	[illegible]	[illegible]	[illegible]	[illegible]	[illegible]	[illegible]	[illegible]	[illegible]	[illegible]	[illegible]	[illegible]	[illegible]	[illegible]	[illegible]	[illegible]	[illegible]	[illegible]	[illegible]	[illegible]	[illegible]	[illegible]	[illegible]	[illegible]	[illegible]	[illegible]	[illegible]
Armagh:																															
[illegible] (R.C.)	[illegible]	[illegible]	[illegible]	[illegible]	[illegible]	[illegible]	[illegible]	[illegible]	[illegible]	[illegible]	[illegible]	[illegible]	[illegible]	[illegible]	[illegible]	[illegible]	[illegible]	[illegible]	[illegible]	[illegible]	[illegible]	[illegible]	[illegible]	[illegible]	[illegible]	[illegible]	[illegible]	[illegible]	[illegible]	[illegible]	[illegible]
Cavan:																															
St. Joseph's, Cavan (R.C.)	[illegible]	[illegible]	[illegible]	[illegible]	[illegible]	[illegible]	[illegible]	[illegible]	[illegible]	[illegible]	[illegible]	[illegible]	[illegible]	[illegible]	[illegible]	[illegible]	[illegible]	[illegible]	[illegible]	[illegible]	[illegible]	[illegible]	[illegible]	[illegible]	[illegible]	[illegible]	[illegible]	[illegible]	[illegible]	[illegible]	[illegible]
Clare:																															
Ennis	[illegible]	[illegible]	[illegible]	[illegible]	[illegible]	[illegible]	[illegible]	[illegible]	[illegible]	[illegible]	[illegible]	[illegible]	[illegible]	[illegible]	[illegible]	[illegible]	[illegible]	[illegible]	[illegible]	[illegible]	[illegible]	[illegible]	[illegible]	[illegible]	[illegible]	[illegible]	[illegible]	[illegible]	[illegible]	[illegible]	[illegible]
Cork:																															
St. Aloysius', Clonakilty (R.C.)	[illegible]	[illegible]	[illegible]	[illegible]	[illegible]	[illegible]	[illegible]	[illegible]	[illegible]	[illegible]	[illegible]	[illegible]	[illegible]	[illegible]	[illegible]	[illegible]	[illegible]	[illegible]	[illegible]	[illegible]	[illegible]	[illegible]	[illegible]	[illegible]	[illegible]	[illegible]	[illegible]	[illegible]	[illegible]	[illegible]	[illegible]
St. Colman's, Queenstown (R.C.)	[illegible]	[illegible]	[illegible]	[illegible]	[illegible]	[illegible]	[illegible]	[illegible]	[illegible]	[illegible]	[illegible]	[illegible]	[illegible]	[illegible]	[illegible]	[illegible]	[illegible]	[illegible]	[illegible]	[illegible]	[illegible]	[illegible]	[illegible]	[illegible]	[illegible]	[illegible]	[illegible]	[illegible]	[illegible]	[illegible]	[illegible]
Our Lady of Mercy, Kinsale (R.C.)	[illegible]	[illegible]	[illegible]	[illegible]	[illegible]	[illegible]	[illegible]	[illegible]	[illegible]	[illegible]	[illegible]	[illegible]	[illegible]	[illegible]	[illegible]	[illegible]	[illegible]	[illegible]	[illegible]	[illegible]	[illegible]	[illegible]	[illegible]	[illegible]	[illegible]	[illegible]	[illegible]	[illegible]	[illegible]	[illegible]	[illegible]
[illegible] Home, [illegible] (Protestant)	[illegible]	[illegible]	[illegible]	[illegible]	[illegible]	[illegible]	[illegible]	[illegible]	[illegible]	[illegible]	[illegible]	[illegible]	[illegible]	[illegible]	[illegible]	[illegible]	[illegible]	[illegible]	[illegible]	[illegible]	[illegible]	[illegible]	[illegible]	[illegible]	[illegible]	[illegible]	[illegible]	[illegible]	[illegible]	[illegible]	[illegible]
Mallow	[illegible]	[illegible]	[illegible]	[illegible]	[illegible]	[illegible]	[illegible]	[illegible]	[illegible]	[illegible]	[illegible]	[illegible]	[illegible]	[illegible]	[illegible]	[illegible]	[illegible]	[illegible]	[illegible]	[illegible]	[illegible]	[illegible]	[illegible]	[illegible]	[illegible]	[illegible]	[illegible]	[illegible]	[illegible]	[illegible]	[illegible]
St. [illegible], Cork (R.C.)	[illegible]	[illegible]	[illegible]	[illegible]	[illegible]	[illegible]	[illegible]	[illegible]	[illegible]	[illegible]	[illegible]	[illegible]	[illegible]	[illegible]	[illegible]	[illegible]	[illegible]	[illegible]	[illegible]	[illegible]	[illegible]	[illegible]	[illegible]	[illegible]	[illegible]	[illegible]	[illegible]	[illegible]	[illegible]	[illegible]	[illegible]
Training Home, Cork (Protestant)	[illegible]	[illegible]	[illegible]	[illegible]	[illegible]	[illegible]	[illegible]	[illegible]	[illegible]	[illegible]	[illegible]	[illegible]	[illegible]	[illegible]	[illegible]	[illegible]	[illegible]	[illegible]	[illegible]	[illegible]	[illegible]	[illegible]	[illegible]	[illegible]	[illegible]	[illegible]	[illegible]	[illegible]	[illegible]	[illegible]	[illegible]
Dublin:																															
Booterstown, Dublin (R.C.)	[illegible]	[illegible]	[illegible]	[illegible]	[illegible]	[illegible]	[illegible]	[illegible]	[illegible]	[illegible]	[illegible]	[illegible]	[illegible]	[illegible]	[illegible]	[illegible]	[illegible]	[illegible]	[illegible]	[illegible]	[illegible]	[illegible]	[illegible]	[illegible]	[illegible]	[illegible]	[illegible]	[illegible]	[illegible]	[illegible]	[illegible]
[illegible]	[illegible]	[illegible]	[illegible]	[illegible]	[illegible]	[illegible]	[illegible]	[illegible]	[illegible]	[illegible]	[illegible]	[illegible]	[illegible]	[illegible]	[illegible]	[illegible]	[illegible]	[illegible]	[illegible]	[illegible]	[illegible]	[illegible]	[illegible]	[illegible]	[illegible]	[illegible]	[illegible]	[illegible]	[illegible]	[illegible]	[illegible]
Lakelands, Sandymount (R.C.)	[illegible]	[illegible]	[illegible]	[illegible]	[illegible]	[illegible]	[illegible]	[illegible]	[illegible]	[illegible]	[illegible]	[illegible]	[illegible]	[illegible]	[illegible]	[illegible]	[illegible]	[illegible]	[illegible]	[illegible]	[illegible]	[illegible]	[illegible]	[illegible]	[illegible]	[illegible]	[illegible]	[illegible]	[illegible]	[illegible]	[illegible]
Merrion (R.C.)	[illegible]	[illegible]	[illegible]	[illegible]	[illegible]	[illegible]	[illegible]	[illegible]	[illegible]	[illegible]	[illegible]	[illegible]	[illegible]	[illegible]	[illegible]	[illegible]	[illegible]	[illegible]	[illegible]	[illegible]	[illegible]	[illegible]	[illegible]	[illegible]	[illegible]	[illegible]	[illegible]	[illegible]	[illegible]	[illegible]	[illegible]
[illegible], Dublin (Protestant)	[illegible]	[illegible]	[illegible]	[illegible]	[illegible]	[illegible]	[illegible]	[illegible]	[illegible]	[illegible]	[illegible]	[illegible]	[illegible]	[illegible]	[illegible]	[illegible]	[illegible]	[illegible]	[illegible]	[illegible]	[illegible]	[illegible]	[illegible]	[illegible]	[illegible]	[illegible]	[illegible]	[illegible]	[illegible]	[illegible]	[illegible]
Galway:																															
Ballinasloe	[illegible]	[illegible]	[illegible]	[illegible]	[illegible]	[illegible]	[illegible]	[illegible]	[illegible]	[illegible]	[illegible]	[illegible]	[illegible]	[illegible]	[illegible]	[illegible]	[illegible]	[illegible]	[illegible]	[illegible]	[illegible]	[illegible]	[illegible]	[illegible]	[illegible]	[illegible]	[illegible]	[illegible]	[illegible]	[illegible]	[illegible]
Loughrea (R.C.)	[illegible]	[illegible]	[illegible]	[illegible]	[illegible]	[illegible]	[illegible]	[illegible]	[illegible]	[illegible]	[illegible]	[illegible]	[illegible]	[illegible]	[illegible]	[illegible]	[illegible]	[illegible]	[illegible]	[illegible]	[illegible]	[illegible]	[illegible]	[illegible]	[illegible]	[illegible]	[illegible]	[illegible]	[illegible]	[illegible]	[illegible]
Clifden (R.C.)	[illegible]	[illegible]	[illegible]	[illegible]	[illegible]	[illegible]	[illegible]	[illegible]	[illegible]	[illegible]	[illegible]	[illegible]	[illegible]	[illegible]	[illegible]	[illegible]	[illegible]	[illegible]	[illegible]	[illegible]	[illegible]	[illegible]	[illegible]	[illegible]	[illegible]	[illegible]	[illegible]	[illegible]	[illegible]	[illegible]	[illegible]
Oughterard (R.C.)	[illegible]	[illegible]	[illegible]	[illegible]	[illegible]	[illegible]	[illegible]	[illegible]	[illegible]	[illegible]	[illegible]	[illegible]	[illegible]	[illegible]	[illegible]	[illegible]	[illegible]	[illegible]	[illegible]	[illegible]	[illegible]	[illegible]	[illegible]	[illegible]	[illegible]	[illegible]	[illegible]	[illegible]	[illegible]	[illegible]	[illegible]
St. Anne's, Galway (R.C.)	[illegible]	[illegible]	[illegible]	[illegible]	[illegible]	[illegible]	[illegible]	[illegible]	[illegible]	[illegible]	[illegible]	[illegible]	[illegible]	[illegible]	[illegible]	[illegible]	[illegible]	[illegible]	[illegible]	[illegible]	[illegible]	[illegible]	[illegible]	[illegible]	[illegible]	[illegible]	[illegible]	[illegible]	[illegible]	[illegible]	[illegible]

* [illegible]
† [illegible]

[illegible]	[illegible]	[illegible]
[illegible]	[illegible]	[illegible]
[illegible]	[illegible]	[illegible]

[illegible]	[illegible]	[illegible]	[illegible]	[illegible]	[illegible]	[illegible]	[illegible]	[illegible]
[illegible]	[illegible]	[illegible]	[illegible]	[illegible]	[illegible]	[illegible]	[illegible]	[illegible]
[illegible]	[illegible]	[illegible]	[illegible]	[illegible]	[illegible]	[illegible]	[illegible]	[illegible]
[illegible]	[illegible]	[illegible]	[illegible]	[illegible]	[illegible]	[illegible]	[illegible]	[illegible]
[illegible]	[illegible]	[illegible]	–			[illegible]	[illegible]	[illegible]
[illegible]	[illegible]	[illegible]	[illegible]	[illegible]	[illegible]	[illegible]	[illegible]	[illegible]
[illegible]	[illegible]	[illegible]	[illegible]	[illegible]	[illegible]	[illegible]	[illegible]	[illegible]
[illegible]	[illegible]	[illegible]	[illegible]	[illegible]	[illegible]	[illegible]	[illegible]	[illegible]
[illegible]	[illegible]	[illegible]	[illegible]	[illegible]	[illegible]	[illegible]	[illegible]	[illegible]
[illegible]	[illegible]	[illegible]	[illegible]	[illegible]	[illegible]	[illegible]	[illegible]	[illegible]
[illegible]	[illegible]	[illegible]	[illegible]	[illegible]	[illegible]	[illegible]	[illegible]	[illegible]
[illegible]	[illegible]	[illegible]	[illegible]	[illegible]	[illegible]	[illegible]	[illegible]	[illegible]
[illegible]	[illegible]	[illegible]	[illegible]	[illegible]	[illegible]	[illegible]	[illegible]	[illegible]
[illegible]	[illegible]	[illegible]	[illegible]	[illegible]	[illegible]	[illegible]	[illegible]	[illegible]
[illegible]	[illegible]	[illegible]	[illegible]	[illegible]	[illegible]	[illegible]	[illegible]	[illegible]
[illegible]	[illegible]	[illegible]	[illegible]	[illegible]	[illegible]	[illegible]	[illegible]	[illegible]
[illegible]	[illegible]	[illegible]	[illegible]	[illegible]	[illegible]	[illegible]	[illegible]	[illegible]
[illegible]	[illegible]	[illegible]	[illegible]	[illegible]	[illegible]	[illegible]	[illegible]	[illegible]
[illegible]	[illegible]	[illegible]	[illegible]	[illegible]	[illegible]	[illegible]	[illegible]	[illegible]

TABLE [illegible].—LUNATIC ASYLUMS.—AS TO CRIMINAL LUNATICS and DANGEROUS LUNATICS CHARGED WITH INTENT TO COMMIT CRIME.—A RETURN showing for each Asylum—I. The Number of these under Detention at the end of the Year [illegible], and whether Committed by Lord Lieutenant's Warrant or by Justices; II. The Periods of their Detention, whether in Asylum or Prison; III. The Number for each Asylum of those Detentions during the Year who had been Committed for each Class of Offence Committed or as Dangerous Lunatics apparently intended to be Committed; and IV. The Number Committed during the Year under each class of authority. Made by Inspectors of Lunatic Asylums.

—	Total.			Armagh. County of Armagh		Ballinasloe. County and Town of Galway and Roscommon County		Belfast. County of Antrim and County-Town [illegible]		Carlow. Counties of Carlow and Kildare		Castlebar. County of Mayo		Clonmel. County of Tipperary	
	M. & W.	M.	W.	M.	W.	M.	W.	M.	W.	M.	W.	M.	W.	M.	W.
PART I.—AUTHORITY FOR COMMITMENT OF THOSE IN CONFINEMENT AT THE END OF THE YEAR [illegible]															
Total number in confinement at end of year [illegible]	[illegible]	[illegible]	[illegible]	[illegible]	[illegible]	[illegible]	[illegible]	[illegible]	[illegible]	[illegible]	[illegible]	[illegible]	[illegible]	[illegible]	[illegible]
Total number committed by Justices,	[illegible]	[illegible]	[illegible]	[illegible]	[illegible]	[illegible]	[illegible]	[illegible]	[illegible]	[illegible]	[illegible]	[illegible]	[illegible]	[illegible]	[illegible]
Total number held in confinement by Warrant of Lord Lieutenant	[illegible]	[illegible]	[illegible]	[illegible]	[illegible]	[illegible]	[illegible]	[illegible]	[illegible]	[illegible]	[illegible]	[illegible]	[illegible]	[illegible]	[illegible]
Total number transferred by Secretary of State for War	[illegible]	[illegible]	[illegible]	[illegible]	[illegible]	[illegible]	[illegible]	[illegible]	[illegible]	[illegible]	[illegible]	[illegible]	[illegible]	[illegible]	[illegible]
PART II.—PERIOD OF DETENTION IN ASYLUM OR PRISON OF THOSE UNDER DETENTION AT END OF THE YEAR [illegible]															
Number who have been detained as Lunatics—															
One year and under,	[illegible]	[illegible]	[illegible]	[illegible]	[illegible]	[illegible]	[illegible]	[illegible]	[illegible]	[illegible]	[illegible]	[illegible]	[illegible]	[illegible]	[illegible]
Two years and above one,	[illegible]	[illegible]	[illegible]	[illegible]	[illegible]	[illegible]	[illegible]	[illegible]	[illegible]	[illegible]	[illegible]	[illegible]	[illegible]	[illegible]	[illegible]
Three years and above two,	[illegible]	[illegible]	[illegible]	[illegible]	[illegible]	[illegible]	[illegible]	[illegible]	[illegible]	[illegible]	[illegible]	[illegible]	[illegible]	[illegible]	[illegible]
Five years and above three,	[illegible]	[illegible]	[illegible]	[illegible]	[illegible]	[illegible]	[illegible]	[illegible]	[illegible]	[illegible]	[illegible]	[illegible]	[illegible]	[illegible]	[illegible]
Ten years and above five,	[illegible]	[illegible]	[illegible]	[illegible]	[illegible]	[illegible]	[illegible]	[illegible]	[illegible]	[illegible]	[illegible]	[illegible]	[illegible]	[illegible]	[illegible]
Fifteen years and above ten,	[illegible]	[illegible]	[illegible]	[illegible]	[illegible]	[illegible]	[illegible]	[illegible]	[illegible]	[illegible]	[illegible]	[illegible]	[illegible]	[illegible]	[illegible]
Twenty years and above fifteen,	[illegible]	[illegible]	[illegible]	[illegible]	[illegible]	[illegible]	[illegible]	[illegible]	[illegible]	[illegible]	[illegible]	[illegible]	[illegible]	[illegible]	[illegible]
Above twenty years,	[illegible]	[illegible]	[illegible]	[illegible]	[illegible]	[illegible]	[illegible]	[illegible]	[illegible]	[illegible]	[illegible]	[illegible]	[illegible]	[illegible]	[illegible]
Total in confinement at end of year [illegible],	[illegible]	[illegible]	[illegible]	[illegible]	[illegible]	[illegible]	[illegible]	[illegible]	[illegible]	[illegible]	[illegible]	[illegible]	[illegible]	[illegible]	[illegible]
PART III.—OFFENCES OF LUNATICS COMMITTED TO ASYLUMS DURING THE YEAR [illegible]															
Murder of Infants aged one year and under,	[illegible]	[illegible]	[illegible]	[illegible]	[illegible]	[illegible]	[illegible]	[illegible]	[illegible]	[illegible]	[illegible]	[illegible]	[illegible]	[illegible]	[illegible]
Other Murders,	[illegible]	[illegible]	[illegible]	[illegible]	[illegible]	[illegible]	[illegible]	[illegible]	[illegible]	[illegible]	[illegible]	[illegible]	[illegible]	[illegible]	[illegible]
Attempts to Murder, Wounding, Stabbing, &c.,	[illegible]	[illegible]	[illegible]	[illegible]	[illegible]	[illegible]	[illegible]	[illegible]	[illegible]	[illegible]	[illegible]	[illegible]	[illegible]	[illegible]	[illegible]
Concealing Birth,	[illegible]	[illegible]	[illegible]	[illegible]	[illegible]	[illegible]	[illegible]	[illegible]	[illegible]	[illegible]	[illegible]	[illegible]	[illegible]	[illegible]	[illegible]
Manslaughter,	[illegible]	[illegible]	[illegible]	[illegible]	[illegible]	[illegible]	[illegible]	[illegible]	[illegible]	[illegible]	[illegible]	[illegible]	[illegible]	[illegible]	[illegible]
Rape,	[illegible]	[illegible]	[illegible]	[illegible]	[illegible]	[illegible]	[illegible]	[illegible]	[illegible]	[illegible]	[illegible]	[illegible]	[illegible]	[illegible]	[illegible]
Assault with intent to Ravish,	[illegible]	[illegible]	[illegible]	[illegible]	[illegible]	[illegible]	[illegible]	[illegible]	[illegible]	[illegible]	[illegible]	[illegible]	[illegible]	[illegible]	[illegible]
Unnatural Offences,	[illegible]	[illegible]	[illegible]	[illegible]	[illegible]	[illegible]	[illegible]	[illegible]	[illegible]	[illegible]	[illegible]	[illegible]	[illegible]	[illegible]	[illegible]
Treasonable and Seditious Offences,	[illegible]	[illegible]	[illegible]	[illegible]	[illegible]	[illegible]	[illegible]	[illegible]	[illegible]	[illegible]	[illegible]	[illegible]	[illegible]	[illegible]	[illegible]
Assault,	[illegible]	[illegible]	[illegible]	[illegible]	[illegible]	[illegible]	[illegible]	[illegible]	[illegible]	[illegible]	[illegible]	[illegible]	[illegible]	[illegible]	[illegible]
Indecent Exposure of the Person,	[illegible]	[illegible]	[illegible]	[illegible]	[illegible]	[illegible]	[illegible]	[illegible]	[illegible]	[illegible]	[illegible]	[illegible]	[illegible]	[illegible]	[illegible]
Burglary and Housebreaking,	[illegible]	[illegible]	[illegible]	[illegible]	[illegible]	[illegible]	[illegible]	[illegible]	[illegible]	[illegible]	[illegible]	[illegible]	[illegible]	[illegible]	[illegible]
Robbery on the Highway, &c.,	[illegible]	[illegible]	[illegible]	[illegible]	[illegible]	[illegible]	[illegible]	[illegible]	[illegible]	[illegible]	[illegible]	[illegible]	[illegible]	[illegible]	[illegible]
Horse, Cattle, and Sheep Stealing,	[illegible]	[illegible]	[illegible]	[illegible]	[illegible]	[illegible]	[illegible]	[illegible]	[illegible]	[illegible]	[illegible]	[illegible]	[illegible]	[illegible]	[illegible]
Larceny and Petty Thefts,	[illegible]	[illegible]	[illegible]	[illegible]	[illegible]	[illegible]	[illegible]	[illegible]	[illegible]	[illegible]	[illegible]	[illegible]	[illegible]	[illegible]	[illegible]
[illegible]	[illegible]	[illegible]	[illegible]	[illegible]	[illegible]	[illegible]	[illegible]	[illegible]	[illegible]	[illegible]	[illegible]	[illegible]	[illegible]	[illegible]	[illegible]
Receiving Stolen Goods,	[illegible]	[illegible]	[illegible]	[illegible]	[illegible]	[illegible]	[illegible]	[illegible]	[illegible]	[illegible]	[illegible]	[illegible]	[illegible]	[illegible]	[illegible]
Arson and Malicious Burning,	[illegible]	[illegible]	[illegible]	[illegible]	[illegible]	[illegible]	[illegible]	[illegible]	[illegible]	[illegible]	[illegible]	[illegible]	[illegible]	[illegible]	[illegible]
Wilful Damage and other Malicious Offences,	[illegible]	[illegible]	[illegible]	[illegible]	[illegible]	[illegible]	[illegible]	[illegible]	[illegible]	[illegible]	[illegible]	[illegible]	[illegible]	[illegible]	[illegible]
Perjury,	[illegible]	[illegible]	[illegible]	[illegible]	[illegible]	[illegible]	[illegible]	[illegible]	[illegible]	[illegible]	[illegible]	[illegible]	[illegible]	[illegible]	[illegible]
Convicted of having in possession Counterfeit Coin,	[illegible]	[illegible]	[illegible]	[illegible]	[illegible]	[illegible]	[illegible]	[illegible]	[illegible]	[illegible]	[illegible]	[illegible]	[illegible]	[illegible]	[illegible]
[illegible] Breach of the Peace,	[illegible]	[illegible]	[illegible]	[illegible]	[illegible]	[illegible]	[illegible]	[illegible]	[illegible]	[illegible]	[illegible]	[illegible]	[illegible]	[illegible]	[illegible]
Under the Vagrant Laws,	[illegible]	[illegible]	[illegible]	[illegible]	[illegible]	[illegible]	[illegible]	[illegible]	[illegible]	[illegible]	[illegible]	[illegible]	[illegible]	[illegible]	[illegible]
Dangerous Persons at Large,	[illegible]	[illegible]	[illegible]	[illegible]	[illegible]	[illegible]	[illegible]	[illegible]	[illegible]	[illegible]	[illegible]	[illegible]	[illegible]	[illegible]	[illegible]
[illegible]	[illegible]	[illegible]	[illegible]	[illegible]	[illegible]	[illegible]	[illegible]	[illegible]	[illegible]	[illegible]	[illegible]	[illegible]	[illegible]	[illegible]	[illegible]
Deserters from the Army or Navy,	[illegible]	[illegible]	[illegible]	[illegible]	[illegible]	[illegible]	[illegible]	[illegible]	[illegible]	[illegible]	[illegible]	[illegible]	[illegible]	[illegible]	[illegible]
For want of Sureties,	[illegible]	[illegible]	[illegible]	[illegible]	[illegible]	[illegible]	[illegible]	[illegible]	[illegible]	[illegible]	[illegible]	[illegible]	[illegible]	[illegible]	[illegible]
Attempts at Suicide,	[illegible]	[illegible]	[illegible]	[illegible]	[illegible]	[illegible]	[illegible]	[illegible]	[illegible]	[illegible]	[illegible]	[illegible]	[illegible]	[illegible]	[illegible]
Threatening Language,	[illegible]	[illegible]	[illegible]	[illegible]	[illegible]	[illegible]	[illegible]	[illegible]	[illegible]	[illegible]	[illegible]	[illegible]	[illegible]	[illegible]	[illegible]
Drunkenness,	[illegible]	[illegible]	[illegible]	[illegible]	[illegible]	[illegible]	[illegible]	[illegible]	[illegible]	[illegible]	[illegible]	[illegible]	[illegible]	[illegible]	[illegible]
[illegible]	[illegible]	[illegible]	[illegible]	[illegible]	[illegible]	[illegible]	[illegible]	[illegible]	[illegible]	[illegible]	[illegible]	[illegible]	[illegible]	[illegible]	[illegible]
Offences not stated,	[illegible]	[illegible]	[illegible]	[illegible]	[illegible]	[illegible]	[illegible]	[illegible]	[illegible]	[illegible]	[illegible]	[illegible]	[illegible]	[illegible]	[illegible]
Total number committed during the year [illegible],	[illegible]	[illegible]	[illegible]	[illegible]	[illegible]	[illegible]	[illegible]	[illegible]	[illegible]	[illegible]	[illegible]	[illegible]	[illegible]	[illegible]	[illegible]
PART IV.—AUTHORITY UNDER WHICH LUNATICS COMMITTED TO ASYLUMS DURING THE YEAR [illegible]															
Transferred from Prison by Lord Lieutenant's Warrant—															
Insane [illegible] Committal and before Trial,	[illegible]	[illegible]	[illegible]	[illegible]	[illegible]	[illegible]	[illegible]	[illegible]	[illegible]	[illegible]	[illegible]	[illegible]	[illegible]	[illegible]	[illegible]
Found or declared Insane,	[illegible]	[illegible]	[illegible]	[illegible]	[illegible]	[illegible]	[illegible]	[illegible]	[illegible]	[illegible]	[illegible]	[illegible]	[illegible]	[illegible]	[illegible]
Acquitted as Insane,	[illegible]	[illegible]	[illegible]	[illegible]	[illegible]	[illegible]	[illegible]	[illegible]	[illegible]	[illegible]	[illegible]	[illegible]	[illegible]	[illegible]	[illegible]
[illegible]	[illegible]	[illegible]	[illegible]	[illegible]	[illegible]	[illegible]	[illegible]	[illegible]	[illegible]	[illegible]	[illegible]	[illegible]	[illegible]	[illegible]	[illegible]
Committed to Asylums by Justices as Dangerous, under [illegible]	[illegible]	[illegible]	[illegible]	[illegible]	[illegible]	[illegible]	[illegible]	[illegible]	[illegible]	[illegible]	[illegible]	[illegible]	[illegible]	[illegible]	[illegible]
Committed by Secretary of State for War,	[illegible]	[illegible]	[illegible]	[illegible]	[illegible]	[illegible]	[illegible]	[illegible]	[illegible]	[illegible]	[illegible]	[illegible]	[illegible]	[illegible]	[illegible]
Total number committed during the year [illegible]	[illegible]	[illegible]	[illegible]	[illegible]	[illegible]	[illegible]	[illegible]	[illegible]	[illegible]	[illegible]	[illegible]	[illegible]	[illegible]	[illegible]	[illegible]

[illegible]

TABLE [illegible].—CRIMINAL LUNATICS IN ASYLUMS.—Showing for each Asylum—I. The Number of those under [illegible]

	Asylums, &c.																	
—	Cork. — County and City of Cork.		Derry. — County of Derry.		Dundrum, Co. Dublin. — Central Criminal for Ireland.		Ennis. — County of Clare.		Enniscorthy. — County of Wexford.		Kilkenny. — County and City of Kilkenny.		Killarney. — County of Kerry.		Letterkenny. — County of Donegal.	
	M.	W.	M.	W.	M.	W.	M.	W.	M.	W.	M.	W.	M.	W.	M.	W.
PART I.—AUTHORITY FOR CONFINEMENT OF THOSE IN CONFINEMENT AT THE END OF THE YEAR [illegible].																
Total number in confinement at end of year [illegible]	[illegible]	[illegible]	[illegible]	[illegible]	[illegible]	[illegible]	[illegible]	[illegible]	[illegible]	[illegible]	[illegible]	[illegible]	[illegible]	[illegible]	[illegible]	[illegible]
Total number committed by Justices	[illegible]	[illegible]	[illegible]	[illegible]	[illegible]	[illegible]	[illegible]	[illegible]	[illegible]	[illegible]	[illegible]	[illegible]	[illegible]	[illegible]	[illegible]	[illegible]
Total number held in confinement by Warrant of Lord Lieutenant	[illegible]	[illegible]	[illegible]	[illegible]	[illegible]	[illegible]	[illegible]	[illegible]	[illegible]	[illegible]	[illegible]	[illegible]	[illegible]	[illegible]	[illegible]	[illegible]
Total number committed by Secretary of State for War	[illegible]	[illegible]	[illegible]	[illegible]	[illegible]	[illegible]	[illegible]	[illegible]	[illegible]	[illegible]	[illegible]	[illegible]	[illegible]	[illegible]	[illegible]	[illegible]
PART II.—PERIOD OF DETENTION IN ASYLUM OF THOSE IN THEIR DETENTION AT END OF THE YEAR [illegible].																
Number who have been detained in Lunatic Asylums— One year and under,	[illegible]	[illegible]	[illegible]	[illegible]	[illegible]	[illegible]	[illegible]	[illegible]	[illegible]	[illegible]	[illegible]	[illegible]	[illegible]	[illegible]	[illegible]	[illegible]
Two years and above one,	[illegible]	[illegible]	[illegible]	[illegible]	[illegible]	[illegible]	[illegible]	[illegible]	[illegible]	[illegible]	[illegible]	[illegible]	[illegible]	[illegible]	[illegible]	[illegible]
Three years and above two,	[illegible]	[illegible]	[illegible]	[illegible]	[illegible]	[illegible]	[illegible]	[illegible]	[illegible]	[illegible]	[illegible]	[illegible]	[illegible]	[illegible]	[illegible]	[illegible]
Three years and above three,	[illegible]	[illegible]	[illegible]	[illegible]	[illegible]	[illegible]	[illegible]	[illegible]	[illegible]	[illegible]	[illegible]	[illegible]	[illegible]	[illegible]	[illegible]	[illegible]
Five years and above [illegible],	[illegible]	[illegible]	[illegible]	[illegible]	[illegible]	[illegible]	[illegible]	[illegible]	[illegible]	[illegible]	[illegible]	[illegible]	[illegible]	[illegible]	[illegible]	[illegible]
Ten years and above five,	[illegible]	[illegible]	[illegible]	[illegible]	[illegible]	[illegible]	[illegible]	[illegible]	[illegible]	[illegible]	[illegible]	[illegible]	[illegible]	[illegible]	[illegible]	[illegible]
Fifteen years and above ten,	[illegible]	[illegible]	[illegible]	[illegible]	[illegible]	[illegible]	[illegible]	[illegible]	[illegible]	[illegible]	[illegible]	[illegible]	[illegible]	[illegible]	[illegible]	[illegible]
Twenty years and above fifteen,	[illegible]	[illegible]	[illegible]	[illegible]	[illegible]	[illegible]	[illegible]	[illegible]	[illegible]	[illegible]	[illegible]	[illegible]	[illegible]	[illegible]	[illegible]	[illegible]
Above twenty years,	[illegible]	[illegible]	[illegible]	[illegible]	[illegible]	[illegible]	[illegible]	[illegible]	[illegible]	[illegible]	[illegible]	[illegible]	[illegible]	[illegible]	[illegible]	[illegible]
Total in confinement at end of year [illegible],	[illegible]	[illegible]	[illegible]	[illegible]	[illegible]	[illegible]	[illegible]	[illegible]	[illegible]	[illegible]	[illegible]	[illegible]	[illegible]	[illegible]	[illegible]	[illegible]
PART III.—OFFENCES OF LUNATICS COMMITTED TO ASYLUMS DURING THE YEAR [illegible].																
Murder of Infants aged one year and under,	[illegible]	[illegible]	[illegible]	[illegible]	[illegible]	[illegible]	[illegible]	[illegible]	[illegible]	[illegible]	[illegible]	[illegible]	[illegible]	[illegible]	[illegible]	[illegible]
Other Murders,	[illegible]	[illegible]	[illegible]	[illegible]	[illegible]	[illegible]	[illegible]	[illegible]	[illegible]	[illegible]	[illegible]	[illegible]	[illegible]	[illegible]	[illegible]	[illegible]
Attempts to Murder, Stab, Shooting, &c.,	[illegible]	[illegible]	[illegible]	[illegible]	[illegible]	[illegible]	[illegible]	[illegible]	[illegible]	[illegible]	[illegible]	[illegible]	[illegible]	[illegible]	[illegible]	[illegible]
Concealing Birth,	[illegible]	[illegible]	[illegible]	[illegible]	[illegible]	[illegible]	[illegible]	[illegible]	[illegible]	[illegible]	[illegible]	[illegible]	[illegible]	[illegible]	[illegible]	[illegible]
Manslaughter,	[illegible]	[illegible]	[illegible]	[illegible]	[illegible]	[illegible]	[illegible]	[illegible]	[illegible]	[illegible]	[illegible]	[illegible]	[illegible]	[illegible]	[illegible]	[illegible]
Rape,	[illegible]	[illegible]	[illegible]	[illegible]	[illegible]	[illegible]	[illegible]	[illegible]	[illegible]	[illegible]	[illegible]	[illegible]	[illegible]	[illegible]	[illegible]	[illegible]
Assault with intent to Ravish,	[illegible]	[illegible]	[illegible]	[illegible]	[illegible]	[illegible]	[illegible]	[illegible]	[illegible]	[illegible]	[illegible]	[illegible]	[illegible]	[illegible]	[illegible]	[illegible]
Unnatural Offences,	[illegible]	[illegible]	[illegible]	[illegible]	[illegible]	[illegible]	[illegible]	[illegible]	[illegible]	[illegible]	[illegible]	[illegible]	[illegible]	[illegible]	[illegible]	[illegible]
[illegible] Offences,	[illegible]	[illegible]	[illegible]	[illegible]	[illegible]	[illegible]	[illegible]	[illegible]	[illegible]	[illegible]	[illegible]	[illegible]	[illegible]	[illegible]	[illegible]	[illegible]
Assaults,	[illegible]	[illegible]	[illegible]	[illegible]	[illegible]	[illegible]	[illegible]	[illegible]	[illegible]	[illegible]	[illegible]	[illegible]	[illegible]	[illegible]	[illegible]	[illegible]
Indecent Exposure of the Person,	[illegible]	[illegible]	[illegible]	[illegible]	[illegible]	[illegible]	[illegible]	[illegible]	[illegible]	[illegible]	[illegible]	[illegible]	[illegible]	[illegible]	[illegible]	[illegible]
Burglary and Housebreaking,	[illegible]	[illegible]	[illegible]	[illegible]	[illegible]	[illegible]	[illegible]	[illegible]	[illegible]	[illegible]	[illegible]	[illegible]	[illegible]	[illegible]	[illegible]	[illegible]
Robbery on the Person, &c.,	[illegible]	[illegible]	[illegible]	[illegible]	[illegible]	[illegible]	[illegible]	[illegible]	[illegible]	[illegible]	[illegible]	[illegible]	[illegible]	[illegible]	[illegible]	[illegible]
Horse, Cattle, and Sheep Stealing,	[illegible]	[illegible]	[illegible]	[illegible]	[illegible]	[illegible]	[illegible]	[illegible]	[illegible]	[illegible]	[illegible]	[illegible]	[illegible]	[illegible]	[illegible]	[illegible]
Larceny and Petty Thefts,	[illegible]	[illegible]	[illegible]	[illegible]	[illegible]	[illegible]	[illegible]	[illegible]	[illegible]	[illegible]	[illegible]	[illegible]	[illegible]	[illegible]	[illegible]	[illegible]
Frauds and Embezzlements,	[illegible]	[illegible]	[illegible]	[illegible]	[illegible]	[illegible]	[illegible]	[illegible]	[illegible]	[illegible]	[illegible]	[illegible]	[illegible]	[illegible]	[illegible]	[illegible]
Receiving Stolen Goods,	[illegible]	[illegible]	[illegible]	[illegible]	[illegible]	[illegible]	[illegible]	[illegible]	[illegible]	[illegible]	[illegible]	[illegible]	[illegible]	[illegible]	[illegible]	[illegible]
Arson and Malicious Burning,	[illegible]	[illegible]	[illegible]	[illegible]	[illegible]	[illegible]	[illegible]	[illegible]	[illegible]	[illegible]	[illegible]	[illegible]	[illegible]	[illegible]	[illegible]	[illegible]
Wilful Damage and other Malicious Offences,	[illegible]	[illegible]	[illegible]	[illegible]	[illegible]	[illegible]	[illegible]	[illegible]	[illegible]	[illegible]	[illegible]	[illegible]	[illegible]	[illegible]	[illegible]	[illegible]
Forgery,	[illegible]	[illegible]	[illegible]	[illegible]	[illegible]	[illegible]	[illegible]	[illegible]	[illegible]	[illegible]	[illegible]	[illegible]	[illegible]	[illegible]	[illegible]	[illegible]
Uttering or having in possession Counterfeit Coin,	[illegible]	[illegible]	[illegible]	[illegible]	[illegible]	[illegible]	[illegible]	[illegible]	[illegible]	[illegible]	[illegible]	[illegible]	[illegible]	[illegible]	[illegible]	[illegible]
Riot and Breach of the Peace,	[illegible]	[illegible]	[illegible]	[illegible]	[illegible]	[illegible]	[illegible]	[illegible]	[illegible]	[illegible]	[illegible]	[illegible]	[illegible]	[illegible]	[illegible]	[illegible]
Under the Vagrant Laws,	[illegible]	[illegible]	[illegible]	[illegible]	[illegible]	[illegible]	[illegible]	[illegible]	[illegible]	[illegible]	[illegible]	[illegible]	[illegible]	[illegible]	[illegible]	[illegible]
Dangerous Persons at Large,	[illegible]	[illegible]	[illegible]	[illegible]	[illegible]	[illegible]	[illegible]	[illegible]	[illegible]	[illegible]	[illegible]	[illegible]	[illegible]	[illegible]	[illegible]	[illegible]
[illegible],	[illegible]	[illegible]	[illegible]	[illegible]	[illegible]	[illegible]	[illegible]	[illegible]	[illegible]	[illegible]	[illegible]	[illegible]	[illegible]	[illegible]	[illegible]	[illegible]
Deserters from the Army or Navy,	[illegible]	[illegible]	[illegible]	[illegible]	[illegible]	[illegible]	[illegible]	[illegible]	[illegible]	[illegible]	[illegible]	[illegible]	[illegible]	[illegible]	[illegible]	[illegible]
For want of Sureties,	[illegible]	[illegible]	[illegible]	[illegible]	[illegible]	[illegible]	[illegible]	[illegible]	[illegible]	[illegible]	[illegible]	[illegible]	[illegible]	[illegible]	[illegible]	[illegible]
Attempts at Suicide,	[illegible]	[illegible]	[illegible]	[illegible]	[illegible]	[illegible]	[illegible]	[illegible]	[illegible]	[illegible]	[illegible]	[illegible]	[illegible]	[illegible]	[illegible]	[illegible]
Threatening Letters,	[illegible]	[illegible]	[illegible]	[illegible]	[illegible]	[illegible]	[illegible]	[illegible]	[illegible]	[illegible]	[illegible]	[illegible]	[illegible]	[illegible]	[illegible]	[illegible]
Drunkenness,	[illegible]	[illegible]	[illegible]	[illegible]	[illegible]	[illegible]	[illegible]	[illegible]	[illegible]	[illegible]	[illegible]	[illegible]	[illegible]	[illegible]	[illegible]	[illegible]
Felony not classed,	[illegible]	[illegible]	[illegible]	[illegible]	[illegible]	[illegible]	[illegible]	[illegible]	[illegible]	[illegible]	[illegible]	[illegible]	[illegible]	[illegible]	[illegible]	[illegible]
Offences not classed,	[illegible]	[illegible]	[illegible]	[illegible]	[illegible]	[illegible]	[illegible]	[illegible]	[illegible]	[illegible]	[illegible]	[illegible]	[illegible]	[illegible]	[illegible]	[illegible]
Total number committed during the year [illegible]	[illegible]	[illegible]	[illegible]	[illegible]	[illegible]	[illegible]	[illegible]	[illegible]	[illegible]	[illegible]	[illegible]	[illegible]	[illegible]	[illegible]	[illegible]	[illegible]
PART IV.—AUTHORITY UNDER WHICH LUNATICS COMMITTED TO ASYLUMS DURING THE YEAR [illegible].																
Transmitted from Prisons by Lord Lieutenant's Warrant—																
Became Insane after Committal and before Trial,	[illegible]	[illegible]	[illegible]	[illegible]	[illegible]	[illegible]	[illegible]	[illegible]	[illegible]	[illegible]	[illegible]	[illegible]	[illegible]	[illegible]	[illegible]	[illegible]
Found at Arraignment Insane,	[illegible]	[illegible]	[illegible]	[illegible]	[illegible]	[illegible]	[illegible]	[illegible]	[illegible]	[illegible]	[illegible]	[illegible]	[illegible]	[illegible]	[illegible]	[illegible]
Acquitted on Insanity,	[illegible]	[illegible]	[illegible]	[illegible]	[illegible]	[illegible]	[illegible]	[illegible]	[illegible]	[illegible]	[illegible]	[illegible]	[illegible]	[illegible]	[illegible]	[illegible]
Became Insane while undergoing Sentence of Imprisonment,	[illegible]	[illegible]	[illegible]	[illegible]	[illegible]	[illegible]	[illegible]	[illegible]	[illegible]	[illegible]	[illegible]	[illegible]	[illegible]	[illegible]	[illegible]	[illegible]
Committed to Asylums by Justices as Dangerous, under [illegible]	[illegible]	[illegible]	[illegible]	[illegible]	[illegible]	[illegible]	[illegible]	[illegible]	[illegible]	[illegible]	[illegible]	[illegible]	[illegible]	[illegible]	[illegible]	[illegible]
Committed by Secretary of State for War,	[illegible]	[illegible]	[illegible]	[illegible]	[illegible]	[illegible]	[illegible]	[illegible]	[illegible]	[illegible]	[illegible]	[illegible]	[illegible]	[illegible]	[illegible]	[illegible]
Total number admitted during the year [illegible].	[illegible]	[illegible]	[illegible]	[illegible]	[illegible]	[illegible]	[illegible]	[illegible]	[illegible]	[illegible]	[illegible]	[illegible]	[illegible]	[illegible]	[illegible]	[illegible]

	County and City of Glasgow		[illegible]		[illegible]		Counties of [illegible]		Counties of [illegible]		[illegible]		Town of [illegible] and Counties of [illegible]		Counties of [illegible]		County and City of [illegible]	
	M.	W.	M.	W.	M.	W.	M.	W.	M.	W.	M.	W.	M.	W.	M.	W.	M.	W.
PART I.—APPREHENSIONS AND COMMITMENTS [illegible] THE YEAR 1869.																		
Total number in confinement at end of year 1868	[illegible]	[illegible]	[illegible]	[illegible]	[illegible]	[illegible]	[illegible]	[illegible]	[illegible]	[illegible]	[illegible]	[illegible]	[illegible]	[illegible]	[illegible]	[illegible]	[illegible]	[illegible]
Total number committed by Justices.	[illegible]	[illegible]	[illegible]	[illegible]	[illegible]	[illegible]	[illegible]	[illegible]	[illegible]	[illegible]	[illegible]	[illegible]	[illegible]	[illegible]	[illegible]	[illegible]	[illegible]	[illegible]
Total number held in confinement by Warrant of Lord Lieutenant	[illegible]	[illegible]	[illegible]	[illegible]	[illegible]	[illegible]	[illegible]	[illegible]	[illegible]	[illegible]	[illegible]	[illegible]	[illegible]	[illegible]	[illegible]	[illegible]	[illegible]	[illegible]
Total number committed by Secretary of State for War.	[illegible]	[illegible]	[illegible]	[illegible]	[illegible]	[illegible]	[illegible]	[illegible]	[illegible]	[illegible]	[illegible]	[illegible]	[illegible]	[illegible]	[illegible]	[illegible]	[illegible]	[illegible]
PART II.—PERIODS OF DETENTION [illegible] OF THOSE [illegible] DETENTION AT END OF THE YEAR 1869.																		
Periods [illegible]																		
One year and under	[illegible]	[illegible]	[illegible]	[illegible]	[illegible]	[illegible]	[illegible]	[illegible]	[illegible]	[illegible]	[illegible]	[illegible]	[illegible]	[illegible]	[illegible]	[illegible]	[illegible]	[illegible]
Two years and above one.	[illegible]	[illegible]	[illegible]	[illegible]	[illegible]	[illegible]	[illegible]	[illegible]	[illegible]	[illegible]	[illegible]	[illegible]	[illegible]	[illegible]	[illegible]	[illegible]	[illegible]	[illegible]
Three years and above two.	[illegible]	[illegible]	[illegible]	[illegible]	[illegible]	[illegible]	[illegible]	[illegible]	[illegible]	[illegible]	[illegible]	[illegible]	[illegible]	[illegible]	[illegible]	[illegible]	[illegible]	[illegible]
Five years and above three.	[illegible]	[illegible]	[illegible]	[illegible]	[illegible]	[illegible]	[illegible]	[illegible]	[illegible]	[illegible]	[illegible]	[illegible]	[illegible]	[illegible]	[illegible]	[illegible]	[illegible]	[illegible]
Ten years and above five.	[illegible]	[illegible]	[illegible]	[illegible]	[illegible]	[illegible]	[illegible]	[illegible]	[illegible]	[illegible]	[illegible]	[illegible]	[illegible]	[illegible]	[illegible]	[illegible]	[illegible]	[illegible]
Fifteen years and above ten.	[illegible]	[illegible]	[illegible]	[illegible]	[illegible]	[illegible]	[illegible]	[illegible]	[illegible]	[illegible]	[illegible]	[illegible]	[illegible]	[illegible]	[illegible]	[illegible]	[illegible]	[illegible]
Twenty years and above fifteen.	[illegible]	[illegible]	[illegible]	[illegible]	[illegible]	[illegible]	[illegible]	[illegible]	[illegible]	[illegible]	[illegible]	[illegible]	[illegible]	[illegible]	[illegible]	[illegible]	[illegible]	[illegible]
Above twenty years.	[illegible]	[illegible]	[illegible]	[illegible]	[illegible]	[illegible]	[illegible]	[illegible]	[illegible]	[illegible]	[illegible]	[illegible]	[illegible]	[illegible]	[illegible]	[illegible]	[illegible]	[illegible]
Total in confinement at end of year 1869	[illegible]	[illegible]	[illegible]	[illegible]	[illegible]	[illegible]	[illegible]	[illegible]	[illegible]	[illegible]	[illegible]	[illegible]	[illegible]	[illegible]	[illegible]	[illegible]	[illegible]	[illegible]
PART III.—OFFENCES OF LUNATICS [illegible] TO ASYLUMS DURING THE YEAR 1869.																		
Number of Lunatics [illegible]																		
Other Murders	[illegible]	[illegible]	[illegible]	[illegible]	[illegible]	[illegible]	[illegible]	[illegible]	[illegible]	[illegible]	[illegible]	[illegible]	[illegible]	[illegible]	[illegible]	[illegible]	[illegible]	[illegible]
Attempts to Murder, Maim, Stabbing, &c.	[illegible]	[illegible]	[illegible]	[illegible]	[illegible]	[illegible]	[illegible]	[illegible]	[illegible]	[illegible]	[illegible]	[illegible]	[illegible]	[illegible]	[illegible]	[illegible]	[illegible]	[illegible]
Concealing Birth.	[illegible]	[illegible]	[illegible]	[illegible]	[illegible]	[illegible]	[illegible]	[illegible]	[illegible]	[illegible]	[illegible]	[illegible]	[illegible]	[illegible]	[illegible]	[illegible]	[illegible]	[illegible]
Manslaughter	[illegible]	[illegible]	[illegible]	[illegible]	[illegible]	[illegible]	[illegible]	[illegible]	[illegible]	[illegible]	[illegible]	[illegible]	[illegible]	[illegible]	[illegible]	[illegible]	[illegible]	[illegible]
Rape	[illegible]	[illegible]	[illegible]	[illegible]	[illegible]	[illegible]	[illegible]	[illegible]	[illegible]	[illegible]	[illegible]	[illegible]	[illegible]	[illegible]	[illegible]	[illegible]	[illegible]	[illegible]
Assault with intent to Ravish	[illegible]	[illegible]	[illegible]	[illegible]	[illegible]	[illegible]	[illegible]	[illegible]	[illegible]	[illegible]	[illegible]	[illegible]	[illegible]	[illegible]	[illegible]	[illegible]	[illegible]	[illegible]
Unnatural Offences	[illegible]	[illegible]	[illegible]	[illegible]	[illegible]	[illegible]	[illegible]	[illegible]	[illegible]	[illegible]	[illegible]	[illegible]	[illegible]	[illegible]	[illegible]	[illegible]	[illegible]	[illegible]
[illegible] and [illegible] Offences	[illegible]	[illegible]	[illegible]	[illegible]	[illegible]	[illegible]	[illegible]	[illegible]	[illegible]	[illegible]	[illegible]	[illegible]	[illegible]	[illegible]	[illegible]	[illegible]	[illegible]	[illegible]
Assaults	[illegible]	[illegible]	[illegible]	[illegible]	[illegible]	[illegible]	[illegible]	[illegible]	[illegible]	[illegible]	[illegible]	[illegible]	[illegible]	[illegible]	[illegible]	[illegible]	[illegible]	[illegible]
[illegible] of the Person.	[illegible]	[illegible]	[illegible]	[illegible]	[illegible]	[illegible]	[illegible]	[illegible]	[illegible]	[illegible]	[illegible]	[illegible]	[illegible]	[illegible]	[illegible]	[illegible]	[illegible]	[illegible]
Burglary and Housebreaking	[illegible]	[illegible]	[illegible]	[illegible]	[illegible]	[illegible]	[illegible]	[illegible]	[illegible]	[illegible]	[illegible]	[illegible]	[illegible]	[illegible]	[illegible]	[illegible]	[illegible]	[illegible]
Robbery on the Highway, &c.	[illegible]	[illegible]	[illegible]	[illegible]	[illegible]	[illegible]	[illegible]	[illegible]	[illegible]	[illegible]	[illegible]	[illegible]	[illegible]	[illegible]	[illegible]	[illegible]	[illegible]	[illegible]
Sheep, Cattle, and Horse Stealing	[illegible]	[illegible]	[illegible]	[illegible]	[illegible]	[illegible]	[illegible]	[illegible]	[illegible]	[illegible]	[illegible]	[illegible]	[illegible]	[illegible]	[illegible]	[illegible]	[illegible]	[illegible]
Larceny and Petty Thefts	[illegible]	[illegible]	[illegible]	[illegible]	[illegible]	[illegible]	[illegible]	[illegible]	[illegible]	[illegible]	[illegible]	[illegible]	[illegible]	[illegible]	[illegible]	[illegible]	[illegible]	[illegible]
Frauds and Embezzlements	[illegible]	[illegible]	[illegible]	[illegible]	[illegible]	[illegible]	[illegible]	[illegible]	[illegible]	[illegible]	[illegible]	[illegible]	[illegible]	[illegible]	[illegible]	[illegible]	[illegible]	[illegible]
Receiving Stolen Goods	[illegible]	[illegible]	[illegible]	[illegible]	[illegible]	[illegible]	[illegible]	[illegible]	[illegible]	[illegible]	[illegible]	[illegible]	[illegible]	[illegible]	[illegible]	[illegible]	[illegible]	[illegible]
[illegible]	[illegible]	[illegible]	[illegible]	[illegible]	[illegible]	[illegible]	[illegible]	[illegible]	[illegible]	[illegible]	[illegible]	[illegible]	[illegible]	[illegible]	[illegible]	[illegible]	[illegible]	[illegible]
Wilful Damage and other Malicious Offences	[illegible]	[illegible]	[illegible]	[illegible]	[illegible]	[illegible]	[illegible]	[illegible]	[illegible]	[illegible]	[illegible]	[illegible]	[illegible]	[illegible]	[illegible]	[illegible]	[illegible]	[illegible]
Forgery	[illegible]	[illegible]	[illegible]	[illegible]	[illegible]	[illegible]	[illegible]	[illegible]	[illegible]	[illegible]	[illegible]	[illegible]	[illegible]	[illegible]	[illegible]	[illegible]	[illegible]	[illegible]
Uttering or having in possession Counterfeit Coin	[illegible]	[illegible]	[illegible]	[illegible]	[illegible]	[illegible]	[illegible]	[illegible]	[illegible]	[illegible]	[illegible]	[illegible]	[illegible]	[illegible]	[illegible]	[illegible]	[illegible]	[illegible]
Breach of the Peace	[illegible]	[illegible]	[illegible]	[illegible]	[illegible]	[illegible]	[illegible]	[illegible]	[illegible]	[illegible]	[illegible]	[illegible]	[illegible]	[illegible]	[illegible]	[illegible]	[illegible]	[illegible]
Under the Vagrant Laws	[illegible]	[illegible]	[illegible]	[illegible]	[illegible]	[illegible]	[illegible]	[illegible]	[illegible]	[illegible]	[illegible]	[illegible]	[illegible]	[illegible]	[illegible]	[illegible]	[illegible]	[illegible]
Dangerous Persons at Large	[illegible]	[illegible]	[illegible]	[illegible]	[illegible]	[illegible]	[illegible]	[illegible]	[illegible]	[illegible]	[illegible]	[illegible]	[illegible]	[illegible]	[illegible]	[illegible]	[illegible]	[illegible]
Lunatics, [illegible]	[illegible]	[illegible]	[illegible]	[illegible]	[illegible]	[illegible]	[illegible]	[illegible]	[illegible]	[illegible]	[illegible]	[illegible]	[illegible]	[illegible]	[illegible]	[illegible]	[illegible]	[illegible]
Deserters from the Army or Navy.	[illegible]	[illegible]	[illegible]	[illegible]	[illegible]	[illegible]	[illegible]	[illegible]	[illegible]	[illegible]	[illegible]	[illegible]	[illegible]	[illegible]	[illegible]	[illegible]	[illegible]	[illegible]
For Breach of [illegible]	[illegible]	[illegible]	[illegible]	[illegible]	[illegible]	[illegible]	[illegible]	[illegible]	[illegible]	[illegible]	[illegible]	[illegible]	[illegible]	[illegible]	[illegible]	[illegible]	[illegible]	[illegible]
Attempts at Suicide	[illegible]	[illegible]	[illegible]	[illegible]	[illegible]	[illegible]	[illegible]	[illegible]	[illegible]	[illegible]	[illegible]	[illegible]	[illegible]	[illegible]	[illegible]	[illegible]	[illegible]	[illegible]
[illegible]	[illegible]	[illegible]	[illegible]	[illegible]	[illegible]	[illegible]	[illegible]	[illegible]	[illegible]	[illegible]	[illegible]	[illegible]	[illegible]	[illegible]	[illegible]	[illegible]	[illegible]	[illegible]
[illegible]	[illegible]	[illegible]	[illegible]	[illegible]	[illegible]	[illegible]	[illegible]	[illegible]	[illegible]	[illegible]	[illegible]	[illegible]	[illegible]	[illegible]	[illegible]	[illegible]	[illegible]	[illegible]
Felony not stated	[illegible]	[illegible]	[illegible]	[illegible]	[illegible]	[illegible]	[illegible]	[illegible]	[illegible]	[illegible]	[illegible]	[illegible]	[illegible]	[illegible]	[illegible]	[illegible]	[illegible]	[illegible]
Offences not [illegible]	[illegible]	[illegible]	[illegible]	[illegible]	[illegible]	[illegible]	[illegible]	[illegible]	[illegible]	[illegible]	[illegible]	[illegible]	[illegible]	[illegible]	[illegible]	[illegible]	[illegible]	[illegible]
Total number committed during the year 1869.	[illegible]	[illegible]	[illegible]	[illegible]	[illegible]	[illegible]	[illegible]	[illegible]	[illegible]	[illegible]	[illegible]	[illegible]	[illegible]	[illegible]	[illegible]	[illegible]	[illegible]	[illegible]
PART IV.—[illegible] COMMITTED TO ASYLUMS DURING THE YEAR 1869.																		
Transmitted from Prisons by Lord Lieutenant's Warrant—																		
Became Insane after Committal or before Trial.	[illegible]	[illegible]	[illegible]	[illegible]	[illegible]	[illegible]	[illegible]	[illegible]	[illegible]	[illegible]	[illegible]	[illegible]	[illegible]	[illegible]	[illegible]	[illegible]	[illegible]	[illegible]
Found or declared Insane	[illegible]	[illegible]	[illegible]	[illegible]	[illegible]	[illegible]	[illegible]	[illegible]	[illegible]	[illegible]	[illegible]	[illegible]	[illegible]	[illegible]	[illegible]	[illegible]	[illegible]	[illegible]
Acquitted as Insane	[illegible]	[illegible]	[illegible]	[illegible]	[illegible]	[illegible]	[illegible]	[illegible]	[illegible]	[illegible]	[illegible]	[illegible]	[illegible]	[illegible]	[illegible]	[illegible]	[illegible]	[illegible]
Became Insane while undergoing the terms of Imprisonment	[illegible]	[illegible]	[illegible]	[illegible]	[illegible]	[illegible]	[illegible]	[illegible]	[illegible]	[illegible]	[illegible]	[illegible]	[illegible]	[illegible]	[illegible]	[illegible]	[illegible]	[illegible]
Committed to Asylums by Justices [illegible]	[illegible]	[illegible]	[illegible]	[illegible]	[illegible]	[illegible]	[illegible]	[illegible]	[illegible]	[illegible]	[illegible]	[illegible]	[illegible]	[illegible]	[illegible]	[illegible]	[illegible]	[illegible]
Committed by Secretary of State for War.	[illegible]	[illegible]	[illegible]	[illegible]	[illegible]	[illegible]	[illegible]	[illegible]	[illegible]	[illegible]	[illegible]	[illegible]	[illegible]	[illegible]	[illegible]	[illegible]	[illegible]	[illegible]

TABLE [illegible].—HIGH COURT OF JUSTICE.—CHANCERY DIVISION.—RETURN of PROCEEDINGS in the OFFICE of the REGISTRARS, in the Year [illegible], made by the Registrars.

NATURE OF PROCEEDINGS.	Total.	Lord Chancellor.	Master of the Rolls.	Vice-Chancellor.	[illegible]
1. [illegible]—					
Awaiting a hearing at commencement of year,	-	-	-	-	-
Set down during the year,	[illegible]	-	[illegible]	[illegible]	-
Heard during the year,	[illegible]	-	-	[illegible]	-
Otherwise disposed of,	[illegible]	-	[illegible]	-	-
Awaiting a hearing at end of year,	-	-	-	-	-
2. [illegible]—					
Awaiting a hearing at commencement of year,	-	-	-	-	-
Set down during the year,	-	-	-	-	-
Heard during the year,	-	-	-	-	-
Otherwise disposed of,	-	-	-	-	-
Awaiting a hearing at end of year,	-	-	-	-	-
3. [illegible]—					
Awaiting a hearing at commencement of year,	-	-	-	-	-
Set down during the year,	-	-	-	-	-
Heard during the year,	-	-	-	-	-
Otherwise disposed of,	-	-	-	-	-
Awaiting a hearing at end of year,	-	-	-	-	-
4. Causes—					
Awaiting a hearing at commencement of year,	-	-	-	-	-
Set down during the year,	-	-	-	-	-
Heard during the year,	-	-	-	-	-
Otherwise disposed of,	-	-	-	-	-
Awaiting a hearing at end of year,	-	-	-	-	-
5. Causes for Trial—					
Awaiting a hearing at commencement of year,	-	-	-	-	-
Set down during the year,	-	-	-	-	-
Heard during the year,	-	-	-	-	-
Otherwise disposed of,	-	-	-	-	-
Awaiting a hearing at end of year,	-	-	-	-	-
6. Actions for Trial—					
Awaiting a hearing at commencement of year,	[illegible]	-	[illegible]	[illegible]	-
Set down during the year,	[illegible]	-	[illegible]	[illegible]	-
Heard during the year,	[illegible]	-	[illegible]	[illegible]	-
Otherwise disposed of,	[illegible]	-	[illegible]	[illegible]	-
Awaiting a hearing at end of year,	[illegible]	-	[illegible]	[illegible]	-
7. [illegible] for Judgment—					
Awaiting a hearing at commencement of year,	[illegible]	-	-	[illegible]	-
Set down during the year,	[illegible]	-	[illegible]	[illegible]	-
Heard during the year,	[illegible]	-	[illegible]	[illegible]	-
Otherwise disposed of,	[illegible]	-	[illegible]	[illegible]	-
Awaiting a hearing at end of year,	[illegible]	-	[illegible]	[illegible]	-
8. Special Cases, and Questions of Law or Fact—					
Awaiting a hearing at commencement of year,	-	-	-	-	-
Set down during the year,	[illegible]	-	[illegible]	[illegible]	-
Heard during the year,	[illegible]	-	[illegible]	[illegible]	-
Otherwise disposed of,	-	-	-	-	-
Awaiting a hearing at end of year,	-	-	-	-	-
9. Causes, Actions, and Causes and Matters for further Consideration—					
Awaiting a hearing at commencement of year,	[illegible]	-	[illegible]	[illegible]	-
Set down during the year,	[illegible]	-	[illegible]	[illegible]	-
Heard during the year,	[illegible]	-	[illegible]	[illegible]	-
Otherwise disposed of,	[illegible]	-	[illegible]	-	-
Awaiting a hearing at end of year,	[illegible]	-	[illegible]	[illegible]	-

NATURE OF PROCEEDINGS.	Total.	Lord Chancellor.	Master of the Rolls.	Vice-Chancellor.	[illegible]
10. Petitions of Right—					
Awaiting a hearing at commencement of year,	-	-	-	-	-
Set down during the year,	-	-	-	-	-
Heard during the year,	-	-	-	-	-
Otherwise disposed of,	-	-	-	-	-
Awaiting a hearing at end of year,	-	-	-	-	-
11. Orders made on the hearing of Petitions under the Companies' Acts, [illegible] and [illegible],	[illegible]	-	[illegible]	[illegible]	-
12. Orders made on the hearing of other Petitions,	[illegible]	[illegible]	[illegible]	[illegible]	-
13. Orders made on the hearing of Special Motions,	[illegible]	[illegible]	[illegible]	[illegible]	-
14. Orders made in Chambers [illegible] drawn up by the Registrars,	[illegible]	-	-	[illegible]	-
15. Orders made in Court on motions adjourned from Chambers,	[illegible]	-	[illegible]	[illegible]	-
16. (a) Orders made on Hearing of Causes,	[illegible]	[illegible]	[illegible]	[illegible]	-
(b) On Petitions of Course,	-	-	-	-	-
(c) [illegible],	[illegible]	-	-	-	[illegible]
(d) Orders made on Judges' fiat, without a hearing,	[illegible]	-	[illegible]	[illegible]	-
(e) Orders made in Chambers and entered in Registrars' Office,	[illegible]	[illegible]	[illegible]	[illegible]	-
(f) Orders made by the [illegible] Judges and entered in Registrars' Office,	[illegible]	-	-	-	[illegible]
(g) Orders made on County Court appeals,	[illegible]	-	-	[illegible]	-
(h) Orders made in [illegible] Act, and entered in Registrars' Office,	[illegible]	-	-	-	[illegible]
17. [illegible] of Judgments signed,	[illegible]	[illegible]	[illegible]	[illegible]	-
18. Accountant General's drafts [illegible],*	-	-	-	-	-
19. Cases standing for Judgment at commencement of year,	[illegible]	[illegible]	[illegible]	-	-
20. Cases standing for Judgment at end of year,	[illegible]	-	-	[illegible]	-
21. Number of days the Judges sat in Court during the year,	[illegible]	[illegible]	[illegible]	[illegible]	
22. Number of Causes transferred from each Judge to other branches of the Court, viz.:	[illegible]	-	-	-	-
Judges from whom transferred,	-	-	[illegible]	[illegible]	-
Judges to whom transferred,	-	-	[illegible]	[illegible]	-
23. [illegible] Number of Deeds settled by Conveyancing Counsel employed by [illegible] of Court,	-	-	-	-	-
24. Number of cases referred to Official [illegible],	-	-	-	-	-
25. Amount of Fees received by Stamps in the Chancery Registrar's office,	[illegible]				

* [illegible]

† [illegible]

‡ [illegible]

TABLE 41.—HIGH COURT OF JUSTICE.—CHANCERY DIVISION.—RETURN of PROCEEDINGS in the CHAMBERS of the LORD CHANCELLOR, MASTER of the ROLLS, and VICE-CHANCELLOR, for the year 18[illegible], made by the Chief Clerks to the Judges.

NATURE OF PROCEEDINGS	Total. No.	Total. Amount.	Lord Chancellor. No.	Lord Chancellor. Amount.	Master of the Rolls. No.	Master of the Rolls. Amount.	Vice-Chancellor. No.	Vice-Chancellor. Amount.
		£ s. d.		£ s. d.		£ s. d.		£ s. d.
Number issued of Summonses to originate Proceedings, viz.:—								
To make Infants Wards,	[illegible]	—	[illegible]	—	.	—	.	—
For the Administration of Estates,	[illegible]	—	[illegible]	—	[illegible]	—	[illegible]	—
Under the Charitable Trusts Act,	.	—	.	—	.	—	.	—
For the Appointment of Guardians and Maintenance of Infants,	[illegible]	—	[illegible]	—	.	—	.	—
For other purposes,	[illegible]	—	[illegible]	—	[illegible]	—	[illegible]	—
Number issued of Summonses, not being Summonses to originate Proceedings,	[illegible]	—	.	—	[illegible]	—	[illegible]	—
Number of Orders made, viz.:—								
Of the class drawn up by the Registrars,		—		—		—	.	—
Of the class drawn up in Chambers,	[illegible]	—	[illegible]	—	[illegible]	—	[illegible]	—
Number of Orders brought into Chambers for prosecution, other than Orders for winding up Companies,	[illegible]	—	[illegible]	—	[illegible]	—	[illegible]	—
Number of Orders brought into Chambers for winding up Companies,	[illegible]	—	[illegible]	—	[illegible]	—	[illegible]	—
Number of Advertisements issued,	[illegible]	—	[illegible]	—	[illegible]	—	[illegible]	—
Number of Debts claimed and adjudicated on,	[illegible]	—	—	—	[illegible]	—	[illegible]	—
Amount of Debts proved,	.	[illegible]		—		[illegible]	.	[illegible]
Number of Contributories included in Lists of Contributories,	[illegible]	—	.	—	[illegible]	—	.	—
Number of Contributories excluded from Lists of Contributories,	[illegible]	—	.	—	[illegible]	—	.	—
Amount of Calls made under Orders for winding up Companies,	.	—	.	—	.	—	.	—
Amount of Dividends ordered to be paid to Creditors,	.	—	.	—	.	—	.	—
Amount ordered to be refunded to Contributories,	.	—	.	—	.	—	.	—
Number of Accounts passed, other than Receivers' Accounts,	[illegible]	—	[illegible]	—	[illegible]	—	[illegible]	—
Amount of Receipts thereon,	.	[illegible]	.	[illegible]	.	[illegible]	.	[illegible]
Amount of Disbursements and Allowances thereon,		[illegible]	.	[illegible]	.	[illegible]	.	[illegible]
Number of Receivers' Accounts passed,	[illegible]	—	[illegible]	—	.	—	[illegible]	—
Amount of Receipts thereon,		[illegible]	.	[illegible]	.	—	.	[illegible]
Amount of Disbursements and Allowances thereon,	.	[illegible]	.	[illegible]	.	—	.	[illegible]
Number of Receivers' and other Accounts referred to Land Judge,	[illegible]	—	[illegible]	—	.	—	.	—
Number of Sales of Estates under Orders of Court,	[illegible]	—	.	—	.	—	[illegible]	—
Amount realised by Sales of Estates,	.	[illegible]	.	—		—	.	[illegible]
Number of Purchases of Estates under Orders of Court,	[illegible]	—	.	—	.	—	[illegible]	—
Number of Certificates filed,	[illegible]	—	[illegible]	—	[illegible]	—	[illegible]	—
Number of Appointments (by Summonses, Adjournment, or otherwise) disposed of,	[illegible]	—	[illegible]	—	[illegible]	—	[illegible]	—
[illegible] before Lord Chancellor,	.	—	.	—	.	—		—
Number of Orders under which Accounts and Inquiries were pending on 1st January, 18[illegible],	[illegible]	—	.	—	[illegible]	—	.	—
Number of Orders for winding up Companies then pending,	[illegible]	—		—	[illegible]	—	[illegible]	—
Amount of Fees collected in Chambers by Stamps,	.	[illegible]	.	[illegible]	.	[illegible]	.	[illegible]
Number of Days Chief Clerk sitting in Court or Judge's Chambers on Chamber Business,	[illegible]	—	[illegible]	—	[illegible]	—	[illegible]	—
Number of new Cases of Lunacy Matters,	[illegible]	—	[illegible]	—	[illegible]	—	.	—
Number of new Wards in Lunacy Matters,	[illegible]	—	[illegible]	—	[illegible]	—	.	—
Number of Cases, Petitions and Minor Matters transferred to Lord Chancellor's Chambers from Masters in Lunacy Offices,	[illegible]	—	[illegible]	—		—	.	—
Number of Marriage Settlements and other Deeds approved,	[illegible]	—	[illegible]	—	.	—	.	—
Number of Minor Matters at end of year,	.	—	.	—	[illegible]	—	[illegible]	—
Number of Wards of Court at end of year,	[illegible]	—	[illegible]	—	[illegible]	—	[illegible]	—
Number of Bills of Costs taxed in Chambers,	[illegible]	—	[illegible]	—	.	—	[illegible]	—
Amount of Costs taxed,	.	[illegible]	.	[illegible]	.	—	.	[illegible]
Number of Amended Actions under 40 & 41 Vic. ch. 54,	.	—	.	—	.	—	.	—

* [illegible]

[illegible] of Justice. [illegible]	[illegible]	[illegible]	[illegible]	[illegible]	[illegible]
[illegible]	[illegible]	[illegible]	[illegible]	[illegible]	[illegible]

[illegible] Bus. [illegible]

[illegible] Little Orders, [illegible]

TABLE [illegible].—HIGH COURT OF JUSTICE.—CHANCERY DIVISION.—RETURN of PROCEEDINGS in the OFFICE of the LORD CHANCELLOR'S SECRETARY, made by the LORD CHANCELLOR'S SECRETARY, and in the OFFICE of the SECRETARY at the ROLLS, made by the SECRETARY at the ROLLS, in the Year 1886.

Proceedings in the Office of the Lord Chancellor's Secretary	Number
Orders on Petitions as to Lunatics,	[illegible]
Orders on Petitions as to Commissioners for Administering Oaths for High Court of Justice,	[illegible]
Orders as to other Petitions referred to Lord Chancellor, [illegible] Petitions,	[illegible]
Total Number of Orders,	[illegible]
Warrants for Commissioners of the Peace,	[illegible]
Warrants as to Coroners,	[illegible]
Other Warrants to the Hanaper Office,	[illegible]
Total Number of Warrants,	[illegible]

Proceedings in the Office of the Secretary at the Rolls	Number
Petitions set down for Hearing.	
In Minor Matters,	[illegible]
Under Acts relating to Public Charities,	[illegible]
Under Trustee Acts, [illegible],	[illegible]
Under Trustee Relief Act ([illegible] Vict. c. [illegible]),	[illegible]
Under Trustee Relief Act (11 & 12 Vict. c. [illegible]),	[illegible]
Under Leases and Sales of Settled Estates Act, 1877,	[illegible]
Under Public Works and Railway Acts,	[illegible]
Under Renewable Leasehold Conversion Act,	[illegible]
Under Winding-up Acts,	[illegible]
Under Infants' Settlements Acts ([illegible] Vict. c. [illegible], and [illegible] Vict. c. [illegible]),	[illegible]
Under [illegible] Vict. c. [illegible] for Charitable Trusts?,	[illegible]
Under [illegible] Act ([illegible] Vict. c. [illegible]),	[illegible]
For Transfer under Title [illegible] Act ([illegible] Vict. c. [illegible]),	[illegible]
By [illegible] under [illegible] and Public Works Acts,	[illegible]
Under Parliamentary Deposits Act ([illegible] Vict. c. [illegible]),	[illegible]
In [illegible] Matters,	[illegible]
In other Matters,	[illegible]
Total Number of Petitions set down for Hearing, Viz.—On the Higher Scale, [illegible]; On the Lower Scale, [illegible]	[illegible]

TABLE 41.—HIGH COURT OF JUSTICE.—CHANCERY DIVISION.—RETURN of PROCEEDINGS in the CROWN and HANAPER OFFICE for the Year 1886, made by the CLERK of the CROWN and HANAPER.

Proceedings	Number
Patents for appointment of Peers,	[illegible]
Patents for appointment of [illegible] Lords Justices [illegible],	[illegible]
Patents connected with the appointment of the Lord Chancellor, Judges, Law Officers, &c.,	[illegible]
Patents appointing Lieutenants and Custos Rotulorum for the several Counties in Ireland,	[illegible]
Patents granting Charters, Fairs and Markets, Licences for Theatres, and other Patents not connected with the foregoing,	[illegible]
Commissions of Assize and Gaol Delivery,	[illegible]
Commissions of Lunacy,	[illegible]
Commissions appointing Commissioners for administering Oaths,	[illegible]
Commissions connected with the appointment of Justices of the Peace,	[illegible]
Writs to supersede Justices of the Peace,	[illegible]
[illegible] Justices of the Peace, &c.,	[illegible]
Attested Copies of all Documents [illegible],	[illegible]
Writs of [illegible], and other Writs,	[illegible]
Writs for the Election of Coroners,	[illegible]
Writs for the Election of Members of Parliament,	[illegible]

Proceedings	Number
Writs for the Election of Representative Peers,	[illegible]
Exemplifications of Orders to Lord [illegible],	[illegible]
Moneys paid for the Return of Representative Peers,	[illegible]
Transmitting Records to Queen's Bench, &c.,	[illegible]
Number of persons to whom Oaths were administered by the Clerk of the Crown and Hanaper, before Lord Chancellor,	[illegible]
Entering Rules and Orders on Roll of Proceedings of the Petty Bag Side of the Chancery Division,	[illegible]
Filing [illegible] Letters and other Documents,	[illegible]
[illegible] and Companies,	[illegible]
Recognizances,	[illegible]
Enrolling Judgments,	[illegible]
Commissions of Inquiry,	[illegible]
Special Commissions of Oyer and Terminer,	[illegible]
Commissions Appointing [illegible] Funds,	[illegible]
Inspection of [illegible] Documents by order of the Court,	[illegible]
Total,	[illegible]
Amount of Fees collected by means of Stamps, £[illegible]	

TABLE [illegible].—HIGH COURT OF JUSTICE.—CHANCERY DIVISION.—LAND JUDGE.

(a.) Judicial Proceedings in the year ended [illegible] November, [illegible].

Proceedings.	Number.	Proceedings.	Number.
Number of Cases pending in Chamber of Judges—at commencement of year,	[illegible]	Number of Cases in which Final Schedules have been settled,	[illegible]
" " at end of year,	[illegible]	" Conveyances or Declarations of Title executed,	[illegible]
" " referred to Chamber of Judges,	[illegible]	" Petitions dismissed and cases wound up,	[illegible]
" " for Sale of Incumbered Estates [illegible]	[illegible]	Proceedings under Tenure and Improvement of Land (Ireland) Act, [illegible]	
" " for Sale of Unincumbered Estates,	[illegible]	Amount of [illegible] of Limited Owners' Improvements lodged,	[illegible]
" " Settled Estates,	[illegible]	Number of Orders charging Annuities for Limited Owners' Improvements,	[illegible]
" " Declarations of Title,	[illegible]	Number of Orders made on such Petitions,	[illegible]
" " Partitions,	[illegible]		
" " Drainage and allotments of [illegible] Lands,	[illegible]		
" " Apportionment of Rent,	[illegible]		
" " Special jurisdiction of Conveyance of Sale,	[illegible]		
" " Appointment of New Trustees,	[illegible]		[illegible]
Proceedings under Landlord and Tenant Act, [illegible], Part III,	[illegible]	Amount of duty paid on account of business transacted in the Court during the year,	[illegible]
[illegible] Leases sanctioned,	[illegible]	Amount of money paid and lodged [illegible],	[illegible]
Petitions to authorise Leases [illegible]	[illegible]	Amount of Value of Estates whose Title declared,	[illegible]
Cases in which Titles approved of,	[illegible]	Net Rental, or Annual Value [illegible], of Estates sold,	[illegible]
" " Sales have been had, or Declarations of Title executed,	[illegible]	Amount of the Purchase-money,	[illegible]

(b.) Sales to Tenants under Part III. of the Land Act, [illegible].

	[illegible]	[illegible]	[illegible]
Amount of Purchase-money in cases in which Charging Orders have been made in favour of the Board of Works, in the years [illegible]	[illegible]	[illegible]	[illegible]
In Cases of Sales of Land in Ulster,	[illegible]	[illegible]	[illegible]
" " Munster,	—	[illegible]	[illegible]
" " Leinster,	[illegible]	[illegible]	[illegible]
" " Connaught,	[illegible]	[illegible]	[illegible]
Number of Tenant Purchasers in each Province—			
In Sales of Land in Ulster,	[illegible]	[illegible]	[illegible]
" " Munster,	—	[illegible]	[illegible]
" " Leinster,	[illegible]	[illegible]	[illegible]
" " Connaught,	[illegible]	[illegible]	[illegible]
Area of Holdings in Sales to Tenant Purchasers—			
Holdings under [illegible] Acres,	[illegible]	[illegible]	[illegible]
" [illegible] Acres and under [illegible],	[illegible]	[illegible]	[illegible]
" [illegible] " [illegible],	[illegible]	[illegible]	[illegible]
" [illegible] " [illegible],	[illegible]	[illegible]	[illegible]
" [illegible] " [illegible],	[illegible]	[illegible]	[illegible]
" [illegible] " [illegible],	[illegible]	[illegible]	[illegible]
" [illegible] Acres and upwards,	[illegible]	—	[illegible]

TABLE [illegible].—HIGH COURT OF JUSTICE—QUEEN'S BENCH DIVISION.—Returns of the Proceedings at the Courts on the Pleas Side in the Year [illegible], made by the Masters of the Court, the Registrar, and the Clerk of Writs.

PROCEEDINGS.	Total.		Quarter ending 31st March.		Quarter ending 30th June.		Quarter ending 30th September.		Quarter ending 31st December.	
	No.	Matters Heard on Return.	No.	Matters Heard on Return.	No.	Matters Heard on Return.	No.	Matters Heard on Return.	No.	Matters Heard on Return.
Entered by Clerk of Writs.										
Writs of Summons issued,	[illegible]	.	[illegible]	.	[illegible]	.	[illegible]	.	[illegible]	-
Writs of Revivor,	-	.	.	.	.	.	.	.	.	.
Writs of [illegible],	.	.	.	.	.	.	.	.	.	.
Registries, Suggestions, &c.	[illegible]	.	[illegible]		[illegible]	.	.	.	.	.
Proceedings and Records under Old System,	.	.	.	.	-	.	.	.	.	.
Entered by Master.										
Appearances entered,	[illegible]	.	[illegible]	.	[illegible]	.	[illegible]	-	[illegible]	.
Judgments entered:										
On Affidavit of Service (in default of Appearance),	[illegible]	.	[illegible]	.	[illegible]	.	[illegible]	.	[illegible]	.
By default (other than default of Appearance) for Plaintiff,	[illegible]	.	[illegible]	.	[illegible]	.	[illegible]	.	[illegible]	-
On Judge's Order, for unconditional leave,	[illegible]	.	[illegible]	.	[illegible]	.	[illegible]	.	[illegible]	-
(Summary) under Order 14, Rule 1,	[illegible]	.	[illegible]	.	[illegible]	.	[illegible]	.	[illegible]	.
On Cognovit, for Plaintiff,	.	.	.	.	.	.	.	.	.	.
On Cognovit, for Defendant,	.	.	.	.	.	.	.	.	.	.
For Plaintiff on Verdict, or Writ of Inquiry,	[illegible]	.	[illegible]	.	[illegible]	.	[illegible]	.	[illegible]	.
For Defendant on Verdict, or Non-suit,	[illegible]	.	[illegible]	.	[illegible]	.	[illegible]	.	[illegible]	.
For [illegible] on Consent Order,	[illegible]	.	[illegible]	.	[illegible]	.	.	.	[illegible]	.
Of Non pros for Defendant,	[illegible]	.	[illegible]	.	[illegible]	.	.	.	.	.
On Special Case for Plaintiff,	.	.	.	.	.	.	.	.	.	.
On Special Case for Defendant,	.	.	.	.	.	.	.	.	.	.
On Judge's Order to stay Proceedings,	.	.	.	.	.	.	.	.	.	.
On Warrant of Attorney,	[illegible]	.	[illegible]	.	[illegible]	.	[illegible]	.	[illegible]	.
On Certificates of Master,	[illegible]	.	[illegible]	.	[illegible]	.	[illegible]	.	[illegible]	.
Other Judgments entered,	[illegible]	.	[illegible]	.	[illegible]	.	[illegible]	.	[illegible]	-
Executions:										
Writs of Fieri Facias,	[illegible]	.	[illegible]	-	[illegible]	.	[illegible]	.	[illegible]	.
Writs of Possession,	[illegible]	.	[illegible]	.	[illegible]	.	[illegible]	.	[illegible]	.
Writs of Elegit,	.	.	.	.	.	.	.	.	.	.
Entered by the Registrar.										
Motions for New Trial, or to enter Judgment (Heard):										
Refused,	.	[illegible]	.	[illegible]	.	[illegible]	.	.	.	[illegible]
Rules [illegible] granted,	-	[illegible]	.	[illegible]	.	[illegible]	.	.	.	[illegible]
Rules Absolute,	-	[illegible]	.	[illegible]	.	[illegible]	.	.	.	[illegible]
Rules Discharged,	.	[illegible]	.	.	.	[illegible]	.	.	.	[illegible]
Other Motions (Heard):										
Refused,	.	[illegible]	.	[illegible]	.	[illegible]	.	.	.	[illegible]
Granted,	.	[illegible]	.	[illegible]	.	[illegible]	.	.	.	[illegible]
Special Cases (Heard):										
Judgment for Plaintiff,	.	[illegible]	.	.	.	.	.	.	.	[illegible]
Judgment for Defendant,	.	.	.	.	.	.	.	.	.	.
Demurrers (Heard):										
Judgment for Plaintiff,	.	[illegible]	.	.	.	.	.	.	.	[illegible]
Judgment for Defendant,	.	[illegible]	.	.	.	[illegible]	.	.	.	[illegible]
Side Bar Rules,	[illegible]	.	[illegible]	.	[illegible]	.	[illegible]	-	[illegible]	.
Matters heard on which the Court decided,	.	[illegible]	.	[illegible]	.	.	.	.	[illegible]	.
Other Proceedings,	.	.	.	.	.	.	.	.	.	-
Entered by the Master.										
Causes referred to Master under Common Law Procedure Acts, 1852 and 1854, and to other Matters,	[illegible]	-	[illegible]	.	[illegible]	.	[illegible]	.	[illegible]	.
Bills of Sale,	[illegible]	.	[illegible]	-	[illegible]	.	[illegible]	-	[illegible]	.
Affidavits filed,	[illegible]	.	[illegible]	-	[illegible]	-	[illegible]	.	[illegible]	.

TABLE [illegible].—HIGH COURT OF JUSTICE.—COMMON PLEAS DIVISION.—Return of the Proceedings of the Court on the Plea Side in the Year [illegible], made by the Master of the Court, the Registrar, and the Clerk of Writs.

PROCEEDINGS.	Total.		Quarter ending 31st March.		Quarter ending 30th June.		Quarter ending 30th September.		Quarter ending 31st December.	
	No.	Matters heard in Banco.	No.	Matters heard in Banco.	No.	Matters heard in Banco.	No.	Matters heard in Banco.	No.	Matters heard in Banco.
Returned by Clerk of Writs.										
Writs of Summons issued,	[illegible]	.	[illegible]	.	[illegible]	.	[illegible]	.	[illegible]	.
Writs of Revivor,	.	.	.	.	.	.	.	.	.	.
Writs of Subpoena,	.	.	.	.	.	.	.	.	.	.
[illegible]	[illegible]	.	.	.	[illegible]	.	.	.	.	.
[illegible] under Old System,	.	.	.	.	.	.	.	.	.	.
Returned by Master.										
Appearances entered,	[illegible]	.	[illegible]	.	[illegible]	.	[illegible]	.	[illegible]	.
Judgments entered:										
On Affidavit of Service (in default of Appearance),	[illegible]	.	[illegible]	.	[illegible]	.	[illegible]	.	[illegible]	.
By default (other than default of Appearance) for Plaintiff,	[illegible]	.	[illegible]	.	[illegible]	.	[illegible]	.	[illegible]	.
On Judge's Order, for substituted Service,	[illegible]	.	[illegible]	.	[illegible]	.	[illegible]	.	[illegible]	.
[illegible] under Order [illegible],	[illegible]	.	[illegible]	.	[illegible]	.	[illegible]	.	[illegible]	.
On Demurrer for Plaintiff,	.	.	.	.	.	.	.	.	.	.
On Demurrer for Defendant,	.	.	.	.	.	.	.	.	.	.
For Plaintiff on Verdict, or Writ of Inquiry,	[illegible]	.	[illegible]	.	[illegible]	.	[illegible]	.	[illegible]	.
For Defendant on Verdict, or Nonsuit,	[illegible]	.	[illegible]	.	[illegible]	.	[illegible]	.	[illegible]	.
For Defendant on Counter Claim,	.	.	.	.	.	.	.	.	.	.
Of [illegible] for Defendant,	[illegible]	.	[illegible]	.	[illegible]	.	[illegible]	.	[illegible]	.
On Special Case for Plaintiff,	.	.	.	.	.	.	.	.	.	.
On Special Case for Defendant,	.	.	.	.	.	.	.	.	.	.
On Judge's Orders in [illegible],	[illegible]	.	[illegible]	.	[illegible]	.	[illegible]	.	[illegible]	.
On Warrants of Attorney,	[illegible]	.	[illegible]	.	[illegible]	.	[illegible]	.	[illegible]	.
On Certificates of Master,	[illegible]	.	[illegible]	.	[illegible]	.	[illegible]	.	[illegible]	.
Other Judgments entered,	[illegible]	.	[illegible]	.	[illegible]	.	[illegible]	.	[illegible]	.
Executions:										
Writs of Fieri Facias,	[illegible]	.	[illegible]	.	[illegible]	.	[illegible]	.	[illegible]	.
Writs of Possession,	[illegible]	.	[illegible]	.	[illegible]	.	[illegible]	.	[illegible]	.
Writs of [illegible],	.	.	.	.	.	.	.	.	.	.
Miscellaneous Writs,	[illegible]	.	[illegible]	.	[illegible]	.	.	.	.	.

TABLE [illegible].—HIGH COURT OF JUSTICE.—EXCHEQUER DIVISION.—Return of the Proceedings of the Court on the Plea Side in the Year [illegible], made by the Masters of the Court, the Registrar, and the Clerk of Writs.

PROCEEDINGS.	Total. No.	Total. Matters Heard or Before.	Quarter ending 31st March. No.	Quarter ending 31st March. Matters Heard or Before.	Quarter ending 30th June. No.	Quarter ending 30th June. Matters Heard or Before.	Quarter ending 30th September. No.	Quarter ending 30th September. Matters Heard or Before.	Quarter ending 31st December. No.	Quarter ending 31st December. Matters Heard or Before.
Returned by Clerk of Writs										
Writs of Summons issued,	[illegible]	-	[illegible]	-	[illegible]	-	[illegible]	-	[illegible]	-
Writs of Revivor,	-	-	-	-	-	-	-	-	-	-
Writs of [illegible],	-	-	-	-	-	-	-	-	-	-
[illegible], &c.,	[illegible]	-	[illegible]	-	[illegible]	-	-	-	[illegible]	-
Executions and [illegible] under Old System,	[illegible]	-	[illegible]	-	[illegible]	-	-	-	[illegible]	-
Returned by Masters.										
Appointments attended,	[illegible]	-	[illegible]	-	[illegible]	-	[illegible]	-	[illegible]	-
Judgments entered:										
On Affidavit of Service (default of Appearance),	[illegible]	-	[illegible]	-	[illegible]	-	[illegible]	-	[illegible]	-
On Affidavit of Service (default of Defence),	[illegible]	-	[illegible]	-	[illegible]	-	[illegible]	-	[illegible]	-
On Order for [illegible] (Summary) under Order [illegible],	[illegible]	-	[illegible]	-	[illegible]	-	[illegible]	-	[illegible]	-
For Plaintiff on Verdict, or Writ of Inquiry,	[illegible]	-	[illegible]	-	[illegible]	-	[illegible]	-	[illegible]	-
On Non pros for Defendant,	[illegible]	-	-	-	[illegible]	-	-	-	-	-
On Warrants of Attorney,	[illegible]	-	[illegible]	-	[illegible]	-	[illegible]	-	[illegible]	-
On Certificates of Master,	[illegible]	-	[illegible]	-	[illegible]	-	[illegible]	-	[illegible]	-
Other Judgments entered,	[illegible]	-	[illegible]	-	[illegible]	-	[illegible]	-	[illegible]	-
Executions:										
Writs of Fieri Facias issued,	[illegible]	-	[illegible]	-	[illegible]	-	[illegible]	-	[illegible]	-
Writs of Possession,	[illegible]	-	[illegible]	-	[illegible]	-	[illegible]	-	[illegible]	-
Returned by the Registrar										
Motions for New Trial, or to enter Judgment (Heard):										
Refused,	-	-	-	-	-	-	-	-	-	-
Rules Nisi granted,	-	[illegible]	-	[illegible]	-	[illegible]	-	-	-	[illegible]
Rules Absolute,	-	[illegible]	-	[illegible]	-	[illegible]	-	-	-	[illegible]
Rules Discharged,	-	[illegible]	-	[illegible]	-	[illegible]	-	-	-	-
Other Motions (Heard):										
Refused,	-	[illegible]	-	[illegible]	-	[illegible]	-	[illegible]	-	[illegible]
Granted,	-	[illegible]	-	[illegible]	-	[illegible]	-	[illegible]	-	[illegible]
Special Cases (Heard):										
Judgment for Plaintiff,	-	[illegible]	-	[illegible]	-	-	-	-	-	-
Judgment for Defendant,	-	[illegible]	-	[illegible]	-	-	-	-	-	-
Demurrers (Heard):										
Judgment for Plaintiff,	-	[illegible]	-	[illegible]	-	-	-	-	-	-
Judgment for Defendant,	-	[illegible]	-	[illegible]	-	-	-	-	-	[illegible]
Side Bar Rules,	[illegible]	-	[illegible]	-	[illegible]	-	[illegible]	-	[illegible]	-
Matters heard in which the Court divided,	-	[illegible]	-	[illegible]	-	-	-	-	-	[illegible]
Other Proceedings,	-	-	-	-	-	-	-	-	-	-
Returned by Master										
Causes entered for Trial or [illegible],	[illegible]	-	[illegible]	-	[illegible]	-	[illegible]	-	[illegible]	-
Affidavits filed,	[illegible]	-	[illegible]	-	[illegible]	-	[illegible]	-	[illegible]	-
Other Documents filed, viz.:										
Writs of Summons,	[illegible]	-	[illegible]	-	[illegible]	-	[illegible]	-	[illegible]	-
Pleadings,	[illegible]	-	[illegible]	-	[illegible]	-	[illegible]	-	[illegible]	-
Statements of Claim, Defences, Replies, Counterclaims, Demurrers,	[illegible]	-	[illegible]	-	[illegible]	-	[illegible]	-	[illegible]	-
Judge's Certificates,	[illegible]	-	[illegible]	-	[illegible]	-	[illegible]	-	[illegible]	-
Recognizances,	[illegible]	-	[illegible]	-	[illegible]	-	[illegible]	-	[illegible]	-
Memorials of Satisfaction of Judgments,	[illegible]	-	[illegible]	-	[illegible]	-	[illegible]	-	[illegible]	-
[illegible],	[illegible]	-	[illegible]	-	[illegible]	-	[illegible]	-	[illegible]	-
Miscellaneous Documents,	[illegible]	-	[illegible]	-	[illegible]	-	-	-	[illegible]	-

TABLE 41.—EXCHEQUER DIVISION.—Return of Proceedings in the [illegible], and in [illegible] and [illegible] Duty Cases, in 188[illegible].

PROCEEDINGS.	Number.
[illegible] by Clerk of [illegible]	
Writs Issued,	[illegible]
[illegible] by the Registrar.	
[illegible] Rules,	[illegible]
[illegible] in Court,	[illegible]
Motions for [illegible] without Argument,	[illegible]
[illegible] in Equity and [illegible],	[illegible]

TABLE 42.—HIGH COURT OF JUSTICE.—QUEEN'S BENCH, COMMON PLEAS, AND EXCHEQUER DIVISIONS.—RETURN of BUSINESS at CHAMBERS and Before a SINGLE JUDGE in COURT in the Year 188[illegible], made by the [illegible].

PARTICULARS.	Total of the Three Divisions.	Queen's Bench Division: Total in Year	Quarter ending [illegible]	[illegible]	[illegible]	[illegible]	Common Pleas Division: Total in Year	Quarter ending [illegible]	[illegible]	[illegible]	[illegible]	Exchequer Division: Total in Year	Quarter ending [illegible]	[illegible]	[illegible]	[illegible]
At Chambers:																
[illegible],	[illegible]	[illegible]	[illegible]	[illegible]	[illegible]	[illegible]	[illegible]	[illegible]	[illegible]	[illegible]	[illegible]	[illegible]	[illegible]	[illegible]	[illegible]	[illegible]
Before a Single Judge in Court or at Chambers.																
[illegible] Motions [illegible] Granted,	[illegible]	[illegible]	[illegible]	[illegible]	[illegible]	[illegible]	[illegible]	[illegible]	[illegible]	[illegible]	[illegible]	[illegible]	[illegible]	[illegible]	[illegible]	[illegible]
[illegible] on Notice:																
Granted,	[illegible]	[illegible]	[illegible]	[illegible]	[illegible]	[illegible]	[illegible]	[illegible]	[illegible]	[illegible]	[illegible]	[illegible]	[illegible]	[illegible]	[illegible]	[illegible]
Refused, or no Rule,	[illegible]	[illegible]	[illegible]	[illegible]	[illegible]	[illegible]	[illegible]	[illegible]	[illegible]	[illegible]	[illegible]	[illegible]	[illegible]	[illegible]	[illegible]	[illegible]
Withdrawn,	[illegible]	[illegible]	.	.	[illegible]	[illegible]	[illegible]	.	[illegible]	[illegible]	[illegible]	[illegible]	[illegible]	.	[illegible]	.
[illegible],	[illegible]	[illegible]	[illegible]	.	[illegible]		[illegible]	[illegible]	[illegible]	.	[illegible]	[illegible]	[illegible]	[illegible]	[illegible]	.

NATURE OF THE SUITS TRIED OR OTHERWISE DISPOSED OF IN COURT.	[illegible]	Verdict for Plaintiff	Verdict for Plaintiff [illegible]	Referred	Verdict for Defendant	[illegible]	[illegible]	[illegible]	[illegible]	[illegible]	[illegible]	[illegible]	[illegible]	[illegible]	[illegible]	[illegible]	[illegible]	[illegible]	[illegible]
Promissory Notes, Bills of Exchange, &c.	[illegible]	[illegible]	[illegible]	[illegible]	[illegible]	[illegible]	[illegible]	[illegible]	[illegible]	[illegible]	[illegible]	[illegible]	[illegible]	[illegible]	[illegible]	[illegible]	[illegible]	[illegible]	[illegible]
Goods sold and delivered, and bargained and sold,	[illegible]	[illegible]	[illegible]	[illegible]	[illegible]	[illegible]	[illegible]	[illegible]	[illegible]	[illegible]	[illegible]	[illegible]	[illegible]	[illegible]	[illegible]	[illegible]	[illegible]	[illegible]	[illegible]
Work and Labour done,	[illegible]	[illegible]	[illegible]	[illegible]	[illegible]	[illegible]	[illegible]	[illegible]	[illegible]	[illegible]	[illegible]	[illegible]	[illegible]	[illegible]	[illegible]	[illegible]	[illegible]	[illegible]	[illegible]
Money paid, [illegible]	[illegible]	[illegible]	[illegible]	[illegible]	[illegible]	[illegible]	[illegible]	[illegible]	[illegible]	[illegible]	[illegible]	[illegible]	[illegible]	[illegible]	[illegible]	[illegible]	[illegible]	[illegible]	[illegible]
Compensation for Personal Injuries, and Compensation	[illegible]	[illegible]	[illegible]	[illegible]	[illegible]	[illegible]	[illegible]	[illegible]	[illegible]	[illegible]	[illegible]	[illegible]	[illegible]	[illegible]	[illegible]	[illegible]	[illegible]	[illegible]	[illegible]
[illegible] Lord Campbell's Act,	[illegible]	[illegible]	[illegible]	[illegible]	[illegible]	[illegible]	[illegible]	[illegible]	[illegible]	[illegible]	[illegible]	[illegible]	[illegible]	[illegible]	[illegible]	[illegible]	[illegible]	[illegible]	[illegible]
[illegible] Carriage for Negligence,	[illegible]	[illegible]	[illegible]	[illegible]	[illegible]	[illegible]	[illegible]	[illegible]	[illegible]	[illegible]	[illegible]	[illegible]	[illegible]	[illegible]	[illegible]	[illegible]	[illegible]	[illegible]	[illegible]
[illegible] for Negligence,	[illegible]	[illegible]	[illegible]	[illegible]	[illegible]	[illegible]	[illegible]	[illegible]	[illegible]	[illegible]	[illegible]	[illegible]	[illegible]	[illegible]	[illegible]	[illegible]	[illegible]	[illegible]	[illegible]
Compensation for other Injuries from Negligence,	[illegible]	[illegible]	[illegible]	[illegible]	[illegible]	[illegible]	[illegible]	[illegible]	[illegible]	[illegible]	[illegible]	[illegible]	[illegible]	[illegible]	[illegible]	[illegible]	[illegible]	[illegible]	[illegible]
[illegible] in respect of Distress,	[illegible]	[illegible]	[illegible]	[illegible]	[illegible]	[illegible]	[illegible]	[illegible]	[illegible]	[illegible]	[illegible]	[illegible]	[illegible]	[illegible]	[illegible]	[illegible]	[illegible]	[illegible]	[illegible]
[illegible] in the Nature of Actions of Trover or Detinue,	[illegible]	[illegible]	[illegible]	[illegible]	[illegible]	[illegible]	[illegible]	[illegible]	[illegible]	[illegible]	[illegible]	[illegible]	[illegible]	[illegible]	[illegible]	[illegible]	[illegible]	[illegible]	[illegible]
Breach of Contract,	[illegible]	[illegible]	[illegible]	[illegible]	[illegible]	[illegible]	[illegible]	[illegible]	[illegible]	[illegible]	[illegible]	[illegible]	[illegible]	[illegible]	[illegible]	[illegible]	[illegible]	[illegible]	[illegible]
Recovery of Land (Ejectment),	[illegible]	[illegible]	[illegible]	[illegible]	[illegible]	[illegible]	[illegible]	[illegible]	[illegible]	[illegible]	[illegible]	[illegible]	[illegible]	[illegible]	[illegible]	[illegible]	[illegible]	[illegible]	[illegible]
[illegible] relating to Land, Houses, &c.	[illegible]	[illegible]	[illegible]	[illegible]	[illegible]	[illegible]	[illegible]	[illegible]	[illegible]	[illegible]	[illegible]	[illegible]	[illegible]	[illegible]	[illegible]	[illegible]	[illegible]	[illegible]	[illegible]
Breach of Promise of Marriage,	[illegible]	[illegible]	[illegible]	[illegible]	[illegible]	[illegible]	[illegible]	[illegible]	[illegible]	[illegible]	[illegible]	[illegible]	[illegible]	[illegible]	[illegible]	[illegible]	[illegible]	[illegible]	[illegible]
[illegible]	[illegible]	[illegible]	[illegible]	[illegible]	[illegible]	[illegible]	[illegible]	[illegible]	[illegible]	[illegible]	[illegible]	[illegible]	[illegible]	[illegible]	[illegible]	[illegible]	[illegible]	[illegible]	[illegible]
[illegible]	[illegible]	[illegible]	[illegible]	[illegible]	[illegible]	[illegible]	[illegible]	[illegible]	[illegible]	[illegible]	[illegible]	[illegible]	[illegible]	[illegible]	[illegible]	[illegible]	[illegible]	[illegible]	[illegible]
[illegible]	[illegible]	[illegible]	[illegible]	[illegible]	[illegible]	[illegible]	[illegible]	[illegible]	[illegible]	[illegible]	[illegible]	[illegible]	[illegible]	[illegible]	[illegible]	[illegible]	[illegible]	[illegible]	[illegible]
[illegible] Imprisonment,	[illegible]	[illegible]	[illegible]	[illegible]	[illegible]	[illegible]	[illegible]	[illegible]	[illegible]	[illegible]	[illegible]	[illegible]	[illegible]	[illegible]	[illegible]	[illegible]	[illegible]	[illegible]	[illegible]
[illegible]	[illegible]	[illegible]	[illegible]	[illegible]	[illegible]	[illegible]	[illegible]	[illegible]	[illegible]	[illegible]	[illegible]	[illegible]	[illegible]	[illegible]	[illegible]	[illegible]	[illegible]	[illegible]	[illegible]
[illegible] Issues,	[illegible]	[illegible]	[illegible]	[illegible]	[illegible]	[illegible]	[illegible]	[illegible]	[illegible]	[illegible]	[illegible]	[illegible]	[illegible]	[illegible]	[illegible]	[illegible]	[illegible]	[illegible]	[illegible]
[illegible]	[illegible]	[illegible]	[illegible]	[illegible]	[illegible]	[illegible]	[illegible]	[illegible]	[illegible]	[illegible]	[illegible]	[illegible]	[illegible]	[illegible]	[illegible]	[illegible]	[illegible]	[illegible]	[illegible]
Recovery of Rent, and [illegible]	[illegible]	[illegible]	[illegible]	[illegible]	[illegible]	[illegible]	[illegible]	[illegible]	[illegible]	[illegible]	[illegible]	[illegible]	[illegible]	[illegible]	[illegible]	[illegible]	[illegible]	[illegible]	[illegible]
Life, Fire, and Marine Policies,	[illegible]	[illegible]	[illegible]	[illegible]	[illegible]	[illegible]	[illegible]	[illegible]	[illegible]	[illegible]	[illegible]	[illegible]	[illegible]	[illegible]	[illegible]	[illegible]	[illegible]	[illegible]	[illegible]
[illegible] Representations,	[illegible]	[illegible]	[illegible]	[illegible]	[illegible]	[illegible]	[illegible]	[illegible]	[illegible]	[illegible]	[illegible]	[illegible]	[illegible]	[illegible]	[illegible]	[illegible]	[illegible]	[illegible]	[illegible]
[illegible] Dismissal,	[illegible]	[illegible]	[illegible]	[illegible]	[illegible]	[illegible]	[illegible]	[illegible]	[illegible]	[illegible]	[illegible]	[illegible]	[illegible]	[illegible]	[illegible]	[illegible]	[illegible]	[illegible]	[illegible]
[illegible] viz.:—	[illegible]	[illegible]	[illegible]	[illegible]	[illegible]	[illegible]	[illegible]	[illegible]	[illegible]	[illegible]	[illegible]	[illegible]	[illegible]	[illegible]	[illegible]	[illegible]	[illegible]	[illegible]	[illegible]
False Return,	[illegible]	[illegible]	[illegible]	[illegible]	[illegible]	[illegible]	[illegible]	[illegible]	[illegible]	[illegible]	[illegible]	[illegible]	[illegible]	[illegible]	[illegible]	[illegible]	[illegible]	[illegible]	[illegible]
On a [illegible],	[illegible]	[illegible]	[illegible]	[illegible]	[illegible]	[illegible]	[illegible]	[illegible]	[illegible]	[illegible]	[illegible]	[illegible]	[illegible]	[illegible]	[illegible]	[illegible]	[illegible]	[illegible]	[illegible]
Slander of Title,	[illegible]	[illegible]	[illegible]	[illegible]	[illegible]	[illegible]	[illegible]	[illegible]	[illegible]	[illegible]	[illegible]	[illegible]	[illegible]	[illegible]	[illegible]	[illegible]	[illegible]	[illegible]	[illegible]
Issues from Queen's Bench and Exchequer Divisions,	[illegible]	[illegible]	[illegible]	[illegible]	[illegible]	[illegible]	[illegible]	[illegible]	[illegible]	[illegible]	[illegible]	[illegible]	[illegible]	[illegible]	[illegible]	[illegible]	[illegible]	[illegible]	[illegible]
Attorney,	[illegible]	[illegible]	[illegible]	[illegible]	[illegible]	[illegible]	[illegible]	[illegible]	[illegible]	[illegible]	[illegible]	[illegible]	[illegible]	[illegible]	[illegible]	[illegible]	[illegible]	[illegible]	[illegible]
[illegible]	[illegible]	[illegible]	[illegible]	[illegible]	[illegible]	[illegible]	[illegible]	[illegible]	[illegible]	[illegible]	[illegible]	[illegible]	[illegible]	[illegible]	[illegible]	[illegible]	[illegible]	[illegible]	[illegible]
Establishing Plaintiff's Title,	[illegible]	[illegible]	[illegible]	[illegible]	[illegible]	[illegible]	[illegible]	[illegible]	[illegible]	[illegible]	[illegible]	[illegible]	[illegible]	[illegible]	[illegible]	[illegible]	[illegible]	[illegible]	[illegible]
Balance of Account,	[illegible]	[illegible]	[illegible]	[illegible]	[illegible]	[illegible]	[illegible]	[illegible]	[illegible]	[illegible]	[illegible]	[illegible]	[illegible]	[illegible]	[illegible]	[illegible]	[illegible]	[illegible]	[illegible]
Recovery of Costs,	[illegible]	[illegible]	[illegible]	[illegible]	[illegible]	[illegible]	[illegible]	[illegible]	[illegible]	[illegible]	[illegible]	[illegible]	[illegible]	[illegible]	[illegible]	[illegible]	[illegible]	[illegible]	[illegible]
Wages,	[illegible]	[illegible]	[illegible]	[illegible]	[illegible]	[illegible]	[illegible]	[illegible]	[illegible]	[illegible]	[illegible]	[illegible]	[illegible]	[illegible]	[illegible]	[illegible]	[illegible]	[illegible]	[illegible]
Refusing to lodge Plaintiff in an Inn,	[illegible]	[illegible]	[illegible]	[illegible]	[illegible]	[illegible]	[illegible]	[illegible]	[illegible]	[illegible]	[illegible]	[illegible]	[illegible]	[illegible]	[illegible]	[illegible]	[illegible]	[illegible]	[illegible]

TABLE [illegible].—QUEEN'S BENCH, COMMON PLEAS, AND EXCHEQUER DIVISIONS OF THE HIGH COURT OF JUSTICE.—RETURN of CASES of [illegible] under Stat. 30 & 31 Vic., cap. [illegible], secs. [illegible], for the year [illegible], made by the [illegible].

[illegible]	Queen's Bench.		Common Pleas.		Exchequer.		Total three Courts.		
	[illegible]	[illegible]	[illegible]	[illegible]	[illegible]	[illegible]	[illegible]	[illegible]	Total.
Number of Applications to refer Cases of Contract to County Court (sec. [illegible])	[illegible]	[illegible]	[illegible]	[illegible]	[illegible]	[illegible]	[illegible]	[illegible]	[illegible]
Applications granted,	[illegible]	[illegible]	[illegible]	[illegible]	[illegible]	[illegible]	[illegible]	[illegible]	[illegible]
" refused,	[illegible]	[illegible]	[illegible]	[illegible]	[illegible]	[illegible]	[illegible]	[illegible]	[illegible]
Number of Applications to refer cases of Tort to County Court (sec. [illegible])	[illegible]	[illegible]	[illegible]	[illegible]	[illegible]	[illegible]	[illegible]	[illegible]	[illegible]
Applications refused,	[illegible]	[illegible]	[illegible]	[illegible]	[illegible]	[illegible]	[illegible]	[illegible]	[illegible]
" granted,	[illegible]	[illegible]	[illegible]	[illegible]	[illegible]	[illegible]	[illegible]	[illegible]	[illegible]
" [illegible] security for costs, and remaining in Superior Court.	[illegible]	[illegible]	[illegible]	[illegible]	[illegible]	[illegible]	[illegible]	[illegible]	[illegible]
" failing to give Security, and [illegible]	[illegible]	[illegible]	[illegible]	[illegible]	[illegible]	[illegible]	[illegible]	[illegible]	[illegible]

* The [illegible] of the Queen's Bench Division states that the number of these applications is [illegible].

TABLE 67.—HIGH COURT OF JUSTICE. QUEEN'S BENCH DIVISION, CROWN SIDE.—(a.) Proceedings other than Causes entered for Jury Trial.—Returns of Queen's Coroner, Attorney, and Master of the Crown Office, for the Year 1886.

Proceedings in Crown Office:	Number.	Proceedings against a Summary Return (other than Trials by Jury).	Number.	Amount in £ s. d.
Writs or Rules applied for, viz.:—				£ s. d.
Articles of the Peace (granted),	1	Fiscal Presentments "Traversed"—City of Dublin,	[illegible]	[illegible]
Attachment,	-	County of Dublin,	[illegible]	[illegible]
[illegible],	[illegible]	Claims for [illegible]—		
Quo Warranto,	[illegible]	[illegible],	[illegible]	[illegible]
Habeas Corpus ad Subjiciendum,	[illegible]	[illegible],	-	
[illegible],	-	Applications for [illegible]—	[illegible]	
Certiorari,	[illegible]	Allowed,		
[illegible],	-	Disallowed,		
New Trial,	[illegible]	Applications for [illegible]—	[illegible]	
Jury Process,	[illegible]	Allowed,		
Other Special Rules,	[illegible]	[illegible],		
Total Writs or Rules applied for,	[illegible]	[illegible]—	[illegible]	
"Traversing" Grand Jury [illegible],	[illegible]	Allowed,		
Applications to present Grand Jury Bills,	-	Disallowed,		
Grand Jury under "The [illegible] (Ireland) Act, 18[illegible],"	-			
Informations—(1) Filed [illegible],	-	Proceedings in Banco:		
(2) Leave to file, applied for,	[illegible]	Special [illegible]—Opened,	[illegible]	-
Trial by Jury—Criminal Cases—at Bar,	-	[illegible],	[illegible]	-
by Single Judge,	-	[illegible]—[illegible],	[illegible]	-
[illegible],	[illegible]	[illegible],	[illegible]	-
[illegible] Proceedings [illegible],	[illegible]	[illegible],	[illegible]	-
[illegible],	[illegible]	[illegible],	-	-
[illegible]—		[illegible],	-	-
[illegible],	[illegible]	[illegible]—Allowed,	-	-
[illegible],	[illegible]	Overruled,	-	-
Quo Warranto [illegible],	-	[illegible]—Allowed,	-	-
Writs of Certiorari [illegible],	[illegible]	Overruled,	-	-
[illegible],	-	Appeals—[illegible],	[illegible]	-
Habeas ad [illegible],	[illegible]	Special Cases—[illegible],	-	-
[illegible],	[illegible]	[illegible],	-	-
[illegible],	[illegible]	[illegible],	[illegible]	-
[illegible],	-	Orders—[illegible],	[illegible]	-
[illegible],	-	[illegible],	-	-
[illegible],	[illegible]			

(b.) Nature of the Causes entered for Trial, and Results of the Causes Tried in Court, together with the Amounts Recovered by Traversers and the Number of each Class of Amounts.

Nature of the Causes entered for Trial.	[illegible]	Results of Causes Tried and Amounts Tried: [illegible]										Number of each Class of Amounts [illegible]															Total Amount Recovered by Traversers.
[illegible]	[illegible]	[illegible]	[illegible]	[illegible]	[illegible]	[illegible]	[illegible]	[illegible]	[illegible]	[illegible]	[illegible]	[illegible]	[illegible]	[illegible]	[illegible]	[illegible]	[illegible]	[illegible]	[illegible]	[illegible]	[illegible]	[illegible]	[illegible]	[illegible]	[illegible]	[illegible]	£ s. d.
[illegible]	[illegible]	[illegible]	[illegible]	[illegible]	[illegible]	[illegible]	[illegible]	[illegible]	[illegible]	[illegible]	[illegible]	[illegible]	[illegible]	[illegible]	[illegible]	[illegible]	[illegible]	[illegible]	[illegible]	[illegible]	[illegible]	[illegible]	[illegible]	[illegible]	[illegible]	[illegible]	£1,171 0 0
[illegible]	[illegible]	[illegible]	[illegible]	[illegible]	[illegible]	[illegible]	[illegible]	[illegible]	[illegible]	[illegible]	[illegible]	[illegible]	[illegible]	[illegible]	[illegible]	[illegible]	[illegible]	[illegible]	[illegible]	[illegible]	[illegible]	[illegible]	[illegible]	[illegible]	[illegible]	[illegible]	[illegible]
Total,	4	[illegible]	[illegible]	[illegible]	[illegible]	[illegible]	[illegible]	[illegible]	[illegible]	[illegible]	[illegible]	[illegible]	[illegible]	[illegible]	[illegible]	[illegible]	[illegible]	[illegible]	[illegible]	[illegible]	[illegible]	[illegible]	[illegible]	[illegible]	[illegible]	[illegible]	£1,171 0 0

	Number.
[illegible],	[illegible]
[illegible],	-
[illegible],	-
[illegible],	-
[illegible],	-
[illegible],	[illegible]
[illegible],	-
	[illegible]

Note.—[illegible]

TABLE [illegible].—PROCEEDINGS as to ELECTION PETITIONS. Return of Petitions lodged in 1886, made by the Master of the Common Pleas Division of the High Court of Justice.

Number of each Petition lodged	County or Borough in which the Election took place	Ground of Petition	Result of Petition: For Petitioner	Result of Petition: For Respondent	[illegible]	Petition [illegible]	Costs of Petitioner	Costs of Respondent	[illegible]
							£ s. d.	£ s. d.	
1	County of Louth, North Division.	Intimidation, undue influence, [illegible], and bribery.	—	—	—	By reason of [illegible] being [illegible] of an [illegible].	—	—	—
2	City of Londonderry.	[illegible], undue influence, [illegible], bribery, &c.	For Petitioner.	—	—	—	[illegible] Taxed	—	—
3	Borough of Belfast, West Division.	Bribery, treating, undue influence, &c.	—	For Respondent.	—	—	—	[illegible] Taxed	—

TABLE [illegible].—HIGH COURT OF JUSTICE, COMMON PLEAS DIVISION.—Return of Proceedings relating to the Acknowledgment of Deeds by Married Women, in the year 1886, made by the Registrar of Certificates and Affidavits of Acknowledgments, under 3 and 4 Wm. IV., cap. [illegible].

Proceedings.	Number
Acknowledgments [illegible] question.*	[illegible]
Number Acknowledgment before Perpetual Commissioners	[illegible]
" " Special Commissioners,	[illegible]
" " Judges of High Court of Justice,	[illegible]
" " County Court Judges [illegible] County Courts and [illegible]	[illegible]
Perpetual Commissioners appointed,	[illegible]
Special Commissioners [illegible],	14
[illegible]	[illegible]

* Under the provisions of the Conveyancing Act, [illegible] [illegible] the Commission and Affidavit of acknowledgment [illegible] [illegible] of the Act.

TABLE [illegible].—HIGH COURT OF JUSTICE, EXCHEQUER DIVISION.—REVENUE SIDE.—Return of Proceedings in the year 1886, made by the Master of the Division.

Proceedings	Number.
By [illegible]—	
Informations filed,	[illegible]
Records of Informations [illegible],	[illegible]
[illegible],	[illegible]
Writs of [illegible],	[illegible]
[illegible],	[illegible]
Judgments signed,	[illegible]
Writs of [illegible],	[illegible]
Appearances,	[illegible]
[illegible],	[illegible]
Crown Bonds and Recognizances,	[illegible]
Writs of [illegible] for Legacy and [illegible] duty issued,	[illegible]
[illegible] Records filed,	[illegible]
[illegible],	[illegible]
Appointment of Under Sheriffs,	[illegible]
Warrants of Appointment by Lord Lieutenant of Sheriffs,	[illegible]
[illegible] issued,	[illegible]

TABLE [illegible].—REGISTRY OF JUDGMENTS.—Return of Proceedings in the Office for the Year 1886, made by the Registrar of Judgments.

Proceedings.	[illegible]	[illegible]	Total.	Proceedings.	[illegible]	[illegible]	Total.
Judgments of Superior Courts [illegible] before 14th July, 1850,	–	[illegible]	[illegible]	Recognizances,	[illegible]	[illegible]	[illegible]
Judgments of Superior Courts [illegible] 14th July, 1850,	[illegible]	[illegible]	[illegible]	Crown Bonds,	[illegible]	[illegible]	[illegible]
Rules, &c.,	–	–	–	Judgments [illegible] of Crown,	–	–	–
Decrees, Rules, and Orders,	–	–	–	Statutes,	–	–	–
Lis pendens,	[illegible]	–	[illegible]	Inquisitions,	–	–	–
Civil Bill Decrees [illegible],	–	–	–	Acceptances of Office,	–	–	–
Judgments from Courts in England and Scotland,	[illegible]	–	[illegible]	Total,	[illegible]	[illegible]	[illegible]
Total	[illegible]	[illegible]	[illegible]				
Satisfactions of Judgments,			[illegible]	Negative Searches [illegible],			[illegible]
Vacates of Re-registrations,			[illegible]	Do. do. [illegible] do.,			[illegible]
Cancellations of Crown Bonds,			–	Requisitions for Search [illegible] made by Public,			[illegible]
Negative Searches on [illegible],			–	Duplicate [illegible] issued,			[illegible]

Number of [illegible] Certificates issued upon which the Registrar, [illegible] 10 & 11 Vic., c. [illegible], [illegible] Fees, . . . [illegible]

TABLE [illegible].—HIGH COURT OF JUSTICE.—CHANCERY DIVISION.—LAND JUDGE.—RETURN of PROCEEDINGS in the RECORD of TITLE OFFICE for the Year ended [illegible] November, [illegible], made by the [illegible] Officer.

—	[illegible]			[illegible]		
	Number.	[illegible]	[illegible]	Number	[illegible]	[illegible]
[illegible]	[illegible]	[illegible]	[illegible]	[illegible]	[illegible]	[illegible]
[illegible]	[illegible]	—	—	[illegible]	—	—
[illegible]	[illegible]	—	—	[illegible]	—	—
[illegible]	[illegible]	—	—	[illegible]	—	—
[illegible]	[illegible]	—	—	[illegible]	—	—
[illegible]	[illegible]	—	—	[illegible]	—	—
[illegible]	[illegible]	—	—	[illegible]	—	—
[illegible]	[illegible]					

* [illegible]

TABLE [illegible].—REGISTRY OF DEEDS, IRELAND.—RETURN showing STATE of BUSINESS in [illegible], made by the Registrar.

—	Number	—	At Commencement of Year.	At End of Year.
[illegible]	[illegible]	[illegible]	[illegible]	[illegible]
[illegible]	[illegible]	[illegible]	[illegible]	[illegible]
[illegible]	[illegible]	[illegible]	[illegible]	[illegible]
[illegible]	[illegible]	[illegible]	[illegible]	[illegible]
[illegible]	[illegible]	[illegible]	[illegible]	[illegible]
[illegible]	[illegible]	[illegible]	[illegible]	[illegible]
[illegible]	[illegible]	[illegible]	[illegible]	[illegible]
[illegible]	[illegible]			[illegible]
[illegible]				[illegible]

TABLE [illegible].—HIGH COURT OF JUSTICE.—CONSOLIDATED TAXING OFFICES.—Return of [illegible] in the Offices for the Year [illegible], made by the Masters.

NATURE OF PROCEEDINGS	[illegible]	[illegible]	[illegible]	[illegible]	[illegible]	[illegible]
[illegible]				£ s. d.	£ s. d.	£ s. d.
[illegible]	[illegible]	[illegible]	[illegible]	[illegible]	[illegible]	[illegible]
[illegible]	[illegible]	[illegible]	[illegible]	—	[illegible]	[illegible]
[illegible]	[illegible]	[illegible]	[illegible]	[illegible]	[illegible]	[illegible]
[illegible]	[illegible]	[illegible]	[illegible]	[illegible]	[illegible]	[illegible]
[illegible]	[illegible]	[illegible]	[illegible]	[illegible]	[illegible]	[illegible]
[illegible]	[illegible]	[illegible]	[illegible]	[illegible]	[illegible]	[illegible]
[illegible]	[illegible]	[illegible]	[illegible]	—	[illegible]	[illegible]

TABLE [illegible].—HIGH COURT OF JUSTICE—CHANCERY DIVISION.—(1.) RECEIVERS' OFFICE OF LAND JUDGE —RETURN for the Year 188[illegible], made by the Examiner.

Number of Receivers appointed by Land Judge during 188[illegible],	[illegible]
" " by other Judges of the High Court of Justice during 18[illegible], but continuing before Land Judge,	(No means of ascertaining.)
" " previously appointed, still under Land Judge,	[illegible]
Total number of Receivers under Land Judge at end of 188[illegible],	[illegible]
Number of Lettings for [illegible], pending the Cause,	[illegible]
" " for [illegible] periods,	[illegible]
" " by biddings,	[illegible]
" " by proposal without biddings,	[illegible]
Number of Accounts passed,	[illegible]
" A [illegible] filed,	[illegible]
" [illegible],	[illegible]
" [illegible],	[illegible]
" Leases,	[illegible]
" Agreements for Letting of Land,	[illegible]
" [illegible] or Adjudications of Land Judge,*	[illegible]
" Orders of Land Judge,	[illegible]

* Including certificates and adjudications of Examiner under General Orders I and VI.

(2.) RECEIVERS and GUARDIANS' ACCOUNTS passed, which are filed in CONSOLIDATED RECORD and WRIT OFFICE, by CLERK of RECORDS and WRITS.

—	Number of Accounts passed in 188[illegible].	Amount of such Accounts.
By [illegible] of Receivers or [illegible],	[illegible]	[illegible]
By [illegible] in other Actions and Suits,	[illegible]	[illegible]
Total,	[illegible]	[illegible]

TABLE [illegible].—LUNACY DEPARTMENT.—RETURN of PROCEEDINGS in the OFFICE of the REGISTRAR in LUNACY for the Year ended 31st December, 188[illegible], made by the CHIEF CLERK.

PROCEEDINGS.	Number.	PROCEEDINGS.	Number.
Number of Lunatics under Court, 31st December, 18[illegible], [illegible]	[illegible]	Number of Medical Visitors' Reports [illegible], [illegible]	
Number of Lunacy Matters under Court, 31st December, 18[illegible], [illegible]	[illegible]	Number of Medical Visitors' Reports [illegible] and [illegible], [illegible]	[illegible]
Orders for [illegible] of Lunacy, [illegible]	[illegible]	Certificates of Medical Visitors' [illegible], [illegible]	[illegible]
[illegible] of Lunacy [illegible] of Commissioners, and [illegible] under the [illegible] of the Lunacy Regulation (Ireland) Act, 18[illegible], [illegible]	[illegible]	[illegible]	[illegible]
Reports from [illegible] the Lord Chancellor by the Registrar in Lunacy [illegible] Property, [illegible], and Maintenance of Lunatics and [illegible], and [illegible] and [illegible], and for [illegible] Maintenance [illegible] of Lunatics, and [illegible] Leases, and for Repairs of Lunatics' Estates, and other Miscellaneous Matters, [illegible]	[illegible]	[illegible]	[illegible]
Orders by Lord Chancellor, [illegible] Reports, [illegible]	[illegible]	[illegible]	[illegible]
Affidavits filed, [illegible]	[illegible]	[illegible] Reports of Committees and [illegible], [illegible]	[illegible]
Number of Applications to Committee of [illegible], [illegible]	[illegible]	Accounts and [illegible] of Committees and [illegible] passed by the Land Judge, [illegible]	[illegible]
[illegible] from Committee of [illegible], [illegible]	[illegible]	[illegible] passed by the Registrar in Lunacy, [illegible]	[illegible]
Number of Applications to Committee of [illegible], [illegible]	[illegible]	Number of Lunatics under Court, 31st December, 18[illegible], [illegible]	[illegible]
[illegible] from Committee of [illegible], [illegible]	[illegible]	Number of Lunacy Matters under Court, 31st December, 18[illegible], [illegible]	[illegible]
Number of Applications for Reports of Medical Visitors, [illegible]	[illegible]	[illegible] of Lunatics under Control of the Lord Chancellor, [illegible], [illegible] 31st December, 18[illegible], [illegible]	[illegible]
Number of Applications for Reports of Medical Visitors, [illegible] section [illegible] of Lunacy Regulation (Ireland) Act, 18[illegible], [illegible]	[illegible]		
	[illegible]		

TABLE [illegible].—PROBATE AND MATRIMONIAL DIVISION OF THE HIGH COURT OF JUSTICE.—MATRIMONIAL BUSINESS. RETURN of PROCEEDINGS in [illegible] under "The Legitimacy Declaration Act (Ireland), [illegible]," during the Year 1884, and for Matrimonial Causes and Matters, under [illegible] Vic., c. [illegible].

PROCEEDINGS.	Number.	PROCEEDINGS.	Number.
Petitions filed:		Motions,	[illegible]
In Special Property,	[illegible]	Causes heard before Judge on oral evidence,	[illegible]
For Divorce a mensa et thoro,	14	" " affidavits,	[illegible]
For Nullity of Marriage,	2	" " with Special Jury,	[illegible]
For Restitution of Conjugal Rights,	[illegible]	" " with Common Jury,	[illegible]
Jactitation of Marriage,	—	Decrees for Divorce a mensa et thoro,	[illegible]
Declaration under Legitimacy Declaration Act,	[illegible]	" Nullity of Marriage,	[illegible]
For Alimony, pendente lite,	7	" Restitution of Conjugal Rights,	[illegible]
For Alimony, permanent,	[illegible]	" Jactitation of Marriage,	[illegible]
Citations issued,	[illegible]	" under Legitimacy Declaration Act,	[illegible]
Appearances entered,	[illegible]	Applications for new Trial,	[illegible]
Affidavits filed,	[illegible]	Appeals to H. M. Court of Appeal,	[illegible]
Replies filed by Petitioners,	[illegible]	Dismissal of Petitions,	[illegible]
Rejoinders by Respondents,	[illegible]	Other orders made by the Principal Registrar, and not included in the above returns,	[illegible]

Total amount of Fees received (Matrimonial Causes), £ s. d. [illegible]

TABLE [illegible].—AFFIDAVIT DUTY FOR GRANTS OF PROBATE AND ADMINISTRATION.—RETURN by the CONTROLLER OF STAMPS.

—	[illegible], 1883.	Property upon which payable, [illegible] 1883.*	[illegible], 1884.	Property upon which payable, 1884.*
	£ s. d.	£	£ s. d.	£
Received in Dublin,	[illegible]	—	[illegible]	—
" the country,	[illegible]	—	[illegible]	—
Total,	[illegible]	—	[illegible]	—

* The Controller of Stamps states that it is not [illegible] to give this information.

TABLE [illegible].—HIGH COURT OF ADMIRALTY.—1. RETURN of PROCEEDINGS in the HIGH COURT of ADMIRALTY of IRELAND for the Year ended 31st December, 1884, made by the [illegible].

CAUSES INSTITUTED DURING YEAR.	Number.	Amount.	CAUSES INSTITUTED DURING YEAR.	Number.	Amount.
		£ s. d.	Position of Cases—continued.		
Salvage,	[illegible]	[illegible]	III. Defendants' Costs in contested Causes.—		£ s. d.
Damage by Collision,	[illegible]	[illegible]	Amount of Plaintiffs' and Defendants' Bills submitted for Taxation,	[illegible]	[illegible]
Bottomry,	—	—	Disallowed,	[illegible]	[illegible]
Necessaries,	[illegible]	[illegible]	Reported due,	—	[illegible]
Towage,	[illegible]	[illegible]	IV. Costs in default Causes.—		
Seamen's Wages,	[illegible]	[illegible]	Amount of Plaintiffs' and Defendants' Bills submitted for Taxation,	—	—
Masters' Wages and Disbursements,	—	—	Disallowed,	—	—
Freight on the Cargo,	—	—	Reported due,	—	—
Ownership,	[illegible]	[illegible]	V. Marshal's Bills (excluding Counsel Charges).—		
Use or Hire of Ship, Carriage of Goods, or cost in account of Goods,	[illegible]	[illegible]	Amount claimed,	[illegible]	[illegible]
Other Causes,	[illegible]	[illegible]	Disallowed,		—
Total Causes during year,	[illegible]	[illegible]			
Causes pending at beginning of year,	[illegible]	[illegible]			
Total Causes,	[illegible]	[illegible]			

BALANCES of Suitors' and other Moneys in Hand at the beginning and end of the Year 18[illegible], and TOTALS of AMOUNTS RECEIVED and PAID during the same Year.

	£ s. d.	£ s. d.
Balance in hand at the beginning of the year —		
Remaining to the credit of the Admiralty Court Deposit Fund,	—	—
Remaining to the credit of the Registrar's Account at the Bank of Ireland,	—	[illegible]
Received during the year —		
Proceeds of Ships, Cargoes, and Freight paid in,	[illegible]	
Tenders for Salvage, &c.,	[illegible]	
Deposits in lieu of Bail,	[illegible]	
Other receipts,	[illegible]	[illegible]
Received the Amount voted by Parliament for Salaries and other Expenses of Office for the year [illegible],	[illegible]	
Received for the excess of expenditure incurred beyond the amount voted by Parliament for the said year,	—	
Received on account of the Amount voted by Parliament for the year [illegible],	[illegible]	[illegible]
Total,		[illegible]

	£ s. d.	£ s. d.
Paid during the year —		
To Salvors,	—	
For Damage by Collision,	[illegible]	
To Bottomry Bondholders,	—	
For Necessaries,	—	
For Towage,	[illegible]	
To Masters for Wages and Disbursements,	—	
To Seamen for Wages,	[illegible]	
To Mortgagees,	—	
Freight on Cargo transhipped,	—	
For Breach of Duty and Contract,	—	
For Damage to Cargo,	—	
To Owners, including Balance after payment of other claims,	[illegible]	
Payment of Tenders,	[illegible]	
Do. of Deposits in lieu of Bail,	—	
To Proctors for Costs,	[illegible]	
To the Marshal for charges and disbursements, including Dock Dues, Brokerage, &c., on Ships and Goods sold by Order of the Court,	[illegible]	
Repayments on account of "Other Receipts,"	[illegible]	
″ of Expense Account Payments,	—	[illegible]
Balance in hand at the end of the year —		
Remaining to the credit of the Admiralty Court Deposit Fund,	—	—
Remaining to the credit of the Registrar's Account at the Bank of Ireland,	—	[illegible]
Salaries and other Expenses of Office for the year ended 31st December, 18[illegible],	[illegible]	
Balance to credit of Parliamentary Vote, 31st December, 18[illegible],	[illegible]	[illegible]
Total,		[illegible]

GENERAL BUSINESS OF THE COURT.

	No.
Number of Days on which the Court sat for Hearing Causes,	[illegible]
″ Days on which the Registrar and Merchants sat for hearing References,	[illegible]
Commissions, &c., certified at the Registry —	
Appointing Judge of the High Court of Admiralty,	—
Appointing Queen's Advocate,	—
Appointments of Commissioners to administer Oaths, and Bail,	[illegible]

	No.	Amount £ s. d.
Appointments of Surrogates,	—	—
Claims referred and heard by the Registrar,	[illegible]	[illegible]
″ allowed in full,	[illegible]	—
″ varied or altered,	[illegible]	—
″ disallowed in toto,	—	—
Awards appealed against to the Judge,	[illegible]	—
Total Amount claimed for Compensation,	—	[illegible]
Total Amount disallowed,	—	[illegible]
Total Amount found due,	—	[illegible]

IRELAND.

TABLE 63.—THE COURT OF BANKRUPTCY IN IRELAND.—RETURN of PROCEEDINGS in BANKRUPTCY for the Year 1886, made by the Chief Registrar.

PROCEEDINGS IN BANKRUPTCY.	Number.	Amount.
		£ s. d.
Petitions of Bankruptcy:—		
By Creditors, [illegible]		
By Debtors, [illegible]	[illegible]	—
Private Arrangements turned into Bankruptcy, [illegible]		
Applications by Debtors for Private Arrangements under the control of the Court,	[illegible]	—
Debtor Summonses [illegible],	[illegible]	—
Sittings before the Judges of the Court,	[illegible]	—
Sittings before the Chief Registrar and the Chief Clerk,	[illegible]	—
Number of Bills of Costs [illegible],	[illegible]	—
Number of [illegible],	[illegible]	—
Amount of Costs as [illegible],	—	[illegible]
Deductions on Taxation,	—	[illegible]
Amount as taxed,	—	[illegible]
Number of Solicitors who attended [illegible] in the Court,	[illegible]	—
Amount of Government Stock standing to the credit of the [illegible] Account in the Bank of Ireland, with Privity of Chief Registrar, 31st December, 1886,	—	—
Amount of Cash [illegible],	—	[illegible]
Number of cases of Bankruptcy referred to [illegible],	—	—
Number of Warrants [illegible],	—	—
Number of Orders [illegible] by Trustees,	—	—

(a) The [illegible] "Private Arrangements turned into Bankruptcy" are included herein.
(b) This does not include "Motions of Course" made before the Judges.

TABLE 64.—THE COURT OF BANKRUPTCY IN IRELAND.—RETURN of PROCEEDINGS in INSOLVENCY in the Year 1886, made by the First Clerk in Insolvency.

PROCEEDINGS IN INSOLVENCY.	Number.	Amount.
		£ s. d.
Petitions of Insolvency in which Dividends declared,	4	—
Amount of [illegible],	—	[illegible]
Amount of Debts upon which Dividends declared,	—	[illegible]
Average Dividend in the £,	—	[illegible]
Amount of remuneration allowed to the Official Assignee in the above cases of Dividend,	—	[illegible]
Amount of Law Costs of the Assignees in the above cases of Dividend, being the Law Expenses of realisation and distribution,	—	[illegible]
Average Cost of each case,	—	[illegible]
Amount of remuneration allowed to Official Assignee in other cases,	—	—
Sittings before the Court in Dublin for all purposes in Insolvency,	[illegible]	—
Sittings before the First Clerk or other Officer for all purposes in Insolvency,	[illegible]	—
Bills of Costs Taxed,	[illegible]	—
Number of Items,	[illegible]	—
Amount as Furnished,	—	[illegible]
Deductions on Taxation,	—	[illegible]
Amount as certified,	—	[illegible]

TABLE 65.—HIGH COURT OF JUSTICE—CHANCERY DIVISION.—RETURN of PROCEEDINGS in the Office of the Accountant-General for the Year ended 31st October, 1886, made by the Accountant-General.

Cash, Securities, and other Effects paid and transferred.	Into Court.	Out of Court.	Other Proceedings in the Office.	No.	Amount.
	£ s. d.	£ s. d.			£ s. d.
			Total Cheques signed,	[illegible]	—
Cash,	[illegible]	[illegible]	Amount of Cash, Securities, and other effects payable over in the Accountant-General's books, being the balance of year ended 31st October, 1886:—		
Government New £3 per cent. Stock,	[illegible]	[illegible]	Cash,		[illegible]
Government £3 per cent. Consols,	[illegible]	[illegible]	Securities,	—	[illegible]
Bank of Ireland Stock,	[illegible]	[illegible]	Indian [illegible] Currency,	—	[illegible]
Government £3 per cent. Reduced Annuities,	—	[illegible]	Powers of Attorney received, [illegible]:—		
Accountant's Bills,	—	—	Lodgment [illegible] by [illegible],	[illegible]	—
			[illegible]		
			Total number of Accounts,	[illegible]	—
Amount of Fees collected, [illegible]					

* The Accountant-General states that the accounts of the Probate and Matrimonial Divisions have ceased to be kept separately from the other accounts under his charge. The information respecting them [illegible] is now included in the present return.

Q

	£ s. d.	£ s. d.	£ s. d.
[illegible] of Cash and Securities standing in the name of the Accountant-General of the Supreme Court of Judicature in Ireland, on 30th September, [illegible], viz.:—			
Cash (Bank of Ireland) — Chancery, &c., Division	[illegible]		
Cash (Bank of Ireland) — Land Judges' Division	[illegible]	[illegible]	—
Securities — Chancery, &c., Division	[illegible]		
Securities — Land Judges' Division	[illegible]	—	[illegible]
[illegible] and transfers into Court in the Year to 30th September, [illegible]:—			
Chancery and Common Law Division.			
Dividends on Securities in Court	[illegible]		
Cash proceeds of sale of Securities in Court (as per contra)	[illegible]		
Other Cash brought into Court	[illegible]	[illegible]	—
Securities purchased with money in Court	[illegible]		
Other Securities brought into Court	[illegible]	—	[illegible]
Land Judges' Division.			
Dividends on Securities in Court	[illegible]		
Cash proceeds of sale of Securities in Court (as per contra)	[illegible]		
Other Cash brought into Court	[illegible]	[illegible]	—
Securities purchased with money in Court	[illegible]		
Other Securities brought into Court	[illegible]	—	[illegible]

	£ s. d.	£ s. d.	£ s. d.
Payments and transfers out of Court in the Year to 30th September, [illegible], viz.:—			
Chancery and Common Law Division.			
Cash paid for securities purchased (as per contra)	[illegible]		
Other Cash paid out of Court	[illegible]	[illegible]	—
Securities sold	[illegible]		
Other Securities transferred out of Court	[illegible]	—	[illegible]
Land Judges' Division.			
Cash paid for Securities purchased (as per contra)	[illegible]		
Other Cash paid out of Court	[illegible]	[illegible]	—
Securities sold	[illegible]		
Other Securities transferred out of Court	[illegible]	—	[illegible]
Balance of Cash and Securities standing in the name of the Accountant-General of the Supreme Court of Judicature in Ireland, on 30th September, [illegible], viz.:—			
Cash (Bank of Ireland) — Chancery, &c., Division	[illegible]		
Cash (Bank of Ireland) — Land Judges' Division	[illegible]	[illegible]	—
Securities — Chancery, &c., Division	[illegible]		
Securities — Land Judges' Division	[illegible]		

SUPREME COURT OF JUDICATURE, IRELAND—continued.

(a.) Statement of Liabilities and Assets in respect of the Funds of Suitors in the Supreme Court of Judicature in Ireland, on the [illegible] September, 188[illegible].

Liabilities.	Cash.	Securities.	Assets.	Cash.	Securities.
	£ s. d.	£ s. d.		£ s. d.	£ s. d.
[illegible]	[illegible]	[illegible]	[illegible]	[illegible]	[illegible]
Chancery and Common Law Division Accounts	[illegible]	[illegible]	Chancery and Common Law Division Accounts	[illegible]	[illegible]
Land Judges' Division Accounts	[illegible]	[illegible]	Land Judges' Division Accounts	[illegible]	[illegible]
			[illegible]	[illegible]	—
			[illegible]	[illegible]	—
	[illegible]	[illegible]		[illegible]	[illegible]
[illegible] Chancery Division	—	[illegible]	[illegible] Chancery Division	—	[illegible]

[illegible]

(b.) Particulars of Securities appearing by the Books of the Accountant-General to be in Court on the [illegible] September, 188[illegible].

—	Chancery Division.	Land Judges' Division.	—	Chancery Division.	Land Judges' Division.
	£ s. d.	£ s. d.		£ s. d.	£ s. d.
[illegible]	[illegible]	[illegible]	[illegible]	[illegible]	[illegible]

TABLE [illegible].—HIGH COURT OF JUSTICE.—STAMPS AND TAXES.—(1.) A RETURN showing the Amount received in respect of the following denominations of Stamps for the year ended 31st Dec., [illegible], viz., Judicature, Judgment Registry, Registry of Deeds, Admiralty Court, Bankruptcy, and Chancery Fund in Lunacy Matters, by Commissioners of Stamps.

Denomination.	Gross Amount.	Discount.	Net Amount.
	£ s. d.	£ s. d.	£ s. d.
1. Judicature (including Probate Courts),	[illegible]	—	[illegible]
2. Judgment Registry,	[illegible]	—	[illegible]
3. Registry of Deeds,	[illegible]	—	[illegible]
4. Admiralty Court,	[illegible]	—	[illegible]
5. Bankruptcy Fund,	[illegible]	—	[illegible]
6. Chancery Fund (Lunacy),	[illegible]	—	[illegible]

(2.) RETURN BY ACCOUNTANT-GENERAL.

	£ s. d.
Amount of percentage on Lunatics' Income in Year [illegible]—	
Cash,	[illegible]
Government Stocks and Shares,	[illegible]

TABLE [illegible].—SUPREME COURTS OF APPEAL.—HER MAJESTY'S COURT OF APPEAL, IRELAND.—RETURN of PROCEEDINGS for the Year [illegible], made by the REGISTRARS of the CHANCERY DIVISION.

I. APPEALS FROM DIVISIONS OF HIGH COURT OF JUSTICE.

NATURE OF PROCEEDINGS.	Totals	Chancery Division.	Queen's Bench Division.	Common Pleas Division.	Exchequer Division.	Probate and Matrimonial Division.
1. Appeals from Final Judgments:						
Awaiting Judgment,	[illegible]	[illegible]	[illegible]	[illegible]	[illegible]	[illegible]
Awaiting a hearing at commencement of year,	[illegible]	[illegible]	[illegible]	[illegible]	[illegible]	[illegible]
Set down during the year,	[illegible]	[illegible]	[illegible]	[illegible]	[illegible]	[illegible]
Heard, and Judgment delivered during the year,	[illegible]	[illegible]	[illegible]	[illegible]	[illegible]	[illegible]
Otherwise disposed of,	[illegible]	[illegible]	[illegible]	[illegible]	[illegible]	[illegible]
Awaiting a hearing at end of year,	[illegible]	[illegible]	[illegible]	[illegible]	[illegible]	[illegible]
Awaiting Judgment,	[illegible]	[illegible]	[illegible]	[illegible]	[illegible]	[illegible]
2. Appeals from Interlocutory Orders:						
Awaiting a hearing at commencement of year,	[illegible]	[illegible]	[illegible]	[illegible]	[illegible]	[illegible]
Set down during the year,	[illegible]	[illegible]	[illegible]	[illegible]	[illegible]	[illegible]
Heard during the year,	[illegible]	[illegible]	[illegible]	[illegible]	[illegible]	[illegible]
Otherwise disposed of,	[illegible]	[illegible]	[illegible]	[illegible]	[illegible]	[illegible]
Awaiting a hearing at end of year,	[illegible]	[illegible]	[illegible]	[illegible]	[illegible]	[illegible]
[illegible]	[illegible]	[illegible]	[illegible]	[illegible]	[illegible]	[illegible]
3. Original Motions:						
Awaiting a hearing at commencement of year,	[illegible]	[illegible]	[illegible]	[illegible]	[illegible]	[illegible]
Heard during the year,	[illegible]	[illegible]	[illegible]	[illegible]	[illegible]	[illegible]
Otherwise disposed of,	[illegible]	[illegible]	[illegible]	[illegible]	[illegible]	[illegible]
Awaiting a hearing at end of year,	[illegible]	[illegible]	[illegible]	[illegible]	[illegible]	[illegible]

TABLE [illegible].—SUPREME COURTS OF APPEAL.—COURT FOR CROWN CASES RESERVED.—RETURN showing CASES reserved for the consideration of the Court in the Year 1886, the COURT before which the Case stood for Trial, the OFFENCES CHARGED, and JUDGMENT of the Court in each Case. By the Master of the Crown Office, Queen's Bench Division.

No.	Court before which Case stood for Trial.	Offence charged.	Judgment of the Court.	Observations.
1	[illegible] Winter Assizes, 18[illegible], County of [illegible].	Under 1 and 2 Wm. IV., c. [illegible], commonly called the "[illegible] Act."	Conviction [illegible]. [illegible] to the Court.	

TABLE [illegible].—SUPREME COURT OF APPEAL.—CASES RESERVED by the JUDGES of QUEEN'S BENCH, COMMON PLEAS, and EXCHEQUER DIVISIONS as to PRESENTMENT and other CASES not within the 11 & 12 Vic., c. [illegible], in the Year 1886, by the Master of the Crown Office, Queen's Bench Division.

No.	Name of Case.	[illegible]	Observations.
1	County [illegible] Spring Assizes, [illegible] [illegible]'s Presentment—[illegible].	6 & 7 Wm. IV., c. 116, s. [illegible], . .	Presentment affirmed.
2	County Kerry Summer Assizes, 18[illegible], Tralee and [illegible] Pier and Railway Presentment.	[illegible] Vic., c. [illegible], and [illegible] Vic. c. [illegible].	Presentment quashed.
[illegible]			

TABLE [illegible].—SUPREME COURTS OF APPEAL.—PRIVY COUNCIL IN IRELAND.—RETURN of JUDICIAL PROCEEDINGS of the PRIVY COUNCIL in the Year 1886.

NATURE OF PROCEEDINGS.	No.	Remaining from 18[illegible].	RESULT. Applications on Appeal. Granted.	Refused.	Withdrawn.	Order Confirmed.	Order Varied.	Pending at close of Year.
Applications under The Tramways and Public Companies (Ireland) Act, 18[illegible], .	1	1	1	1	1	.	.	.
Applications under The Tramways (Ireland) Acts, 18[illegible], and 18[illegible], . . .	3*	.	3	.				.
Applications under The Fairs (Ireland) Act, 18[illegible], ...	1	.	1	.				.
Applications under The Labourers (Ireland) Act, 18[illegible], for confirmation of Provisional Orders made by the Local Government Board for Ireland ([illegible] Vic. cap. [illegible], s. [illegible]), ...	1[illegible]	.	.	.	1	1	[illegible]	[illegible]

* One of these was an Application for the abandonment of an undertaking, under Sec. [illegible] of the Act of 18[illegible].

TABLE 7[illegible].—SUPREME COURTS OF APPEAL—HOUSE OF LORDS.—RETURN of APPEALS from IRELAND for the Year [illegible], made by the Clerk of the Parliaments.

—	Total.
Number of Appeals presented in matters of	
Real Property, [illegible]	[illegible]
Personal Property, [illegible]	
Causes dismissed for want of prosecution,	[illegible]
Judgments delivered in Appeals—	
Causes affirmed, [illegible]	[illegible]
Do. reversed, [illegible]	
Causes standing over:—	
For judgment,	[illegible]
For hearing,	[illegible]
	£ s. d.
Fees,	[illegible]

TABLE 7[illegible].—LOCAL COURTS OF ADMIRALTY.—PROCEEDINGS in the Year [illegible], from Returns made by the Registrars.

PLACE WHERE COURT HELD	Total Number of Admiralty Actions or Proceedings	Arrests of Vessels	Final Decrees	Amount of Claims	Amount of Successors' Costs allowed	Suitors' Money: Paid under Order of Court	Suitors' Money: In Bank [illegible] Order at end of year	Instruments Executed	Notices of Bail
				£ s. d.	£ s. d.	£ s. d.	£ s. d.		
1. Belfast,	6	6	2	[illegible]	[illegible]	—	[illegible]	[illegible]	—
2. Cork,	11	[illegible]	[illegible]	[illegible]	[illegible]	[illegible]	—	—	1

TABLE 7[illegible].—HIGH COURT OF JUSTICE—PROBATE AND MATRIMONIAL DIVISION.—LOCAL PROBATE BUSINESS.—TABLE of PROCEEDINGS before the DISTRICT REGISTRARS in the Year [illegible], and of the AMOUNT of PROBATE DUTY received, from Returns made by the District Registrars.

DISTRICT REGISTRIES	Total Number of Grants issued in Year	Granted in Common Form: Probates	Granted in Common Form: Letters of Administration with the Will annexed	Granted in Common Form: Letters of Administration: Granted under Intestate Widows' Act, [illegible]	Granted in Common Form: Letters of Administration: Others	Granted under Direction of Judge: Probates	Granted under Direction of Judge: Letters of Administration with the Will annexed	Granted under Direction of Judge: Letters of Administration	Refused under direction of Judge: Probates	Refused under direction of Judge: Letters of Administration
Armagh,	[illegible]	[illegible]	[illegible]	[illegible]	[illegible]	[illegible]	[illegible]	[illegible]	[illegible]	[illegible]
Ballina,	[illegible]	[illegible]	[illegible]	[illegible]	[illegible]	[illegible]	[illegible]	[illegible]	[illegible]	[illegible]
Belfast,	[illegible]	[illegible]	[illegible]	[illegible]	[illegible]	[illegible]	[illegible]	[illegible]	[illegible]	[illegible]
Cavan,	[illegible]	[illegible]	[illegible]	[illegible]	[illegible]	[illegible]	[illegible]	[illegible]	[illegible]	[illegible]
Cork,	[illegible]	[illegible]	[illegible]	[illegible]	[illegible]	[illegible]	[illegible]	[illegible]	[illegible]	[illegible]
Kilkenny,	[illegible]	[illegible]	[illegible]	[illegible]	[illegible]	[illegible]	[illegible]	[illegible]	[illegible]	[illegible]
Limerick,	[illegible]	[illegible]	[illegible]	[illegible]	[illegible]	[illegible]	[illegible]	[illegible]	[illegible]	[illegible]
Londonderry,	[illegible]	[illegible]	[illegible]	[illegible]	[illegible]	[illegible]	[illegible]	[illegible]	[illegible]	[illegible]
Mullingar,	[illegible]	[illegible]	[illegible]	[illegible]	[illegible]	[illegible]	[illegible]	[illegible]	[illegible]	[illegible]
Tuam,	[illegible]	[illegible]	[illegible]	[illegible]	[illegible]	[illegible]	[illegible]	[illegible]	[illegible]	[illegible]
Waterford,	[illegible]	[illegible]	[illegible]	[illegible]	[illegible]	[illegible]	[illegible]	[illegible]	[illegible]	[illegible]
Total,	[illegible]	[illegible]	[illegible]	[illegible]	[illegible]	[illegible]	[illegible]	[illegible]	[illegible]	[illegible]

DISTRICT REGISTRIES	Granted on Decision of County Court Judges: Probates	Granted on Decision of County Court Judges: Letters of Administration with the Will annexed	Granted on Decision of County Court Judges: Letters of Administration	Resealed or signed: Probates	Resealed or signed: Letters of Administration	Caveats against Grant of Probates and Letters of Administration	Amount of Fees received on Grants	Fees on [illegible]	Total of all Fees received in Registry	Amount of Duty on Schedules lodged for Grants
							£ s. d.	£ s. d.	£ s. d.	£ s. d.
Armagh,	[illegible]	[illegible]	[illegible]	[illegible]	[illegible]	[illegible]	[illegible]	[illegible]	[illegible]	[illegible]
Ballina,	[illegible]	[illegible]	[illegible]	[illegible]	[illegible]	[illegible]	[illegible]	[illegible]	[illegible]	[illegible]
Belfast,	[illegible]	[illegible]	[illegible]	[illegible]	[illegible]	[illegible]	[illegible]	[illegible]	[illegible]	[illegible]
Cavan,	[illegible]	[illegible]	[illegible]	[illegible]	[illegible]	[illegible]	[illegible]	[illegible]	[illegible]	[illegible]
Cork,	[illegible]	[illegible]	[illegible]	[illegible]	[illegible]	[illegible]	[illegible]	[illegible]	[illegible]	[illegible]
Kilkenny,	[illegible]	[illegible]	[illegible]	[illegible]	[illegible]	[illegible]	[illegible]	[illegible]	[illegible]	[illegible]
Limerick,	[illegible]	[illegible]	[illegible]	[illegible]	[illegible]	[illegible]	[illegible]	[illegible]	[illegible]	[illegible]
Londonderry,	[illegible]	[illegible]	[illegible]	[illegible]	[illegible]	[illegible]	[illegible]	[illegible]	[illegible]	[illegible]
Mullingar,	[illegible]	[illegible]	[illegible]	[illegible]	[illegible]	[illegible]	[illegible]	[illegible]	[illegible]	[illegible]
Tuam,	[illegible]	[illegible]	[illegible]	[illegible]	[illegible]	[illegible]	[illegible]	[illegible]	[illegible]	[illegible]
Waterford,	[illegible]	[illegible]	[illegible]	[illegible]	[illegible]	[illegible]	[illegible]	[illegible]	[illegible]	[illegible]
Total,	[illegible]	[illegible]	[illegible]	[illegible]	[illegible]	[illegible]	[illegible]	[illegible]	[illegible]	[illegible]

	—	—
	—	—
	—	—
	—	—
	—	—
	—	—
[illegible]	[illegible]	[illegible]
	—	—
	—	—
	—	—
	—	—
	—	—
	—	—
	—	—
	—	—
	—	—
	—	—
	—	—
	—	—
	—	—
	—	—
	—	—
[illegible]	[illegible]	[illegible]
	—	—
	—	—
	—	—

[illegible]			[illegible]	[illegible]	[illegible]
[illegible]	[illegible]	[illegible]	[illegible]	[illegible]	[illegible]

TABLE [illegible].—HIGH COURT OF JUSTICE.—PROCEEDINGS ON CIRCUIT.—APPEALS from COUNTY COURT JUDGES and RECORDERS in [illegible], from Returns made by Clerks of the Peace and Registrars of [illegible].

Counties and Counties of Cities and of Towns, arranged in Circuits.	Appeals from County Court Judges and Recorders.			
	Entered.	Heard.		Struck Out, Withdrawn, Settled, &c.
		Affirmed.	Varied or Reversed.	
Leinster Circuit:				
Carlow,	[illegible]	[illegible]	[illegible]	[illegible]
Kildare,	[illegible]	[illegible]	[illegible]	[illegible]
Kilkenny,	[illegible]	[illegible]	[illegible]	[illegible]
Queen's County,	[illegible]	[illegible]	[illegible]	[illegible]
Tipperary, North Riding, / Tipperary, South Riding,	[illegible]	[illegible]	[illegible]	[illegible]
Waterford,	[illegible]	[illegible]	[illegible]	[illegible]
Wexford,	[illegible]	[illegible]	[illegible]	[illegible]
Wicklow,	[illegible]	[illegible]	[illegible]	[illegible]
Total,	[illegible]	[illegible]	[illegible]	[illegible]
Munster Circuit:				
Clare,	[illegible]	[illegible]	[illegible]	[illegible]
Cork, East Riding,	[illegible]	[illegible]	[illegible]	[illegible]
Cork, West Riding,	[illegible]	[illegible]	[illegible]	[illegible]
Kerry,	[illegible]	[illegible]	[illegible]	[illegible]
Limerick,	[illegible]	[illegible]	[illegible]	[illegible]
Total,	[illegible]	[illegible]	[illegible]	[illegible]
North-East Circuit:				
Antrim,	[illegible]	[illegible]	[illegible]	[illegible]
Armagh,	[illegible]	[illegible]	[illegible]	[illegible]
Down,	[illegible]	[illegible]	[illegible]	[illegible]
Louth,	[illegible]	[illegible]	[illegible]	[illegible]
Meath,	[illegible]	[illegible]	[illegible]	[illegible]
Monaghan,	[illegible]	[illegible]	[illegible]	[illegible]
Total,	[illegible]	[illegible]	[illegible]	[illegible]
North-West Circuit:				
Cavan,	[illegible]	[illegible]	[illegible]	[illegible]
Donegal,	[illegible]	[illegible]	[illegible]	[illegible]
Fermanagh,	[illegible]	[illegible]	[illegible]	[illegible]
Londonderry,	[illegible]	[illegible]	[illegible]	[illegible]
Longford,	[illegible]	[illegible]	[illegible]	[illegible]
Tyrone,	[illegible]	[illegible]	[illegible]	[illegible]
Westmeath,	[illegible]	[illegible]	[illegible]	[illegible]
Total,	[illegible]	[illegible]	[illegible]	[illegible]
Connaught Circuit:				
Galway,	[illegible]	[illegible]	[illegible]	[illegible]
King's County,	[illegible]	[illegible]	[illegible]	[illegible]
Leitrim,	[illegible]	[illegible]	[illegible]	[illegible]
Mayo,	[illegible]	[illegible]	[illegible]	[illegible]
Roscommon,	[illegible]	[illegible]	[illegible]	[illegible]
Sligo,	[illegible]	[illegible]	[illegible]	[illegible]
Total,	[illegible]	[illegible]	[illegible]	[illegible]
Belfast, North-east Circuit,	[illegible]	[illegible]	[illegible]	[illegible]
Cork City, Munster Circuit,	[illegible]	[illegible]	[illegible]	[illegible]
Galway Town, Connaught Circuit,	[illegible]	[illegible]	[illegible]	[illegible]
Londonderry City, North-west Circuit,	[illegible]	[illegible]	[illegible]	[illegible]
Total,	[illegible]	[illegible]	[illegible]	[illegible]
Total of Ireland,	[illegible]	[illegible]	[illegible]	[illegible]

TABLE 61.—COUNTY COURTS AND RECORDER'S COURTS.—CIVIL BILL EJECTMENTS, REPLEVINS, and other CIVIL BILLS served in [illegible], from Returns made by Process Servers appointed by COUNTY COURT JUDGES and RECORDERS.

Counties, and Counties of Cities or of Towns.	Number of Process Servers appointed.	Number of Process Servers who have made Returns.	Number of Process Servers who have not made Returns.	Served by Process Servers.		
				Civil Bill Ejectments.	Replevins.	Other Civil Bills.
Leinster.						
Carlow,	[illegible]	[illegible]	[illegible]	[illegible]	.	[illegible]
Dublin,	[illegible]	[illegible]	[illegible]	[illegible]	.	[illegible]
Dublin City,	[illegible]	[illegible]	[illegible]	[illegible]	[illegible]	[illegible]
Kildare,	[illegible]	[illegible]	[illegible]	[illegible]	[illegible]	[illegible]
Kilkenny, and City,	[illegible]	[illegible]	.	[illegible]	[illegible]	[illegible]
King's County,	[illegible]	[illegible]	[illegible]	[illegible]	[illegible]	[illegible]
Longford,	[illegible]	[illegible]	[illegible]	[illegible]	[illegible]	[illegible]
Louth, and Drogheda Town,	[illegible]	[illegible]	.	[illegible]	[illegible]	[illegible]
Meath,	[illegible]	[illegible]	[illegible]	[illegible]	.	[illegible]
Queen's County,	[illegible]	[illegible]	.	[illegible]	.	[illegible]
Westmeath,	[illegible]	[illegible]	.	[illegible]	[illegible]	[illegible]
Wexford,	[illegible]	[illegible]	.	[illegible]	.	[illegible]
Wicklow,	[illegible]	[illegible]	[illegible]	[illegible]	.	[illegible]
Total of Province,	[illegible]	[illegible]	[illegible]	[illegible]	[illegible]	[illegible]
Munster.						
Clare,	[illegible]	[illegible]	[illegible]	[illegible]	[illegible]	[illegible]
Cork, East Riding,	[illegible]	[illegible]	[illegible]	[illegible]	[illegible]	[illegible]
Cork, West Riding,	[illegible]	[illegible]	[illegible]	[illegible]	[illegible]	[illegible]
Cork City (Recorder's Court),	[illegible]	[illegible]	.	[illegible]	.	[illegible]
Kerry,	[illegible]	[illegible]	.	[illegible]	[illegible]	[illegible]
Limerick, and City,	[illegible]	[illegible]	.	[illegible]	.	[illegible]
Tipperary,	[illegible]	[illegible]	[illegible]	[illegible]	[illegible]	[illegible]
Waterford, and City,	[illegible]	[illegible]	[illegible]	[illegible]	[illegible]	[illegible]
Total of Province,	[illegible]	[illegible]	[illegible]	[illegible]	[illegible]	[illegible]
Ulster.						
Antrim (including Carrickfergus),	[illegible]	[illegible]	[illegible]	[illegible]	[illegible]	[illegible]
Armagh,	[illegible]	[illegible]	.	[illegible]	[illegible]	[illegible]
Cavan,	[illegible]	[illegible]	[illegible]	[illegible]	.	[illegible]
Donegal,	[illegible]	[illegible]	.	[illegible]	.	[illegible]
Down,	[illegible]	[illegible]	.	[illegible]	[illegible]	[illegible]
Fermanagh,	[illegible]	[illegible]	.	[illegible]	[illegible]	[illegible]
Londonderry,	[illegible]	[illegible]	.	[illegible]	[illegible]	[illegible]
Monaghan,	[illegible]	[illegible]	.	[illegible]	.	[illegible]
Tyrone,	[illegible]	[illegible]	[illegible]	[illegible]	[illegible]	[illegible]
Total of Province,	[illegible]	[illegible]	[illegible]	[illegible]	[illegible]	[illegible]
Connaught.						
Galway, and Town,	[illegible]	[illegible]	[illegible]	[illegible]	[illegible]	[illegible]
Leitrim,	[illegible]	[illegible]	[illegible]	[illegible]	[illegible]	[illegible]
Mayo,	[illegible]	[illegible]	[illegible]	[illegible]	[illegible]	[illegible]
Roscommon,	[illegible]	[illegible]	[illegible]	[illegible]	[illegible]	[illegible]
Sligo,	[illegible]	[illegible]	[illegible]	[illegible]	.	[illegible]
Total of Province,	[illegible]	[illegible]	[illegible]	[illegible]	[illegible]	[illegible]
Total of Ireland [illegible]	[illegible]	[illegible]	[illegible]	[illegible]	[illegible]	[illegible]

TABLE [illegible].—COUNTY COURTS AND RECORDERS' COURTS—PROCEEDINGS in all SUITS ([illegible]

Returns made by Clerks of the Peace

COUNTIES.	Number of Places at which Courts are held	[illegible]				Cases [illegible]	For Plaintiff.				For Defendant.			
		Total Number	[illegible]	[illegible]	Other [illegible]		[illegible]	[illegible]	[illegible]	[illegible]	[illegible]	[illegible]	[illegible]	[illegible]
Leinster:														
Carlow,	[illegible]	[illegible]	[illegible]	[illegible]	[illegible]	[illegible]	[illegible]	[illegible]	[illegible]	[illegible]	[illegible]	[illegible]	[illegible]	[illegible]
Dublin,	[illegible]	[illegible]	[illegible]	[illegible]	[illegible]	[illegible]	[illegible]	[illegible]	[illegible]	[illegible]	[illegible]	[illegible]	[illegible]	[illegible]
Dublin City (Recorder's Court),	[illegible]	[illegible]	[illegible]	[illegible]	[illegible]	[illegible]	[illegible]	[illegible]	[illegible]	[illegible]	[illegible]	[illegible]	[illegible]	[illegible]
Kildare,	[illegible]	[illegible]	[illegible]	[illegible]	[illegible]	[illegible]	[illegible]	[illegible]	[illegible]	[illegible]	[illegible]	[illegible]	[illegible]	[illegible]
Kilkenny,	[illegible]	[illegible]	[illegible]	[illegible]	[illegible]	[illegible]	[illegible]	[illegible]	[illegible]	[illegible]	[illegible]	[illegible]	[illegible]	[illegible]
King's County,	[illegible]	[illegible]	[illegible]	[illegible]	[illegible]	[illegible]	[illegible]	[illegible]	[illegible]	[illegible]	[illegible]	[illegible]	[illegible]	[illegible]
Longford,	[illegible]	[illegible]	[illegible]	[illegible]	[illegible]	[illegible]	[illegible]	[illegible]	[illegible]	[illegible]	[illegible]	[illegible]	[illegible]	[illegible]
Louth,	[illegible]	[illegible]	[illegible]	[illegible]	[illegible]	[illegible]	[illegible]	[illegible]	[illegible]	[illegible]	[illegible]	[illegible]	[illegible]	[illegible]
Meath,	[illegible]	[illegible]	[illegible]	[illegible]	[illegible]	[illegible]	[illegible]	[illegible]	[illegible]	[illegible]	[illegible]	[illegible]	[illegible]	[illegible]
Queen's County,	[illegible]	[illegible]	[illegible]	[illegible]	[illegible]	[illegible]	[illegible]	[illegible]	[illegible]	[illegible]	[illegible]	[illegible]	[illegible]	[illegible]
Westmeath,	[illegible]	[illegible]	[illegible]	[illegible]	[illegible]	[illegible]	[illegible]	[illegible]	[illegible]	[illegible]	[illegible]	[illegible]	[illegible]	[illegible]
Wexford,	[illegible]	[illegible]	[illegible]	[illegible]	[illegible]	[illegible]	[illegible]	[illegible]	[illegible]	[illegible]	[illegible]	[illegible]	[illegible]	[illegible]
Wicklow,	[illegible]	[illegible]	[illegible]	[illegible]	[illegible]	[illegible]	[illegible]	[illegible]	[illegible]	[illegible]	[illegible]	[illegible]	[illegible]	[illegible]
Total of Leinster,	[illegible]	[illegible]	[illegible]	[illegible]	[illegible]	[illegible]	[illegible]	[illegible]	[illegible]	[illegible]	[illegible]	[illegible]	[illegible]	[illegible]
Munster:														
Clare,	[illegible]	[illegible]	[illegible]	[illegible]	[illegible]	[illegible]	[illegible]	[illegible]	[illegible]	[illegible]	[illegible]	[illegible]	[illegible]	[illegible]
Cork, E.R.,	[illegible]	[illegible]	[illegible]	[illegible]	[illegible]	[illegible]	[illegible]	[illegible]	[illegible]	[illegible]	[illegible]	[illegible]	[illegible]	[illegible]
Cork, W.R.,	[illegible]	[illegible]	[illegible]	[illegible]	[illegible]	[illegible]	[illegible]	[illegible]	[illegible]	[illegible]	[illegible]	[illegible]	[illegible]	[illegible]
Cork City (Recorder's Court),	[illegible]	[illegible]	[illegible]	[illegible]	[illegible]	[illegible]	[illegible]	[illegible]	[illegible]	[illegible]	[illegible]	[illegible]	[illegible]	[illegible]
Kerry,	[illegible]	[illegible]	[illegible]	[illegible]	[illegible]	[illegible]	[illegible]	[illegible]	[illegible]	[illegible]	[illegible]	[illegible]	[illegible]	[illegible]
Limerick,	[illegible]	[illegible]	[illegible]	[illegible]	[illegible]	[illegible]	[illegible]	[illegible]	[illegible]	[illegible]	[illegible]	[illegible]	[illegible]	[illegible]
Tipperary,	[illegible]	[illegible]	[illegible]	[illegible]	[illegible]	[illegible]	[illegible]	[illegible]	[illegible]	[illegible]	[illegible]	[illegible]	[illegible]	[illegible]
Waterford,	[illegible]	[illegible]	[illegible]	[illegible]	[illegible]	[illegible]	[illegible]	[illegible]	[illegible]	[illegible]	[illegible]	[illegible]	[illegible]	[illegible]
Total of Munster,	[illegible]	[illegible]	[illegible]	[illegible]	[illegible]	[illegible]	[illegible]	[illegible]	[illegible]	[illegible]	[illegible]	[illegible]	[illegible]	[illegible]
Ulster:														
Antrim,	[illegible]	[illegible]	[illegible]	[illegible]	[illegible]	[illegible]	[illegible]	[illegible]	[illegible]	[illegible]	[illegible]	[illegible]	[illegible]	[illegible]
Armagh,	[illegible]	[illegible]	[illegible]	[illegible]	[illegible]	[illegible]	[illegible]	[illegible]	[illegible]	[illegible]	[illegible]	[illegible]	[illegible]	[illegible]
Belfast (Recorder's Court),	[illegible]	[illegible]	[illegible]	[illegible]	[illegible]	[illegible]	[illegible]	[illegible]	[illegible]	[illegible]	[illegible]	[illegible]	[illegible]	[illegible]
Cavan,	[illegible]	[illegible]	[illegible]	[illegible]	[illegible]	[illegible]	[illegible]	[illegible]	[illegible]	[illegible]	[illegible]	[illegible]	[illegible]	[illegible]
Donegal,	[illegible]	[illegible]	[illegible]	[illegible]	[illegible]	[illegible]	[illegible]	[illegible]	[illegible]	[illegible]	[illegible]	[illegible]	[illegible]	[illegible]
Down,	[illegible]	[illegible]	[illegible]	[illegible]	[illegible]	[illegible]	[illegible]	[illegible]	[illegible]	[illegible]	[illegible]	[illegible]	[illegible]	[illegible]
Fermanagh,	[illegible]	[illegible]	[illegible]	[illegible]	[illegible]	[illegible]	[illegible]	[illegible]	[illegible]	[illegible]	[illegible]	[illegible]	[illegible]	[illegible]
Londonderry City (Recorder's Court),	[illegible]	[illegible]	[illegible]	[illegible]	[illegible]	[illegible]	[illegible]	[illegible]	[illegible]	[illegible]	[illegible]	[illegible]	[illegible]	[illegible]
Londonderry,	[illegible]	[illegible]	[illegible]	[illegible]	[illegible]	[illegible]	[illegible]	[illegible]	[illegible]	[illegible]	[illegible]	[illegible]	[illegible]	[illegible]
Monaghan,	[illegible]	[illegible]	[illegible]	[illegible]	[illegible]	[illegible]	[illegible]	[illegible]	[illegible]	[illegible]	[illegible]	[illegible]	[illegible]	[illegible]
Tyrone,	[illegible]	[illegible]	[illegible]	[illegible]	[illegible]	[illegible]	[illegible]	[illegible]	[illegible]	[illegible]	[illegible]	[illegible]	[illegible]	[illegible]
Total of Ulster,	[illegible]	[illegible]	[illegible]	[illegible]	[illegible]	[illegible]	[illegible]	[illegible]	[illegible]	[illegible]	[illegible]	[illegible]	[illegible]	[illegible]
Connaught:														
Galway,	[illegible]	[illegible]	[illegible]	[illegible]	[illegible]	[illegible]	[illegible]	[illegible]	[illegible]	[illegible]	[illegible]	[illegible]	[illegible]	[illegible]
Galway Town (Recorder's Court),	[illegible]	[illegible]	[illegible]	[illegible]	[illegible]	[illegible]	[illegible]	[illegible]	[illegible]	[illegible]	[illegible]	[illegible]	[illegible]	[illegible]
Leitrim,	[illegible]	[illegible]	[illegible]	[illegible]	[illegible]	[illegible]	[illegible]	[illegible]	[illegible]	[illegible]	[illegible]	[illegible]	[illegible]	[illegible]
Mayo,	[illegible]	[illegible]	[illegible]	[illegible]	[illegible]	[illegible]	[illegible]	[illegible]	[illegible]	[illegible]	[illegible]	[illegible]	[illegible]	[illegible]
Roscommon,	[illegible]	[illegible]	[illegible]	[illegible]	[illegible]	[illegible]	[illegible]	[illegible]	[illegible]	[illegible]	[illegible]	[illegible]	[illegible]	[illegible]
Sligo,	[illegible]	[illegible]	[illegible]	[illegible]	[illegible]	[illegible]	[illegible]	[illegible]	[illegible]	[illegible]	[illegible]	[illegible]	[illegible]	[illegible]
Total of Connaught,	[illegible]	[illegible]	[illegible]	[illegible]	[illegible]	[illegible]	[illegible]	[illegible]	[illegible]	[illegible]	[illegible]	[illegible]	[illegible]	[illegible]
Total of Ireland,	[illegible]	[illegible]	[illegible]	[illegible]	[illegible]	[illegible]	[illegible]	[illegible]	[illegible]	[illegible]	[illegible]	[illegible]	[illegible]	[illegible]

[illegible] (Land [illegible], [illegible], and under Land [illegible] Act) in the Year 18[illegible], from [illegible] and Registrars of [illegible].

[illegible]						[illegible]								COUNTIES
[illegible]		[illegible]		[illegible]		[illegible]		[illegible]		[illegible]		[illegible]		
[illegible]	[illegible]	[illegible]	[illegible]	[illegible]	[illegible]	[illegible]	[illegible]	[illegible]	[illegible]	[illegible]	[illegible]	[illegible]	[illegible]	
[illegible]	[illegible]	[illegible]	[illegible]	[illegible]	[illegible]									LEINSTER.
[illegible]	[illegible]	[illegible]	[illegible]	[illegible]	[illegible]	[illegible]	[illegible]	[illegible]	[illegible]	[illegible]	[illegible]	[illegible]	[illegible]	Carlow.
[illegible]	[illegible]	[illegible]	[illegible]	[illegible]	[illegible]	[illegible]	[illegible]	[illegible]	[illegible]	[illegible]	[illegible]	[illegible]	[illegible]	Dublin.
[illegible]	[illegible]	[illegible]	[illegible]	[illegible]	[illegible]	[illegible]	[illegible]	[illegible]	[illegible]	[illegible]	[illegible]	[illegible]	[illegible]	Dublin City (Recorder's Court).
[illegible]	[illegible]	[illegible]	[illegible]	[illegible]	[illegible]	[illegible]	[illegible]	[illegible]	[illegible]	[illegible]	[illegible]	[illegible]	[illegible]	Kildare.
[illegible]	[illegible]	[illegible]	[illegible]	[illegible]	[illegible]	[illegible]	[illegible]	[illegible]	[illegible]	[illegible]	[illegible]	[illegible]	[illegible]	Kilkenny.
[illegible]	[illegible]	[illegible]	[illegible]	[illegible]	[illegible]	[illegible]	[illegible]	[illegible]	[illegible]	[illegible]	[illegible]	[illegible]	[illegible]	King's County.
[illegible]	[illegible]	[illegible]	[illegible]	[illegible]	[illegible]	[illegible]	[illegible]	[illegible]	[illegible]	[illegible]	[illegible]	[illegible]	[illegible]	Longford.
[illegible]	[illegible]	[illegible]	[illegible]	[illegible]	[illegible]	[illegible]	[illegible]	[illegible]	[illegible]	[illegible]	[illegible]	[illegible]	[illegible]	Louth.
[illegible]	[illegible]	[illegible]	[illegible]	[illegible]	[illegible]	[illegible]	[illegible]	[illegible]	[illegible]	[illegible]	[illegible]	[illegible]	[illegible]	Meath.
[illegible]	[illegible]	[illegible]	[illegible]	[illegible]	[illegible]	[illegible]	[illegible]	[illegible]	[illegible]	[illegible]	[illegible]	[illegible]	[illegible]	Queen's County.
[illegible]	[illegible]	[illegible]	[illegible]	[illegible]	[illegible]	[illegible]	[illegible]	[illegible]	[illegible]	[illegible]	[illegible]	[illegible]	[illegible]	Westmeath.
[illegible]	[illegible]	[illegible]	[illegible]	[illegible]	[illegible]	[illegible]	[illegible]	[illegible]	[illegible]	[illegible]	[illegible]	[illegible]	[illegible]	Wexford.
[illegible]	[illegible]	[illegible]	[illegible]	[illegible]	[illegible]	[illegible]	[illegible]	[illegible]	[illegible]	[illegible]	[illegible]	[illegible]	[illegible]	Wicklow.
[illegible]	[illegible]	[illegible]	[illegible]	[illegible]	[illegible]	[illegible]	[illegible]	[illegible]	[illegible]	[illegible]	[illegible]	[illegible]	[illegible]	Total of Leinster.
														MUNSTER.
[illegible]	[illegible]	[illegible]	[illegible]	[illegible]	[illegible]	[illegible]	[illegible]	[illegible]	[illegible]	[illegible]	[illegible]	[illegible]	[illegible]	Clare.
[illegible]	[illegible]	[illegible]	[illegible]	[illegible]	[illegible]	[illegible]	[illegible]	[illegible]	[illegible]	[illegible]	[illegible]	[illegible]	[illegible]	Cork, E. R.
[illegible]	[illegible]	[illegible]	[illegible]	[illegible]	[illegible]	[illegible]	[illegible]	[illegible]	[illegible]	[illegible]	[illegible]	[illegible]	[illegible]	Cork, W. R.
[illegible]	[illegible]	[illegible]	[illegible]	[illegible]	[illegible]	[illegible]	[illegible]	[illegible]	[illegible]	[illegible]	[illegible]	[illegible]	[illegible]	Cork City (Recorder's Court).
[illegible]	[illegible]	[illegible]	[illegible]	[illegible]	[illegible]	[illegible]	[illegible]	[illegible]	[illegible]	[illegible]	[illegible]	[illegible]	[illegible]	Kerry.
[illegible]	[illegible]	[illegible]	[illegible]	[illegible]	[illegible]	[illegible]	[illegible]	[illegible]	[illegible]	[illegible]	[illegible]	[illegible]	[illegible]	Limerick.
[illegible]	[illegible]	[illegible]	[illegible]	[illegible]	[illegible]	[illegible]	[illegible]	[illegible]	[illegible]	[illegible]	[illegible]	[illegible]	[illegible]	Tipperary.
[illegible]	[illegible]	[illegible]	[illegible]	[illegible]	[illegible]	[illegible]	[illegible]	[illegible]	[illegible]	[illegible]	[illegible]	[illegible]	[illegible]	Waterford.
[illegible]	[illegible]	[illegible]	[illegible]	[illegible]	[illegible]	[illegible]	[illegible]	[illegible]	[illegible]	[illegible]	[illegible]	[illegible]	[illegible]	Total of Munster.
														ULSTER.
[illegible]	[illegible]	[illegible]	[illegible]	[illegible]	[illegible]	[illegible]	[illegible]	[illegible]	[illegible]	[illegible]	[illegible]	[illegible]	[illegible]	Antrim.
[illegible]	[illegible]	[illegible]	[illegible]	[illegible]	[illegible]	[illegible]	[illegible]	[illegible]	[illegible]	[illegible]	[illegible]	[illegible]	[illegible]	Armagh.
[illegible]	[illegible]	[illegible]	[illegible]	[illegible]	[illegible]	[illegible]	[illegible]	[illegible]	[illegible]	[illegible]	[illegible]	[illegible]	[illegible]	Belfast (Recorder's Court).
[illegible]	[illegible]	[illegible]	[illegible]	[illegible]	[illegible]	[illegible]	[illegible]	[illegible]	[illegible]	[illegible]	[illegible]	[illegible]	[illegible]	Cavan.
[illegible]	[illegible]	[illegible]	[illegible]	[illegible]	[illegible]	[illegible]	[illegible]	[illegible]	[illegible]	[illegible]	[illegible]	[illegible]	[illegible]	Donegal.
[illegible]	[illegible]	[illegible]	[illegible]	[illegible]	[illegible]	[illegible]	[illegible]	[illegible]	[illegible]	[illegible]	[illegible]	[illegible]	[illegible]	Down.
[illegible]	[illegible]	[illegible]	[illegible]	[illegible]	[illegible]	[illegible]	[illegible]	[illegible]	[illegible]	[illegible]	[illegible]	[illegible]	[illegible]	Fermanagh.
[illegible]	[illegible]	[illegible]	[illegible]	[illegible]	[illegible]	[illegible]	[illegible]	[illegible]	[illegible]	[illegible]	[illegible]	[illegible]	[illegible]	Londonderry City (Recorder's Court).
[illegible]	[illegible]	[illegible]	[illegible]	[illegible]	[illegible]	[illegible]	[illegible]	[illegible]	[illegible]	[illegible]	[illegible]	[illegible]	[illegible]	Londonderry.
[illegible]	[illegible]	[illegible]	[illegible]	[illegible]	[illegible]	[illegible]	[illegible]	[illegible]	[illegible]	[illegible]	[illegible]	[illegible]	[illegible]	Monaghan.
[illegible]	[illegible]	[illegible]	[illegible]	[illegible]	[illegible]	[illegible]	[illegible]	[illegible]	[illegible]	[illegible]	[illegible]	[illegible]	[illegible]	Tyrone.
[illegible]	[illegible]	[illegible]	[illegible]	[illegible]	[illegible]	[illegible]	[illegible]	[illegible]	[illegible]	[illegible]	[illegible]	[illegible]	[illegible]	Total of Ulster.
														CONNAUGHT.
[illegible]	[illegible]	[illegible]	[illegible]	[illegible]	[illegible]	[illegible]	[illegible]	[illegible]	[illegible]	[illegible]	[illegible]	[illegible]	[illegible]	Galway.
[illegible]	[illegible]	[illegible]	[illegible]	[illegible]	[illegible]	[illegible]	[illegible]	[illegible]	[illegible]	[illegible]	[illegible]	[illegible]	[illegible]	Galway Town (Recorder's Court).
[illegible]	[illegible]	[illegible]	[illegible]	[illegible]	[illegible]	[illegible]	[illegible]	[illegible]	[illegible]	[illegible]	[illegible]	[illegible]	[illegible]	Leitrim.
[illegible]	[illegible]	[illegible]	[illegible]	[illegible]	[illegible]	[illegible]	[illegible]	[illegible]	[illegible]	[illegible]	[illegible]	[illegible]	[illegible]	Mayo.
[illegible]	[illegible]	[illegible]	[illegible]	[illegible]	[illegible]	[illegible]	[illegible]	[illegible]	[illegible]	[illegible]	[illegible]	[illegible]	[illegible]	Roscommon.
[illegible]	[illegible]	[illegible]	[illegible]	[illegible]	[illegible]	[illegible]	[illegible]	[illegible]	[illegible]	[illegible]	[illegible]	[illegible]	[illegible]	Sligo.
[illegible]	[illegible]	[illegible]	[illegible]	[illegible]	[illegible]	[illegible]	[illegible]	[illegible]	[illegible]	[illegible]	[illegible]	[illegible]	[illegible]	Total of Connaught.
[illegible]	[illegible]	[illegible]	[illegible]	[illegible]	[illegible]	[illegible]	[illegible]	[illegible]	[illegible]	[illegible]	[illegible]	[illegible]	[illegible]	Total of Ireland.

TABLE [illegible].—COUNTY COURTS AND RECORDERS' COURTS.—RESULTS of EQUITY CIVIL [illegible]

COUNTIES.	Number of Places where a County Court is held [illegible]	[illegible] Total.	For [illegible]	For [illegible]	For the [illegible]	For any other purpose.	[illegible] Total.	For any purpose under the Trustee Acts.	For the [illegible]	For any other purpose.	Lunacy: Number of [illegible]	Number of Orders made.
Leinster:												
Carlow,	[illegible]	[illegible]	-	-	-	[illegible]	[illegible]	-	-	[illegible]	-	-
Dublin,	[illegible]	[illegible]	[illegible]	[illegible]	-	[illegible]	[illegible]	[illegible]	[illegible]	[illegible]	-	-
Dublin City,	[illegible]	[illegible]	[illegible]	[illegible]	-	[illegible]	[illegible]	[illegible]	-	[illegible]	-	-
Kildare,	[illegible]	[illegible]	[illegible]	-	-	[illegible]	-	-	-	-	-	[illegible]
Kilkenny,	[illegible]	[illegible]	[illegible]	-	-	[illegible]	-	-	-	-	-	-
King's County,	[illegible]	[illegible]	[illegible]	-	-	[illegible]	-	-	-	-	-	-
Longford,	[illegible]	[illegible]	[illegible]	-	[illegible]	[illegible]	-	-	-	-	[illegible]	[illegible]
Louth,	[illegible]	[illegible]	[illegible]	-	-	[illegible]	[illegible]	[illegible]	-	-	-	-
Meath,	[illegible]	[illegible]	[illegible]	[illegible]	[illegible]	[illegible]	[illegible]	[illegible]	[illegible]	[illegible]	-	-
Queen's County,	[illegible]	[illegible]	[illegible]	[illegible]	-	[illegible]	-	-	-	-	-	-
Westmeath,	[illegible]	[illegible]	[illegible]	[illegible]	-	[illegible]	[illegible]	-	[illegible]	-	-	[illegible]
Wexford,	[illegible]	[illegible]	[illegible]	[illegible]	[illegible]	[illegible]	-	-	-	-	-	-
Wicklow,	[illegible]	[illegible]	[illegible]	-	-	[illegible]	[illegible]	-	-	[illegible]	-	-
Total,	[illegible]	[illegible]	[illegible]	[illegible]	[illegible]	[illegible]	[illegible]	[illegible]	[illegible]	[illegible]	[illegible]	[illegible]
Munster:												
Clare,	[illegible]	[illegible]	[illegible]	-	-	[illegible]	-	-	-	-	-	-
Cork, East Riding,	[illegible]	[illegible]	[illegible]	[illegible]	-	[illegible]	[illegible]	[illegible]	-	-	[illegible]	[illegible]
Cork, West Riding,	[illegible]	[illegible]	[illegible]	[illegible]	-	[illegible]	-	-	-	-	-	-
Kerry,	[illegible]	[illegible]	[illegible]	-	-	[illegible]	[illegible]	-	[illegible]	-	-	-
Limerick,	[illegible]	[illegible]	[illegible]	-	-	[illegible]	[illegible]	-	-	[illegible]	-	[illegible]
Tipperary,	[illegible]	[illegible]	[illegible]	[illegible]	[illegible]	[illegible]	[illegible]	[illegible]	-	[illegible]	[illegible]	[illegible]
Waterford,	[illegible]	[illegible]	[illegible]	-	[illegible]	[illegible]	[illegible]	[illegible]	-	[illegible]	-	-
Total,	[illegible]	[illegible]	[illegible]	[illegible]	[illegible]	[illegible]	[illegible]	[illegible]	[illegible]	[illegible]	[illegible]	[illegible]
Ulster:												
Antrim,	[illegible]	[illegible]	[illegible]	[illegible]	[illegible]	[illegible]	[illegible]	[illegible]	[illegible]	-	-	[illegible]
Armagh,	[illegible]	[illegible]	[illegible]	-	-	[illegible]	-	-	-	-	-	-
Cavan,	[illegible]	[illegible]	[illegible]	-	[illegible]	[illegible]	[illegible]	[illegible]	[illegible]	[illegible]	[illegible]	[illegible]
Donegal,	[illegible]	[illegible]	[illegible]	-	-	[illegible]	[illegible]	-	[illegible]	[illegible]	-	-
Down,	[illegible]	[illegible]	[illegible]	[illegible]	-	[illegible]	-	-	-	-	-	-
Fermanagh,	[illegible]	[illegible]	[illegible]	-	-	[illegible]	-	-	-	-	-	-
Londonderry,	[illegible]	[illegible]	[illegible]	-	-	[illegible]	[illegible]	[illegible]	-	-	-	-
Monaghan,	[illegible]	[illegible]	[illegible]	-	-	[illegible]	[illegible]	[illegible]	-	-	-	-
Tyrone,	[illegible]	[illegible]	[illegible]	-	-	[illegible]	-	-	-	-	-	[illegible]
Total,	[illegible]	[illegible]	[illegible]	[illegible]	[illegible]	[illegible]	[illegible]	[illegible]	[illegible]	[illegible]	[illegible]	[illegible]
Connaught:												
Galway,	[illegible]	[illegible]	[illegible]	-	-	[illegible]	-	-	-	-	-	-
Leitrim,	[illegible]	[illegible]	[illegible]	[illegible]	-	-	[illegible]	-	[illegible]	-	-	-
Mayo,	[illegible]	[illegible]	[illegible]	[illegible]	-	[illegible]	-	-	-	-	-	-
Roscommon,	[illegible]	[illegible]	[illegible]	[illegible]	-	[illegible]	-	-	-	-	[illegible]	[illegible]
Sligo,	[illegible]	[illegible]	[illegible]	-	-	[illegible]	[illegible]	-	-	[illegible]	-	[illegible]
Total,	[illegible]	[illegible]	[illegible]	[illegible]	-	[illegible]	[illegible]	-	[illegible]	[illegible]	[illegible]	[illegible]
Total of Ireland,	[illegible]	[illegible]	[illegible]	[illegible]	[illegible]	[illegible]	[illegible]	[illegible]	[illegible]	[illegible]	[illegible]	[illegible]

(a) The Clerk of the Peace states that the lunatics have about £[illegible] in [illegible] and lands.
(b) [illegible]
(c) The Clerk of the Peace states that he has no means of obtaining this information.

[illegible] of PROCEEDINGS in the Year [illegible], from Returns made by the Clerks of the Peace.

[illegible]	[illegible]	[illegible]	[illegible]	[illegible]	[illegible]	[illegible]	[illegible]	[illegible]	[illegible]	[illegible]	COUNTIES.
	£ s. d.			£ s. d.	£ s. d.						LEINSTER:
.	—	.	.	[illegible]	—	[illegible]	.	.	.	.	Carlow.
.	[illegible]	[illegible]	[illegible]	[illegible]	[illegible]	[illegible]	.	.	.	.	Dublin.
—	—	.	[illegible]	—	—	[illegible]	.	.	.	.	Dublin City
.	[illegible]	[illegible]	[illegible]	[illegible]	[illegible]	[illegible]	.	.	.	.	Kildare.
.	—	.	.	—	[illegible]	.	.	.	.	.	Kilkenny.
.	—	.	.	[illegible]	—	[illegible]	[illegible]	.	.	.	King's County.
.	—	[illegible]	.	[illegible]	—	[illegible]	.	.	.	.	Longford.
.	—	.	.	[illegible]	[illegible]	[illegible]	.	.	[illegible]	.	Louth.
.	—	.	.	—	—	.	.	.	.	.	Meath.
.	—	[illegible]	.	[illegible]	[illegible]	[illegible]	[illegible]	.	.	.	Queen's County.
[illegible]	—	[illegible]	.	—	[illegible]	[illegible]	.	.	.	—	Westmeath.
—	—	—	.	[illegible]	[illegible]	[illegible]	—	.	.	.	Wexford.
.	—	.	.	[illegible]	[illegible]	[illegible]	.	.	[illegible]	.	Wicklow.
[illegible]	[illegible]	[illegible]	[illegible]	[illegible]	[illegible]	[illegible]	[illegible]	.	[illegible]	.	Total.
											MUNSTER:
.	[illegible] —	[illegible]	.	[illegible]	[illegible]	[illegible]	.	.	.	.	Clare.
.	—	.	.	[illegible]	[illegible]	[illegible]	.	.	.	.	Cork, East Riding.
.	—	.	.	[illegible]	—	[illegible]	.	.	[illegible]	—	Cork, West Riding.
.	—	.	[illegible]	[illegible]	[illegible]	[illegible]	[illegible]	.	[illegible]	.	Kerry.
[illegible]	[illegible]	[illegible]	.	[illegible]	[illegible]	[illegible]	.	.	[illegible]	[illegible]	Limerick.
[illegible]	[illegible] —	[illegible]	[illegible]	[illegible]	[illegible]	[illegible]	.	[illegible]	[illegible]	.	Tipperary.
.	—	.	.	[illegible]	[illegible]	[illegible]	.	.	.	.	Waterford.
[illegible]	[illegible]	[illegible]	[illegible]	[illegible]	[illegible]	[illegible]	[illegible]	[illegible]	[illegible]	[illegible]	Total.
											ULSTER:
[illegible]	[illegible]	[illegible]	[illegible]	[illegible] —	—	[illegible]	.	.	[illegible]	.	Antrim.
.	—	.	.	[illegible]	[illegible]	[illegible]	.	.	[illegible]	.	Armagh.
.	—	[illegible]	.	[illegible] —	[illegible]	[illegible]	.	[illegible]	.	—	Cavan.
.	—	.	—	[illegible]	[illegible]	[illegible]	—	.	.	.	Donegal.
.	—	.	[illegible]	[illegible]	[illegible]	[illegible]	[illegible]	.	.	.	Down.
—	—	.	.	[illegible]	[illegible]	[illegible]	[illegible]	.	.	.	Fermanagh.
.	[illegible]	[illegible]	[illegible]	[illegible]	[illegible]	[illegible]	.	.	—	.	Londonderry.
.	—	.	.	[illegible]	[illegible]	[illegible]	[illegible]	[illegible]	[illegible]	.	Monaghan.
.	—	[illegible]	.	[illegible]	[illegible]	[illegible]	.	.	.	.	Tyrone.
[illegible]	[illegible]	[illegible]	[illegible]	[illegible]	[illegible]	[illegible]	[illegible]	[illegible]	[illegible]	.	Total.
											CONNAUGHT:
.	—	.	.	[illegible] —	—	[illegible]	[illegible]	.	.	[illegible]	Galway.
.	—	.	.	[illegible]	—	[illegible]	.	.	.	.	Leitrim.
.	—	.	.	[illegible]	—	[illegible]	.	[illegible]	.	.	Mayo.
.	[illegible] —	[illegible]	.	[illegible]	[illegible]	[illegible]	[illegible]	.	—	.	Roscommon.
.	—	[illegible]	.	[illegible] —	[illegible]	[illegible]	.	.	.	.	Sligo.
—	—	[illegible]	.	[illegible]	[illegible]	[illegible]	[illegible]	[illegible]	.	[illegible]	Total.
[illegible]	—	[illegible]	[illegible]	[illegible]	[illegible]	.	[illegible]	[illegible]	[illegible]	[illegible]	Total of Ireland.

(a) Besides this number, there were [illegible] cases from the previous year.

TABLE 64.—COUNTY COURTS.—LAND SESSIONS—PROCEEDINGS in the year 1886, under the

COUNTIES ARRANGED IN PROVINCES.	[illegible]	Land Sessions. Land Claim Court.					Applications of Parents to sanction Leases.				Applications of Tenants [illegible]				Appeals.			Result of Appeals [illegible]			
	[illegible]	[illegible]	[illegible]	[illegible]	[illegible]	[illegible]	[illegible]	[illegible]	[illegible]	[illegible]	[illegible]	[illegible]	[illegible]	[illegible]	Entered	[illegible]	Heard	[illegible]	[illegible]	[illegible]	[illegible]
LEINSTER:																					
Carlow,	-	-	-	-	-	-	-	-	-	-	-	-	-	-	-	-	-	-	-	-	-
Dublin,	-	-	-	-	-	-	-	-	-	-	-	-	-	-	-	-	-	-	-	-	-
Kildare,	-	-	-	-	-	-	-	-	-	-	-	-	-	-	-	-	-	-	-	-	-
Kilkenny,	-	-	-	-	-	-	-	-	-	-	-	-	-	-	-	-	-	-	-	-	-
King's County,	-	-	-	-	-	-	-	-	-	-	-	-	-	-	-	-	-	-	-	-	-
Longford,	-	-	-	-	-	-	-	-	-	-	-	-	-	-	-	-	-	-	-	-	-
Louth,	-	-	-	-	-	-	-	-	-	-	-	-	-	-	-	-	-	-	-	-	-
Meath,	-	-	-	-	-	-	-	-	-	-	-	-	-	-	-	-	-	-	-	-	-
Queen's County,	1	1	-	-	-	1	-	-	-	-	-	-	-	-	-	-	-	-	-	-	-
Westmeath,	-	-	-	-	-	-	-	-	-	-	-	-	-	-	-	-	-	-	-	-	-
Wexford,	-	-	-	-	-	-	-	-	-	-	-	-	-	-	-	-	-	-	-	-	-
Wicklow,	-	-	-	-	-	-	-	-	-	-	-	-	-	-	-	-	-	-	-	-	-
Total of Leinster,	1	1	-	-	-	1	-	-	-	-	-	-	-	-	-	-	-	-	-	-	-
MUNSTER:																					
Clare,	3	3	1	-	2	-	-	-	-	-	-	-	-	-	-	-	-	-	-	-	-
Cork, E. R.,	4	1	-	1	1	1	-	-	-	-	-	-	-	-	-	-	-	-	-	-	-
Cork, W. R.,	-	-	-	-	-	-	-	-	-	-	-	-	-	-	-	-	-	-	-	-	-
Kerry,	1	1	-	-	1	-	-	-	-	-	-	-	-	-	-	-	-	-	-	-	-
Limerick,	-	-	-	-	-	-	-	-	-	-	-	-	-	-	-	-	-	-	-	-	-
Tipperary,	-	-	-	-	-	-	-	-	-	-	-	-	-	-	-	-	-	-	-	-	-
Waterford,	1	4	1	2	1	-	-	-	-	-	-	-	-	-	1	1	-	-	-	-	-
Total of Munster,	8	11	2	1	4	1	-	-	-	-	-	-	-	-	1	1	-	-	-	-	-
ULSTER:																					
Antrim,	1	1	1	1	-	-	-	-	-	-	-	-	-	-	-	-	-	-	-	-	-
Armagh,	1	1	2	-	-	-	-	-	-	-	-	-	-	-	-	-	-	-	-	-	-
Cavan,	-	-	-	-	-	-	-	-	-	-	-	-	-	-	-	-	-	-	-	-	-
Donegal,	-	-	-	-	-	-	-	-	-	-	-	-	-	-	-	-	-	-	-	-	-
Down,	-	-	-	-	-	-	-	-	-	-	-	-	-	-	-	-	-	-	-	-	-
Fermanagh,	-	-	-	-	-	-	-	-	-	-	-	-	-	-	-	-	-	-	-	-	-
Londonderry,	1	1	1	-	1	1	-	-	-	-	-	-	-	-	-	-	-	-	-	-	-
Monaghan,	-	-	-	-	-	-	-	-	-	-	-	-	-	-	-	-	-	-	-	-	-
Tyrone,	-	-	-	-	-	-	-	-	-	-	-	-	-	-	-	-	-	-	-	-	-
Total of Ulster,	4	4	1	1	1	1	-	-	-	-	-	-	-	-	-	-	-	-	-	-	-
CONNAUGHT:																					
Galway,	-	-	-	-	-	-	-	-	-	-	-	-	-	-	-	-	-	-	-	-	-
Leitrim,	-	-	-	-	-	-	-	-	-	-	-	-	-	-	-	-	-	-	-	-	-
Mayo,	4	3	1	-	-	1	-	-	-	-	-	-	-	-	1	1	-	-	-	-	-
Roscommon,	-	-	-	-	-	-	-	-	-	-	-	-	-	-	-	-	-	-	-	-	-
Sligo,	-	-	-	-	-	-	-	-	-	-	-	-	-	-	-	-	-	-	-	-	-
Total of Connaught,	4	3	1	-	-	2	-	-	-	-	-	-	-	-	1	1	-	-	-	-	-
Total of Ireland,	21	17	6	4	6	5	-	-	-	-	-	-	-	-	3	7	-	-	-	-	-

Landlord and Tenant (Ireland) Act, 1870, from Returns made by the Clerks of the Peace.

Amount Charged.					Amount [illegible], with Costs.					Sub Loans [illegible]						COUNTIES, ARRANGED IN PROVINCES.
[illegible]	[illegible]	[illegible]	[illegible]	[illegible]	[illegible]	[illegible]	[illegible]	[illegible]	[illegible]	[illegible]	[illegible]	[illegible]	[illegible]	[illegible]	[illegible]	
£	£	£	£	£	£	£	£	£	£	£	£	£	£	£	£	LEINSTER:
-	-	-	-	-	-	-	-	-	-	-	-	-	-	-	-	Carlow.
-	-	-	-	-	-	-	-	-	-	-	-	-	-	-	-	Dublin.
-	-	-	-	-	-	-	-	-	-	-	-	-	-	-	-	Kildare.
-	-	-	-	-	-	-	-	-	-	-	-	-	-	-	-	Kilkenny.
-	-	-	-	-	-	-	-	-	-	-	-	-	-	-	-	King's County.
-	-	-	-	-	-	-	-	-	-	-	-	-	-	-	-	Longford.
-	-	-	-	-	-	-	-	-	-	-	-	-	-	-	-	Louth.
-	-	-	-	-	-	-	-	-	-	-	-	-	-	-	-	Meath.
[illegible]	-	-	-	[illegible]	-	-	-	-	-	-	-	-	-	-	-	Queen's County.
-	-	-	-	-	-	-	-	-	-	-	-	-	-	-	-	Westmeath.
-	-	-	-	-	-	-	-	-	-	-	-	-	-	-	-	Wexford.
-	-	-	-	-	-	-	-	-	-	-	-	-	-	-	-	Wicklow.
[illegible]	-	-	-	[illegible]	-	-	-	-	-	-	-	-	-	-	-	Total of Leinster.
																MUNSTER:
[illegible]	[illegible]	[illegible]	-	-	[illegible]	-	[illegible]	-	-	[illegible]	[illegible]	-	-	-	-	Clare.
[illegible]	[illegible]	-	-	[illegible]	-	-	-	-	[illegible]	-	-	-	-	-	-	Cork, E.R.
-	-	-	-	-	-	-	-	-	-	-	-	-	-	-	-	Cork, W.R.
[illegible]	[illegible]	-	-	-	-	-	-	-	-	-	-	-	-	-	-	Kerry.
-	-	-	-	-	-	-	-	-	-	-	-	-	-	-	-	Limerick.
-	-	-	-	-	-	-	-	-	-	-	-	-	-	-	-	Tipperary.
[illegible]	[illegible]	[illegible]	[illegible]	-	[illegible]	[illegible]	[illegible]	[illegible]	-	-	-	-	-	-	-	Waterford.
[illegible]	[illegible]	[illegible]	[illegible]	[illegible]	[illegible]	[illegible]	[illegible]	[illegible]	[illegible]	[illegible]	[illegible]	-	-	-	-	Total of Munster.
																ULSTER:
[illegible]	-	[illegible]	[illegible]	-	[illegible]	[illegible]	[illegible]	[illegible]	[illegible]	[illegible]	-	-	[illegible]	-	-	Antrim.
[illegible]	-	[illegible]	-	-	[illegible]	[illegible]	[illegible]	[illegible]	-	-	-	-	-	-	-	Armagh.
-	-	-	-	-	-	-	-	-	-	-	-	-	-	-	-	Cavan.
-	-	-	-	-	-	-	-	-	-	-	-	-	-	-	-	Donegal.
-	-	-	-	-	-	-	-	-	-	-	-	-	-	-	-	Down.
-	-	-	-	-	-	-	-	-	-	-	-	-	-	-	-	Fermanagh.
[illegible]	[illegible]	[illegible]	-	[illegible]	[illegible]	[illegible]	[illegible]	[illegible]	-	[illegible]	[illegible]	[illegible]	-	-	[illegible]	Londonderry.
-	-	-	-	-	-	-	-	-	-	-	-	-	-	-	-	Monaghan.
-	-	-	-	-	-	-	-	-	-	-	-	-	-	-	-	Tyrone.
[illegible]	[illegible]	[illegible]	[illegible]	[illegible]	[illegible]	[illegible]	[illegible]	[illegible]	[illegible]	[illegible]	[illegible]	[illegible]	[illegible]	-	[illegible]	Total of Ulster.
																CONNAUGHT:
-	-	-	-	-	-	-	-	-	-	-	-	-	-	-	-	Galway.
-	-	-	-	-	-	-	-	-	-	-	-	-	-	-	-	Leitrim.
[illegible]	-	[illegible]	-	[illegible]	[illegible]	[illegible]	[illegible]	-	-	-	-	-	-	-	-	Mayo.
-	-	-	-	-	-	-	-	-	-	-	-	-	-	-	-	Roscommon.
-	-	-	-	-	-	-	-	-	-	-	-	-	-	-	-	Sligo.
[illegible]	-	[illegible]	-	[illegible]	[illegible]	[illegible]	[illegible]	-	-	-	-	-	-	-	-	Total of Connaught.
[illegible]	[illegible]	[illegible]	[illegible]	[illegible]	[illegible]	[illegible]	[illegible]	[illegible]	[illegible]	[illegible]	[illegible]	[illegible]	[illegible]	-	[illegible]	Total of Ireland.

TABLE 64.—continued.—COUNTY COURTS.—LAND SESSIONS.—PROCEEDINGS in the year 18[illegible]

Counties arranged in Provinces.	For Improvements, [illegible] (Amount Claimed)					[illegible]	For Loss or [illegible] (Amount Claimed)					[illegible]	For [illegible] (Amount Claimed)					[illegible]
	[illegible]	[illegible]	[illegible]	[illegible]	[illegible]	[illegible]	[illegible]	[illegible]	[illegible]	[illegible]	[illegible]	[illegible]	[illegible]	[illegible]	[illegible]	[illegible]	[illegible]	[illegible]
LEINSTER:	£	£	£	£	£	£	£	£	£	£	£	£	£	£	£	£	£	£
Carlow,	–	–	–	–	–	–	–	–	–	–	–	–	–	–	–	–	–	–
Dublin,	–	–	–	–	–	–	–	–	–	–	–	–	–	–	–	–	–	–
Kildare,	–	–	–	–	–	–	–	–	–	–	–	–	–	–	–	–	–	–
Kilkenny,	–	–	–	–	–	–	–	–	–	–	–	–	–	–	–	–	–	–
King's County,	–	–	–	–	–	–	–	–	–	–	–	–	–	–	–	–	–	–
Longford,	–	–	–	–	–	–	–	–	–	–	–	–	–	–	–	–	–	–
Louth,	–	–	–	–	–	–	–	–	–	–	–	–	–	–	–	–	–	–
Meath,	–	–	–	–	–	–	–	–	–	–	–	–	–	–	–	–	–	–
Queen's County,	[illegible]	–	–	–	[illegible]	–	–	–	–	–	–	–	–	–	–	–	–	–
Westmeath,	–	–	–	–	–	–	–	–	–	–	–	–	–	–	–	–	–	–
Wexford,	–	–	–	–	–	–	–	–	–	–	–	–	–	–	–	–	–	–
Wicklow,	–	–	–	–	–	–	–	–	–	–	–	–	–	–	–	–	–	–
Total of Leinster,	[illegible]	–	–	–	[illegible]	–	–	–	–	–	–	–	–	–	–	–	–	–
MUNSTER:																		
Clare,	[illegible]	[illegible]	[illegible]	–	–	[illegible]	–	–	–	–	–	–	–	–	–	–	–	–
Cork, E.R.,	[illegible]	[illegible]	–	–	[illegible]	–	–	–	–	–	–	–	–	–	–	–	–	–
Cork, W.R.,	–	–	–	–	–	–	–	–	–	–	–	–	–	–	–	–	–	–
Kerry,	[illegible]	[illegible]	–	–	–	–	–	–	–	–	–	–	–	–	–	–	–	–
Limerick,	–	–	–	–	–	–	–	–	–	–	–	–	–	–	–	–	–	–
Tipperary,	–	–	–	–	–	–	–	–	–	–	–	–	–	–	–	–	–	–
Waterford,	[illegible]	[illegible]	[illegible]	[illegible]	–	[illegible]	–	–	–	–	–	–	–	–	–	–	–	–
Total of Munster,	[illegible]	[illegible]	[illegible]	[illegible]	[illegible]	[illegible]	–	–	–	–	–	–	–	–	–	–	–	–
ULSTER:																		
Antrim,	[illegible]	–	[illegible]	–	–	[illegible]	[illegible]	–	[illegible]	–	–	[illegible]	–	–	–	–	–	–
Armagh,	–	–	–	–	–	–	[illegible]	–	[illegible]	–	–	[illegible]	–	–	–	–	–	–
Cavan,	–	–	–	–	–	–	–	–	–	–	–	–	–	–	–	–	–	–
Donegal,	–	–	–	–	–	–	–	–	–	–	–	–	–	–	–	–	–	–
Down,	–	–	–	–	–	–	–	–	–	–	–	–	–	–	–	–	–	–
Fermanagh,	–	–	–	–	–	–	–	–	–	–	–	–	–	–	–	–	–	–
Londonderry,	[illegible]	–	[illegible]	–	–	[illegible]	–	–	–	–	–	–	[illegible]	–	–	–	[illegible]	–
Monaghan,	–	–	–	–	–	–	–	–	–	–	–	–	–	–	–	–	–	–
Tyrone,	–	–	–	–	–	–	–	–	–	–	–	–	–	–	–	–	–	–
Total of Ulster,	[illegible]	–	[illegible]	–	–	[illegible]	[illegible]	–	[illegible]	–	–	[illegible]	[illegible]	–	–	–	[illegible]	–
CONNAUGHT:																		
Galway,	–	–	–	–	–	–	–	–	–	–	–	–	–	–	–	–	–	–
Leitrim,	–	–	–	–	–	–	–	–	–	–	–	–	–	–	–	–	–	–
Mayo,	[illegible]	–	[illegible]	–	–	[illegible]	[illegible]	–	–	–	[illegible]	–	–	–	–	–	–	–
Roscommon,	–	–	–	–	–	–	–	–	–	–	–	–	–	–	–	–	–	–
Sligo,	–	–	–	–	–	–	–	–	–	–	–	–	–	–	–	–	–	–
Total of Connaught,	[illegible]	–	[illegible]	–	–	[illegible]	[illegible]	–	–	–	[illegible]	–	–	–	–	–	–	–
Total of Ireland,	[illegible]	[illegible]	[illegible]	[illegible]	[illegible]	[illegible]	[illegible]	–	[illegible]	–	[illegible]	[illegible]	[illegible]	–	–	–	[illegible]	–

under the Landlord and Tenant (Ireland) Act, 1870, from Returns made by the Clerks of the Peace.

[illegible]	[illegible]	[illegible]	[illegible]	[illegible]	[illegible]	[illegible]	[illegible]	[illegible]	[illegible]	[illegible]	[illegible]	[illegible]	[illegible]	[illegible]	COUNTIES, ARRANGED IN PROVINCES.
[illegible]	[illegible]	[illegible]	[illegible]	[illegible]	[illegible]	[illegible]	[illegible]	[illegible]	[illegible]	[illegible]	[illegible]	[illegible]	[illegible]	[illegible]	LEINSTER:
-	-	-	-	-	-	-	-	-	-	-	-	-	-	-	Carlow.
-	-	-	-	-	-	-	-	-	-	-	-	-	-	-	Dublin.
-	-	-	-	-	-	-	-	-	-	-	-	-	-	-	Kildare.
-	-	-	-	-	-	-	-	-	-	-	-	-	-	-	Kilkenny.
-	-	-	-	-	-	-	-	-	-	-	-	-	-	-	King's County.
-	-	-	-	-	-	-	-	-	-	-	-	-	-	-	Longford.
-	-	-	-	-	-	-	-	-	-	-	-	-	-	-	Louth.
-	-	-	-	-	-	-	-	-	-	-	-	-	-	-	Meath.
-	-	-	-	-	-	-	-	-	-	-	-	-	-	-	Queen's County.
-	-	-	-	-	-	-	-	-	-	-	-	-	-	-	Westmeath.
-	-	-	-	-	-	-	-	-	-	-	-	-	-	-	Wexford.
-	-	-	-	-	-	-	-	-	-	-	-	-	-	-	Wicklow.
-	-	-	-	-	-	-	-	-	-	-	-	-	-	-	Total of Leinster
															MUNSTER:
-	-	-	-	-	-	-	-	-	-	-	-	-	-	-	Clare.
-	-	-	-	-	-	-	-	-	-	-	-	-	-	-	Cork, E.R.
-	-	-	-	-	-	-	-	-	-	-	-	-	-	-	Cork, W.R.
-	-	-	-	-	-	-	-	-	-	-	-	-	-	-	Kerry.
-	-	-	-	-	-	-	-	-	-	-	-	-	-	-	Limerick.
-	-	-	-	-	-	-	-	-	-	-	-	-	-	-	Tipperary.
87	-	-	-	-	-	-	-	-	-	-	-	-	-	-	Waterford.
87	-	-	-	-	-	-	-	-	-	-	-	-	-	-	Total of Munster
															ULSTER:
-	-	-	-	-	-	-	-	-	-	-	-	-	-	-	Antrim.
-	-	-	-	-	-	-	-	-	-	-	-	-	-	-	Armagh.
-	-	-	-	-	-	-	-	-	-	-	-	-	-	-	Cavan.
-	-	-	-	-	-	-	-	-	-	-	-	-	-	-	Donegal.
-	-	-	-	-	-	-	-	-	-	-	-	-	-	-	Down.
-	-	-	-	-	-	-	-	-	-	-	-	-	-	-	Fermanagh.
-	-	-	-	-	-	-	-	-	-	-	-	-	-	-	Londonderry.
-	-	-	-	-	-	-	-	-	-	-	-	-	-	-	Monaghan.
-	-	-	-	-	-	-	-	-	-	-	-	-	-	-	Tyrone.
-	-	-	-	-	-	-	-	-	-	-	-	-	-	-	Total of Ulster
															CONNAUGHT:
-	-	-	-	-	-	-	-	-	-	-	-	-	-	-	Galway.
-	-	-	-	-	-	-	-	-	-	-	-	-	-	-	Leitrim.
78	98	-	-	-	-	-	-	-	-	-	-	-	-	-	Mayo.
-	-	-	-	-	-	-	-	-	-	-	-	-	-	-	Roscommon.
-	-	-	-	-	-	-	-	-	-	-	-	-	-	-	Sligo.
78	98	-	-	-	-	-	-	-	-	-	-	-	-	-	Total of Connaught.
[illegible]	98	-	-	-	-	-	-	-	-	-	-	-	-	-	Total of Ireland.

* The Clerks of the Peace [illegible] Land Law (Ireland) [illegible]

TABLE 14.—RETURN of PROCEEDINGS (a) under the

Counties arranged in Provinces	Applications to have Fair Rent Fixed: In Court: Number entered and lodged	In Court: Number of Rents fixed	In Court: Dismissed or struck out	In Court: Withdrawn	In Court: Pending at end of year	Out of Court: Number of Agreements lodged, Fair Rents fixed	Total Number of Fair Rents fixed in Court and out of Court	Applications to fix Date Leases: [illegible]	[illegible]	Withdrawn [illegible]	Pending at end of year	Miscellaneous Originating Motions: Number lodged	Disposed of	Pending at end of year	Appeals to Land Court, &c.: Number lodged	Heard	Withdrawn	Pending at end of year
Leinster																		
Carlow,	[illegible]	[illegible]	[illegible]	[illegible]	[illegible]	[illegible]	[illegible]	[illegible]	[illegible]	[illegible]	[illegible]	[illegible]	[illegible]	[illegible]	[illegible]	[illegible]	[illegible]	[illegible]
Dublin,	[illegible]	[illegible]	[illegible]	[illegible]	[illegible]	[illegible]	[illegible]	[illegible]	[illegible]	[illegible]	[illegible]	[illegible]	[illegible]	[illegible]	[illegible]	[illegible]	[illegible]	[illegible]
Kildare,	[illegible]	[illegible]	[illegible]	[illegible]	[illegible]	[illegible]	[illegible]	[illegible]	[illegible]	[illegible]	[illegible]	[illegible]	[illegible]	[illegible]	[illegible]	[illegible]	[illegible]	[illegible]
Kilkenny,	[illegible]	[illegible]	[illegible]	[illegible]	[illegible]	[illegible]	[illegible]	[illegible]	[illegible]	[illegible]	[illegible]	[illegible]	[illegible]	[illegible]	[illegible]	[illegible]	[illegible]	[illegible]
King's County,	[illegible]	[illegible]	[illegible]	[illegible]	[illegible]	[illegible]	[illegible]	[illegible]	[illegible]	[illegible]	[illegible]	[illegible]	[illegible]	[illegible]	[illegible]	[illegible]	[illegible]	[illegible]
Longford,	[illegible]	[illegible]	[illegible]	[illegible]	[illegible]	[illegible]	[illegible]	[illegible]	[illegible]	[illegible]	[illegible]	[illegible]	[illegible]	[illegible]	[illegible]	[illegible]	[illegible]	[illegible]
Louth,	[illegible]	[illegible]	[illegible]	[illegible]	[illegible]	[illegible]	[illegible]	[illegible]	[illegible]	[illegible]	[illegible]	[illegible]	[illegible]	[illegible]	[illegible]	[illegible]	[illegible]	[illegible]
Meath,	[illegible]	[illegible]	[illegible]	[illegible]	[illegible]	[illegible]	[illegible]	[illegible]	[illegible]	[illegible]	[illegible]	[illegible]	[illegible]	[illegible]	[illegible]	[illegible]	[illegible]	[illegible]
Queen's County,	[illegible]	[illegible]	[illegible]	[illegible]	[illegible]	[illegible]	[illegible]	[illegible]	[illegible]	[illegible]	[illegible]	[illegible]	[illegible]	[illegible]	[illegible]	[illegible]	[illegible]	[illegible]
Westmeath,	[illegible]	[illegible]	[illegible]	[illegible]	[illegible]	[illegible]	[illegible]	[illegible]	[illegible]	[illegible]	[illegible]	[illegible]	[illegible]	[illegible]	[illegible]	[illegible]	[illegible]	[illegible]
Wexford,	[illegible]	[illegible]	[illegible]	[illegible]	[illegible]	[illegible]	[illegible]	[illegible]	[illegible]	[illegible]	[illegible]	[illegible]	[illegible]	[illegible]	[illegible]	[illegible]	[illegible]	[illegible]
Wicklow,	[illegible]	[illegible]	[illegible]	[illegible]	[illegible]	[illegible]	[illegible]	[illegible]	[illegible]	[illegible]	[illegible]	[illegible]	[illegible]	[illegible]	[illegible]	[illegible]	[illegible]	[illegible]
Total of Leinster,	[illegible]	[illegible]	[illegible]	[illegible]	[illegible]	[illegible]	[illegible]	[illegible]	[illegible]	[illegible]	[illegible]	[illegible]	[illegible]	[illegible]	[illegible]	[illegible]	[illegible]	[illegible]
Munster																		
Clare,	[illegible]	[illegible]	[illegible]	[illegible]	[illegible]	[illegible]	[illegible]	[illegible]	[illegible]	[illegible]	[illegible]	[illegible]	[illegible]	[illegible]	[illegible]	[illegible]	[illegible]	[illegible]
Cork,	[illegible]	[illegible]	[illegible]	[illegible]	[illegible]	[illegible]	[illegible]	[illegible]	[illegible]	[illegible]	[illegible]	[illegible]	[illegible]	[illegible]	[illegible]	[illegible]	[illegible]	[illegible]
Kerry,	[illegible]	[illegible]	[illegible]	[illegible]	[illegible]	[illegible]	[illegible]	[illegible]	[illegible]	[illegible]	[illegible]	[illegible]	[illegible]	[illegible]	[illegible]	[illegible]	[illegible]	[illegible]
Limerick,	[illegible]	[illegible]	[illegible]	[illegible]	[illegible]	[illegible]	[illegible]	[illegible]	[illegible]	[illegible]	[illegible]	[illegible]	[illegible]	[illegible]	[illegible]	[illegible]	[illegible]	[illegible]
Tipperary,	[illegible]	[illegible]	[illegible]	[illegible]	[illegible]	[illegible]	[illegible]	[illegible]	[illegible]	[illegible]	[illegible]	[illegible]	[illegible]	[illegible]	[illegible]	[illegible]	[illegible]	[illegible]
Waterford,	[illegible]	[illegible]	[illegible]	[illegible]	[illegible]	[illegible]	[illegible]	[illegible]	[illegible]	[illegible]	[illegible]	[illegible]	[illegible]	[illegible]	[illegible]	[illegible]	[illegible]	[illegible]
Total of Munster,	[illegible]	[illegible]	[illegible]	[illegible]	[illegible]	[illegible]	[illegible]	[illegible]	[illegible]	[illegible]	[illegible]	[illegible]	[illegible]	[illegible]	[illegible]	[illegible]	[illegible]	[illegible]
Ulster																		
Antrim,	[illegible]	[illegible]	[illegible]	[illegible]	[illegible]	[illegible]	[illegible]	[illegible]	[illegible]	[illegible]	[illegible]	[illegible]	[illegible]	[illegible]	[illegible]	[illegible]	[illegible]	[illegible]
Armagh,	[illegible]	[illegible]	[illegible]	[illegible]	[illegible]	[illegible]	[illegible]	[illegible]	[illegible]	[illegible]	[illegible]	[illegible]	[illegible]	[illegible]	[illegible]	[illegible]	[illegible]	[illegible]
Cavan,	[illegible]	[illegible]	[illegible]	[illegible]	[illegible]	[illegible]	[illegible]	[illegible]	[illegible]	[illegible]	[illegible]	[illegible]	[illegible]	[illegible]	[illegible]	[illegible]	[illegible]	[illegible]
Donegal,	[illegible]	[illegible]	[illegible]	[illegible]	[illegible]	[illegible]	[illegible]	[illegible]	[illegible]	[illegible]	[illegible]	[illegible]	[illegible]	[illegible]	[illegible]	[illegible]	[illegible]	[illegible]
Down,	[illegible]	[illegible]	[illegible]	[illegible]	[illegible]	[illegible]	[illegible]	[illegible]	[illegible]	[illegible]	[illegible]	[illegible]	[illegible]	[illegible]	[illegible]	[illegible]	[illegible]	[illegible]
Fermanagh,	[illegible]	[illegible]	[illegible]	[illegible]	[illegible]	[illegible]	[illegible]	[illegible]	[illegible]	[illegible]	[illegible]	[illegible]	[illegible]	[illegible]	[illegible]	[illegible]	[illegible]	[illegible]
Londonderry,	[illegible]	[illegible]	[illegible]	[illegible]	[illegible]	[illegible]	[illegible]	[illegible]	[illegible]	[illegible]	[illegible]	[illegible]	[illegible]	[illegible]	[illegible]	[illegible]	[illegible]	[illegible]
Monaghan,	[illegible]	[illegible]	[illegible]	[illegible]	[illegible]	[illegible]	[illegible]	[illegible]	[illegible]	[illegible]	[illegible]	[illegible]	[illegible]	[illegible]	[illegible]	[illegible]	[illegible]	[illegible]
Tyrone,	[illegible]	[illegible]	[illegible]	[illegible]	[illegible]	[illegible]	[illegible]	[illegible]	[illegible]	[illegible]	[illegible]	[illegible]	[illegible]	[illegible]	[illegible]	[illegible]	[illegible]	[illegible]
Total of Ulster,	[illegible]	[illegible]	[illegible]	[illegible]	[illegible]	[illegible]	[illegible]	[illegible]	[illegible]	[illegible]	[illegible]	[illegible]	[illegible]	[illegible]	[illegible]	[illegible]	[illegible]	[illegible]
Connaught																		
Galway,	[illegible]	[illegible]	[illegible]	[illegible]	[illegible]	[illegible]	[illegible]	[illegible]	[illegible]	[illegible]	[illegible]	[illegible]	[illegible]	[illegible]	[illegible]	[illegible]	[illegible]	[illegible]
Leitrim,	[illegible]	[illegible]	[illegible]	[illegible]	[illegible]	[illegible]	[illegible]	[illegible]	[illegible]	[illegible]	[illegible]	[illegible]	[illegible]	[illegible]	[illegible]	[illegible]	[illegible]	[illegible]
Mayo,	[illegible]	[illegible]	[illegible]	[illegible]	[illegible]	[illegible]	[illegible]	[illegible]	[illegible]	[illegible]	[illegible]	[illegible]	[illegible]	[illegible]	[illegible]	[illegible]	[illegible]	[illegible]
Roscommon,	[illegible]	[illegible]	[illegible]	[illegible]	[illegible]	[illegible]	[illegible]	[illegible]	[illegible]	[illegible]	[illegible]	[illegible]	[illegible]	[illegible]	[illegible]	[illegible]	[illegible]	[illegible]
Sligo,	[illegible]	[illegible]	[illegible]	[illegible]	[illegible]	[illegible]	[illegible]	[illegible]	[illegible]	[illegible]	[illegible]	[illegible]	[illegible]	[illegible]	[illegible]	[illegible]	[illegible]	[illegible]
Total of Connaught,	[illegible]	[illegible]	[illegible]	[illegible]	[illegible]	[illegible]	[illegible]	[illegible]	[illegible]	[illegible]	[illegible]	[illegible]	[illegible]	[illegible]	[illegible]	[illegible]	[illegible]	[illegible]
Total of Ireland,	[illegible]	[illegible]	[illegible]	[illegible]	[illegible]	[illegible]	[illegible]	[illegible]	[illegible]	[illegible]	[illegible]	[illegible]	[illegible]	[illegible]	[illegible]	[illegible]	[illegible]	[illegible]

Land Law (Ireland) Act, 1881, for the Year [illegible]

Results of Appeals Heard.				Fair Rents Fixed.				Totals.		Counties arranged in Provinces.
				In Court.		Out of Court.				
[illegible]	[illegible]	[illegible]	[illegible]	Former Rent.	Judicial Rent.	Former Rent.	Judicial Rent.	Former Rent.	Judicial Rent.	
				£ s. d.	£ s. d.	£ s. d.	£ s. d.	£ s. d.	£ s. d.	Leinster:
[illegible]	[illegible]	[illegible]	[illegible]	[illegible]	[illegible]	[illegible]	[illegible]	[illegible]	[illegible]	Carlow.
[illegible]	[illegible]	[illegible]	[illegible]	[illegible]	[illegible]	[illegible]	[illegible]	[illegible]	[illegible]	Dublin.
[illegible]	[illegible]	[illegible]	[illegible]	[illegible]	[illegible]	[illegible]	[illegible]	[illegible]	[illegible]	Kildare.
[illegible]	[illegible]	[illegible]	[illegible]	[illegible]	[illegible]	[illegible]	[illegible]	[illegible]	[illegible]	Kilkenny.
[illegible]	[illegible]	[illegible]	[illegible]	[illegible]	[illegible]	[illegible]	[illegible]	[illegible]	[illegible]	King's County.
[illegible]	[illegible]	[illegible]	[illegible]	[illegible]	[illegible]	[illegible]	[illegible]	[illegible]	[illegible]	Longford.
[illegible]	[illegible]	[illegible]	[illegible]	[illegible]	[illegible]	[illegible]	[illegible]	[illegible]	[illegible]	Louth.
[illegible]	[illegible]	[illegible]	[illegible]	[illegible]	[illegible]	[illegible]	[illegible]	[illegible]	[illegible]	Meath.
[illegible]	[illegible]	[illegible]	[illegible]	[illegible]	[illegible]	[illegible]	[illegible]	[illegible]	[illegible]	Queen's County.
[illegible]	[illegible]	[illegible]	[illegible]	[illegible]	[illegible]	[illegible]	[illegible]	[illegible]	[illegible]	Westmeath.
[illegible]	[illegible]	[illegible]	[illegible]	[illegible]	[illegible]	[illegible]	[illegible]	[illegible]	[illegible]	Wexford.
[illegible]	[illegible]	[illegible]	[illegible]	[illegible]	[illegible]	[illegible]	[illegible]	[illegible]	[illegible]	Wicklow.
[illegible]	[illegible]	[illegible]	[illegible]	[illegible]	[illegible]	[illegible]	[illegible]	[illegible]	[illegible]	Total of Leinster.
										Munster:
[illegible]	[illegible]	[illegible]	[illegible]	[illegible]	[illegible]	[illegible]	[illegible]	[illegible]	[illegible]	Clare.
[illegible]	[illegible]	[illegible]	[illegible]	[illegible]	[illegible]	[illegible]	[illegible]	[illegible]	[illegible]	Cork.
[illegible]	[illegible]	[illegible]	[illegible]	[illegible]	[illegible]	[illegible]	[illegible]	[illegible]	[illegible]	Kerry.
[illegible]	[illegible]	[illegible]	[illegible]	[illegible]	[illegible]	[illegible]	[illegible]	[illegible]	[illegible]	Limerick.
[illegible]	[illegible]	[illegible]	[illegible]	[illegible]	[illegible]	[illegible]	[illegible]	[illegible]	[illegible]	Tipperary.
[illegible]	[illegible]	[illegible]	[illegible]	[illegible]	[illegible]	[illegible]	[illegible]	[illegible]	[illegible]	Waterford.
[illegible]	[illegible]	[illegible]	[illegible]	[illegible]	[illegible]	[illegible]	[illegible]	[illegible]	[illegible]	Total of Munster.
										Ulster:
[illegible]	[illegible]	[illegible]	[illegible]	[illegible]	[illegible]	[illegible]	[illegible]	[illegible]	[illegible]	Antrim.
[illegible]	[illegible]	[illegible]	[illegible]	[illegible]	[illegible]	[illegible]	[illegible]	[illegible]	[illegible]	Armagh.
[illegible]	[illegible]	[illegible]	[illegible]	[illegible]	[illegible]	[illegible]	[illegible]	[illegible]	[illegible]	Cavan.
[illegible]	[illegible]	[illegible]	[illegible]	[illegible]	[illegible]	[illegible]	[illegible]	[illegible]	[illegible]	Donegal.
[illegible]	[illegible]	[illegible]	[illegible]	[illegible]	[illegible]	[illegible]	[illegible]	[illegible]	[illegible]	Down.
[illegible]	[illegible]	[illegible]	[illegible]	[illegible]	[illegible]	[illegible]	[illegible]	[illegible]	[illegible]	Fermanagh.
[illegible]	[illegible]	[illegible]	[illegible]	[illegible]	[illegible]	[illegible]	[illegible]	[illegible]	[illegible]	Londonderry.
[illegible]	[illegible]	[illegible]	[illegible]	[illegible]	[illegible]	[illegible]	[illegible]	[illegible]	[illegible]	Monaghan.
[illegible]	[illegible]	[illegible]	[illegible]	[illegible]	[illegible]	[illegible]	[illegible]	[illegible]	[illegible]	Tyrone.
[illegible]	[illegible]	[illegible]	[illegible]	[illegible]	[illegible]	[illegible]	[illegible]	[illegible]	[illegible]	Total of Ulster.
										Connaught:
[illegible]	[illegible]	[illegible]	[illegible]	[illegible]	[illegible]	[illegible]	[illegible]	[illegible]	[illegible]	Galway.
[illegible]	[illegible]	[illegible]	[illegible]	[illegible]	[illegible]	[illegible]	[illegible]	[illegible]	[illegible]	Leitrim.
[illegible]	[illegible]	[illegible]	[illegible]	[illegible]	[illegible]	[illegible]	[illegible]	[illegible]	[illegible]	Mayo.
[illegible]	[illegible]	[illegible]	[illegible]	[illegible]	[illegible]	[illegible]	[illegible]	[illegible]	[illegible]	Roscommon.
[illegible]	[illegible]	[illegible]	[illegible]	[illegible]	[illegible]	[illegible]	[illegible]	[illegible]	[illegible]	Sligo.
[illegible]	[illegible]	[illegible]	[illegible]	[illegible]	[illegible]	[illegible]	[illegible]	[illegible]	[illegible]	Total of Connaught.
[illegible]	[illegible]	[illegible]	[illegible]	[illegible]	[illegible]	[illegible]	[illegible]	[illegible]	[illegible]	Total of Ireland.

[illegible]

TABLE [illegible].—SHERIFFS' PROCEEDINGS in the Year [illegible].

from Returns by Sheriffs of Counties and of Counties of Cities and of Towns.

Westmeath.	Wexford.	Wicklow.	MUNSTER. Total of Munster.	Clare.	Cork.	Cork City.	Kerry.	Limerick.	Limerick City.	Tipperary.	Waterford.	Waterford City.	PROCEEDINGS.
													I.—Proceedings other than those for Delivery or Taking Possession of Land.
-	-	-	[illegible]	-	-	-	[illegible]	-	-	[illegible]	-	-	Courts held for Election of Coroners.
[illegible]	[illegible]	[illegible]	[illegible]	-	[illegible]	[illegible]	[illegible]	-	[illegible]	[illegible]	[illegible]	1	Courts held for Election of Members of Parliament.
	-	-	[illegible]	[illegible]	-	-	-	-	-	-	-	-	Courts held under Writs of Trial or Inquiry.
-	-	-	-	-	-	-	-	-	-	-	-	-	Courts held under Land Clauses, Companies Act, &c.
[illegible]	[illegible]	[illegible]	[illegible]	[illegible]	[illegible]	[illegible]	[illegible]	[illegible]	[illegible]	[illegible]	[illegible]	[illegible]	Civil Bill Decrees and Dismisses executed by Sheriff.
[illegible]	[illegible]	[illegible]	[illegible]	[illegible]	[illegible]	[illegible]	[illegible]	[illegible]	[illegible]	-	[illegible]	1	" " " by Special Bailiffs.
-	[illegible]	-	[illegible]	-	[illegible]	-	[illegible]	-	-	-	[illegible]	-	Prison Conveyances taken.[1]
													Persons conveyed to Queen's Bench:—
-	-	-	-	-	-	-	-	-	-	-	-	-	(1) Bankrupts.
-	-	-	-	-	-	-	-	-	-	-	-	-	(2) Wrecks of the Sea.
-	-	-	-	-	-	-	-	-	-	-	-	-	(3) All other Cases.
-	-	-	-	-	-	-	-	-	-	-	-	-	Writs of Habeas Corpus, Proceedings in.
-	-	-	-	-	-	-	-	-	-	-	-	-	Writs of De Excommunicato Capiendo, Proceedings in.
[illegible]	-	[illegible]	[illegible]	-	-	-	[illegible]	-	-	-	-	-	All other Writs, not being Writs of Execution.
-	-	[illegible]	[illegible]	[illegible]	[illegible]	-	[illegible]	-	-	[illegible]	-	1	Applications to Court or Proceedings by way of Interpleader.
-	-	-	[illegible]	[illegible]	[illegible]	-	[illegible]	-	-	-	-	-	Issues directed thereon.
-	-	-	[illegible]	[illegible]	-	-	[illegible]	-	-	-	-	-	Replevin Bonds taken, or Affidavits of Value drawn.
													Writs of Execution from High Court of Justice:—
[illegible]	[illegible]	[illegible]	[illegible]	[illegible]	[illegible]	[illegible]	[illegible]	[illegible]	[illegible]	[illegible]	[illegible]	[illegible]	Fieri Facias.
-	[illegible]	-	[illegible]	[illegible]	-	[illegible]	-	-	[illegible]	[illegible]	-	-	Writs of Attachment under Railway Act.
													II.—For Delivery or Taking Possession of Land.
[illegible]	[illegible]	[illegible]	[illegible]	[illegible]	[illegible]	[illegible]	[illegible]	[illegible]	[illegible]	[illegible]	[illegible]	[illegible]	Total number of Ejectments for Non-payment of Rent.
[illegible]	[illegible]	[illegible]	[illegible]	[illegible]	[illegible]	[illegible]	[illegible]	[illegible]	[illegible]	[illegible]	[illegible]	[illegible]	Viz.:—Writs of Habere of High Court of Justice executed by Sheriff.
[illegible]	-	-	[illegible]	-	-	-	[illegible]	[illegible]	-	-	[illegible]	-	Writs of Habere of High Court of Justice executed by Special Bailiffs.
[illegible]	[illegible]	[illegible]	[illegible]	[illegible]	[illegible]	[illegible]	[illegible]	[illegible]	[illegible]	[illegible]	[illegible]	[illegible]	Civil Bill Ejectments executed.
[illegible]	[illegible]	[illegible]	[illegible]	-	[illegible]	[illegible]	[illegible]	[illegible]	[illegible]	[illegible]	-	-	Total Number of Ejectments between Landlord and Tenant, other than for Non-payment of Rent.
-	-	[illegible]	[illegible]	-	[illegible]	-	-	-	[illegible]	[illegible]	-	-	Viz.:—Writs of Habere of High Court of Justice executed by Sheriff.
[illegible]	[illegible]	-	[illegible]	-	-	-	[illegible]	-	-	-	-	-	Writs of Habere of High Court of Justice executed by Special Bailiffs.
[illegible]	[illegible]	[illegible]	[illegible]	-	-	[illegible]	-	[illegible]	[illegible]	-	-	-	Civil Bill Ejectments executed.
[illegible]	-	[illegible]	[illegible]	-	[illegible]	-	[illegible]	-	[illegible]	-	-	-	Total Number of Ejectments other than between Landlord and Tenant.
-	-	[illegible]	[illegible]	-	-	-	-	-	[illegible]	-	-	-	Viz.:—Writs of Habere of High Court of Justice executed by Sheriff.
-	-	-	[illegible]	-	-	-	[illegible]	-	-	-	-	-	Writs of Habere of High Court of Justice executed by Special Bailiffs.
[illegible]	-	[illegible]	-	-	-	-	-	-	-	-	-	-	Civil Bill Ejectments executed.
[illegible]	[illegible]	[illegible]	[illegible]	[illegible]	[illegible]	[illegible]	[illegible]	[illegible]	[illegible]	[illegible]	[illegible]	[illegible]	Total Number of Ejectments of all Classes.
-	-	[illegible]	[illegible]	-	-	[illegible]	-	[illegible]	-	-	[illegible]	-	Writs of Habere and Decrees executed by consent in cases of [illegible] [illegible] [illegible]
-	-	[illegible]	[illegible]	-	-	-	[illegible]	-	-	-	[illegible]	-	[illegible]
-	-	-	-	-	-	-	-	-	-	-	-	-	Number of Writs of Restitution after Partial Execution, [illegible]
-	[illegible]	-	[illegible]	-	-	-	-	-	-	-	-	-	[illegible]
-	-	-	-	-	-	-	-	-	-	-	-	-	Writs of Assistance from the Chancery Division.
-	-	-	-	-	-	-	-	-	-	-	-	-	Writs of Assistance from the Probate and Matrimonial Division.
-	[illegible]	-	[illegible]	-	[illegible]	-	-	-	-	-	[illegible]	-	Injunctions from Land Judges.
-	-	-	-	-	[illegible]	-	-	-	-	-	-	-	Process under Land Clauses Acts.
-	-	[illegible]	[illegible]	-	-	-	[illegible]	-	-	-	-	-	Other Process or Order.

[1] Prison Conveyances taken on every occasion.

PROCEEDINGS.	ULSTER.							
	Town of Belfast.	Antrim.	Armagh.	Carrickfergus.	Cavan.	Donegal.	Down.	Fermanagh.
I.—PROCEEDINGS OTHER THAN THOSE FOR DELIVERY OR TAKING POSSESSION OF LAND.								
Courts held for Election of Coroners,	1	1	.	.	.	.	.	.
Courts held for Election of Members of Parliament,	[illegible]	[illegible]	[illegible]	.	[illegible]	[illegible]	[illegible]	[illegible]
Courts held under Writs of Trial or Inquiry,	[illegible]	[illegible]	.	.	.	.	.	.
Juries held under Land Clauses Consolidation Act, &c.,	.	.	.	.	.	.	.	.
Civil Bill Decrees and Dismisses executed by Sheriff,	[illegible]	[illegible]	[illegible]	[illegible]	[illegible]	[illegible]	[illegible]	[illegible]
" " " by Special Bailiffs,	[illegible]	[illegible]	[illegible]	[illegible]	.	[illegible]	[illegible]	[illegible]
Securities taken,	.	.	.	.	.	.	.	.
Persons removed to County Gaol —								
(1.) [illegible]	.	.	.	.	.	.	.	.
(2.) [illegible]	.	.	.	.	.	.	.	.
(3.) All other Cases,	.	.	.	.	.	.	.	.
Writs of Habeas Corpus, Proceedings on,	.	.	.	.	.	.	.	.
Writs of Ne Exeat Regno, Proceedings on,	.	.	.	.	.	.	.	.
Other Writs, and [illegible] Writs of Execution,	.	.	.	.	.	.	.	.

[illegible] Returns by Sheriffs of Counties and of Counties of Cities and of Towns.

[illegible]	Wicklow.	Total of Connaught.	Galway.	Galway, Town of.	Leitrim.	Mayo.	Roscommon.	Sligo.	PROCEEDINGS.
									I.—Proceedings other than those for Enforcing or Taking Possession of Land.
.	.	.	.	.	.	.	.	.	Courts held for Election of Coroners.
.	[illegible]	[illegible]	.	.	.	.	[illegible]	7	Courts held for Election of Members of Parliament.
.	.	.	.	.	.	.	.	.	Courts held under Writs of Trial or Inquiry.
.	.	.	.	.	.	.	.	.	Courts held under Land Clauses Consolidation Act, &c.
[illegible]	[illegible]	[illegible]	[illegible]	[illegible]	[illegible]	[illegible]	[illegible]	[illegible]	Civil Bill Decrees and Dismisses executed by Sheriff.
[illegible]	.	[illegible]	[illegible]		[illegible]	[illegible]	[illegible]	[illegible]	" " " by Special Bailiffs.
.	.	[illegible]	.	.	[illegible]	.	[illegible]	.	Fines Commitments taken.
									Property executed at Crown's Suit:—
.	.	.	.	.	.	.	.	.	(1) Forfeitures.
.	.	.	.	.	.	.	.	.	(2) Wrecks of the Sea.
.	.	.	.	.	.	.	.	.	(3) All other Cases.
.	.	.	.	.	.	.	.	.	Writs of Habeas Corpus, Proceedings in.
.	.	.	.	.	.	.	.	.	Writs of Ne Exeat or [illegible], Proceedings in.
.	.	.	.	.	.	.	.	.	All other Writs, not being Writs of Execution.
.	.	[illegible]	.	.	.	[illegible]	[illegible]	.	Applications to Court as Proceedings by way of Interpleader.
.	.	[illegible]	.	.	.	[illegible]	[illegible]	.	Issues [illegible] Damages.
.	.	.	.	.	.	.	.	.	Replevin Bonds taken, or Affidavits of Value drawn.
									Writs of Execution from High Court of Justice, or

16	776
24	872
4	[illegible]
9	[illegible]
10	[illegible]
14	[illegible]
1	[illegible]
6	[illegible]
[illegible]	[illegible]
[illegible]	[illegible]
4	[illegible]
[illegible]	[illegible]
8	745
[illegible]	[illegible]
4	[illegible]
[illegible]	[illegible]
[illegible]	[illegible]
[illegible]	[illegible]
-	[illegible]
[illegible]	[illegible]
[illegible]	[illegible]
[illegible]	[illegible]
[illegible]	[illegible]
-	[illegible]
[illegible]	[illegible]
[illegible]	[illegible]
[illegible]	[illegible]
[illegible]	[illegible]
[illegible]	[illegible]
[illegible]	[illegible]
-	[illegible]

in respect of the Preparation, Revision, and Correction, in 18[illegible], of Jurors' Lists and Jurors' Books, from Returns of the Clerks of the Peace.

[illegible]					[illegible]					
On List as prepared by Clerk of Peace.	Added by Revising Court.	Struck off by Revising Court.	Removed by Clerk of Peace.	Struck off Book by Judges.	Total on Book when handed to Sheriff.	General Jurors fined.	General Jurors exempted or struck off.	Special Jurors fined.	Special Jurors exempted or struck off.	COUNTIES, COUNTIES OF CITIES AND TOWNS AND BOROUGHS HAVING SEPARATE COMMISSIONS OF THE PEACE, ARRANGED IN PROVINCES.
										LEINSTER.
[illegible]	-	[illegible]	-	-	[illegible]	-	-	-	-	Carlow.
[illegible]	-	[illegible]	-	-	[illegible]	-	-	-	-	Drogheda, Town of
[illegible]	[illegible]	-	[illegible]	-	[illegible]	-	-	-	-	Dublin.
[illegible]	[illegible]	[illegible]	-	-	[illegible]	-	-	-	-	" City.
[illegible]	-	[illegible]	-	-	[illegible]	-	-	-	-	Kildare.
[illegible]	-	[illegible]	-	-	[illegible]	-	-	-	-	Kilkenny.
[illegible]	[illegible]	[illegible]	-	-	[illegible]	-	-	-	-	" City.
[illegible]	-	[illegible]	-	-	[illegible]	-	-	-	-	King's County.
[illegible]	-	-	-	-	[illegible]	-	-	-	-	Longford.
[illegible]	-	[illegible]	[illegible]	-	[illegible]	-	[illegible]	-	[illegible]	Louth.
[illegible]	-	[illegible]	-	-	[illegible]	-	-	-	-	Meath.
[illegible]	-	[illegible]	-	-	[illegible]	-	-	-	-	Queen's County.
[illegible]	[illegible]	[illegible]	-	-	[illegible]	-	[illegible]	-	[illegible]	Westmeath.
[illegible]	-	[illegible]	-	-	[illegible]	-	-	-	-	Wexford.
[illegible]	-	[illegible]	[illegible]	-	[illegible]	-	-	-	-	Wicklow.
[illegible]	[illegible]	[illegible]	[illegible]	-	[illegible]	-	[illegible]	-	[illegible]	Total of Leinster.
										MUNSTER.
[illegible]	-	-	-	-	[illegible]	6	[illegible]	[illegible]	[illegible]	Clare.
[illegible]	-	[illegible]	-	-	[illegible]	-	-	-	-	Cork, E.R.
[illegible]	-	[illegible]	-	-	[illegible]	-	-	-	-	" W.R.
[illegible]	-	[illegible]	-	-	[illegible]	-	-	-	-	" City.
[illegible]	-	[illegible]	-	-	[illegible]	[illegible]	[illegible]	[illegible]	-	Kerry.
[illegible]	-	[illegible]	-	-	[illegible]	-	-	-	-	Limerick.
[illegible]	[illegible]	[illegible]	-	-	[illegible]	-	-	-	-	" City.
[illegible]	-	[illegible]	-	[illegible]	[illegible]	-	-	-	-	Tipperary.
[illegible]	-	[illegible]	[illegible]	-	[illegible]	-	-	-	-	Waterford.
[illegible]	-	[illegible]	-	-	[illegible]	-	-	-	-	" City.
[illegible]	[illegible]	[illegible]	[illegible]	[illegible]	[illegible]	[illegible]	[illegible]	[illegible]	[illegible]	Total of Munster.
										ULSTER.
[illegible]	-	[illegible]	-	-	[illegible]	-	-	-	-	Antrim.
[illegible]	-	[illegible]	-	-	[illegible]	-	-	-	-	Armagh.
*	-	-	-	-	-	-	-	-	-	Belfast, Borough.
[illegible]	-	[illegible]	-	-	[illegible]	-	-	-	-	Carrickfergus, Town of.
[illegible]	-	[illegible]	-	-	[illegible]	-	-	-	-	Cavan.
[illegible]	[illegible]	[illegible]	-	-	[illegible]	-	[illegible]	-	[illegible]	Donegal.
[illegible]	-	-	-	-	[illegible]	-	-	-	-	Down.
[illegible]	-	[illegible]	-	-	[illegible]	-	-	-	-	Fermanagh.
[illegible]	-	[illegible]	-	-	[illegible]	-	-	-	-	Londonderry.
[illegible]	-	[illegible]	-	-	[illegible]	-	-	-	-	" Borough.
[illegible]	-	[illegible]	-	-	[illegible]	-	-	-	-	Monaghan.
[illegible]	-	[illegible]	-	-	[illegible]	-	-	-	-	Tyrone.
[illegible]	[illegible]	[illegible]	-	-	[illegible]	-	[illegible]	-	[illegible]	Total of Ulster.
										CONNAUGHT.
[illegible]	-	[illegible]	-	-	[illegible]	-	-	-	-	Galway.
[illegible]	-	-	-	-	[illegible]	-	-	-	-	" Town of.
[illegible]	-	[illegible]	-	-	[illegible]	-	-	-	-	Leitrim.
[illegible]	[illegible]	[illegible]	-	-	[illegible]	-	-	-	-	Mayo.
[illegible]	-	[illegible]	-	-	[illegible]	-	-	-	-	Roscommon.
[illegible]	-	[illegible]	-	-	[illegible]	-	-	-	-	Sligo.
[illegible]	[illegible]	[illegible]	-	-	[illegible]	-	-	-	-	Total of Connaught.
[illegible]	[illegible]	[illegible]	[illegible]	[illegible]	[illegible]	11	[illegible]	[illegible]	[illegible]	Total of Ireland.

* No special jurors' lists or book for the Recorder's court.

TABLE [illegible].—JURORS.—PROCEEDINGS of SHERIFFS in summoning JURORS in the Year of [illegible] by the Clerks.

COUNTIES, COUNTIES OF CITIES AND TOWNS, AND BOROUGHS HAVING SEPARATE COMMISSIONS OF THE PEACE, ARRANGED IN PROVINCES.	Total Number of Jurors summoned during the year.	For Assizes, Commissions, and Sessions Courts.								
		Grand Jurors.			Petty and Common Jurors.			Special Jurors.		
		January to June.	July to December.	Total.	January to June.	July to December.	Total.	January to June.	July to December.	Total.
LEINSTER:										
Dublin:										
Crown Side of Queen's Bench Division, Winter Assizes, and Commission Court	.	[illegible]	[illegible]	[illegible]	[illegible]	[illegible]	[illegible]	.	.	.
Civil Side of Queen's Bench Division, Common Pleas Division, Exchequer Division,	.	[illegible]	[illegible]	[illegible]	[illegible]	[illegible]	[illegible]	.	.	.
Probate and Matrimonial Division,	.	.	.	.	.	.	.	.	.	.
Bankruptcy,	.	.	.	.	.	.	.	.	.	.
Recorder,	.	.	.	.	.	.	.	.	.	.
Other purposes than Quarter Sessions or Civil Bills before County Court Judges	.	.	.	.	.	.	.	.	.	.
Total of Dublin County,	[illegible]	[illegible]	[illegible]	[illegible]	[illegible]	[illegible]	[illegible]	.	.	.
Dublin City:										
Crown Side of Queen's Bench Division, Winter Assizes, and Commission Court	.	[illegible]	[illegible]	[illegible]	[illegible]	[illegible]	[illegible]	.	.	.
Civil Side of Queen's Bench Division, Common Pleas Division, Exchequer Division,	.	[illegible]	[illegible]	[illegible]	[illegible]	[illegible]	[illegible]	.	.	.
Probate and Matrimonial Division,	.	[illegible]	[illegible]	[illegible]	[illegible]	[illegible]	[illegible]	.	.	.
Bankruptcy,	.	.	.	.	.	.	.	.	.	.
Recorder,	.	.	.	.	[illegible]	[illegible]	[illegible]	.	.	.
Other purposes than Quarter Sessions or Civil Bills before Recorder	.	.	.	.	.	.	.	.	.	.
Total of Dublin City,	[illegible]	[illegible]	[illegible]	[illegible]	[illegible]	[illegible]	[illegible]	.	.	.
Carlow,	[illegible]	[illegible]	[illegible]	[illegible]	[illegible]	[illegible]	[illegible]	[illegible]	[illegible]	[illegible]
Drogheda, Town of,	[illegible]	[illegible]	[illegible]	[illegible]	[illegible]	[illegible]	[illegible]	[illegible]	[illegible]	[illegible]
Kildare,	[illegible]	[illegible]	[illegible]	[illegible]	[illegible]	[illegible]	[illegible]	[illegible]	[illegible]	[illegible]
Kilkenny,	[illegible]	[illegible]	[illegible]	[illegible]	[illegible]	[illegible]	[illegible]	[illegible]	[illegible]	[illegible]
" City,	[illegible]	[illegible]	[illegible]	[illegible]	[illegible]	[illegible]	[illegible]	[illegible]	[illegible]	[illegible]
King's County,	[illegible]	[illegible]	[illegible]	[illegible]	[illegible]	[illegible]	[illegible]	[illegible]	[illegible]	[illegible]
Longford,	[illegible]	[illegible]	[illegible]	[illegible]	[illegible]	[illegible]	[illegible]	[illegible]	[illegible]	[illegible]
Louth,	[illegible]	[illegible]	[illegible]	[illegible]	[illegible]	[illegible]	[illegible]	[illegible]	[illegible]	[illegible]
Meath,	[illegible]	[illegible]	[illegible]	[illegible]	[illegible]	[illegible]	[illegible]	[illegible]	[illegible]	[illegible]
Queen's County,	[illegible]	[illegible]	[illegible]	[illegible]	[illegible]	[illegible]	[illegible]	[illegible]	[illegible]	[illegible]
Westmeath,	[illegible]	[illegible]	[illegible]	[illegible]	[illegible]	[illegible]	[illegible]	[illegible]	[illegible]	[illegible]
Wexford,	[illegible]	[illegible]	[illegible]	[illegible]	[illegible]	[illegible]	[illegible]	[illegible]	[illegible]	[illegible]
Wicklow,	[illegible]	[illegible]	[illegible]	[illegible]	[illegible]	[illegible]	[illegible]	[illegible]	[illegible]	[illegible]
Total of Leinster,	[illegible]	[illegible]	[illegible]	[illegible]	[illegible]	[illegible]	[illegible]	[illegible]	[illegible]	[illegible]
MUNSTER:										
Clare,	[illegible]	[illegible]	[illegible]	[illegible]	[illegible]	[illegible]	[illegible]	[illegible]	[illegible]	[illegible]
Cork,	[illegible]	[illegible]	[illegible]	[illegible]	[illegible]	[illegible]	[illegible]	[illegible]	[illegible]	[illegible]
" City,	[illegible]	[illegible]	[illegible]	[illegible]	[illegible]	[illegible]	[illegible]	[illegible]	[illegible]	[illegible]
Kerry,	[illegible]	[illegible]	[illegible]	[illegible]	[illegible]	[illegible]	[illegible]	[illegible]	[illegible]	[illegible]
Limerick,	[illegible]	[illegible]	[illegible]	[illegible]	[illegible]	[illegible]	[illegible]	[illegible]	[illegible]	[illegible]
" City,	[illegible]	[illegible]	[illegible]	[illegible]	[illegible]	[illegible]	[illegible]	[illegible]	[illegible]	[illegible]
Tipperary,	[illegible]	[illegible]	[illegible]	[illegible]	[illegible]	[illegible]	[illegible]	[illegible]	[illegible]	[illegible]
Waterford,	[illegible]	[illegible]	[illegible]	[illegible]	[illegible]	[illegible]	[illegible]	[illegible]	[illegible]	[illegible]
" City,	[illegible]	[illegible]	[illegible]	[illegible]	[illegible]	[illegible]	[illegible]	[illegible]	[illegible]	[illegible]
Total of Munster,	[illegible]	[illegible]	[illegible]	[illegible]	[illegible]	[illegible]	[illegible]	[illegible]	[illegible]	[illegible]
ULSTER:										
Antrim,	[illegible]	[illegible]	[illegible]	[illegible]	[illegible]	[illegible]	[illegible]	[illegible]	[illegible]	[illegible]
Armagh,	[illegible]	[illegible]	[illegible]	[illegible]	[illegible]	[illegible]	[illegible]	[illegible]	[illegible]	[illegible]
Belfast, Borough,	[illegible]	[illegible]	[illegible]	[illegible]	[illegible]	[illegible]	[illegible]	[illegible]	[illegible]	[illegible]
Carrickfergus, Town of,	[illegible]	[illegible]	[illegible]	[illegible]	[illegible]	[illegible]	[illegible]	[illegible]	[illegible]	[illegible]
Cavan,	[illegible]	[illegible]	[illegible]	[illegible]	[illegible]	[illegible]	[illegible]	[illegible]	[illegible]	[illegible]
Donegal,	[illegible]	[illegible]	[illegible]	[illegible]	[illegible]	[illegible]	[illegible]	[illegible]	[illegible]	[illegible]
Down,	[illegible]	[illegible]	[illegible]	[illegible]	[illegible]	[illegible]	[illegible]	[illegible]	[illegible]	[illegible]
Fermanagh,	[illegible]	[illegible]	[illegible]	[illegible]	[illegible]	[illegible]	[illegible]	[illegible]	[illegible]	[illegible]
Londonderry,	[illegible]	[illegible]	[illegible]	[illegible]	[illegible]	[illegible]	[illegible]	[illegible]	[illegible]	[illegible]
" City,	[illegible]	[illegible]	[illegible]	[illegible]	[illegible]	[illegible]	[illegible]	[illegible]	[illegible]	[illegible]
Monaghan,	[illegible]	[illegible]	[illegible]	[illegible]	[illegible]	[illegible]	[illegible]	[illegible]	[illegible]	[illegible]
Tyrone,	[illegible]	[illegible]	[illegible]	[illegible]	[illegible]	[illegible]	[illegible]	[illegible]	[illegible]	[illegible]
Total of Ulster,	[illegible]	[illegible]	[illegible]	[illegible]	[illegible]	[illegible]	[illegible]	[illegible]	[illegible]	[illegible]
CONNAUGHT:										
Galway,	[illegible]	[illegible]	[illegible]	[illegible]	[illegible]	[illegible]	[illegible]	[illegible]	[illegible]	[illegible]
" Town of,	[illegible]	[illegible]	[illegible]	[illegible]	[illegible]	[illegible]	[illegible]	[illegible]	[illegible]	[illegible]
Leitrim,	[illegible]	[illegible]	[illegible]	[illegible]	[illegible]	[illegible]	[illegible]	[illegible]	[illegible]	[illegible]
Mayo,	[illegible]	[illegible]	[illegible]	[illegible]	[illegible]	[illegible]	[illegible]	[illegible]	[illegible]	[illegible]
Roscommon,	[illegible]	[illegible]	[illegible]	[illegible]	[illegible]	[illegible]	[illegible]	[illegible]	[illegible]	[illegible]
Sligo,	[illegible]	[illegible]	[illegible]	[illegible]	[illegible]	[illegible]	[illegible]	[illegible]	[illegible]	[illegible]
Total of Connaught,	[illegible]	[illegible]	[illegible]	[illegible]	[illegible]	[illegible]	[illegible]	[illegible]	[illegible]	[illegible]
Total of Ireland,	[illegible]	[illegible]	[illegible]	[illegible]	[illegible]	[illegible]	[illegible]	[illegible]	[illegible]	[illegible]

[illegible] 1876–77, from Returns by the [illegible], and, in the case of Belfast and Londonderry Boroughs, of the Peace.

[illegible] Quarter Sessions: Grand Juries: January to June	Grand Juries: July to December	Grand Juries: Total	Petty Sessions: January to June	Petty Sessions: July to December	Petty Sessions: Total	Civil Bills before County Court Judges or Recorders: January to June	July to December	Total	Other Purposes	Counties, Counties of Cities and Towns, and [illegible] Separate Commissions of the Peace, arranged in Provinces
										Leinster:
										Dublin:
.	.	.	.	.	.	.	.	.	.	Crown Side of Queen's Bench Division, Winter Assizes, and Commission Court
.	.	.	.	.	.	.	.	.	.	Civil Side of Queen's Bench Division
.	.	.	.	.	.	.	.	.	.	Common Pleas Division
.	.	.	.	.	.	.	.	.	.	Exchequer Division
.	.	.	.	.	.	.	.	.	.	Probate and Matrimonial Division
.	.	.	.	.	.	.	.	.	.	Bankruptcy
.	.	.	.	.	.	.	.	.	.	[illegible]
.	.	.	.	.	.	.	.	.	.	Other purposes than Quarter Sessions or Civil Bills before County Court Judge
[illegible]	[illegible]	[illegible]	[illegible]	[illegible]	[illegible]	[illegible]	[illegible]	[illegible]	.	Total of Dublin County.
										Dublin City:
.	.	.	.	.	.	.	.	.	.	Crown Side of Queen's Bench Division, Winter Assizes, and Commission Court
.	.	.	.	.	.	.	.	.	.	Civil Side of Queen's Bench Division
.	.	.	.	.	.	.	.	.	.	Common Pleas Division
.	.	.	.	.	.	.	.	.	.	Exchequer Division
.	.	.	.	.	.	.	.	.	.	Probate and Matrimonial Division
.	.	.	.	.	.	.	.	.	.	Bankruptcy
.	.	.	.	.	.	.	.	.	.	[illegible]
.	.	.	.	.	.	.	.	.	.	Other purposes than Quarter Sessions or Civil Bills before Recorder.
[illegible]	[illegible]	[illegible]	[illegible]	[illegible]	[illegible]	[illegible]	[illegible]	[illegible]	.	Total of Dublin City.
[illegible]	[illegible]	[illegible]	[illegible]	[illegible]	[illegible]	[illegible]	[illegible]	[illegible]	[illegible]	Carlow
[illegible]	[illegible]	[illegible]	[illegible]	[illegible]	[illegible]	[illegible]	[illegible]	[illegible]	[illegible]	Drogheda, Town of
[illegible]	[illegible]	[illegible]	[illegible]	[illegible]	[illegible]	[illegible]	[illegible]	[illegible]	[illegible]	Kildare
[illegible]	[illegible]	[illegible]	[illegible]	[illegible]	[illegible]	[illegible]	[illegible]	[illegible]	[illegible]	Kilkenny
[illegible]	[illegible]	[illegible]	[illegible]	[illegible]	[illegible]	[illegible]	[illegible]	[illegible]	[illegible]	„ City
[illegible]	[illegible]	[illegible]	[illegible]	[illegible]	[illegible]	[illegible]	[illegible]	[illegible]	[illegible]	King's County
[illegible]	[illegible]	[illegible]	[illegible]	[illegible]	[illegible]	[illegible]	[illegible]	[illegible]	[illegible]	Longford
[illegible]	[illegible]	[illegible]	[illegible]	[illegible]	[illegible]	[illegible]	[illegible]	[illegible]	[illegible]	Louth
[illegible]	[illegible]	[illegible]	[illegible]	[illegible]	[illegible]	[illegible]	[illegible]	[illegible]	[illegible]	Meath
[illegible]	[illegible]	[illegible]	[illegible]	[illegible]	[illegible]	[illegible]	[illegible]	[illegible]	[illegible]	Queen's County
[illegible]	[illegible]	[illegible]	[illegible]	[illegible]	[illegible]	[illegible]	[illegible]	[illegible]	[illegible]	Westmeath
[illegible]	[illegible]	[illegible]	[illegible]	[illegible]	[illegible]	[illegible]	[illegible]	[illegible]	[illegible]	Wexford
[illegible]	[illegible]	[illegible]	[illegible]	[illegible]	[illegible]	[illegible]	[illegible]	[illegible]	[illegible]	Wicklow
[illegible]	[illegible]	[illegible]	[illegible]	[illegible]	[illegible]	[illegible]	[illegible]	[illegible]	[illegible]	Total of Leinster.
										Munster.
[illegible]	[illegible]	[illegible]	[illegible]	[illegible]	[illegible]	[illegible]	[illegible]	[illegible]	[illegible]	Clare
[illegible]	[illegible]	[illegible]	[illegible]	[illegible]	[illegible]	[illegible]	[illegible]	[illegible]	[illegible]	Cork
[illegible]	[illegible]	[illegible]	[illegible]	[illegible]	[illegible]	[illegible]	[illegible]	[illegible]	[illegible]	„ City
[illegible]	[illegible]	[illegible]	[illegible]	[illegible]	[illegible]	[illegible]	[illegible]	[illegible]	[illegible]	Kerry
[illegible]	[illegible]	[illegible]	[illegible]	[illegible]	[illegible]	[illegible]	[illegible]	[illegible]	[illegible]	Limerick
[illegible]	[illegible]	[illegible]	[illegible]	[illegible]	[illegible]	[illegible]	[illegible]	[illegible]	[illegible]	„ City
[illegible]	[illegible]	[illegible]	[illegible]	[illegible]	[illegible]	[illegible]	[illegible]	[illegible]	[illegible]	Tipperary
[illegible]	[illegible]	[illegible]	[illegible]	[illegible]	[illegible]	[illegible]	[illegible]	[illegible]	[illegible]	Waterford
[illegible]	[illegible]	[illegible]	[illegible]	[illegible]	[illegible]	[illegible]	[illegible]	[illegible]	[illegible]	„ City.
[illegible]	[illegible]	[illegible]	[illegible]	[illegible]	[illegible]	[illegible]	[illegible]	[illegible]	.	Total of Munster.
										Ulster.
[illegible]	[illegible]	[illegible]	[illegible]	[illegible]	[illegible]	[illegible]	[illegible]	[illegible]	[illegible]	Antrim
[illegible]	[illegible]	[illegible]	[illegible]	[illegible]	[illegible]	[illegible]	[illegible]	[illegible]	[illegible]	Armagh
[illegible]	[illegible]	[illegible]	[illegible]	[illegible]	[illegible]	[illegible]	[illegible]	[illegible]	[illegible]	Belfast, Borough
[illegible]	[illegible]	[illegible]	[illegible]	[illegible]	[illegible]	[illegible]	[illegible]	[illegible]	[illegible]	Carrickfergus, Town of
[illegible]	[illegible]	[illegible]	[illegible]	[illegible]	[illegible]	[illegible]	[illegible]	[illegible]	[illegible]	Cavan
[illegible]	[illegible]	[illegible]	[illegible]	[illegible]	[illegible]	[illegible]	[illegible]	[illegible]	[illegible]	Donegal
[illegible]	[illegible]	[illegible]	[illegible]	[illegible]	[illegible]	[illegible]	[illegible]	[illegible]	[illegible]	Down
[illegible]	[illegible]	[illegible]	[illegible]	[illegible]	[illegible]	[illegible]	[illegible]	[illegible]	[illegible]	Fermanagh
[illegible]	[illegible]	[illegible]	[illegible]	[illegible]	[illegible]	[illegible]	[illegible]	[illegible]	[illegible]	Londonderry
[illegible]	[illegible]	[illegible]	[illegible]	[illegible]	[illegible]	[illegible]	[illegible]	[illegible]	[illegible]	„ City
[illegible]	[illegible]	[illegible]	[illegible]	[illegible]	[illegible]	[illegible]	[illegible]	[illegible]	[illegible]	Monaghan
[illegible]	[illegible]	[illegible]	[illegible]	[illegible]	[illegible]	[illegible]	[illegible]	[illegible]	[illegible]	Tyrone
[illegible]	[illegible]	[illegible]	[illegible]	[illegible]	[illegible]	[illegible]	[illegible]	[illegible]	[illegible]	Total of Ulster.
										Connaught.
[illegible]	[illegible]	[illegible]	[illegible]	[illegible]	[illegible]	[illegible]	[illegible]	[illegible]	[illegible]	Galway
[illegible]	[illegible]	[illegible]	[illegible]	[illegible]	[illegible]	[illegible]	[illegible]	[illegible]	[illegible]	„ Town of
[illegible]	[illegible]	[illegible]	[illegible]	[illegible]	[illegible]	[illegible]	[illegible]	[illegible]	[illegible]	Leitrim
[illegible]	[illegible]	[illegible]	[illegible]	[illegible]	[illegible]	[illegible]	[illegible]	[illegible]	[illegible]	Mayo
[illegible]	[illegible]	[illegible]	[illegible]	[illegible]	[illegible]	[illegible]	[illegible]	[illegible]	[illegible]	Roscommon
[illegible]	[illegible]	[illegible]	[illegible]	[illegible]	[illegible]	[illegible]	[illegible]	[illegible]	[illegible]	Sligo
[illegible]	[illegible]	[illegible]	[illegible]	[illegible]	[illegible]	[illegible]	[illegible]	[illegible]	.	Total of Connaught.
[illegible]	[illegible]	[illegible]	[illegible]	[illegible]	[illegible]	[illegible]	[illegible]	[illegible]	[illegible]	Total of Ireland.

TABLE ..—TABLE of PROCEEDINGS in the Year 1854, as to the ATTENDANCE of MAGISTRATES and the under STATUTE 23 & 24 VIC., c. 14, and as to OVERHOLDING TENANTS ...

PETTY SESSIONS DISTRICTS, ARRANGED IN COUNTIES, COUNTIES OF CITIES OR OF TOWNS, AND PROVINCES.	No. of places at which Petty Sessions held.	Attendance of Magistrates				Civil Cases arising from Proceedings as to Union Tenants, and Complaining Tenants			

LEINSTER.

Carlow
Drogheda, Town of, . . .
Dublin County, Metropolitan Police District
Dublin Metropolitan Police District, including Enumerators
Kildare,
Kilkenny,
Kilkenny City, . . .
King's County, . . .
Longford,
Louth,
Meath,
Queen's County, . . .
Westmeath, . . .
Wexford,
Wicklow,

 Total, . . .

MUNSTER.

Clare,
Cork,
Cork City,
Kerry,
Limerick,
Limerick City, . . .
Tipperary,
Waterford,
Waterford City and Police Court

 Total, . . .

ULSTER.

Antrim,
Armagh,
Carrickfergus, County of the Town of
Cavan,
Donegal,
Down,
Fermanagh,
Londonderry,

NUMBER of CIVIL CASES other than PROCEEDINGS as to COTTIER TENANTS, and as to COTTIER TENANTS ... TOWNS under 14 & 15 VIC., c. 93, from Returns made by Clerks of Petty Sessions.

[illegible]									[illegible] 14 & 15 Vic., c. 93, s. 15				PETTY SESSIONS DISTRICTS, ARRANGED IN COUNTIES, COUNTIES OF CITIES OR OF TOWNS, AND PROVINCES.
[illegible]	[illegible]	[illegible]	[illegible]	[illegible]	[illegible]	[illegible]	[illegible]	[illegible]	[illegible]	[illegible]	[illegible]	[illegible]	
													LEINSTER.
[illegible]	[illegible]	[illegible]	[illegible]	[illegible]	[illegible]	[illegible]	[illegible]	[illegible]	[illegible]	[illegible]	[illegible]	[illegible]	Carlow.
[illegible]	[illegible]	[illegible]	[illegible]	[illegible]	[illegible]	[illegible]	[illegible]	[illegible]	[illegible]	[illegible]	[illegible]	[illegible]	Drogheda, Town of.
[illegible]	[illegible]	[illegible]	[illegible]	[illegible]	[illegible]	[illegible]	[illegible]	[illegible]	[illegible]	[illegible]	[illegible]	[illegible]	Dublin County (exclusive of Metropolitan Police District).
[illegible]	[illegible]	[illegible]	[illegible]	[illegible]	[illegible]	[illegible]	[illegible]	[illegible]	[illegible]	[illegible]	[illegible]	[illegible]	Dublin Metropolitan Police District, including Kingstown.
[illegible]	[illegible]	[illegible]	[illegible]	[illegible]	[illegible]	[illegible]	[illegible]	[illegible]	[illegible]	[illegible]	[illegible]	[illegible]	Kildare.
[illegible]	[illegible]	[illegible]	[illegible]	[illegible]	[illegible]	[illegible]	[illegible]	[illegible]	[illegible]	[illegible]	[illegible]	[illegible]	Kilkenny.
[illegible]	[illegible]	[illegible]	[illegible]	[illegible]	[illegible]	[illegible]	[illegible]	[illegible]	[illegible]	[illegible]	[illegible]	[illegible]	Kilkenny City.
[illegible]	[illegible]	[illegible]	[illegible]	[illegible]	[illegible]	[illegible]	[illegible]	[illegible]	[illegible]	[illegible]	[illegible]	[illegible]	King's County.
[illegible]	[illegible]	[illegible]	[illegible]	[illegible]	[illegible]	[illegible]	[illegible]	[illegible]	[illegible]	[illegible]	[illegible]	[illegible]	Longford.
[illegible]	[illegible]	[illegible]	[illegible]	[illegible]	[illegible]	[illegible]	[illegible]	[illegible]	[illegible]	[illegible]	[illegible]	[illegible]	Louth.
[illegible]	[illegible]	[illegible]	[illegible]	[illegible]	[illegible]	[illegible]	[illegible]	[illegible]	[illegible]	[illegible]	[illegible]	[illegible]	Meath.
[illegible]	[illegible]	[illegible]	[illegible]	[illegible]	[illegible]	[illegible]	[illegible]	[illegible]	[illegible]	[illegible]	[illegible]	[illegible]	Queen's County.
[illegible]	[illegible]	[illegible]	[illegible]	[illegible]	[illegible]	[illegible]	[illegible]	[illegible]	[illegible]	[illegible]	[illegible]	[illegible]	Westmeath.
[illegible]	[illegible]	[illegible]	[illegible]	[illegible]	[illegible]	[illegible]	[illegible]	[illegible]	[illegible]	[illegible]	[illegible]	[illegible]	Wexford.
[illegible]	[illegible]	[illegible]	[illegible]	[illegible]	[illegible]	[illegible]	[illegible]	[illegible]	[illegible]	[illegible]	[illegible]	[illegible]	Wicklow.
[illegible]	[illegible]	[illegible]	[illegible]	[illegible]	[illegible]	[illegible]	[illegible]	[illegible]	[illegible]	[illegible]	[illegible]	[illegible]	Total
													MUNSTER.
[illegible]	[illegible]	[illegible]	[illegible]	[illegible]	[illegible]	[illegible]	[illegible]	[illegible]	[illegible]	[illegible]	[illegible]	[illegible]	Clare.
[illegible]	[illegible]	[illegible]	[illegible]	[illegible]	[illegible]	[illegible]	[illegible]	[illegible]	[illegible]	[illegible]	[illegible]	[illegible]	Cork.
[illegible]	[illegible]	[illegible]	[illegible]	[illegible]	[illegible]	[illegible]	[illegible]	[illegible]	[illegible]	[illegible]	[illegible]	[illegible]	Cork City
[illegible]	[illegible]	[illegible]	[illegible]	[illegible]	[illegible]	[illegible]	[illegible]	[illegible]	[illegible]	[illegible]	[illegible]	[illegible]	Kerry.
[illegible]	[illegible]	[illegible]	[illegible]	[illegible]	[illegible]	[illegible]	[illegible]	[illegible]	[illegible]	[illegible]	[illegible]	[illegible]	Limerick.
[illegible]	[illegible]	[illegible]	[illegible]	[illegible]	[illegible]	[illegible]	[illegible]	[illegible]	[illegible]	[illegible]	[illegible]	[illegible]	Limerick City.
[illegible]	[illegible]	[illegible]	[illegible]	[illegible]	[illegible]	[illegible]	[illegible]	[illegible]	[illegible]	[illegible]	[illegible]	[illegible]	Tipperary.
[illegible]	[illegible]	[illegible]	[illegible]	[illegible]	[illegible]	[illegible]	[illegible]	[illegible]	[illegible]	[illegible]	[illegible]	[illegible]	Waterford.
[illegible]	[illegible]	[illegible]	[illegible]	[illegible]	[illegible]	[illegible]	[illegible]	[illegible]	[illegible]	[illegible]	[illegible]	[illegible]	Waterford City and Police Court
[illegible]	[illegible]	[illegible]	[illegible]	[illegible]	[illegible]	[illegible]	[illegible]	[illegible]	[illegible]	[illegible]	[illegible]	[illegible]	Total
													ULSTER.
[illegible]	[illegible]	[illegible]	[illegible]	[illegible]	[illegible]	[illegible]	[illegible]	[illegible]	[illegible]	[illegible]	[illegible]	[illegible]	Antrim.
[illegible]	[illegible]	[illegible]	[illegible]	[illegible]	[illegible]	[illegible]	[illegible]	[illegible]	[illegible]	[illegible]	[illegible]	[illegible]	Armagh.
[illegible]	[illegible]	[illegible]	[illegible]	[illegible]	[illegible]	[illegible]	[illegible]	[illegible]	[illegible]	[illegible]	[illegible]	[illegible]	Carrickfergus, County of the Town of.
[illegible]	[illegible]	[illegible]	[illegible]	[illegible]	[illegible]	[illegible]	[illegible]	[illegible]	[illegible]	[illegible]	[illegible]	[illegible]	Cavan.
[illegible]	[illegible]	[illegible]	[illegible]	[illegible]	[illegible]	[illegible]	[illegible]	[illegible]	[illegible]	[illegible]	[illegible]	[illegible]	Donegal.
[illegible]	[illegible]	[illegible]	[illegible]	[illegible]	[illegible]	[illegible]	[illegible]	[illegible]	[illegible]	[illegible]	[illegible]	[illegible]	Down.
[illegible]	[illegible]	[illegible]	[illegible]	[illegible]	[illegible]	[illegible]	[illegible]	[illegible]	[illegible]	[illegible]	[illegible]	[illegible]	Fermanagh.
[illegible]	[illegible]	[illegible]	[illegible]	[illegible]	[illegible]	[illegible]	[illegible]	[illegible]	[illegible]	[illegible]	[illegible]	[illegible]	Londonderry.
[illegible]	[illegible]	[illegible]	[illegible]	[illegible]	[illegible]	[illegible]	[illegible]	[illegible]	[illegible]	[illegible]	[illegible]	[illegible]	Londonderry City.
[illegible]	[illegible]	[illegible]	[illegible]	[illegible]	[illegible]	[illegible]	[illegible]	[illegible]	[illegible]	[illegible]	[illegible]	[illegible]	Monaghan.
[illegible]	[illegible]	[illegible]	[illegible]	[illegible]	[illegible]	[illegible]	[illegible]	[illegible]	[illegible]	[illegible]	[illegible]	[illegible]	Tyrone.
[illegible]	[illegible]	[illegible]	[illegible]	[illegible]	[illegible]	[illegible]	[illegible]	[illegible]	[illegible]	[illegible]	[illegible]	[illegible]	Total.
													CONNAUGHT.
[illegible]	[illegible]	[illegible]	[illegible]	[illegible]	[illegible]	[illegible]	[illegible]	[illegible]	[illegible]	[illegible]	[illegible]	[illegible]	Galway.
[illegible]	[illegible]	[illegible]	[illegible]	[illegible]	[illegible]	[illegible]	[illegible]	[illegible]	[illegible]	[illegible]	[illegible]	[illegible]	Galway, County of Town.
[illegible]	[illegible]	[illegible]	[illegible]	[illegible]	[illegible]	[illegible]	[illegible]	[illegible]	[illegible]	[illegible]	[illegible]	[illegible]	Leitrim.
[illegible]	[illegible]	[illegible]	[illegible]	[illegible]	[illegible]	[illegible]	[illegible]	[illegible]	[illegible]	[illegible]	[illegible]	[illegible]	Mayo.
[illegible]	[illegible]	[illegible]	[illegible]	[illegible]	[illegible]	[illegible]	[illegible]	[illegible]	[illegible]	[illegible]	[illegible]	[illegible]	Roscommon.
[illegible]	[illegible]	[illegible]	[illegible]	[illegible]	[illegible]	[illegible]	[illegible]	[illegible]	[illegible]	[illegible]	[illegible]	[illegible]	Sligo.
[illegible]	[illegible]	[illegible]	[illegible]	[illegible]	[illegible]	[illegible]	[illegible]	[illegible]	[illegible]	[illegible]	[illegible]	[illegible]	Total.
[illegible]	[illegible]	[illegible]	[illegible]	[illegible]	[illegible]	[illegible]	[illegible]	[illegible]	[illegible]	[illegible]	[illegible]	[illegible]	Total of Ireland

TABLE 66.—QUARTER SESSIONS COURTS.—TABLE showing NUMBER of APPEALS from MAGISTRATES and APPLICATIONS for SPIRIT LICENCES in the Year 1880, from Returns made by Clerks of the Peace.

County, County of City or of Town, and Province.	Appeals from Magistrates: Total.	Affirmed.	Reversed.	Varied.	Otherwise disposed of	Applications for Spirit Licences: Total.	At Annual Licensing Sessions: Number Granted or Confirmed: On Original Application.	On Application for Renewal.	Number Refused: On Original Application.	On Application for Renewal.	Otherwise disposed of.	At other Quarter Sessions: Number Granted.	Number Refused.
LEINSTER:													
Carlow,	[illegible]	[illegible]	[illegible]	[illegible]	[illegible]	[illegible]	[illegible]	[illegible]	[illegible]	[illegible]	[illegible]	[illegible]	[illegible]
Drogheda, Town of,	[illegible]	[illegible]	[illegible]	[illegible]	[illegible]	[illegible]	[illegible]	[illegible]	[illegible]	[illegible]	[illegible]	[illegible]	[illegible]
Dublin,	[illegible]	[illegible]	[illegible]	[illegible]	[illegible]	[illegible]	[illegible]	[illegible]	[illegible]	[illegible]	[illegible]	[illegible]	[illegible]
Dublin City,	[illegible]	[illegible]	[illegible]	[illegible]	[illegible]	[illegible]	[illegible]	[illegible]	[illegible]	[illegible]	[illegible]	[illegible]	[illegible]
Kildare,	[illegible]	[illegible]	[illegible]	[illegible]	[illegible]	[illegible]	[illegible]	[illegible]	[illegible]	[illegible]	[illegible]	[illegible]	[illegible]
Kilkenny,	[illegible]	[illegible]	[illegible]	[illegible]	[illegible]	[illegible]	[illegible]	[illegible]	[illegible]	[illegible]	[illegible]	[illegible]	[illegible]
Kilkenny City,	[illegible]	[illegible]	[illegible]	[illegible]	[illegible]	[illegible]	[illegible]	[illegible]	[illegible]	[illegible]	[illegible]	[illegible]	[illegible]
King's County,	[illegible]	[illegible]	[illegible]	[illegible]	[illegible]	[illegible]	[illegible]	[illegible]	[illegible]	[illegible]	[illegible]	[illegible]	[illegible]
Longford,	[illegible]	[illegible]	[illegible]	[illegible]	[illegible]	[illegible]	[illegible]	[illegible]	[illegible]	[illegible]	[illegible]	[illegible]	[illegible]
Louth,	[illegible]	[illegible]	[illegible]	[illegible]	[illegible]	[illegible]	[illegible]	[illegible]	[illegible]	[illegible]	[illegible]	[illegible]	[illegible]
Meath,	[illegible]	[illegible]	[illegible]	[illegible]	[illegible]	[illegible]	[illegible]	[illegible]	[illegible]	[illegible]	[illegible]	[illegible]	[illegible]
Queen's County,	[illegible]	[illegible]	[illegible]	[illegible]	[illegible]	[illegible]	[illegible]	[illegible]	[illegible]	[illegible]	[illegible]	[illegible]	[illegible]
Westmeath,	[illegible]	[illegible]	[illegible]	[illegible]	[illegible]	[illegible]	[illegible]	[illegible]	[illegible]	[illegible]	[illegible]	[illegible]	[illegible]
Wexford,	[illegible]	[illegible]	[illegible]	[illegible]	[illegible]	[illegible]	[illegible]	[illegible]	[illegible]	[illegible]	[illegible]	[illegible]	[illegible]
Wicklow,	[illegible]	[illegible]	[illegible]	[illegible]	[illegible]	[illegible]	[illegible]	[illegible]	[illegible]	[illegible]	[illegible]	[illegible]	[illegible]
Total,	[illegible]	[illegible]	[illegible]	[illegible]	[illegible]	[illegible]	[illegible]	[illegible]	[illegible]	[illegible]	[illegible]	[illegible]	[illegible]
MUNSTER:													
Clare,	[illegible]	[illegible]	[illegible]	[illegible]	[illegible]	[illegible]	[illegible]	[illegible]	[illegible]	[illegible]	[illegible]	[illegible]	[illegible]
Cork, East Riding,	[illegible]	[illegible]	[illegible]	[illegible]	[illegible]	[illegible]	[illegible]	[illegible]	[illegible]	[illegible]	[illegible]	[illegible]	[illegible]
Cork, West Riding,	[illegible]	[illegible]	[illegible]	[illegible]	[illegible]	[illegible]	[illegible]	[illegible]	[illegible]	[illegible]	[illegible]	[illegible]	[illegible]
Cork City,	[illegible]	[illegible]	[illegible]	[illegible]	[illegible]	[illegible]	[illegible]	[illegible]	[illegible]	[illegible]	[illegible]	[illegible]	[illegible]
Kerry,	[illegible]	[illegible]	[illegible]	[illegible]	[illegible]	[illegible]	[illegible]	[illegible]	[illegible]	[illegible]	[illegible]	[illegible]	[illegible]
Limerick,	[illegible]	[illegible]	[illegible]	[illegible]	[illegible]	[illegible]	[illegible]	[illegible]	[illegible]	[illegible]	[illegible]	[illegible]	[illegible]
Limerick City,	[illegible]	[illegible]	[illegible]	[illegible]	[illegible]	[illegible]	[illegible]	[illegible]	[illegible]	[illegible]	[illegible]	[illegible]	[illegible]
Tipperary,	[illegible]	[illegible]	[illegible]	[illegible]	[illegible]	[illegible]	[illegible]	[illegible]	[illegible]	[illegible]	[illegible]	[illegible]	[illegible]
Waterford,	[illegible]	[illegible]	[illegible]	[illegible]	[illegible]	[illegible]	[illegible]	[illegible]	[illegible]	[illegible]	[illegible]	[illegible]	[illegible]
Waterford City,	[illegible]	[illegible]	[illegible]	[illegible]	[illegible]	[illegible]	[illegible]	[illegible]	[illegible]	[illegible]	[illegible]	[illegible]	[illegible]
Total,	[illegible]	[illegible]	[illegible]	[illegible]	[illegible]	[illegible]	[illegible]	[illegible]	[illegible]	[illegible]	[illegible]	[illegible]	[illegible]
ULSTER:													
Antrim,	[illegible]	[illegible]	[illegible]	[illegible]	[illegible]	[illegible]	[illegible]	[illegible]	[illegible]	[illegible]	[illegible]	[illegible]	[illegible]
Armagh,	[illegible]	[illegible]	[illegible]	[illegible]	[illegible]	[illegible]	[illegible]	[illegible]	[illegible]	[illegible]	[illegible]	[illegible]	[illegible]
Belfast, Town of,	[illegible]	[illegible]	[illegible]	[illegible]	[illegible]	[illegible]	[illegible]	[illegible]	[illegible]	[illegible]	[illegible]	[illegible]	[illegible]
Carrickfergus, Town of,	[illegible]	[illegible]	[illegible]	[illegible]	[illegible]	[illegible]	[illegible]	[illegible]	[illegible]	[illegible]	[illegible]	[illegible]	[illegible]
Cavan,	[illegible]	[illegible]	[illegible]	[illegible]	[illegible]	[illegible]	[illegible]	[illegible]	[illegible]	[illegible]	[illegible]	[illegible]	[illegible]
Donegal,	[illegible]	[illegible]	[illegible]	[illegible]	[illegible]	[illegible]	[illegible]	[illegible]	[illegible]	[illegible]	[illegible]	[illegible]	[illegible]
Down,	[illegible]	[illegible]	[illegible]	[illegible]	[illegible]	[illegible]	[illegible]	[illegible]	[illegible]	[illegible]	[illegible]	[illegible]	[illegible]
Fermanagh,	[illegible]	[illegible]	[illegible]	[illegible]	[illegible]	[illegible]	[illegible]	[illegible]	[illegible]	[illegible]	[illegible]	[illegible]	[illegible]
Londonderry,	[illegible]	[illegible]	[illegible]	[illegible]	[illegible]	[illegible]	[illegible]	[illegible]	[illegible]	[illegible]	[illegible]	[illegible]	[illegible]
Londonderry City,	[illegible]	[illegible]	[illegible]	[illegible]	[illegible]	[illegible]	[illegible]	[illegible]	[illegible]	[illegible]	[illegible]	[illegible]	[illegible]
Monaghan,	[illegible]	[illegible]	[illegible]	[illegible]	[illegible]	[illegible]	[illegible]	[illegible]	[illegible]	[illegible]	[illegible]	[illegible]	[illegible]
Tyrone,	[illegible]	[illegible]	[illegible]	[illegible]	[illegible]	[illegible]	[illegible]	[illegible]	[illegible]	[illegible]	[illegible]	[illegible]	[illegible]
Total,	[illegible]	[illegible]	[illegible]	[illegible]	[illegible]	[illegible]	[illegible]	[illegible]	[illegible]	[illegible]	[illegible]	[illegible]	[illegible]
CONNAUGHT:													
Galway,	[illegible]	[illegible]	[illegible]	[illegible]	[illegible]	[illegible]	[illegible]	[illegible]	[illegible]	[illegible]	[illegible]	[illegible]	[illegible]
Galway, Town of,	[illegible]	[illegible]	[illegible]	[illegible]	[illegible]	[illegible]	[illegible]	[illegible]	[illegible]	[illegible]	[illegible]	[illegible]	[illegible]
Leitrim,	[illegible]	[illegible]	[illegible]	[illegible]	[illegible]	[illegible]	[illegible]	[illegible]	[illegible]	[illegible]	[illegible]	[illegible]	[illegible]
Mayo,	[illegible]	[illegible]	[illegible]	[illegible]	[illegible]	[illegible]	[illegible]	[illegible]	[illegible]	[illegible]	[illegible]	[illegible]	[illegible]
Roscommon,	[illegible]	[illegible]	[illegible]	[illegible]	[illegible]	[illegible]	[illegible]	[illegible]	[illegible]	[illegible]	[illegible]	[illegible]	[illegible]
Sligo,	[illegible]	[illegible]	[illegible]	[illegible]	[illegible]	[illegible]	[illegible]	[illegible]	[illegible]	[illegible]	[illegible]	[illegible]	[illegible]
Total,	[illegible]	[illegible]	[illegible]	[illegible]	[illegible]	[illegible]	[illegible]	[illegible]	[illegible]	[illegible]	[illegible]	[illegible]	[illegible]
TOTAL OF IRELAND,	[illegible]	[illegible]	[illegible]	[illegible]	[illegible]	[illegible]	[illegible]	[illegible]	[illegible]	[illegible]	[illegible]	[illegible]	[illegible]

[illegible]

TABLE 67.—LOCAL CHARTER COURTS.—TABLE of PROCEEDINGS in LORD MAYOR'S COURT and COURTS of CONSCIENCE in the Year 1880, from Returns made by the Registrars.

Names of Courts	[illegible]	[illegible]	Number of Decrees: [illegible]	[illegible]	[illegible]	[illegible]	[illegible]	[illegible]	[illegible]	[illegible]	[illegible]	Application of Fees: [illegible]	[illegible]	[illegible]
Clonmel Court of Conscience,	[illegible]	[illegible]	[illegible]	[illegible]	[illegible]	[illegible]	[illegible]	[illegible]	[illegible]	[illegible]	[illegible]	[illegible]	[illegible]	[illegible]
Drogheda do.,	[illegible]	[illegible]	[illegible]	[illegible]	[illegible]	[illegible]	[illegible]	[illegible]	[illegible]	[illegible]	[illegible]	[illegible]	[illegible]	[illegible]
Dublin (Lord Mayor's Court),	[illegible]	[illegible]	[illegible]	[illegible]	[illegible]	[illegible]	[illegible]	[illegible]	[illegible]	[illegible]	[illegible]	[illegible]	[illegible]	[illegible]
Dublin Court of Conscience,	[illegible]	[illegible]	[illegible]	[illegible]	[illegible]	[illegible]	[illegible]	[illegible]	[illegible]	[illegible]	[illegible]	[illegible]	[illegible]	[illegible]
Kilkenny do.,	[illegible]	[illegible]	[illegible]	[illegible]	[illegible]	[illegible]	[illegible]	[illegible]	[illegible]	[illegible]	[illegible]	[illegible]	[illegible]	[illegible]
Limerick do.,	[illegible]	[illegible]	[illegible]	[illegible]	[illegible]	[illegible]	[illegible]	[illegible]	[illegible]	[illegible]	[illegible]	[illegible]	[illegible]	[illegible]
Londonderry do.,	[illegible]	[illegible]	[illegible]	[illegible]	[illegible]	[illegible]	[illegible]	[illegible]	[illegible]	[illegible]	[illegible]	[illegible]	[illegible]	[illegible]
Wexford do.,	[illegible]	[illegible]	[illegible]	[illegible]	[illegible]	[illegible]	[illegible]	[illegible]	[illegible]	[illegible]	[illegible]	[illegible]	[illegible]	[illegible]
Total,	[illegible]	[illegible]	[illegible]	[illegible]	[illegible]	[illegible]	[illegible]	[illegible]	[illegible]	[illegible]	[illegible]	[illegible]	[illegible]	[illegible]

* The Registrar states that it is impossible for him to give this information.

www.ingramcontent.com/pod-product-compliance
Lightning Source LLC
Chambersburg PA
CBHW030558270326
41927CB00007B/975